Investigating Wittgenstein

Investigating Wittgenstein

MERRILL B. HINTIKKA
and
JAAKKO HINTIKKA

Basil Blackwell

First published 1986
Reprinted and first published in paperback 1989

Basil Blackwell Ltd
108 Cowley Road, Oxford OX4 1JF, UK

Basil Blackwell Inc.
432 Park Avenue South, Suite 1503
New York, NY 10016, USA

British Library Cataloguing in Publication Data

Hintikka, Merril B.
  Investigating, Wittgenstein.
  1. Wittgenstein, Ludwig
  I. Title   II. Hintikka, Jaakko
  192   B3376.W564

  ISBN 0–631–14179–0
  ISBN 0–631–14181–2 (Pbk)

Library of Congress Cataloging in Publication Data

Hintikka, Merrill B., 1939–
Investigating Wittgenstein.

Bibliography: p.
Includes index.
1. Wittgenstein, Ludwig, 1889–1951.   I.
Hintikka,
Jaakko, 1929–   . II. Title.
B3376. W564H54 1986   192   86–1102

ISBN 0–631–14179–0
ISBN 0–631–14181–2 (pbk.)

Typeset by Freeman Graphic, Tonbridge, Kent.
Printed in Great Britain by TJ Press, Padstow, Cornwall

To
Georg Henrik von Wright

'Only connect . . .'
(E. M. Forster)

Contents

Preface

How did we ever come to write this book? Neither of us is a follower of Wittgenstein, and initially neither of us took much interest in the details of Wittgensteinian scholarship. Yet the answer is easy. What prompted us is the joy of investigative and interpretive discovery. We both enjoy puzzle-solving and, in particular, enjoy the work of the literary and interpretative detective who is trying to tease out the true meaning of a philosopher's words. Moreover, we enjoy doing such scholarly sleuthing together. In hindsight, our work on this book began when sometime in the winter of 1976 one of us took the other one to task for overlooking certain crucial evidence concerning the interpretation of Wittgenstein's so-called 'private language argument'. Since we were getting together at the time, one thing literally led to another, to Merrill Hintikka's dissertation at Stanford, to a series of joint and individual papers, and eventually to the idea of a co-authored book. The outcome is so much a joint effort that there is no point in trying to separate our respective contributions from each other. More than once, one of us has said to the other, 'Here's a new idea for the Wittgenstein book', only to learn that he or she had forgotten that the other one had come upon and expressed the same idea earlier.

From what was said of our bent of scholarly mind, it follows that our main aim in this book is 'only to connect', that is, to understand Wittgenstein's ideas and their development, not to evaluate them or bring them to bear on subsequent topical discussions. In this book, we are not prosecuting attorneys, defence counsels, or jurors; we are investigators. Admittedly, it would in many instances be both interesting and helpful to relate Wittgenstein's insights to more recent philosophical ideas, be they game-theoretical semantics, causal theories of naming, or speech-act theories. Wittgenstein is still waiting for his Dummett, we might say. But such insights by hindsight are bound to be shaky before someone has performed the much more basic task of understanding Wittgenstein in his own terms. And this task, we believe, simply has not been accomplished before. In any case, comparisons with post-Wittgenstein developments are not what we are attempting here. Admittedly, we shall now and then relate Wittgenstein's ideas to the views of other philosophers and logicians, but the purpose of such confrontations is always to appreciate Wittgenstein's thought better, not to bring it to bear on the doctrines of others.

However, we would not have written this book if we were not convinced of the tremendous interest and depth of many of Wittgenstein's ideas. Even where we disagree with him, for instance with respect to Wittgenstein's extreme form of belief in the ineffability of all matters semantical, we recognize an extraordinarily deep insight hidden underneath exaggerations. We are convinced that the enhanced understanding of Wittgenstein's thought which we hope to bring about has in many cases genuine philosophical value well beyond the historical dimensions of our enterprise, even though we do not claim that it will prove the value or interest of all aspects of his philosophy. We are not convinced, for instance, that Wittgenstein's philosophy of mathematics has anything like the same depth as his philosophy of language or his philosophy of psychology.

Our aim has to some extent dictated our approach. Our strategy of interpretation and argumentation will be to let Wittgenstein speak for himself as much as possible by quoting liberally his published and unpublished writings. This is not due to false piety, nor does it mean that we subscribe to Richard Robinson's canon of interpretation, according to which one must not ascribe to a Plato any views which Plato did not himself state. On the contrary, we are constantly trying to go beyond Wittgenstein's words and look for the questions he is asking himself and for the problems he is trying to solve.

The true function of quotations in interpreting a philosophical writer is not unlike the function of figures in geometrical reasoning. Instead of trying to reason about triangles, circles, tangents and other geometrical objects *in abstracto*, a geometer presents to us an actual example of the geometrical configurations he is arguing about, and carries out his argument by reference to this concrete instantiation of the general concepts he or she is dealing with. Somewhat in the same way, a discussion of a philosopher's views is facilitated enormously by taking a specific proposition he or she actually put forward and discussing his or her general ideas in terms of that paradigmatic proposition. This lends to one's interpretive efforts the kind of concreteness and immediacy Wittgenstein himself valued highly.

It also makes one's exposition more persuasive. Aristotle once said that when the relevant geometrical constructions have been carried out, the theorem to be proved is obvious. In a similar spirit, it seems

to us that the only way of convincing our readers of this or that part of
our interpretation often is to catch Wittgenstein red-handed in the act
of putting forward the very view we are ascribing to him. For instance,
there is no better way of convincing you of our interpretation of how
Wittgenstein proposed to deal with the problem of colour incompatibility in the *Tractatus* than to quote his own subsequent explanation
of that very subject. For this reason, we have indulged in quoting
Wittgenstein more than is perhaps customary.

An additional reason for such extensive quoting is that much of our
evidence comes from Wittgenstein's unpublished writings. A reader
cannot judge our interpretation of Wittgenstein's words unless we
quote them and thereby make them available to our audience.

In fact, a by-product of our efforts may very well be – we hope – a
keener realization by the philosophical community of the embarrass-
ment of riches which the Wittgenstein *Nachlass* amounts to. We hope
that in the future philosophers will no longer try to support their
interpretations of Wittgenstein by haphazard quotes out of their
historical, developmental, and argumentative context, as still is the
case to far too great an extent. In particular, Wittgenstein's *aperçus*
cannot be fully understood without knowing where they belong in
the development of Wittgenstein's ideas and questions, or without
knowing the problems he is wrestling with on a particular occasion.
For instance, we shall argue in chapter 11 below that the address of
one of the most famous Wittgensteinian lines, 'An "inner process" is
in need of external criteria', has been widely misunderstood precisely
because philosophers have not paid enough attention to its problem
context.

If we are successful in this work, we have established the main lines
of development of Wittgenstein's ideas. A full understanding of the
details of Wittgenstein's philosophical biography will need much more
work, and it may also need an easier access to Wittgenstein's unpublished writings than is now available. But without knowing the broad
outlines of the growth of Wittgenstein's ideas which we have sought to
sketch, future scholars cannot easily identify even what questions to
try to answer through their further work.

Our exposition is not strictly chronological, however. Even though
we shall proceed from Wittgenstein's early philosophy to his middle
period and then to his later thought, each chapter of this book is
devoted to one interpretational problem or group of problems. The
overall view of Wittgenstein as a philosopher and of his development
will emerge from the interrelated and mutually supporting results of
the different chapters.

The nature of the subject matter has led us to a somewhat different approach to the different periods of Wittgenstein's philosophical activity. In dealing with his philosophically central works, that is, in dealing with the *Tractatus* and with the *Philosophical Investigations*, one is facing relatively stabilized and articulated philosophical views. Moreover, the most important source material from both periods, that is, from the early period culminating in the *Tractatus* and the later period to which the *Philosophical Investigations* belong, has been published, and will not present any major surprises to our readers. Accordingly, in dealing with these two periods our emphasis will be on careful analysis of the philosophical ideas codified in Wittgenstein's published writings. In contrast, in dealing with Wittenstein's development from the earlier position to the later, the main problem facing any serious scholar is a much more historical one. Since both the precise chronology and even the main outlines of Wittgenstein's development have remained almost completely in the dark in the earlier literature, our first aim in dealing with Wittgenstein's middle period (1929–36) has been to try to grasp the general trend of the history of Wittgenstein's problems and his attempted solutions to them. For this reason, the middle chapters – chapters 6–8 – of this book look somewhat more like straightforward exercises in the history of recent philosophy than the others.

Acknowledgements

In working together on Wittgenstein we have incurred many intellectual and moral debts. The greatest of them is to Georg Henrik von Wright. He has helped our work in many different ways. He has encouraged us throughout our joint work in a way for which we are sincerely and deeply grateful. He has offered us concrete suggestions; he has opened his Wittgenstein archives to us; he has helped us to find a publisher, and given us his permission to quote copyrighted Wittgenstein material. What is even more important, he has made important suggestions that have led us to new perspectives and ideas, and he has read an earlier draft of this work and made a large number of invaluable comments on it, great and small. Even apart from the fact that he was the main philosophy teacher of one of us, there was a foregone conclusion that we would dedicate this book to him.

Others with whom we have – or at least one of us has – had the privilege and the pleasure of discussing our ideas or who have otherwise contributed to our work on this book include Rogers Albritton, Max Black, W. W. Bartley III, Nancy Cartwright, Russell Dancy, Alberto Emiliani, Dagfinn Føllesdal, William Godwin, Warren Goldfarb, Paul Grice, Leila Haaparanta, Ian Hacking, Rudolf Haller, Robert Howell, Hidé Ishiguro, Anthony Kenny, C. G. Luckhardt, André Maury, Linda McAllister, C. J. B. Macmillan, Brian McGuinness, Michel Meyer, Anselm Müller, Heikki Nyman, David Pears, Colin Radford, Hans Sluga, Erik Stenius, David Stern, Barry Stroud, Ralph Walker, Paul Ziff, and undoubtedly many others whom we are unjustly forgetting here. None of them is responsible for our mistakes, however, for none of them is likely to agree at this time with our conclusions. (Of course we hope to persuade all of them through our arguments in this book.) Of the philosophers listed, a few have to be specially mentioned. We have been strongly influenced by David Pears, whose pioneering work on the pre-World War I interaction between Russell and Wittgenstein first opened our eyes to some of the most fundamental aspects of the *Tractatus*. We have nevertheless pushed the line of thought he started further than he has done himself and also in a rather different direction. Heikki Nyman has helped us greatly in finding our bearings among the unpublished Wittgenstein materials, and has made available to us unpublished typescript versions of several works of Wittgenstein's he has edited together with G. H. von Wright. Jim Macmillan and Jaakko Hintikka have had frequent discussions about Wittgenstein over the last few years, many traces of which will undoubtedly be found in the book. David Stern has let us use a re-edited and uncut version of Wittgenstein's 'Notes for Lectures on "Private Language" and "Sense Data"' which he prepared.

The help we have received from the staff of the Department of Philosophy, Florida State University, and from the secretarial staff provided by Academy of Finland for Jaakko Hintikka, goes far beyond routine typing and copyediting. Erkki Kilpinen in Helsinki has greatly facilitated our access to the unpublished materials, among other things by helping us to transcribe Wittgenstein's texts. In Tallahassee, Jayne Moneysmith, Constance Jakubcin and Leigh Garrison (Campbell) have done yeowomen's work in improving the successive drafts of the book, and Florene Ball has deftly turned our drafts into handsome printouts.

We have not received any grants exclusively for the writing of this book, but indirectly and partly our work has been helped financially by a number of donors. Jaakko Hintikka received a Guggenheim Fellowship at an early stage of our efforts in 1980–1. In 1982–4 Jaakko Hintikka was the recipient of NSF grant #BNS–8119033 (Linguistics) for his work in game-theoretical semantics. The role of the grant in facilitating also his work on Wittgenstein's language-games and the semantics Wittgenstein based on them has to be acknowledged here. Support by the Academy of Finland has made it possible for Jaakko Hintikka to undertake several trips to Helsinki, where he has worked in von Wright's Wittgenstein archives and discussed our work with him. One of Jaakko Hintikka's trips to the annual International Wittgenstein Symposia was made possible by a grant from Florida State University. More than once, his participation in these symposia has been facilitated by grants from the Österreische Ludwig Wittgenstein Gesellschaft, their organizers.

In a less material but nevertheless very real sense we owe warm thanks to our colleagues and students at the Department of Philosophy, Florida State University, and especially to its chair, Alan Mabe, for creating an atmosphere in which our work has been able to thrive. Last but not least, we appreciate the interest of our publisher, Basil Blackwell, in our work and for their efficiency in bringing it to fruition.

Unpublished and posthumously published writings by Ludwig Wittgenstein are quoted by permission of the copyright owners, Professors G. E. M. Anscombe, Rush Rhees, and G. H. von Wright. Their kind permission is hereby gratefully acknowledged.

We are grateful to Professor G. H. von Wright for allowing us to use his Wittgenstein archives, and to him and to Mr Heikki Nyman for putting at our disposal edited but unpublished versions of several Wittgenstein manuscripts or typescripts from the *Nachlass*.

Material from the Frank Ramsey Collection has been used and quoted with the permission of Mrs Lettice Ramsey and of The Special Collections Department of the University of Pittsburgh Libraries.

The copyrights of the previously unpublished picture of Wittgenstein used as our frontispiece belong to Professor Knut Erik Tranoy. His kind permission to publish the photograph is acknowledged here with warm thanks.

We have used material from a number of earlier publications as a part of this book, in most cases in a heavily rewritten form. These publications are the following:

Jaakko Hintikka and Merrill B. Hintikka, 'Some remarks on (Wittgensteinian) logical form', *Synthese*, vol. 56, no. 2 (August 1983), pp. 155–70. (Publisher: D. Reidel Publishing Company, Dordrecht. This number was a part of the proceedings of a conference held under the auspices of the Austrian Institute, New York, at Florida State University on 1–3 April 1982.)

Merrill B. Hintikka and Jaakko Hintikka, 'Wittgensteinin Tractatus-teoksen salaisuus' (in Finnish; with an English summary, 'The enigma of Wittgenstein's *Tractatus*'), *Academia Scientiarum Fennica, Vuosikirja – Year Book, 1982–1983*, Helsinki, 1983, pp. 121–33.

Merrill B. Hintikka and Jaakko Hintikka, 'Wittgenstein: some perspectives on the development of his thought', in Ingmar Pörn, editor, *Essays in Philosophical Analysis Dedicated to Erik Stenius* (*Acta Philosophica Fennica*, vol. 32), Societas Philosophica Fennica, Helsinki, 1981, pp. 79–95.

Jaakko Hintikka and Merrill B. Hintikka, 'The development of Ludwig Wittgenstein's philosophy: the hidden unity', in Paul Weingartner and Hans Czermak, editors, *Epistemology and Philosophy of Science, Proceedings of the Seventh International Wittgenstein Symposium*, Hölder-Pichler-Tempsky, Vienna, 1983, pp. 425–37.

Merrill B. Hintikka, 'The objects of Wittgenstein's *Tractatus*', in Elisabeth Leinfellner et al., editors, *Language and Ontology, Proceedings of the Sixth International Wittgenstein Symposium*, Hölder-Pichler-Tempsky, Vienna, 1982, pp. 429–34.

Jaakko Hintikka, 'Wittgenstein's semantical Kantianism', in Edgar Morscher and Rudolf Stranzinger, editors, *Ethics: Foundations, Problems, and Applications, Proceedings of the Fifth International Wittgenstein Symposium*, Hölder-Pichler-Tempsky, Vienna, 1981, pp. 375–90.

Merrill B. Hintikka and Jaakko Hintikka, 'Different language-games in Wittgenstein', in Rudolf Haller and Wolfgang Grassl, editors, *Language, Logic, and Philosophy, Proceedings of the Fourth International Wittgenstein Symposium*, Hölder-Pichler-Tempsky, Vienna, 1980, pp. 417–22.

Jaakko Hintikka and Merrill B. Provence [Hintikka], 'Wittgenstein on privacy and publicity', in E. and W. Leinfellner et al., editors, *Wittgenstein and His Impact on Contemporary Thought, Proceedings of the Second International Wittgenstein Symposium*, Hölder-Pichler-Tempsky, Vienna, 1978, pp. 351–62.

All these materials are used by the appropriate permission of the copyright owners.

Sources

WITTGENSTEIN'S PUBLISHED BOOKS AND PAPERS

We shall refer to Wittgenstein's writings and quote them in the standard English translation or otherwise in the version that seems to us most easily available. All changes from the standard translation have been indicated and, whenever the translation makes a substantial difference, justified by reference to the German original. The following abbreviations will be used: *PI* for the *Philosophical Investigations* and the *Tractatus* for *Tractatus Logico-Philosophicus*. Decimal-point numbers refer to sections of the *Tractatus*, unless otherwise specified. All references not otherwise specified are to works listed below in our list of sources. Bilingual editions are indicated by an asterisk.

'On logic and how not to do it', *Cambridge Review*, vol. 34, no. 853, 6 March 1913 (review of P. Coffey, *The Science of Logic*); reprinted in Eric Homberger et al., editors, *The Cambridge Mind: Ninety Years of the Cambridge Review 1897–1969*, Little, Brown, Boston, 1970, pp. 127–9.

Tractatus Logico-Philosophicus: the German text of Ludwig Wittgenstein's *Logisch-Philosophische Abhandlung* with a new translation by D. F. Pears and B. F. McGuinness and with the Introduction by Bertrand Russell, Routledge & Kegan Paul, London, 1961.

'Some remarks on logical form', *Proceedings of the Aristotelian Society, Supplementary Volume* 9 (1929), pp. 162–71.

Philosophical Investigations, translated by G. E. M. Anscombe, Basil Blackwell, Oxford, 1953.

Remarks on the Foundations of Mathematics, edited by G. H. von Wright, Rush Rhees, and G. E. M. Anscombe, translated by G. E. M. Anscombe, Basil Blackwell, Oxford, 1956.

The Blue and Brown Books (Preliminary Studies for the 'Philosophical Investigations', Generally Known as The Blue and Brown Books), edited by Rush Rhees, Basil Blackwell, Oxford, 1958.

**Notebooks 1914–1916*, second edn, edited by G. H. von Wright and G. E. M. Anscombe, translated by G. E. M. Anscombe, Basil Blackwell, Oxford, 1979. (First edn, 1961.)

Philosophical Remarks, edited by Rush Rhees and translated by Raymond Hargreaves and Roger White, Basil Blackwell, Oxford, 1975. German text under the title *Philosophische Bemerkungen*, same editor and publisher, 1964.

*Zettel, edited by G. E. M. Anscombe and G. H. von Wright, translated by G. E. M. Anscombe, Basil Blackwell, 1967.

Philosophical Grammar, edited by Rush Rhees, translated by Anthony Kenny, Basil Blackwell, Oxford, 1974. German text under the title *Philosophische Grammatik*, same editor and publisher, 1969.

*On Certainty, edited by G. E. M. Anscombe and G. H. von Wright, translated by Denis Paul and G. E. M. Anscombe, Basil Blackwell, Oxford, 1969.

**Prototractatus: An Early Version of 'Tractatus Logico-Philosophicus'*, edited by B. F. McGuinness, T. Nyberg, and G. H. von Wright, with an Introduction by G. H. von Wright, Routledge & Kegan Paul, London, 1971.

**Remarks on Colour*, edited and translated by G. E. M. Anscombe, Basil Blackwell, Oxford, 1977.

Culture and Value, edited by G. H. von Wright in collaboration with Heikki Nyman, translated by Peter Winch, Basil Blackwell, Oxford, 1980. The German text was published in 1977 under the title *Vermischte Bemerkungen* by Suhrkamp Verlag, Frankfurt am Main.

**Remarks on the Philosophy of Psychology* vol. I, edited by G. E. M. Anscombe and G. H. von Wright, translated by G. E. M. Anscombe; vol. II, edited by G. H. von Wright and Heikki Nyman, translated by C. G. Luckhardt and M. A. E. Aue, Basil Blackwell, Oxford, 1980.

Letzte Schriften über die Philosophie der Psychologie (Last Writings on the Philosophy of Psychology), vol. I: Preliminary Studies for Part II of *Philosophical Investigations*, edited by G. H. von Wright and Heikki Nyman, translated by C. G. Luckhardt and M. A. E. Aue, Basil Blackwell, Oxford, 1982.

OTHER PUBLISHED WRITINGS BY WITTGENSTEIN

'Lecture on ethics', with an Introduction by Rush Rhees, *Philosophical Review*, vol. 74 (1965), pp. 3–12.

Paul Engelmann, *Letters from Ludwig Wittgenstein, With a Memoir*, edited by B. F. McGuinness, translated by L. Furtmüller, Basil Blackwell, Oxford, 1967. The German text was published under the title *Ludwig Wittgenstein, Briefe und Begegnungen*, same editor, R. Oldenbourg, Vienna and Munich, 1970.

'Bemerkungen über Frazers *The Golden Bough*', with an introductory note by Rush Rhees, *Synthese*, vol. 17 (1967), pp. 233–53.

'Notes for lectures on "private experience" and "sense data"', edited by Rush Rhees, published in the *Philosophical Review*, vol. 77 (1968), pp. 271–320; reprinted in O. R. Jones, editor, *The Private Language Argument*, Macmillan, London, 1971, pp. 226–75. This publication consists of excerpts from MSS 148, 149, and 151. Omissions are not indicated by the editor and the omitted passages are sometimes fully as important as the included material. We shall refer to the pages of the Jones reprint.

Briefe an Ludwig Ficker, edited by G. H. von Wright in collaboration with W. Methlagl, Otto Müller Verlag, Salzburg, 1969.

Letters to C. K. Ogden, with Comments on the English Translation of the 'Tractatus Logico-Philosophicus', edited with an Introduction by G. H. von Wright, Basil Blackwell, Oxford, and Routledge & Kegan Paul, London, 1973.

Letters to Russell, Keynes and Moore, edited with an Introduction by G. H. von Wright, assisted by B. F. McGuinness, Basil Blackwell, Oxford, 1974.

A number of letters by Wittgenstein have also been published in

Michael Nedo and Michele Ranchetti, editors, *Wittgenstein: Sein Leben in Bildern und Texten*, Suhrkamp Verlag, Frankfurt am Main, 1983.

LECTURE AND DISCUSSION NOTES NOT MADE BY WITTGENSTEIN

G. E. Moore, 'Wittgenstein's lectures in 1930–33' in G. E. Moore, *Philosophical Papers*, Allen & Unwin, London, 1959.

Lectures and Conversations on Aesthetics, Psychology, and Religious Belief, compiled from the notes taken by Yorick Smythies, Rush Rhees, and James Taylor, edited by Cyril Barrett, University of California Press, Berkeley and Los Angeles, 1967.

Wittgenstein's Lectures on the Foundations of Mathematics, Cambridge, 1939, from the notes of R. G. Bosanquet, Norman Malcolm, Rush Rhees, and Yorick Smythies, edited by Cora Diamond, Cornell University Press, Ithaca, N.Y., 1976.

Wittgenstein's Lectures, Cambridge 1932–1935, from the notes of Alice Ambrose and Margaret Macdonald, edited by Alice Ambrose, Basil Blackwell, Oxford, 1979.

Ludwig Wittgenstein and the Vienna Circle: Conversations recorded by Friedrich Waismann, edited by Brian McGuinness, translated by Joachim Schulte and Brian McGuinness, Basil Blackwell, Oxford, 1979.

Wittgenstein's Lectures, Cambridge 1930–1932, from the notes of John King and Desmond Lee, edited by Desmond Lee, Basil Blackwell, Oxford, 1980.

UNPUBLISHED MATERIAL BY WITTGENSTEIN

Wittgenstein's unpublished manuscripts are referred to by their numbers in G. H. von Wright, *Wittgenstein*, Basil Blackwell, Oxford, 1982, and by the pages in the original MSS.

All the translations from untranslated German MSS are by Jaakko Hintikka. Whenever the German text has not been published, the original German is given along with the English translation.

OTHER MS MATERIAL

Frank Ramsey Collection, University of Pittsburgh Libraries, Special Collections.

1
Wittgenstein and Language as the Universal Medium

1 LANGUAGE AS THE UNIVERSAL MEDIUM

We shall begin our investigation of Wittgenstein by presenting, in this first chapter, a viewpoint which helps one to understand not only Wittgenstein but also much of recent philosophy of language. This viewpoint was introduced into scholarly discussion in a special case by Jean van Heijenoort in his perceptive paper on Frege's conception of logic.[1] He characterizes it as a contrast between two conceptions of logic, which he labels 'logic as language' and 'logic as calculus'. He explains the former view in effect as a doctrine of the *universality* (in the sense of *inescapability*) *of logic*. We cannot as it were get outside our logic and its intended interpretation. For instance, an 'important consequence of the universality of logic is that nothing can be, or has to be, said outside of the system.'

In his suggestive paper, van Heijenoort traces several other consequences of the view of logic as language and attributes it to Frege. This view he contrasts to that of 'logic as calculus', according to which we can raise metatheoretic questions about our logic and even think of its interpretation as being changed, for instance, with respect to the domain over which its quantifiers range. His point is thus not that on this view logic is like an uninterpreted calculus, but rather that it is reinterpretable like a calculus.

Jaakko Hintikka has generalized van Heijenoort's contrast into a fundamental opposition between two different ways of looking at one's language.[2] He calls these 'language as the universal medium' and 'language as calculus'. According to the former view, one cannot as it were look at one's language from outside and describe it, as one can do to other objects that can be specified, referred to, described, discussed, and theorized about in language. The reason for this alleged impossibility is that one can use language to talk about something only if one can rely on a given definite interpretation, a given network of meaning relations obtaining between language and the world. Hence one cannot meaningfully and significantly say in language what these meaning relations are, for in any attempt to do so one must already presuppose them. Thus the gist of this view of language as the universal medium lies in the thesis of the *ineffability of semantics*, for it is precisely semantics that deals with those language–reality relationships. In this respect, the consequences of the view of language as the universal medium are especially close to those of the narrower doctrine of logic as language, for (as van Heijenoort noted) all logical semantics (model theory) is impossible if the view of language as the universal medium is correct.

2 SEMANTICISTS WITHOUT SEMANTICS

Several clarificatory comments are in order here. First, it is important to realize that the thesis of language as the universal medium implies primarily the inexpressibility of semantics rather than the impossibility of semantics, in the sense that a believer in language as the universal medium can nevertheless have many and sharp ideas about language–world connections, which are the subject of semantics. However, these relations are inexpressible if one believes in the view of language as the universal medium. In fact, this is, according to van Heijenoort, Frege's actual position. Frege had much more sophisticated ideas about the relation between our language and the world than first meet the eye. Frege is usually credited primarily with the sense-reference theory, which is for him essentially a theory about the meaning of expressions occurring in oblique (intensional) contexts. What is frequently not realized is that Frege also had a definite and articulated set of ideas about the semantics of ordinary extensional language, including truth-functional definitions of propositional connectives, the meaning of quantifiers, etc. However, since he does not believe in the proper linguistic expressibility of such semantical relationships, he does not incorporate them in his 'official' systematic theory, but leaves them on the level of indirect informal explanations.

The first main thesis of this chapter is that Wittgenstein's attitude to the ineffability of semantics was rather like Frege's.[3] Wittgenstein had, in both his early and his late philosophy, a clear and sweeping vision of how language and the world are connected with each other. Like Frege, he did not think that this vision could be expressed in language. Unlike Frege, the young Wittgenstein nevertheless believed that he could convey his vision by an oblique use of language. This nonliteral, secondary employment of language he had to consider as something different from *saying* what the semantics of our language is. This is the origin, it will be argued later, of Wittgenstein's notion of *showing* as distinguished from *saying*.

One specific thing that is inexpressible, according to the view of language as the universal medium, is what *would be* the case *if* the semantical relations between language and the world were different. In other words, one cannot on this view vary the representative relations between our expressions on the one hand and the reality on the other. We are stuck, logically speaking, with our one and only home language. Even the enterprise of learning a new language, in the usual sense of the word, should strictly speaking be conceptualized as extending one's first (and only) language rather than as acquiring a radically new one. After all, the only way in which one could learn the 'new' language is by means of the old one, according to this view. In brief, the view of language as the universal medium implies a thesis of the *universality of language* reminiscent of the universality of logic to which Frege was committed.

The impossibility of varying the interpretation of our language is an important additional reason why all model theory is impossible on the view of language as the universal medium. For a systematic variation of the representative relations between language (or at least its non-logical vocabulary) and the world is a conceptual cornerstone of all logical semantics. Indeed, the development of logical semantics and its technical twin, model theory, has gone hand in hand with a gradual transition from the view of language as the universal medium to the view of language as calculus. It is striking that those logicians, notably Quine, who have remained committed to the view of language as the universal medium have completely failed (or refused) to contribute to model theory or to use it in their work.

This situation leads a commentator to a terminological dilemma. In describing Frege's, Wittgenstein's, or Quine's views about language–world relationships, it is very tempting to speak of their views about semantics. Is it not precisely semantics that studies these links between our expressions and their targets in reality? Yes, but all semantics, as it is practised as a systematic enterprise whose results are codifiable in language, is committed to the view of language as calculus, for reasons just noted. Yet these philosophers do not share this presuppositition. Hence it will sound strange to speak of the semantical views of such philosopher-logicians, since they rejected the very idea of systematic, codified semantics. For instance, Jaakko Hintikka has been led to speak of Frege as a 'semanticist who did not believe in semantics'.[4] The paradox is in reality only a terminological one, and need not mislead one who keeps in mind what has to be meant by terms like 'semantics' in the case of someone who is committed to language as the universal medium.

3 LANGUAGE AS THE UNIVERSAL MEDIUM IN WITTGENSTEIN'S PREDECESSORS

In the case of Bertrand Russell, the consequences of his qualified adoption of the view of language as the universal medium have been studied by Peter Hylton, and to some extent also by Warren Goldfarb.[5] These consequences need not concern us here, except for one particular area where they impinge on Wittgenstein, namely, Russell's Introduction to Wittgenstein's *Tractatus Logico-Philosophicus*. There Russell puts forward, as a solution to the problem of the inexpressibility of language, the idea of metalanguage, i.e., a language in which we can speak about a given language (later termed the *object language*).

For us latter-day readers, Russell's suggestion may too easily seem trite, since it is practically the first idea that we would expect to occur to a competent logician or philosopher of language. In reality, it was for Russell a radical and daring departure from his earlier position, in which he had been deeply committed to the universality of language. The depth of Wittgenstein's impact on Russell may be measured in part by the sharpness of this departure from Russell's own earlier views. One of the consequences of the idea of 'logic as language', which van Heijenoort registered in the case of Frege, is precisely the impossibility (and the consequent absence) of metalogical considerations. The same point has been argued in the case of the early Russell by Peter Hylton. The novelty of Russell's proposal in his Introduction to the *Tractatus* can be seen from such observations. Russell's suggestion is an attempt to overcome the view of language as the universal medium, perhaps forced on him when he saw the consequences of the view so explicitly developed by Wittgenstein, who firmly believed in it.

The idea of language as the universal medium can be considered as a linguistic counterpart of certain Kantian doctrines.[6] The connection is pointed out by Wittgenstein:

> The limit of language shows itself in the impossibility of describing the fact that corresponds to a sentence . . . without repeating that very sentence.

> What we are dealing with here is the Kantian solution to the problem of philosophy. (*Vermischte Bemerkungen*, p. 27; translation by Jaakko Hintikka)

What happened on the way from Kant to Wittgenstein is more than a mere linguistic turn, however. The Kantian doctrine of the limits of our knowledge and the unknowability of things in themselves, i.e., things considered independently of our knowledge-seeking activities and of the means they employ, should of course correspond to a doctrine of the limits of language in the sense of a doctrine of the inexpressibility of things independently of some one particular language. This would amount to something like linguistic relativism rather than a thesis of the ineffability of semantics. Or so it seems. However, Jaakko Hintikka has argued that there is an intrinsic link, virtually a mutual implication, between the unknowability of things considered in themselves, independently of our knowledge-seeking activities and the conceptual framework that they utilize, and the unknowability of these activities and of this framework.[7] This 'paradox of transcendental knowledge' is matched on the linguistic side by a similar mutal dependence between the ineffability of things considered in abstraction from language (and of the conceptual system it embodies) and the inexpressibility of those semantical links which are supposed to mediate between language and reality.

Kant does not seem to take cognizance of the paradox of transcendental knowledge. However, there has been a somewhat sharper awareness among subsequent philosophers of the linguistic counterpart of the paradox of transcendental knowledge. This counterpart is the mutual dependence of linguistic relativity (impossibility of expressing reality as it is, considered independently of our language) and the ineffability of semantics. Wittgenstein, for one, held both views. In particular, it will be argued later in this chapter that Wittgenstein maintained the ineffability of semantics throughout his career. His belief in the inexpressibility of reality *an sich* can be seen, e.g., from *Philosophical Remarks*, VIII, sec. 85:

> If someone said: Very well, how do you know that the whole of reality can be represented by propositions? The reply is: I only know that it can be represented by propositions, and to draw a line between a part which can and a part which can't be so represented is something I can't do in language. Language *means* the totality of propositions.

The universality of language – one of the main consequences of the idea of language as the universal medium – is expressed by Wittgenstein among other places in *Notebooks 1914–1916* (entry for 29 May 1915):

> But is *language*: the *only* language?
> Why should there not be a mode of expression through which I can talk *about* language in such a way that it can appear to me in co-ordination with something else?
> Suppose that music were such a mode of expression: then it is at any

rate characteristic of *science* that *no* musical themes can occur in it.
I myself write only sentences down here? And why?
How is language unique?

As one can see, Wittgenstein ends up entertaining the uniqueness of
language here. It is also significant that he connects the uniqueness of
language with the impossibility of describing it from the outside.

A discussion of the role of the idea of language as the universal
medium in Wittgenstein falls naturally into several parts. These
include (a) the consequences of the ineffability of semantics in the
Tractatus; (b) the ineffability of semantics in relation to the idea of
formalism; (c) the ineffability of semantics and the limits of language;
(d) the consequences of the idea of language as the universal medium
for Wittgenstein's ideas of grammar, calculus, and the publicity of language; and (e) language as the universal medium in later Wittgenstein.

4 THE INEFFABILITY OF SEMANTICS IN THE *TRACTATUS*

It is no news that Wittgenstein's *Tractatus* represents a version of the
thesis of the ineffability of semantics. If an example is needed to
illustrate this fact, 3.263 will serve the purpose:

> The meanings of primitive signs can be explained by means of eluci-
> dations. Elucidations are propositions that contain the primitive signs.
> So they can be understood if the meanings of those signs are already
> known.

It is also unmistakable that Wittgenstein's belief in the ineffability
of semantics is a consequence of his adoption of the idea of language
as the universal medium; witness, e.g., the following (4.12):

> In order to be able to represent the logical form, we should have to be
> able to station ourselves with propositions somewhere outside logic,
> that is to say outside the world.

It is likewise clear that the most important consequence of the idea
of language as the universal medium in the *Tractatus* is the contrast
between what can be *said* and what can only be *shown*. What is
perhaps not equally clear is that everything which, according to the
Tractatus, can only be shown involves in the last analysis semantical
relationships. Basically, it is thus the world–language links, and
these links only, that cannot be said but can be shown according to
Wittgenstein.

Here this claim will be argued for in a number of representative cases.

Perhaps the easiest one is the sense of a sentence, which according to 4.022 can only be shown. But what is this sense? A meaningful sentence is understood by Wittgenstein to include both the sentential sign and its 'projective relation to the world' (3.12). Moreover, this 'method of projection is the thinking of the sense of the sentence' (3.11). Along the same lines, he says in 4.2 that 'the sense of a sentence is its agreement and disagreement with the possibilities of atomic facts obtaining or not obtaining.' These relations of agreement are of course just what above have been called semantical relations. Hence, it is impossible to say what the sense of a sentence is because we cannot express in language the semantical or 'projective' relations which connect a sentence with atomic facts according to Wittgenstein.

It follows by the same token that the identity of the meanings of two expressions cannot be asserted in language, as Wittgenstein indeed says in 6.2322.

Another group of consequences of the inexpressibility of semantics in the *Tractatus* is arrived at by considering the meaning of the simples of language (Wittgenstein's 'names'). Their relation to the objects that are their meanings is ineffable, according to the early Wittgenstein. This ineffability is apparently taken by him to imply that we cannot even say in any particular case that there is something at the receiving end of the relation, i.e., that the name in question is not empty, any more than we can say in language what an object *is*, as distinguished from what it is *like* (see 3.221). (But cf. here chapter 3, section 4, below.) In other words, the concept of individual existence is inexpressible. We cannot say: *This* and *this* there is in the world, *that* there is not. (See 5.61.) The existence of an object can only be shown through its name's use in the language. This is taken by Wittgenstein to imply that in a logically correct language all names are non-empty, which implication is confirmed by 5.47 (second paragraph) and by 5.441. Nor can we say in language how many objects there are in the world (see 4.1272). When the elementary sentences are given, the totality of *all* elementary sentences is thereby given (see 5.524); and that totality determines the totality of *all* objects in the world (ibid.). And that totality of elementary sentences, Wittgenstein says explicitly, is determined by the application of logic. From this it follows further, according to Wittgenstein, that the world as a whole is inexpressible, because its boundaries are inexpressible. (Cf. 5.61.) For these boundaries are determined by the totality of objects, or equivalently, the totality of elementary propositions. Furthermore, since ethics and aesthetics deal with the world as a whole (*Notebooks 1914–1916*,

p. 83; cf. 6.43), they, too, are transcendental (6.421), i.e., belong to the realm of what can only be shown, not said.

The ineffability of the simple name–object relations has several further consequences for the early Wittgenstein. It amounts to maintaining that the existence of an individual can only be shown by means of language through the use of its name; it cannot be stated. This view is apparently taken by Wittgenstein to imply that the identity of individuals is also shown by the use of the same name. This leads him to his well-known nonstandard treatment of identity in the *Tractatus*.

Logical forms (forms of representation) comprise another rich class of things that can only be shown, not said.

> 2.172   A picture cannot, however, depict its pictorial form: it displays it [*weist sie auf*].

It is also clear in the *Tractatus* that logical forms – more generally, pictorial forms – are vehicles of semantical language–world relations:

> 2.22   What a picture represents it represents independently of its truth or falsity, by means of its pictorial form.

In particular,

> 2.181   A picture whose pictorial form is logical form is called a logical picture.

Such logical pictures Wittgenstein identifies with propositions. Their forms are inexpressible, because the semantics fo our language is inexpressible. Wittgenstein indicates quite clearly that the reason for this ineffability is the idea of language as our one and only inescapable medium:

> 2.174   A picture cannot, however, place itself outside its representational form.

Hence all matters of logical form belong to the sphere of what can only be shown, not said, because of the ineffability of all semantics. Since questions of logical form are frequent in the *Tractatus*, this observation explains why many of the detailed matters that Wittgenstein considers merely 'showable' are so thought of by him.

Among these more specific matters is the status of tautologies or contradictions as lacking sense (4.461). Since logical operations deal with relations in forms (5.241), they can only manifest themselves in a variable (5.24).

Furthermore, the polyadicity of a relation cannot be expressed in language, although it can of course be shown. Thus one can understand Wittgenstein's denial that there are privileged relations or privileged polyadicities of relations. (See 5.553–5.5541.) Likewise type-distinctions, in which Peter Geach has wanted to see the gist of Wittgenstein's saying–showing distinction,[8] are inexpressible according to Wittgenstein precisely because they are aspects of the logical form of entities of different kinds. Hence they can only be shown. (Cf. 3.331–3.332.) Both polyadicities and type-distinctions are matters of logical form.

There may be even more in common among these different cases than first meets the eye. One of the most striking doctrines of the *Tractatus* is that all logical forms can be built up of the forms of simple objects. We shall return to this doctrine below in chapter 3. Since it is, according to Wittgenstein, impossible to say what a particular object essentially is, it is likewise impossible to say what its logical form is. Hence it is also impossible to say in language what the logical form of a proposition is, since this form consists of ineffable forms of simple objects. Hence it follows that the formal properties of propositions and of objects are inexpressible, which is indeed a familiar doctrine of the *Tractatus* (see 4.12–4.1211; 6.12). Thus the ineffability of logical forms in general is in the *Tractatus* a consequence of Wittgenstein's doctrine of the reducibility of all logical forms to those of simple objects plus the ineffability of those objects themselves.

Thus Wittgenstein's doctrine of showing has two roots in the *Tractatus*, a more general and a more specific one. The more general reason for Wittgenstein's view is the ineffability of all semantical relations. The more specific reason is the inexpressibility of simple objects and their forms. It may even be suspected that all cases of merely showing in the *Tractatus* ultimately reduce to the ineffability of simple objects and their logical forms. Everything else in language consists after all of combinations of simple names. We shall not try to argue for this reduction in this chapter, however. It can be considered a consequence of the results we shall argue for in chapters 3–4 below.

5 LANGUAGE AS THE UNIVERSAL MEDIUM AND THE PARADOX OF FORMALIZATION

There is one particularly subtle manifestation of the assumption of language as the universal medium which is important for the interpretation of both the early and the late philosophy of Wittgenstein and which is also found in Frege.[9] We may call it the paradox of formalization in logic. What it amounts to is the fact that an emphasis on formalism in logic can have two diametrically opposed motivations. Clearly, one who embraces the idea of language as calculus can employ formalism to mark those ingredients of language whose interpretations are, on the occasion in question, thought of as being varied. The rules governing such formulas must then be formulated in purely formal terms.

However, a believer in language as the universal medium is pushed in the same direction by an entirely different line of thought. Such a philosopher typically believes in a fixed universal set of meaning relations between language and the world. That system of semantical relations cannot be varied, and it cannot be discussed in language. Hence, the introduction of formalism cannot be motivated in the same way as in the case of believers in language as calculus. However, even though an adherent of the view of language as the universal medium firmly believes that logic is based on one system of meaning relations, he or she cannot speak of those meaning relations in formulating a system of logic. All that a believer in language as the universal medium can do in his or her logic is to speak of the words and other symbols of language, abstracted from their semantical function. In brief, he or she is led to a purely formalistic conception of logic by a belief in the ineffability of semantics. Hence, the idea of a logical syntax of language as a purely formal enterprise can be motivated in two entirely different ways. Notwithstanding one's initial expectations, this idea also comes eminently naturally to a defender of the undiluted idea of language as the universal medium.

This is precisely what is found in Frege and in early Wittgenstein. It may appear as one of the minor paradoxes of the recent history of logic that the first complete formalization of first-order logic, and indeed the very idea of a formal system of logic, should have been developed by that sworn enemy of formalistic philosophies of logic and mathematics, Gottlob Frege. The paradox disappears, however, as soon as the role of the idea of language as the universal medium in Frege's thought is appreciated. This possible outcome of regarding language as the universal medium also provides a partial explanation of another feature of Frege's thought, the fact that Frege gives up all attempts to assign any semantical (let alone intuitive) content to his logical axioms and rules of proof.[10]

Wittgenstein expresses in his discussions with Waismann (28 December 1930, see *Philosophical Remarks*, p. 320) his agreement with Frege's criticism of the formalists. In other respects, too, one meets in Wittgenstein's *Tractatus* a picture similar to that found in Frege. The introduction of the idea of logical syntax is motivated precisely in terms of the ineffability of semantics:

3.33   In logical syntax the meaning of a sign should never play a role. It must be possible to establish logical syntax without mentioning the *meaning* of a sign: only the description of expressions may be pre-supposed.

Other passages of the *Tractatus* are also relevant here; cf., e.g., 3.331–3.334.

For these reasons, it is incorrect to refer to the *Tractatus* view as asserting the inexpressibility of *language* per se or the inexpressibility of the *structure* of language (as Russell does in his Introduction to the *Tractatus*). The inexpressibility is confined to the *semantics* of our language and its structure. In contrast, the *syntax* of language can be expressed and discussed in language. And in fact, the views expressed in the *Tractatus* amount to a strong incentive to study 'the logical *syntax* of language'.

One symptom of the same abstention from semantical consider-ations as was practised by Wittgenstein is the preference for 'the formal mode' of language by Carnap and some other members of the Vienna Circle. This tendency culminates in Carnap's *Logical Syntax of Language* and is there attributed in so many words to Wittgenstein.[11] In the light of our observations, it is not surprising to find that Wittgenstein himself explicitly draws the connection between the restriction to a 'formal mode of speech' which the Vienna Circle practised for a while and his main ideas in the *Tractatus*. In a letter to Schlick on 8 August 1932,[12] he accuses Carnap of taking over his ideas without any acknowledgement:

> Fifthly, you know very well yourself that Carnap is not taking any step beyond me when he stands for the formal and against the "material mode of speech" [*inhaltliche Redeweise*]. And I cannot imagine that Carnap should have misunderstood so completely the last few prop-ositions of the *Tractatus* – and hence the basic ideas of the entire book [as not to know that, too].

This is also interesting in that it shows that Wittgenstein clearly believed in the ineffability of semantics and in the resulting need of a purely formal approach in 1932.

6 WITTGENSTEIN'S NOTION OF GRAMMAR

This background of Wittgenstein's 'formalistic' ideas in the *Tractatus* does not seem to have prompted any serious misinterpretations. However, similar practices in Wittgenstein's later work have proved somewhat more misleading.

They are exemplified by Wittgenstein's deeply ingrained habit in his later work of speaking of what are obviously semantical rules (rules of relating language to reality) as *grammatical* rules. Here are some examples:

> One is inclined to make a distinction between rules of grammar that set up a connection between language and reality and those that do not. (*Philosophical Grammar*, IV, sec. 46)

> . . . the grammar describes also the application of the language, that which one might call the connection between language and reality.[13]

As long as this peculiar force of Wittgenstein's terms 'grammar' and 'grammatical' is not appreciated, it is very easily thought that by his frequent references to 'grammar' he meant intralinguistic rules of language, i.e., rules for speaking or writing, and not the rules for extralinguistic language-games, i.e., rules for using language for non-linguistic purposes, as was his intention. (For the role of language-games, see chapter 9 below.)

How tempting the potential confusion is here can be seen, e.g., from *PI*, I, sec. 496:

> Grammar does not tell how language must be constructed in order to fulfil its purpose, in order to have such-and-such an effect on human beings. It only describes and in no way explains *the use of signs* [emphasis added].

A priori, the italicized expression could refer to the use of signs inside language – the kind of use that is discussed in books of grammar. This sounds paradoxical, for the very purpose of the language-game idea is to explain the *syntactical* use of signs by spelling out their *semantics*. It is only in a wider context that we can realize what Wittgenstein means, viz. the use of signs in the language-games which connect language and reality. It is language-games that are unanalysable and unexplainable according to Wittgenstein, not the verbal usage.[14]

Historically, Wittgenstein's adoption of the term 'grammar' has to be seen against the background of the ideas he expressed in the *Tractatus*. There he had put forward the 'mirroring' idea which we shall study in chapter 5 below and according to which the admissible combinations of symbols in a fully analysed language match the possible configurations of the entities they represent. In brief, in a logically analysed language, grammar matches ontology. From this thesis it is not a long step to the idea that the grammar of a language reflects also its semantics.

Wittgenstein's extremely wide sense of 'grammar' is paralleled by the inclusive meaning he gives to the word 'language' in his writings. Within the scope of that term, he includes things that are normally taken to be merely helpful paraphernalia for the use of language, such as colour samples in the use of colour-vocabulary. Likewise, the use of language includes for Wittgenstein much more than speaking a language (making utterances). It includes also the role of language in facilitating activities which are in themselves nonlinguistic. No wonder, therefore, that by the 'grammar' of a language Wittgenstein means the rules governing all these various activities, not just the rules for speaking and writing the language. The dangers of this wide use are illustrated in chapter 9, sec. 4, below.

7 WITTGENSTEIN'S NOTION OF CALCULUS

Essentially the same comments as were made in sec. 6 on the force of 'grammar' in Wittgenstein apply also, perhaps even more surprisingly, to Wittgenstein's use of the term 'calculus'. This word seems to refer paradigmatically to the use of signs *inside* language. Do we not mean by 'calculating' essentially just manipulating symbols without regard to their meaning? This is in fact what the terms 'calculus' and 'calculate' are frequently used to highlight in recent philosophy.

This, of course, may be one of the many ideas Wittgenstein wants to capture by his term 'calculus'. But he is also here highlighting, not so much his idea of language–world relationships, as the ineffability of semantics. Since we cannot express in our language its semantics, all we can do is express its syntax. And, as we saw, according to Wittgenstein 'every syntax can be conceived of as a system of rules of a game,' i.e., as a calculus.

However, Wittgenstein's use of the term 'calculus' in his middle period is primarily calculated to emphasize an altogether different facet of the situation. Instead of focusing on the absence of all attention to the meanings of the symbols involved in calculation, Wittgenstein focuses on a completely independent aspect of the analogy. It is that in applying language *we have to do something*, in the same way that in calculating it does not suffice merely to stare at the signs. *We* have to do the calculating. (Alas, the prevalence of pocket calculators is bound to make this point harder for future readers of Wittgenstein to appreciate.) That this in fact is Wittgenstein's point is neatly verified by *Ludwig Wittgenstein and the Vienna Circle*, p. 171, where Wittgenstein says of an example:

> I use the picture like the signs in a calculus, as a point of contact for action.

Likewise, Wittgenstein writes in *Philosophical Grammar*, X, sec. 140:

> Language is for us a calculus; it is characterized by *language acts* [*Sprachhandlungen*; our translation].

Thus the acts Wittgenstein calls attention to by using the term 'calculus' are not intralinguistic, either. He is not inviting his readers to consider a mere game with symbols. Somewhat surprisingly, Wittgenstein is not focusing on what happens in natural language, either:

> It is an incorrect idea that the application of a calculus to the grammar of the actual language lends it a reality which it did not have earlier.[15]

Wittgenstein's emphasis on the activity of calculating is also illustrated by the following titbits:

> Augustine does describe a calculus of our language, only not everything that we call language is this [particular] calculus. (*Philosophical Grammar*, II, sec. 19)

> When someone interprets, or understands, a sign in one sense or another, what he is doing is taking a step in a calculus (like a calculation). What he *does* is roughly what he does if he gives expression to his interpretation. (*Philosophical Grammar*, I, sec. 13)

How elusive this point is may be seen for instance from *PI*, I, sec. 136. There Wittgenstein says:

> what a proposition is is in one sense determined by the rules of sentences formation . . . and in another sense by the use of the sign in the language-game.

Wittgenstein's somewhat unfortunate use of the term 'calculus' can be characterized as an attempt to capture *both* of these ideas by one and the same term, the former by emphasizing the idea of 'mere calculation' or calculus as a purely formal operation and the latter by stressing the idea that in calculating we actually have to do something. This attempt proved unsuccessful in the final analysis. Accordingly, Wittgenstein in the *Philosophical Investigations* almost completely gave up the calculus analogy. But it is important to realize that this was not because he gave up either of the two points he wanted to highlight. He merely came to realize that the term 'calculus' could not serve both purposes at the same time.

The use of 'calculate' involved in Wittgenstein's second point is probably inspired by mathematical usage, more specifically, by the contrast between establishing the existence of a certain number by a purely non-constructive proof and actually being able to calculate it.

In the usage which has been described and which is characteristic of Wittgenstein's middle period, 'calculus' means nearly the same as his famous term 'language-game'. Indeed, the latter term seems to have been adopted by Wittgenstein later than the former. Kenny quotes an instructive passage from *Philosophical Grammar*, II, sec. 31, where Wittgenstein actually passes over from the use of the word 'calculus' to that of 'game'.[16] This is an early stage of the development of the notion of language-game, for the 'game' in question is still a play with words. But undoubtedly the idea of calculus is one of the most important sources of the concept of language-game in Wittgenstein.

In view of this interpretation of the role of language-games in Wittgenstein's late philosophy, it is especially interesting to see that he sometimes says of calculi exactly what we shall maintain later in this book that he thought of language-games:

It is the *calculus* of thought that connects with extramental reality. (*Philosophical Grammar*, VIII, sec. 111)

There are certain differences between the two terms, however, other than that. 'Calculus' seems to have been preferred by Wittgenstein in his writings from the same period as *Philosophical Grammar*, 'language-game' in his later writings. This change may also be partly due to the fact that 'calculus' seems to presuppose the existence of explicit rules in a way which 'language-game' does not. This makes a crucial difference, for (as is spelled out below in chapter 7) Wittgenstein in his last period not only did not believe in sharp rules for language-games (cf., e.g., *PI*, I, secs. 100–8); he went further and firmly believed that language-games were conceptually prior to their rules, however sharp or unsharp. In this respect, there is thus a clear and important contrast between the terms 'language-game' and 'calculus' in late Wittgenstein. This provided him with an additional reason to give up the term 'calculus', except perhaps when calculi with sharp explicit rules are involved. Indeed, one use of the term 'calculus' by the Wittgenstein of the *Philosophical Investigations* is precisely to highlight the fact that an activity has sharp rules. This is what Wittgenstein does, e.g., in *PI*, I, sec. 81. It is nevertheless significant that even here Wittgenstein feels called upon to point out explicitly that he means 'calculi with fixed rules' or 'a calculus according to definite rules'. Moreover, it is clear that the calculi of *PI*, I, sec. 81, are not formal calculi, for they comprise uttering a sentence which the utterer means and understands.

This parentage of the term 'language-game' in Wittgenstein is important to keep in mind because some of the same misleading implications (e.g., the suggestion of involving merely a intralingual game) which attach to the term 'calculus' sometimes also attach to the term 'language-game' in Wittgenstein's later philosophy. In order to correct this biased connotation of the term 'calculus', as Wittgenstein for a while tried to use it, it may be salutary to note his reasons for abandoning it. The main reason does not seem to have been the misleading suggestion of precision, but the misleading suggestion of intralinguistic activity. Speaking of a calculus seems to imply that we are dealing with the manipulation of symbols, whereas Wittgenstein's language-games involve much more than speech-acts or other language-acts. Otherwise, they could not serve their basic purpose of linking language with reality. (Cf. chapter 9 below.)

Did the dangerous connotations of the terms 'calculus' and 'language-game' ever mislead Wittgenstein himself? It seems not. One of the uses of the idea of language as the universal medium as applied to Wittgenstein is to dispel the impression that Wittgenstein might have misled himself here, in the sense of thinking of his language-games as intralinguistic games, by explaining the true motivation on which his usage is based and which does not involve the idea of calculi, or language-games as linguistic calculi.

8 WITTGENSTEIN AND THE LIMITS OF LANGUAGE

Here we shall take up a line of thought from the end of section 4. The inexpressibility of the existence of the particular objects which there are in the world is a special case of what Wittgenstein calls the *limits of language*. This doctrine of Wittgenstein's is intimately related to his belief in language as the universal medium. Since Wittgenstein identified in his early philosophy what can be said and what can be thought, this view appears in the *Tractatus* also as a doctrine of the limits of what is thinkable. It is one of the most important doctrines of Wittgenstein's in his own estimation. In his own preface to the *Tractatus* he writes:

> Thus the aim of the book is to set a limit to thought, or rather – not to thought, but to the expression of thoughts: for in order to be able to set a limit to thought, we should have to find both sides of the limit thinkable (i.e. we should have to be able to think what cannot be thought).
> It will therefore only be in language that the limit can be set, and what lies on the other side of the limit is simply nonsense.

It is largely this task of limiting the realm of the thinkable that makes Wittgenstein's philosophical enterprise not only analogous to but intrinsically similar to Kant's. The main thesis of this section is that those limits were ultimately thought of by Wittgenstein as consequences of the ineffability of semantics.

This thesis is fairly obvious as applied to Wittgenstein's *Tractatus*. There the limits of language are connected explicitly with the doctrine of showing which was argued above to be a consequence of the ineffability of semantics in Wittgenstein's thinking.[17] Furthermore, it can easily be seen that the main limit of language is set by the totality of objects that are named in the language. This view is examined more closely in chapter 3 below. For Wittgenstein, the most important 'limit of language' therefore was, not the external (as it were) boundary of language, but the internal limitation of language, viz. the inevitable restrictions on what one can say in a language about that language.

It might seem less obvious that Wittgenstein also emphasized in his later philosophy, in similar terms, the importance of the limits of language – and also their roots in the inexpressibility of semantical relations. Yet his commitment to these ideas is unmistakable. Thus he writes in MS 108, p. 265 (quoted by Hallett):[18]

> This impossibility of expressing in language the conditions of agreement between a meaningful proposition – a thought – and reality is the solution of the puzzle.

In *PI*, I, sec. 119, we also find reference to the limits of language. This reference is not only one of approval, but one positively in the spirit of Wittgenstein's Kantian enterprise (his 'Critique of Pure Language'):

> The results of philosophy are the uncovering of one or another piece of plain nonsense and of bumps that the understanding has got by running its head against the *limits of language*. These bumps make us see the value of the discovery. [Emphasis added.]

This remark is not an incidental aside on Wittgenstein's part, either. It is an integral part of his most explicit explanation in his later thought of the nature of the whole philosophical enterprise. (This explanation is what *PI*, I, secs. 116–28, amount to.) Hence the importance of the 'limits of language' view for the later Wittgenstein is scarcely smaller than it was for the Wittgenstein of the *Tractatus*.

One way of arguing for the presence of the idea of the limits of language in the late Wittgenstein is to refute the competing interpretations. A convenient and knowledgeable example of the interpretations we are rejecting is offered by G. Hallett's *Companion*.

In his comment on the quoted passage, Hallett claims that in his later thought Wittgenstein 'saw the error in his whole idea' of the limits of language which he had held earlier. Hallett is nevertheless radically mistaken. He does not supply any direct textual evidence for his view. What is more important, his general discussion of Wittgenstein's position in the *Philosophical Investigations* (see Hallett, *Companion*, 'General Introduction', secs. 41 and 43) is predicated on a mistaken idea of what the limits of language are to which Wittgenstein is referring in *PI*, I, sec. 119. Hallett thinks that the limits of language in the *Tractatus* are due to the strictness of the rules that are supposed to govern a logically correct language. Accordingly, Hallett is led to believe that when Wittgenstein gave up strict rules, he thereby gave up the idea of the limits of language. As we have seen, however, the limits of language Wittgenstein is talking about are due to the ineffability of the semantical rules of language. This inexpressibility entails, among other things, the linguistic inaccessibility of the relation of a true sentence to the fact which makes it true. (Cf. Wittgenstein's remark on 'Kant's solution to the problem of philosophy', quoted in sec. 3 above.) Whether such semantical rules are strict or loose does not make the slightest difference. Objectively viewed, all the information Hallett in fact supplied supports this interpretation rather than his.[19]

Further evidence is easily forthcoming. For instance in *Philosophical Grammar*, VI, sec. 71, Wittgenstein writes:

> "But language can expand." Certainly, but if this word "expand" has a sense here, then I know *already* what I mean by it. I must be able to specify how I imagine such an expansion. And what I can't think, I can't now express or even hint at. And in *this* case the word "now" means "in this calculus" or "if the words are used according to *these* grammatical rules" . . .
>
> No sign leads us beyond itself, and no argument either.

9 LANGUAGE AS THE UNIVERSAL MEDIUM AND THE PUBLIC CHARACTER OF LANGUAGE

Wittgenstein's belief in the universality of language also seems to have encouraged him to emphasize the public character of language. Since the link between the two is not one of implication, it is somewhat difficult to see precisely how Wittgenstein made the transition from the idea of language as the universal medium to the status of language as a part of the public physical world. His line of thought can nevertheless be seen in passages like the following (MS 108, p. 277, also MS 116, p. 6):

> What is expressible through language I call thought. Then it can be translated from this language into *another*. I want to say: all thought must then take place in symbols.
>
> But if one says "How am I supposed to know what he means, all I can see are merely his symbols," then I say: "How is *he* supposed to know what he means, all that he has are merely his symbols."
>
> The question "How is that [expression] meant," makes sense only when it amounts to "it is meant *thus*." This "thus" is a linguistic expression.
>
> A language [or, what is said – Wittgenstein's variant] can be explained only by means of a language, wherefore *the language* cannot be explained.
>
> The aim of philosophy is to build a wall where the language simply comes to an end.
>
> One can also put it thus: Since one expresses oneself only in a given language system and since one therefore can explain only in this system what a sentence means, eventually meanings disappear totally from the language and hence from consideration, and the only thing we can consider remains the language [itself].
>
> When we explain the meaning of a sentence, we translate it into a language less prone to misunderstanding.

The German text is given in an appendix to this chapter. This passage shows how Wittgenstein's belief in the ineffability of meanings led him to his idea of the limits of language and also to the idea that somehow all we can consider in philosophy is language as an independent formal structure, which is part of the physical world. Similar passages will be quoted in chapter 7 below.

The basic idea seems to be this: If we are trying to make the words or sentences of one language understandable to a speaker of another language, in the last analysis the only thing we can do is to present a set of rules for translating from the former language to the latter. Those translation rules cannot rely on the meanings of words. Since they cannot be expressed in language, they have to be formal, that is, depend only on the public feature of symbols. Consequently, what is given to us by a foreign sentence is merely a configuration of symbols. And in principle the same holds for one's own language.

This line of thought, modified in different ways and developed further, is in evidence at two crucial junctures of Wittgenstein's later philosophy, first in his decisive initial change of mind in October 1929 and then later in his rejection of private languages in the *Philosophical*

Investigations. We shall cross these interpretational bridges when we come to them. Then we shall also discuss how much philosophical traffic these bridges can really bear.

10 THE INEFFABILITY OF SEMANTICS IN THE *PHILOSOPHICAL INVESTIGATIONS*

Here we shall examine the role of the ineffability of semantics in Wittgenstein's later philosophy. Wittgenstein indicates clearly in an important passage of the *Philosophical Investigations* that he is there, too, accepting the view of language as the universal medium, including prominently its corollary, the universality of (our actual) language:

> When I talk about language (words, sentences, etc.) I must speak the language of every day. Is this language somehow too coarse and material for what we want to say? *Then how is another one to be constructed?* – And how strange that we should be able to do anything at all with the one we have!

> In giving explanations I already have to use language full-blown (not some sort of preparatory, provisional one); this by itself shews that I can adduce only exterior facts about language.

> Yes, but then how can these explanations satisfy us? – Well, your very questions were framed in this language; they had to be expressed in this language, if there was anything to ask!

> And your scruples are misunderstandings.

> Your questions refer to words; so I have to talk about words.

> You say: the point isn't the word, but its meaning, and you think of the meaning as a thing of the same kind as the word, though also different from the word. Here the word, there the meaning. The money, and the cow that you can buy with it. (But contrast: money, and its usefulness.) (*PI*, I, sec. 120)[20]

This is as explicit a statement of the view of language as the universal medium as one can hope to find. The first three paragraphs affirm the thesis of the universality of language. At the end of the second paragraph (and again in the fifth) Wittgenstein subscribes once again to the 'formalistic' consequences of the ineffability of semantics. (Only the 'exterior facts about language' can be expressed in it.) The last paragraph is particularly interesting in that it shows how

Wittgenstein's doctrine of meaning as use was based on his belief in language as the universal medium.

11 LANGUAGE AS THE UNIVERSAL MEDIUM AND LINGUISTIC RELATIVISM

Another prima facie consequence of Wittgenstein's belief in language as the universal medium deserves notice. The inexpressibility of semantical relations alternative to our own encourages a form of linguistic relativism. If lions could speak, we could not understand them, Wittgenstein says. (See *PI*, II, xi, p. 223.) There does not seem to be much reason not to assume that some human societies could in principle likewise have such different 'ways of life' that we could not understand their members. It is such a linguistic relativism, it seems, that Wittgenstein's version of solipsism in the *Tractatus* partly dramatizes. In Wittgenstein's last writings, this individual solipsism is transformed into a 'cultural solipsism', better regarded as linguistic relativism. Such a relativism is strongly suggested, for instance, by *PI*, II, xi, p. 226:

What has to be accepted, what is given, are – one can say – *forms of life*.

Such forms of life have been throughout the *Philosophical Investigations* the highest court of semantical appeal according to Wittgenstein, and now they turn out to be something that can in principle be accepted by us and be given to us. Hence they must be something that alternatively could be rejected by us and not be given to us. In MS 109, p. 196, Wittgenstein confesses as openly his linguistic solipsism as in the *Tractatus* he confessed his experiential solipsism:

A language that I don't understand is no language. [Eine Sprache die ich nicht verstehe ist keine Sprache.]

An apparent counter-example to our attribution of conceptual relativism to Wittgenstein is found in *PI*, I, sec. 206, where the English translation makes Wittgenstein speak of 'the common behaviour of mankind' which enables us to interpret an unknown language. As we shall point out in chapter 8, sec. 5, Wittgenstein's German text does not carry any such anti-relativistic implications.

In MS 109, p. 58 Wittgenstein in so many words professes linguistic relativism:[21]

> The relation . . . between thoughts and reality is reproduced by language through a shared expression. The relation cannot be expressed in other ways.

> We are confronted here by a kind of theory of linguistic relativity. (And the analogy is not accidental.)

It is not hard to see what Wittgenstein means by the analogy with Einstein's theory of relativity. Einstein motivated his theory by discussing the ways in which certain propositions (ascriptions of simultaneity and time) can or cannot be verified. Wittgenstein, too, was at the time of MS 109 preoccupied with the way different propositions are in fact verified.[22]

Wittgenstein's linguistic relativism is rampant in his philosophy of mathematics. Witness, e.g., *Remarks on the Foundations of Mathematics*, Appendix I, sec. 7:

> "But may there not be true propositions which are written in this symbolism, but are not provable in Russell's system?" – 'True propositions', hence propositions which are true in *another* system, i.e. can rightly be asserted in another game. Certainly; why should there not be such propositions; or rather: why should not propositions – of physics, e.g. – be written in Russell's symbolism?

> The question is quite analogous to: Can there be true propositions in the language of Euclid, which are not provable in his system, but are true? – Why, there are even propositions which are provable in Euclid's system, but are *false* in another system.

> . . . . [A] proposition which cannot be proved in Russell's system is "true" or "false" in a different sense from a proposition of *Principia Mathematica*.

Hence there is in mathematics nothing like a 'common behaviour of mankind' which would assign a unique sense even to our concepts of truth and falsity. There is no reason why Wittgenstein should have been any more absolutistic outside mathematical languages.

Nor does an appeal to customary modes of behaviour associated with a language necessarily help us:

> We don't understand Chinese gestures any more than Chinese sentences. (*Zettel*, sec. 219)

12 WITTGENSTEIN OBEYS HIS OWN PRINCIPLES

Still another consequence of the view of language as the universal medium is unmistakably present in Wittgenstein's later writings. It is the idea of the universality of language. Time and again Wittgenstein measures philosophical remarks about language by the same standards as he claims to apply to our ordinary discourse. Philosophical views do not enjoy the privilege of being formulated in a separate metalanguage. They, too, have to be expressed in our everyday language, and hence they are subject to the same limitations as our ordinary (object) language. There are, in fact, many passages in Wittgenstein's later writings where he interprets philosophical meta-statements (of the same kind as most propositions of the *Tractatus*) as if they belonged to our ordinary language. He expresses the principle on which this practice is based (applied to the philosophy of logic) as follows:

As there is no metaphysics, there is no metalogic, either. The word "understand" [and likewise] the expression "understand a proposition" is also not metalogical but an expression on a par with any other one in the language. (MS 110, p. 189.)[23]

Wittgenstein makes a similar point about philosophy in general in *PI*, I, sec. 121:

One might think: if philosophy speaks of the use of the word "philosophy" there must be a second-order philosophy. But it is not so: it is, rather, like the case of orthography, which deals with the word "orthography" among others without then being second-order.

A different formulation is given in *Philosophical Grammar*, VI, sec. 77. Another example is offered by MS 116, p. 2:[24]

[There is] a temptation to think that the word "understand", the expression "understand a proposition", are *metalogical* words.

"Understand" and "mean" are words like all the others.

An instructive application of this principle in the field of the philosophy of psychology is found in *PI*, I, sec. 296:

"Yes, but there is *something* there all the same accompanying my cry of pain. And it is on account of that that I utter it. And this something is what is important – and frightful." Only whom are we informing of this? And on what occasion?

Moves of this kind are in fact a staple part of Wittgenstein's argumentation in his later writings.[25]

Wittgenstein's rejection of metatheoretical ('second-order') considerations is part and parcel of his idea of language as the universal medium. Thus the idea of the universality of language is closely related to one of the most important features of Wittgenstein's argumentative strategy in the *Philosophical Investigations*. This connection provides further evidence for our interpretation.

These observations help to put Wittgenstein's philosophical technique in perspective. This technique involves asking, time and again, 'on what occasion would anyone utter such a sentence?' This technique presupposes that a philosophical discussion is not one of the relevant occasions. Why not? Is Wittgenstein not completely arbitrary in ruling out this kind of occasion? The answer is that Wittgenstein has a theoretical reason for trying to rule out not only all philosophical but also all other metatheoretical contexts. This reason is the universality of language, which implies that the apparently metatheoretical uses of language are not genuine ones. They must be improper or trivial. Hence Wittgenstein can disregard philosophical uses of language, because in the last analysis (he believes) there are no such uses. In order to criticize Wittgenstein on this score, one has to criticize his assumption of the universality of language.

It is important to realize that in this mode of argument Wittgenstein is going farther than in his early philosophy in effectively rejecting philosophical views which cannot be expressed in language. In the *Tractatus*, he distinguished what can only be shown from what can be said in language, and classified most of his own views in that book as being merely showable. Thus the young Wittgenstein of the *Tractatus* is one of the 'semanticists without semantics' mentioned in section 2 above. Here the author of the *Tractatus* is comparable to Frege, who also had quite rich and detailed semantical views but did not think that they could be expressed in language.[26]

In this respect, Frege and the early Wittgenstein were more relaxed than Bertrand Russell. As Peter Hylton has aptly shown,[27] Russell was ready to use the inexpressibility of Frege's theory as a reason for rejecting it. Frege cannot express in language that a concept is essentially predicative, for he claims that 'the concept X' does not refer to a concept, but to an object.[28] For Russell this is enough to show that Frege's theory cannot be true: 'the theory consists of propositions which according to that theory itself cannot be propositions at all, and if they are not propositions, they cannot be true'.[29]

Now Wittgenstein's semantical severity in his later philosophy can be characterized as a return, *mutatis mutandis*, to the stricter standards of early Russell as distinguished from those of Frege and of his own younger self. He no longer wants to be a semanticist without semantics; such an idea is now branded by him as nonsense. This point is particularly important to keep in mind in interpreting the *Philosophical Investigations*. (Cf. chapter 9, sec. 3, below.)

These observations give us an important clue for appreciating several characteristic features of Wittgenstein's later philosophical argumentation and philosophical style. They show why he is paying so much attention to what can be said meaningfully in language, and what circumstances.[30] They also put into perspective Wittgenstein's criticisms of the misleading things that philosophers often say.[31] Most importantly, we are now beginning to understand the purely descriptive emphasis of Wittgenstein's later philosophy. In the *Tractatus* he had not hesitated to go beyond ordinary language. This is shown by such propositons as 3.323. By contrast, in his later philosophy Wittgenstein wants to leave everything as it is (*PI*, I, sec. 124). This characteristic aspect of Wittgenstein's later philosophical methodology can thus be traced back to his attitude to language as the universal medium.

13 LANGUAGE AS THE UNIVERSAL MEDIUM AND WITTGENSTEIN'S PHILOSOPHY OF MATHEMATICS

Even though Wittgenstein's philosophy of mathematics will not be dealt with in this work, it is nevertheless relevant to register an important consequence of his commitment to the idea of language as the universal medium. As we have seen above, according to Wittgenstein's position there cannot be any metatheoretical considerations about language. Now in the special case of the languages (systems, calculi) of mathematics, one important class of attempted metatheoretical results deals with the consistency of mathematical systems. Faithful as he is to the dogma of the universality of language, Wittgenstein is committed to rejecting all attempts to produce consistency proofs or, alternatively and a shade more interestingly, he is committed to considering such proofs as merely another mathematical calculus, on a par with the original mathematical system.

This is a repeated theme in Wittgenstein's philosophy of mathematics. It is, for instance, why he holds that 'what Hilbert is doing is mathematics and not metamathematics. It is another calculus, just like any other one' (*Ludwig Wittgenstein and the Vienna Circle*, p. 121).

Another, even more general, consequence of Wittgenstein's belief in the ineffability of semantics is that Wittgenstein cannot use in mathematics any properly semantical conception of truth different from provability in some one system. This is one of the most character-

istic features of his discussions of the foundations of mathematics. Cf.,
e.g., *PI*, I, sec. 136 or *Remarks on the Foundations of Mathematics*,
Appendix I, secs. 5–6:

> Are there true propositions in Russell's system, which cannot be proved
> in his system? – What is called a true proposition in Russell's system,
> then?
>
> For what does a proposition's *'being true'* mean? *'p'* is *true = p*. (That is
> the answer.)
>
> So we want to ask something like: under what circumstances do we
> assert a proposition?

This tendency to subordinate the notion of truth to other concepts,
such as proof and inference, is but a corollary to Wittgenstein's deep-
seated belief in the ineffability of semantics.

These observations can be generalized further. Wittgenstein's philosophy of mathematics is sometimes characterized as being finitistic,
constructivistic, and anti-platonistic. All these labels are applicable,
but they do not tell the whole story. They do not indicate the true
source of several of these characteristic features of Wittgenstein's
philosophy of mathematics. This source is his belief in the universality
of language. In the same way as the author of the *Tractatus* had for
this reason ended up with a formalistic conception of logic (as was
seen above in sec. 5), the older Wittgenstein embraced a view of
mathematics on which it deals with what is actually done in mathematics – the actual calculation. Thus it is Wittgenstein's belief in
language as the universal medium that is important here, not an
independent commitment to finitism or operationalism as such.

From the same vantage point one can likewise understand the main
feature which distinguishes Wittgenstein's philosophy of mathematics
from other finitistic and operationalist approaches. It is the emphasis
Wittgenstein places on *systems* of calculation.[32] This primacy of
systems in Wittgenstein's philosophy of mathematics is but a special
case of the primacy of language-games over their rules in Wittgenstein's
later philosophy of language.

This section and its predecessor help to explain a puzzling contrast
between Wittgenstein's descriptivistic and apparently resigned attitude to ordinary language and his highly critical attitude to mathematical, especially metamathematical, practice. In reality, the two
originate from the same source, his belief in language as the universal
medium. In both cases, Wittgenstein is criticizing metatheoretical
conceptualizations.

Thus the assumption of language as the universal medium has

extremely important consequences for Wittgenstein's philosophy of mathematics. The source of these consequences has not been diagnosed satisfactorily in the literature. A study of Wittgenstein's philosophy of mathematics from the vantage point we have reached is nevertheless far too large an undertaking to be attempted here.

NOTES

1 See his important paper, 'Logic as language and logic as calculus', *Synthese*, vol. 17 (1967), pp. 324–30.

2 Cf. here also Jaakko Hintikka, 'Frege's hidden semantics', *Revue internationale de philosophie*, vol. 33 (1979), pp. 716–22.

3 Cf. here Jaakko Hintikka, 'Language-Games' in Jaakko Hintikka et al., editors, *Essays on Wittgenstein in Honour of G. H. von Wright* (*Acta Philosophica Fennica*, vol. 28, nos. 1–3), North-Holland, Amsterdam, 1976, pp. 105–25.

4 In his paper 'Semantics: a revolt against Frege' in G. Flöistad, editor, *Contemporary Philosophy: A New Survey*, vol. 1, Martinus Nijhoff, The Hague, 1981, pp. 57–82.

5 Peter Hylton, 'Russell's substitutional theory', *Synthese*, vol. 45 (1980), pp. 1–31; Warren Goldfarb, 'Logic in the Twenties: the nature of the quantifier', *Journal of Symbolic Logic*, vol. 44 (1979), pp. 351–68.

6 Jaakko Hintikka, 'Wittgenstein's semantical Kantianism', in E. Morscher and R. Stranzinger, editors, *Ethics, Proceedings of the Fifth International Wittgenstein Symposium*, Hölder-Pichler-Tempsky, Vienna, 1981, pp. 375–90.

7 Ibid., note 6, and Jaakko Hintikka, 'Das Paradox transzendentaler Erkenntnis', in Eva Schaper and Wilhelm Vossenkuhl, editors, *Bedingungen der Möglichkeit: 'Transcendental Arguments' und transzendentales Denken*, Klett-Cotta, Stuttgart, 1984, pp. 123–49.

8 Peter Geach, 'Saying and showing in Frege and Wittgenstein' in Jaakko Hintikka et al., editors, *Essays on Wittgenstein*, pp. 54–70.

9 See note 3 above.

10 Jaakko Hintikka, 'C. S. Peirce's "First Real Discovery" and its contemporary relevance', *The Monist*, vol. 63 (1980), pp. 304–15.

11 Rudolf Carnap, *The Logical Syntax of Language*, Kegan Paul, London, 1937, p. 282. (The German original appeared in 1934.)

12 This letter has been published in Michael Nedo and Michele Ranchetti, editors, *Wittgenstein: Sein Leben in Bildern und Texten*, Suhrkamp, Frankfurt am Main, 1983, pp. 254–5.

13 This latter quotation is from MS 113, p. 40 (in the actual pagination common to MSS 112–13, p. 310), dated 16 February 1932. The German original reads as follows: 'In der Grammatik wird auch die Andwendung der Sprache beschreibt; das was man den Zusammenhang zwischen Sprache und Wirklichkeit nennen möchte.'

14 In MS 110, pp. 194–5, Wittgenstein acknowledges that his 'grammatical investigations' differ from those of a philologist in that he is interested in rules

which a philologist does not consider at all. Wittgenstein does not specify, however, what these rules are like. What we shall attempt in chapters 7–8 below is to spell out the nature of such rules: they are rules of language-games.

15 The quote is from MS 113, pp. 119–20 (pp. 390–1 in the actual pagination). The German reads: 'Die unrichtige Idee ist, daß die Anwendung eines Kalküls in der Grammatik der wirklichen Sprache ihm eine Realität zuordnet, eine Wirklichkeit gibt, die er früher [vorher] nicht hatte.'

16 See Anthony Kenny, *Wittgenstein*, Penguin Books, Harmondsworth, Middlesex, 1973.

17 For the connection, see *Tractatus* 5.6–5.62, 5.5561.

18 Garth Hallett, *A Companion to Wittgenstein's 'Philosophical Investigations'*, Cornell University Press, Ithaca, N.Y., 1977.

19 The passages which show Wittgenstein's faith in the idea of language as the universal medium during his middle period include the following: MS 108, pp. 192, 260, 265, 269; MS 109, pp. 16, 79, 97, 212, 225, 290; MS 110, pp. 99, 141, 189; MS 111, p. 134. It is also instructive to read *Philosophical Remarks*, XV, sec. 171:

> The basic mistake consists, as in the previous philosophy of logic, in assuming that a word can make a sort of allusion to its object (point at it from a distance) without necessarily going proxy for it . . .
>
> A form cannot be described: it can only be presented.

20 It seems to us that Wittgenstein's point comes across more forcefully if *Nutzen* is translated as 'usefulness' and not as mere 'use', as in the usual translation.

21 The German reads:

> Das Verhältnis, die Beziehung zwischen Gedanken und Wirklichkeit gibt die Sprache durch die Gemeinsamkeit des Ausdrucks wieder. Anders kann sie dies Verhältnis nicht darstellen.
>
> Wir haben hier eine Art Relativitätstheorie der Sprache vor uns. (Und die Analogie ist keine zufällige.)

22 This is verified by what Wittgenstein says in MS 107, p. 143: 'Einstein: the way a quantity is measured, is the quantity.' ['Einstein: Wie eine Größe gemessen wird, das ist sie.']

23 The German text reads: 'Wie es keine Mataphysik gibt, so gibt es keine Metalogik. Das Wort "verstehen", der Ausdruck "einen Satz verstehen" ist auch nicht metalogisch, sondern ein Ausdruck wie jeder andre der Sprache.'

24 The German text reads:

> Eine Versuchung zu glauben, das Wort "verstehen", der Ausdruck: "einen Satz verstehen", seien metalogische Worte.
>
> "Verstehen" und "meinen" sind Worte wie alle anderen.

29

25 Examples are offered inter alia by *PI*, I, secs. 190–2, 209–11, 213, 216, 227, 231, 261, 278, 289, 325, 352, 360, 465, 479, 491, 497, 527, 625, 626, 674, 676, 681, etc. Other examples are found in such works as *Zettel*; cf., e.g., secs. 225, 233, 330.
26 See, e.g., note 2 above.
27 Peter Hylton, 'Russell's substitutional theory', note 5 above.
28 Gottlob Frege, 'Über Begriff und Gegenstand', *Vierteljahrschrift für wissenschaftliche Philosophie*, vol. 16 (1892), pp. 192–205. (See pp. 196–7.)
29 Hylton, 'Russell's substitutional theory', p. 9.
30 See, e.g., *PI*, I, secs. 59–60, 261, 394, 577, etc.
31 Cf., e.g., *PI*, I, secs. 253–4.
32 Cf., e.g., *Remarks on the Foundations of Mathematics*, Appendix I, sec. 7.

APPENDIX MS 108, PP. 277-8

Denken nenne ich das was sich durch eine Sprache ausdrücken läßt. Dann muß es in diese Sprache aus einer *anderen* übersetzt werden. Ich will sagen: alles Denken muß dann in Zeichen vorsichgehen.

Wenn man aber sagt: "Wie soll ich wissen was er meint ich sehe ja nur seine Zeichen" so sage ich: "Wie soll *er* wissen was er meint, er hat ja auch nur seine Zeichen".

Die Frage "*Wie* ist das gemeint", hat nur Sinn wenn es heißt "es ist *so* gemeint". Dieses "so" ist ein sprachlicher Ausdruck.

Die Sprache [Gesprochenes, Wittgenstein's variant] kann man nur durch die Sprache erklären, darum kann man *die Sprache* nicht erklären.

Das Ziel der Philosophie ist es eine Mauer dort zu errichten wo die Sprache ohnehin aufhört.

Man kann es auch so sagen: Wenn man sich nur [immer, Wittgenstein's variant] in einem Sprachsystem ausdrückt und also was ein Satz meint nur durch Sätze dieses Systems erklärt, so fällt am Schluß die Meinung ganz aus der Sprache, also aus der Betrachtung, heraus und es bleibt die Sprache das einzige was wir betrachten können.

Wenn wir jemandem den Sinn eines Satzes erklären so übersetzen wir ihn in eine unmißverständlichere Sprache [weniger mißverständliche Sprache].

2
The Categorial Status of the Objects of Wittgenstein's *Tractatus*

1 ARE THE OBJECTS OF THE *TRACTATUS* LIMITED TO PARTICULARS?

Wittgenstein's early philosophy culminated in his *Tractatus Logico-Philosophicus* (German original 1921, the bilingual edition 1922). Instead of mounting a frontal attack on this remarkable book, we shall examine in this chapter and in each of the next three chapters one particular aspect of the *Tractatus*. Together, these interrelated studies will yield, we hope, an interpretation of the most important aspects of Wittgenstein's early philosophy.

We shall assume that the reader is somewhat familiar with the contents of Wittgenstein's book. In a nutshell, the overall picture Wittgenstein paints there is this: The world consists of the totality of facts. These facts are in the last analysis combinations of (simple) *objects* (*Gegenstände*). These objects – we shall usually drop the epithet 'simple' in what follows – are thus the basic ingredients of the world. They can be combined with each other in different ways so as to form facts. Since the world is the totality of facts, it is limited by the totality of objects that can serve as ingredients of facts. An object is represented in the language (logically explicit language) by a name. By combining names in analogy with the way their objects may be combined we can form propositions. They represent, therefore, facts in virtue of this analogy, which Wittgenstein expresses by speaking of picturing. (This is his famous 'picture theory', which we shall examine more closely in chapter 4 below.)

The crucial subject matter in trying to understand the *Tractatus* is obviously Wittgenstein's conception of object (*Gegenstand*). What are these objects like? One of the most persistent and most pervasive misunderstandings concerning Wittgenstein's *Tractatus* is the idea that what he there calls objects (*Gegenstände*) include only individuals (particulars) but not properties and relations. Instead of 'objects' (*Gegenstände*), Wittgenstein sometimes says 'things' (*Dinge*), cf., e.g., 1.01. Nothing of importance seems to hang on this terminological variation, however.[1] The eminent victims of this misunderstanding include G. E. M. Anscombe, Irving Copi, George Pitcher, Richard Bernstein, and a host of other philosophers.[2] This misunderstanding has been criticized by, among others, Erik Stenius and André Maury.[3] The first and foremost aim of this chapter is to bury it for good.

The terminological counterpart to this mistake is the view that what Wittgenstein calls 'names' in the *Tractatus* are logically speaking all *singular terms*, and hence exclude *predicates* (including relation symbols). (Cf. 3.203: 'A name means an object.')

An additional reason for discussing this misinterpretation is that doing so leads to a sharpened understanding of Wittgenstein's *Tractatus* in several important respects. These include Wittgenstein's notions of relation and simplicity, as well as his use of the contextual principle he inherited from Frege ('only in the nexus of a proposition does a name have meaning'). These will in turn lead us to consider the all-important idea of logical form in relation to Wittgenstein's concept of object.

2 HISTORICAL EVIDENCE

To discuss the purely historical and textual aspects of the problem first, there is excellent prima facie evidence that Wittgenstein included properties and relations among what he called objects (*Gegenstände*). For instance, in his *Notebooks 1914–1916* (p. 61, for 16 June 1915) Wittgenstein writes: 'Relations and properties, etc., are *objects* too' (Wittgenstein's emphasis).

And this remark is more than a fleeting aside. It was penned at a time when Wittgenstein had already recorded in his notebook a large number of what later became propositions of the *Tractatus*. Moreover, six days later (22 June 1915; *Notebooks 1914–1916*, p. 69) Wittgenstein is obviously relying on the same classification. After having discussed the apparently complex entities *Socrates* and *the property of mortality*, Wittgenstein concludes that 'here they just function as simple objects.' Further (indirect) evidence is provided by *Notebooks 1914–1916*, p. 70 (22 June 1915):

> A name designating an object thereby stands in a relation to it which is wholly determined by the logical kind of the object and which signalises that logical kind.

Objects are thus not all of one and the same 'logical kind'.

Further evidence to the effect that Wittgenstein included properties and relations among his 'objects' in his early philosophy is obtained from Wittgenstein's 'Notes dictated to G. E. Moore in Norway' (Appendix II to *Notebooks 1914–1916*). Among other things that can only be shown but not said in language Wittgenstein lists there the 'difference between things, facts, properties, relations' (p. 109). He likewise countenances there subject–predicate propositions (ibid.). Wittgenstein's terminology in these 'Notes' differs from that of the *Tractatus* in that he restricts the term 'thing' to particulars and the term 'name' to linguistic representatives of particulars. Once we realize this terminological peculiarity, we can see that Wittgenstein there admits linguistic relations as perfectly good representatives of relations in the world. For instance, on p. 111 Wittgenstein says that a proposition of the form

(∃x,y,R). xRy

is 'unanalysable'. Yet it contains a relation variable, which according to the Anscombe–Copi view could not occur in an unanalysable proposition.

These observations may seem to close the issue for good before it really gets going. However, it is not quite the end of the story. It has been objected that Wittgenstein could very well have changed his mind between the writing of the *Notebooks* passage and the writing of the *Tractatus*.

If so, he changed his mind twice. For in his middle period writings, he is again happily including properties and relations among objects; witness, e.g., *Philosophical Grammar*, I, sec. 20 (p. 58):

> And this is the origin of the bad expression: a fact is a complex of objects [*Gegenstände*]. Here the fact that a man is sick is compared with a combination of two things [*Dinge*] the one the man and the other the sickness.

As has been pointed out in the literature, there is further evidence in Wittgenstein's later published and unpublished writings that he included properties and relations among his objects.[4]

The improbability of a dual change of terminology in this important respect provides an excellent reason for rejecting the identification of Wittgenstein's 'objects' in the *Tractatus* with individuals (particulars).

But what about the evidence that is offered by the *Tractatus* itself? There are unfortunately no direct statements about the matter to be found there. However, there is good indirect textual evidence for the thesis of this chapter also in the *Tractatus*. Indeed, there is virtually conclusive evidence that in the *Tractatus* Wittgenstein included properties, relations, and functions (in logicians' usual sense, meaning certain kinds of relations) among his 'objects'. In 5.02 he writes:

> The arguments of functions are readily confused with the indices of names . . . For example, when Russell writes '+ $_c$', the '$_c$' is an index which indicates that the sign as a whole is the addition sign for cardinal numbers. But the use of this sign is the result of arbitrary conventions and it would be quite possible to choose a *simple sign* instead of '+ $_c$' . . . (. . . An index is always part of a description of the *object* to whose *name* we affix it . . .). [Emphasis added throughout this quotation.]

Here Wittgenstein implies in two different ways the symbol for addition is a name and hence stands for an object. First, it can have an index, which is a characteristic of names. Second, it is equivalent with a simple sign, i.e., a name. (Cf. 3.202: 'The simple signs employed in a proposition are called names.')

Our interpretation is clinched by Wittgenstein's own explanations (to Desmond Lee) of the first few propositions of the *Tractatus*:[5]

> 'Objects' also include relations; a proposition is not two things connected by a relation. 'Thing' and 'relation' are on the same level. The objects hang as it were in a chain.

After this, the purely exegetical issue can be considered pretty much closed. If more evidence is needed, here is a telling passage:

> Our ordinary language is enough to show that the symbolism which represents a table must be of a completely different nature from that of propositional functions. For ordinary language treats words for objects in a completely different way from words for properties and relations.

This quote is from F. Waismann, *Ludwig Wittgenstein and the Vienna Circle*, p. 254, where Waismann is trying to capture the philosophy of the *Tractatus* as improved by Wittgenstein in the twenties. The clear implication of the passage is that in the language of propositional functions, i.e., in the language of the *Tractatus*, objects include properties and relations.

Further confirmation is obtained from Wittgenstein's own later comments. In the *Philosophical Investigations*, Wittgenstein criticizes his own earlier views in the *Tractatus* concerning objects, especially the ineffability of the existence of particular objects. (For a discussion of this aspect of Wittgenstein's doctrine, see next chapter.) The prime example Wittgenstein uses in his discussion is 'Red exists'. (See *PI*, I, secs. 57–8.) This shows in the light of hindsight not only that Wittgenstein counted colours as objects in the *Tractatus*, but also that it would be less misleading to assimilate all the Tractarian objects to properties than to assimilate them to particulars. For Wittgenstein's doctrine of the indestructibility of objects makes much better sense as applied to properties and relations than as applied to particulars.

> "Something red can be destroyed, but red cannot be destroyed . . ." (*PI*, I, sec. 57)

Appearances notwithstanding, no counter-evidence is forthcoming from Wittgenstein's *Notebooks 1914–1916*, pp. 75–6, either. Admittedly Wittgenstein there says, in the usual English translation:

> Instead of "all objects" we might say: All *particular objects*.

However, Wittgenstein's German word which is rendered 'particular' is *bestimmt*. This word does not mean *particular* as opposed to *general*; it means *determinate* in contradistinction to *indefinite*. This is made clear by Wittgenstein on p. 75:

> The proposition fa speaks of particular objects [*Gegenstände*], the general proposition of *all* objects.

By a general proposition, Wittgenstein clearly means a *quantified* proposition like '(∀x) fx'. It is of course clear that a 'particular object' is an object of the same logical type as the objects that a quantifier like '(∀x)' ranges over. Both *bestimmt* and *unbestimmt* objects can be of any logical type as far as their logical and ontological status is concerned. Hence, what Wittgenstein is saying is not that his objects are particulars rather than universals. What he is saying is that he is dealing with specific objects, bearers of proper names, not merely with unspecified values of quantified variables. In other words, he is making a distinction not unlike Russell's distinction between 'real' and 'apparent' variables, and saying that he proposes to eliminate the 'apparent', i.e., bound, variables. Indeed, by saying that the proposition *fa* speaks of particular objects (note the plural), Wittgenstein indicates in effect that the property *f*, not just the individual *a*, is for him also an object. Far from contradicting our interpretation, the quoted *Notebooks* passage thus strongly supports it.

The *textual* evidence thus confirms the thesis of this chapter conclusively. However, this still leaves one with an *interpretational* (doctrinal) problem. Most of the evidence adduced by the defenders of the view under criticism is indeed doctrinal rather than exegetical. This poses the problem of understanding those views of Wittgenstein's which have been appealed to for this purpose – or at least some of them.

3 OBJECTS AND THE INEFFABILITY OF SEMANTICS

Perhaps the most pressing interpretational problem here is this: If Wittgenstein included properties and relations among the objects of the *Tractatus*, why does he not say so? Once again, the total interpretation of Wittgenstein outlined in this work yields a plausible explanation. Wittgenstein's silence in the *Tractatus* about this important *terminological* point might prima facie seem surprising, but it is in reality a straightforward consequence of his assumption of the ineffability of semantics. (Cf. here chapter 1 above.) One corollary to this assumption (on his view) is that the number of argument-places of the primitive predicates we need in our ideal language cannot be predicted a priori and is in this sense arbitrary. (See 5.553–5.556, especialy 5.554: 'It would be completely arbitrary to give any specific form.') By the same token, the distinction between individuals (relations with zero argument-places), properties (relations with one argument-place), and relations proper is likewise completely arbitrary. No wonder Wittgenstein disregarded it in his terminology.

4 OBJECTS AS VALUES OF QUANTIFIERS

One way of seeing that Wittgenstein must have included more than individuals among what he called objects is to ask: What would the linguistic representatives, the names, of these objects look like? On the view we are criticizing, they must all be on a par. But then we cannot use these names to make type distinctions in the way in which Wittgenstein assumes that we can when he discusses Russell's theory of types (cf. 3.333) and when he discusses the stipulations which determine the ranges of different quantifiers (see 3.316–3.317 and cf. 5.52, which is based on 5.501). If there were no categorical distinctions among Wittgenstein's 'objects', all quantifiers would of necessity have the same range, and no stipulation would be possible.

This is borne out by a closer study of Wittgenstein's logical practice. Here, as in so many other walks of logic, the real evidence does not come so much from what a philosopher says, but from what he does. As Quine has eloquently reminded us, what entities a philosopher countenances is shown by the entities he or she is prepared to quantify over. Now in Wittgenstein's case we can find a passage of the *Tractatus* where he tips his hand in this respect. Not surprisingly, it is the passage where he speaks of fully generalized propositions (5.526–5.5261). In 5.526 he says:

> We can describe the world completely by means of fully generalized propositions, i.e. without first correlating any name with a particular object.
> Then, in order to arrive at the customary mode of expression, we simply need to add, after an expression like, 'There is one and only one *x* such that . . .', the words, 'and this *x* is *a*'.

Here the use of the lower-case symbols '*x*' and '*a*' might prima facie suggest that Wittgenstein is thinking only of generality with respect to individuals. This is in effect assumed by one of the proponents of the view under criticism here, Irving Copi.[6] His argument is strictly circular, however. Wittgenstein never identifies lower-case variables with individual variables. Instead, he explains variables by means of the notion of object, whose interpretation is precisely the moot point here:

> 4.1272   Thus the variable name '*x*' is the proper sign for the pseudo-concept *object*.

In any case, 5.5261 shows conclusively that in discussing fully generalized propositions Wittgenstein is also thinking of quantification over (generality with respect to) properties and relations:

> A fully generalized proposition, like every other proposition, is composite. (This is shown by the fact that in '(∃*x*,ɸ). (ɸ*x*)' we have to mention '*x*' and 'ɸ' separately. They both, independently, stand in signifying relations to the world, just as is the case in ungeneralized proposition.)

In other words, Wittgenstein is accepting as quantified variables, and indeed as variables, all of which independently have 'signifying relations to the world', those ranging over properties and not only those ranging over individuals. It is hard to think of a more revealing statement by a philosopher as to what there is in his universe. (Note also the use of the terms 'object' and 'name' in 5.526.)

There are other clear indications in Wittgenstein's early writings that he is prepared to quantify over properties and relations, and not just over individuals; witness, e.g., 3.331 and section 5 in Wittgenstein's letter to Russell of 19 August 1919 (*Notebooks 1914–1916*, p. 130).

Indeed, Copi himself calls attention to a further passage of this kind. Copi misunderstands Wittgenstein's comments on Russell's axiom of reducibility in 6.1232–6.1233, when he claims that they support his interpretation. Or, rather, he misconstrues the import of the axiom. It does not assert anything of the existence of certain properties and relations *simpliciter*. Hence its possible falsity according to Wittgenstein does not mean that certain actually existing properties and relations can possibly fail to exist, as Copi thinks. Rather, the axiom says that, *given* any property or relation of a certain kind, viz. a higher-order one (in Russell's sense), there exists an equivalent predicative one. In other words, the axiom does not speak of the absolute existence and nonexistence of properties and relations but of the configurations which existing properties and relations of a certain kind in fact exhibit.

Wittgenstein's point in 6.1233 is clearly that even if all the existing properties and relations in fact were so related to each other as to make the axiom of reducibility true, they could exhibit a different structure which would invalidate the axiom. Such an alternative structure of an imaginary simplified universe is in fact described by Wittgenstein in *Notebooks 1914–1916*, p. 127, and in *Letters to Russell, Keynes and Moore*, pp. 39, 42. Hence the axiom of reducibility (Wittgenstein avers) cannot belong to logic. And, on this correct reading, the passage does not offer evidence for Copi, but for our interpretation, for in it Wittgenstein is unmistakably quantifying in effect over properties and relations.

5 THE NAMES OF PROPERTIES AND RELATIONS ARE THEMSELVES PROPERTIES AND RELATIONS

Copi has also been seriously misled by Wittgenstein's concise way of expressing himself in 3.1432:

> Instead of, 'The complex sign "*a*R*b*" says that *a* stands to *b* in the relation R', we ought to put, 'That "*a*" stands to "*b*" in a certain relation says *that a*R*b*.'

Copi takes this to imply that there are only two ingredients (objects) in the fact that is being represented. There is no such implication; rather there must be according to the *Tractatus* the same number of names in an elementary proposition as there are objects in the situation represented by it (4.04). Now what the situation is is not determined by the names '*a*' and '*b*' alone. Therefore, there must be a third element in the proposition, which is somehow determined by 'R'. Hence, there likewise must be three objects in the situation, not two.

Copi thinks that by using the locution 'a certain relation' Wittgenstein is in effect abstracting from the relational sign, as it were generalizing existentially with respect to it. This is a plain misreading of the text;

the words 'a *certain* relation' (*eine gewiße Beziehung*) do not function there as an abstracting or quantifying operator. This is shown by a passage in 'Notes dictated to G. E. Moore in Norway' (*Notebooks 1914–1916*, p. 110, fifth paragraph). From it we can see that there could be a more explicit version of the second half of 3.1432. It might run as follows:

> We ought to put, 'That "*a*" stands to "*b*" in a certain relation, *viz. in the relation of flanking* "R" (*in the relation that obtains when* "R" *stands between* "*a*" *and* "*b*") says *that aRb*'.

This point is verified by other Wittgenstein passages; witness, e.g., *Notebooks 1914–1916*, p. 98:

> Symbols are not what they seem to be. In "*aRb*" "R" looks like a substantive but is not one. What symbolizes in "*aRb*" is that "R" occurs between "*a*" and "*b*". Hence "R" is *not* the indefinable in "*aRb*".

This clearly means that what *is* indefinable in "*aRb*" is the relation which consists of the symbols ("*a*" and "*b*") flanking "R". But indefinables are for Wittgenstein precisely *names*, and they stand for *objects*.

This passage is especially relevant to the interpretation of 3.1432 because it occurs earlier in the very same work, viz. in Wittgenstein's 'Notes on Logic', in which he a little later formulates the very same proposition 3.1432 as is being discussed here (see *Notebooks 1914–1916*, p. 105).

This brings out an important point of exegesis, and an insight into Copi's difficulties. What has been found here is not just that there is a third ingredient in the relational proposition Wittgenstein contemplates in 3.1432. It has been found what this third ingredient is. It is the relation which consists in two individual names' flanking a symbol correlated with a certain relation in the world. Now this third ingredient of the proposition must according to Wittgenstein's *Tractatus* be a *name*. Here what a name is, for Wittgenstein, is not a linguistic *symbol* (e.g., the letter 'R'), but a certain linguistic *relation* (i.e., that of flanking a particular letter). This usage may sound utterly strange. Yet it is merely the precise linguistic counterpart to the idea that a relation obtaining in the world has as its linguistic counterpart a linguistic *relation*. Far from being strange, this idea is almost a matter of course for those who are taking seriously Wittgenstein's idea of an elementary proposition as an isomorphic representation (e.g., Stenius).

In his 'Notes Dictated to Moore' (*Notebooks 1914–1916*, p. 109) Wittgenstein puts this very point as follows:

E.g., in "aRb", "R" is *not* a symbol, but *that* "R" is between one name and another symbolizes. Here we have *not* said: this symbol is not of this type but of that, but only: *This* symbolizes and not that.

Part of the difficulty of accepting the interpretation offered here is terminological. A *name* certainly seems to be always a *word*, not a linguistic *property* or linguistic *relation*. Furthermore, Frege sets up a contrast between saturated entities, which he called *objects*, and unsaturated entities, which he termed *functions*. On the interpretation presented here, Wittgenstein departs sharply from Frege's terminology in this respect, for according to this interpretation Wittgenstein in the *Tractatus* calls both kinds of entities *objects*. These are merely terminological perplexities, however, and have no bearing on the real issues of interpretation.

6 OBJECTS ARE SIMPLE – IN WHAT SENSE?

There nevertheless remains a genuine interpretational hurdle. One of the most important characteristics of the objects of the *Tractatus* is that they are *simple*. And this certainly appears to rule out relations as objects, for a relation does have a structure: in it, we have to distinguish the terms of the relation from the relation that obtains between them, and to distinguish the terms from each other. In the linguistic representative of a relation, one likewise has to distinguish the argument places and the relational letter or word itself ('R' in the example above).

In view of this objection, it is important to see precisely what the simplicity of (basic) objects means for Wittgenstein. There are at least three different things which Wittgenstein could (sight unseen, so to speak) have meant by the simplicity of objects:

  (i) They have no structure. (They are 'of a piece'.)
  (ii) They cannot be analysed further into more basic objects.
  (iii) They are logically independent of each other.

It follows from what has been shown above that Wittgenstein definitely did not mean (i). He seems to have considered (iii) as a corollary to (ii), and in any case he had another, perfectly good term for (iii), viz. 'independence'. Hence he was unlikely to mean just (iii) by 'simplicity'. This leaves (ii) as Wittgenstein's meaning. He in effect confirms this in 3.26, even though he speaks there of names rather than of objects:

A name cannot be analysed further by means of definitions; it is a primitive symbol [*Urzeichen*].

(Cf. here also 3.261.)

In any case, the crucial thing here is that in the important sense (ii), primitive (unanalysable) relations can obviously be 'simple' in Wittgenstein's sense, and hence can be objects.

Furthermore, the kind of complexity which a relation exhibits (e.g., one's being able to distinguish its different terms) concerns only the relation's different possibilities of being combined with other entities into states of affairs. Now this kind of complexity Wittgenstein attributes in so many words to his simple objects:

> 2.0123   If I know an object I also know all its possible occurrences in states of affairs. (Every one of these possibilities must be part of the nature of the object.)

Hence the kind of complexity which a relation instantiates is not the kind of complexity Wittgenstein denies of his objects, and hence is not a reason for not including relations among the objects Wittgenstein countenances in the *Tractatus*.

Moreover, by the same token there can be connections between the different objects in the framework of the *Tractatus*, even though the objects themselves are said by Wittgenstein to be simple. In other words, different objects can be combined with each other in different ways because they have a different 'logical form'. Having such a logical form is not excluded by the simplicity of objects.

Indeed, there must be some sort of form built into Tractarian objects to explain asymmetries between different kinds of objects as far as their possible combinations are concerned, if the main thesis of this chapter is correct that relations and properties are also objects. For an object of one kind, viz. a particular, cannot be combined with another particular object in the same way a different kind of object, viz. a property, can be combined with it, namely, in the sense of being attributed to it. (Cf. 3.333.) This impossibility is obviously thought of by Wittgenstein as being logical in nature. However, it cannot be due to the status of the objects in question qua objects. It is due to their structure, to such features of theirs as were described by Frege in speaking of saturated and unsaturated entities. If so, is it surprising if the allegedly simple objects possess other kinds of structure, including such structure as governs the way they can combine with each other in general?

In the case of type-distinctions (e.g., distinctions between particulars, properties, and relations) Wittgenstein's point is easy to swallow because in the usual logical notation the corresponding 'names' exhibit the right sort of behaviour. As Wittgenstein says in 5.525 in speaking of necessity and possibility:

> The precedent to which one may want to appeal must be constituted by the symbol itself.

For instance, we cannot plug the name of a property, say the unsaturated symbol P(–), into the argument-place of the name for another property, say Q(–); for only saturated symbols can be so substituted. (Cf. 3.333.) Wittgenstein does not produce a similar notation in other cases, e.g., in the case of colour predicates, whose incompatibility prima facie violates Wittgenstein's principle that elementary propositions are independent of each other. Hence we have here an interpretational problem in trying to find out how Wittgenstein thought that colours can exclude others. We shall return to this problem in chapter 5 below. Meanwhile, it is not hard to see how Wittgenstein might have thought that he could solve the problem of colour incompatibility. All he had to do was to find a set of simples (of whatever logical type) underlying the structure of colours such that all their possible combinations are reflected by the admissible combinations of their linguistic representatives. The logical simplicity of colours does not imply that they do not have a 'logical form' which allows only some ways of combining them, not others. The problems is merely to devise an appropriate symbolism to reflect the range of their possible combinations. (This is what Wittgenstein in effect says in 6.3751.)

Even though the details of Wittgenstein's discussion thus can be seen to make good sense, given his overall view of objects and their simplicity, this overall view itself presents a problem. It is not clear that the most fundamental building-blocks of one's ontology (whether one chooses to call them 'simple' or not) should have a built-in structure which governs their interplay with each other. For instance, there does not seem to be any precedent for Wittgenstein's assumption of such structures in Russell. Hence we face the problem of explaining why Wittgenstein adopted his doctrine that his simples (simple objects) have a logical form. We shall return to this problem in the next chapter.

7 WITTGENSTEIN AND FREGE ON SATURATED VS. UNSATURATED ENTITIES

A closely related way of looking at Wittgenstein's view in the *Tractatus* is to suggest that he realized a tacit contradiction which lurks in the contrast Frege drew between saturated and unsaturated symbols and the contextual principle. The principle was accepted both by Frege ('only in a proposition have the words really a meaning,' *Die Grundlagen der Arithmetik*, tr. by J. L. Austin, Basil Blackwell, Oxford, 1959, sec. 60); and by Wittgenstein ('only propositions have sense; only in the nexus of a proposition does a name have meaning,' *Tractatus* 3.3). The contrast is supposed to be between those ('unsaturated') entities ('functions', in Frege's terminology) that need another entity to 'complete' them and those ('saturated') entities ('objects', in Frege's terminology) that do not. This contrast corresponds to an analogous distinction between the linguistic representatives of the two kinds of entities. But the contextual principle says that neither unsaturated nor saturated symbols have independent meaning outside propositions. Either kind of symbol is 'in need of completion' by the other kind. The same will, of course, apply to the corresponding entities. Hence the saturated–unsaturated contrast becomes otiose. There are no other ways of creating an asymmetry between saturated and unsaturated symbols, either. For instance, according to Frege both saturated and unsaturated symbols have references, which are respectively saturated and unsaturated, too. Hence, the Frege distinction between objects and functions becomes a merely correlative one, and there was no reason for Wittgenstein not to call both of them 'objects'.

Moreover, if from this vantage point one wants to assimilate the 'objects' of the *Tractatus* either to Frege's saturated entities ('objects') or to his unsaturated entities ('functions'), we can now see that the better identification is with Frege's functions, for these are for him unsaturated, which we found *all* entities to be in the sense of the contextual principle. Thus the usual identification of the 'objects' of Wittgenstein's *Tractatus* with individuals (saturated entities) is not only mistaken, but diametrically wrong. It is less misleading to think of Wittgenstein's 'objects' as all being functions than to think of them all as individuals. The misunderstanding which was intially called persistent and pervasive is also perverse.

8 STATES OF AFFAIRS AS COMBINATION OF OBJECTS

Our observations concerning the nature of the objects postulated in the *Tractatus* open still another interpretational perspective on Wittgenstein's book. In order to see what it is, we should return to the mistaken interpretation criticized in the beginning of this chapter. The prize specimens for those interpreters who think that Wittgenstein included only individuals among his objects in the *Tractatus* are 2.03–2.031:

> 2.03   In a state of affairs objects fit into one another like the links of a chain.

> 2.031   In a state of affairs objects stand in a determinate relation to one another.

It is nevertheless clear that these statements are perfectly compatible with the view that objects also include properties and relations. The suggestion in 2.03 that there is a kind of symmetry between different kinds of objects occurring in a state of affairs (they are all members of the same chain) will be accounted for later. The point that the relation mentioned in 2.031 cannot be one of Wittgenstein's objects is well taken, but it falters on this question: Is it a *relation* in the sense in which relations are a part of one's ontology? A second look quickly shows that it cannot be. Wittgenstein is not even speaking in 2.031 of any one relation, but of *how objects are related to each other [verhalten sich . . . zueinander]*. A comparison with 2.14–2.15 shows that the relationship which Wittgenstein has in mind is of the kind that constitutes the form of states of affairs and (by isomorphism) pictorial forms. It is eminently clear that these are not constituted by ordinary relations.

Highly relevant evidence here is forthcoming from the *Notebooks 1914–1916*, p. 26. Speaking of the linguistic counterpart of the connection of objects in a state of affairs ('the logical connexion') Wittgenstein says there:

> N.B. that connexion is not a relation but only the *holding* of a relation.

It is also instructive to note that in 2.032 Wittgenstein likewise speaks not of how objects are *related to* each other in a state of affairs, but rather of 'die Art und Weise, wie Gegenstände im Sachverhalt zusammenhängen'.

But even after all this has been said, the quoted propositions remain puzzling. The paradoxical-looking feature of such propositions as 2.03 is that nothing is required in order to make up a state of affairs except a number of objects. This is probably what so forcefully struck Anscombe, Copi and the others who have relied on 2.03 in their denials of objecthood to relations. Now the developmental perspective proposed by Pears and explained in chapter 3 below enables us to understand this aspect of Wittgenstein's point. In moving from his earlier position (which Russell took up after Wittgenstein had given it up himself) to the position of the *Tractatus*, Wittgenstein gave up all complex logical forms, e.g., forms corresponding to complex logical propositions, and even the forms of elementary propositions, as independent entities. All that remains are forms of objects, out of which all the other forms can be constructed. It is this self-sufficiency of objects that is highlighted in propositions like 2.03.

We shall return to the problems discussed here in chapter 4 below. (See especially secs. 7–8.)

NOTES

1 There is nevertheless a sharp difference between the use of the term 'thing' in the *Tractatus* and in Wittgenstein's "Notes dictated to G. E. Moore in Norway" (Appendix II to *Notebooks 1914–1916*), as we shall point out below. In the 'Notes', only particulars are called 'things'. For another difference between the terms 'object' and 'thing' in the *Tractatus*, see chapter 3, sec. 15.

2 See G. E. M. Anscombe, *An Introduction to Wittgenstein's Tractatus*, second, rev. edn, Hutchinson, London, 1963; Irving M. Copi, 'Objects, properties, and relations in the *Tractatus*', *Mind*, vol. 67 (1958), pp. 145–65; G. E. M. Anscombe, 'Mr. Copi on objects, properties, and relations in the *Tractatus*', *Mind*, vol. 68 (1959), p. 404; George Pitcher, *The Philosophy of Wittgenstein*, Prentice-Hall, Englewood Cliffs, 1964, pp. 113–18; Richard J. Bernstein 'Wittgenstein's three languages', *Review of Metaphysics*, vol. 15 (1961), pp. 278–98.

3 Erik Stenius, *Wittgenstein's Tractatus: A Critical Exposition of Its Main Lines of Thought*, Basil Blackwell, Oxford, 1960; André Maury, *The Concepts of Sinn and Gegenstand in Wittgenstein's 'Tractatus'* (*Acta Philosophica Fennica*, vol. 29, no. 4), North-Holland, Amsterdam, 1977.

4 See, e.g., MS 220, p. 85; MS 127, p. 38, quoted by Maury, *Concepts*, pp. 112–14.

5 See *Wittgenstein's Lectures, Cambridge, 1930–1932*, p. 120.

6 Copi, 'Objects, Properties, and Relations'.

3

The Objects of the *Tractatus* as Objects of Acquaintance

1 WHAT ARE THE OBJECTS OF THE *TRACTATUS*?

The main interpretational question which remains open concerning Wittgenstein's *Tractatus* also concerns the objects Wittgenstein assumes and discusses there. It is one of the first to occur to every reader of the book: What is the nature of the (simple) *objects* which he postulates in that famous work? What *are* they anyway? This problem is made pressing by Wittgenstein's silence about this subject in the *Tractatus*, which is prima facie most surprising in view of the central importance of objects in the ontology of the *Tractatus*. Admittedly, according to the official doctrine of early Wittgenstein's, it cannot be *said* what the objects are, only *shown*. (Cf. chapter 1 above.) So his silence might seem explicable. But equally admittedly Wittgenstein breaks his self-imposed vow of silence on a number of much less important occasions and makes a great many comments in the *Tractatus* which, by the same token, convey something to us only by way of showing rather than saying. Hence the silence of the author of the *Tractatus* in this important matter is indeed telling.

But there is a deeper mystery than a mere silence about the objects of the *Tractatus*. Wittgenstein drops contradictory hints as to the nature of objects. On the one hand, they are the persisting, objective (no pun intended) ingredients in the world:

2.021   Objects make up the substance of the world . . .

2.024   Substance is what subsists independently of what is the case.

2.026   There must be objects, if the world is to have an unalterable form.

2.027   Objects, the unalterable, and the subsistent are one and the same.

2.0271   Objects are what is unalterable and subsistent; their configuration is what is changing and unstable.

On the other hand, there are apparent indications to the effect that Wittgenstein thought that the objects of the *Tractatus* included *phenomenological* ones (objects of immediate experience).[1] For instance, several times in the *Notebooks 1914–1916* Wittgenstein mentions points or patches in *visual* space, which are paradigmatically phenomenological entities, as examples of simple objects:

> As examples of the simple I always think of points of the visual space . . . (6 May 1915; p. 45)

> It seems to me perfectly possible that patches in our visual field are simple objects . . . ; the visual appearances of stars even seem certainly to be so. (18 June 1915; p. 64)

2 THE INEFFABILITY OF OBJECTUAL EXISTENCE

This mystery is compounded by another one. Many of Wittgenstein's views in the *Tractatus* are based on an assumption whose importance has not been fully recognized in the literature. It is the thesis that one cannot significantly express the existence or nonexistence of a particular unanalysable object. One can say that there are objects of a certain kind, but not that a certain particular object exists or does not exist. That can only be shown:

> 5.61   So we cannot say in logic: 'The world has this in it, and this, but not that.'

The basis of this thesis is indicated earlier in the *Tractatus*:

> 3.221   Objects can only be *named*. Signs are their representatives. I can only speak *about* them: *I cannot put them into words.*
> A proposition can only say *how* a thing is, not *what* it is. [We have restored Wittgenstein's singular in the last sentence, which Pears and McGuinness translate in the plural.]

As Wittgenstein says elsewhere (5.552), logic is prior to the question *How*, but not prior to the question *What*.

This feature of Wittgenstein's objects is taken by him to be one of their most characteristic properties, perhaps even their defining property. For instance, in criticizing his own earlier views Wittgenstein still writes in *PI*, I, sec. 58, as a formulation of the doctrine he is criticizing:

> "I want to restrict the term 'name' to what cannot occur in the combination 'X exists'. Thus one cannot say 'Red exists', because if there were no red it could not be spoken at all."

Indeed, virtually Wittgenstein's whole discussion in the *Philosophical Investigations* of his former 'objects' is predicated on the assumption that this is their characteristic property; cf. *PI*, I, secs. 50, 55, 58, and 59. Likewise, the impossibility of expressing the existence of objects in language is considered by Wittgenstein their characteristic mark in *Philosophical Remarks*, III, sec. 36.

An important consequence of these views is duly recorded by Wittgenstein:

> 4.1272 (5–6)   So one cannot say, for example, 'There are objects', as one might say, 'There are books'. And it is just as impossible to say, 'There are 100 objects', or, 'There are $\aleph_0$ objects'. And it is non-sensical to speak of the *total number of objects*.

We shall call the view under consideration the *ineffability of objectual existence*. On the level of language this view implies that the existence of a particular simple object is shown by the fact that its name is used in the language. A consequence of this view for the inference rules of one's logic is that all individual constants of a logically well-formed language are assumed to be non-empty.

Prima facie, there might not seem to be anything really puzzling about this doctrine of the *Tractatus*. After all, it merely reproduces a feature of Frege's logical notation. There, too, one could not express the existence or nonexistence of an individual object. Existence is a higher-level predicate; it is expressed only by the existential quantifier. And this Fregean practice can be considered, according to several philosophers, merely as a technical realization of the older idea that existence is not a predicate. Moreover, the Fregean assumption which matches Wittgenstein's was subsequently built into practically all systems of first-order logic (predicate calculus). Hence it is perhaps understandable that philosophers have not paid very much attention to this assumption as an ingredient of the *Tractatus*.

It nevertheless plays an important and interesting role there. However many views Wittgenstein may have taken over from Frege, he adopted none of them uncritically. The ineffability of individual existence was not prejudged by the other doctrines of Frege's which Wittgenstein incorporated into his own thinking, and it can be considered one of the most dubious aspects of Frege's logical notation and his system of logical inference. As has been shown by the ill-named systems of free logic, the Fregean assumption is dispensable on a purely logical level. Admittedly, these were developed much later, but they certainly were not beyond Wittgenstein's acumen.[2] Moreover, the inexpressibility of the existence of an individual may be considered something of an aberration on Frege's part. It violates the principle that existence is expressed solely by the existential quantifier, for it means that existence assumptions are imported into one's logical language by each and every individual constant admitted into it.

Moreover, Wittgenstein pressed the thesis of the ineffability of objectual existence much further than did Frege. For Frege, it is partly a technical decision as to how to handle the concept of existence. For Wittgenstein, it becomes one of the most important doctrines of the whole work. Some of its consequences are worth examining here, albeit briefly. Some others will be examined in the next chapter.

3 SOME CONSEQUENCES OF THE INEFFABILITY

It was already indicated that the technical counterpart to one of the consequences of the thesis of the ineffability of individual existence is the assumption that all 'names', to use Wittgenstein's term in the *Tractatus*, are non-empty. However, this is not all. Unlike Frege, Wittgenstein is envisaging in the *Tractatus* an ontology of possible states of affairs. For this reason, the inexpressibility of individual existence becomes for him a much stronger assumption. Just as we cannot say that a particular object exists or does not exist, so it makes little sense (according to Wittgenstein) to say that it might not exist or could exist even though it does not actually do so. And this Wittgenstein takes to mean that we have to deal with the objects that actually are as if each of them existed necessarily and as if collectively they were exhaustive by necessity. Of course Wittgenstein does not think that he can *say* that objects exist necessarily. This is what he means by the transcendentality of objects, which is for him the gist of the transcendentality of logic (cf. 6.13). It is nevertheless clear that he makes the important but inexpressible assumption of the *necessary* and *necessarily exhaustive existence* of objects.

One of the most important implications of this assumption is that not only all the actually obtaining states of affairs but also all the possible states of affairs must be thought of as having been built out of the same objects:

2.022   It is obvious that an imagined world, however different it may be from the real one, must have *something* – a form – in common with it.

2.023   Objects are just what constitute this unalterable form.

Thus the thesis of the ineffability of objectual existence implies in Wittgenstein's view the striking doctrine mentioned above in sec. 1

according to which it is the objects that constitute the substance of the world. The proposition 2.026, quoted above, is instructive here, and so are the following:

> 2.0124   If all objects are given, then at the same time all *possible* states of affairs are also given.
>
> 2.014   The objects contain the possibility of all situations.
>
> 2.0141   The possibility of its occurring in states of affairs is the form of an object.

Thus Wittgenstein's thesis that the existence of particular objects is ineffable serves to explain why he thought of objects as constituting the substance of the world – of the actual world and of any other possible worlds. The same objects must be the ultimate building-blocks of each such world. It is important to realize that this kind of substantiality has nothing to do with the persistence or ephemerality of objects under the actual course of events.

From the propositions quoted we can see that Wittgenstein gives this idea a twist which is not only unexpected but apparently almost self-contradictory. What we have found, on the basis of Wittgenstein's thesis of the ineffability of objectual existence, is why he should have thought that objects constitute the *substance* or *content* of the world. Yet what he actually says goes further, and goes in an apparently opposite direction. Wittgenstein says that objects are *form* and content (2.025) and that they constitute not just the substance of any possible world, but also its *form*. (Cf. 2.022–2.023, quoted above.) This form of an object he also identifies (cf. 2.0141) with its possibilities of occurring in states of affairs. It is also clear that this form of an object is thought of by Wittgenstein as its *logical* form.

Now this idea of form at first sight seems extremely strange. When a contemporary philosopher thinks of logical form, he or she is likely to think primarily of the different ways in which complex propositions can be formed from simpler ones. Wittgenstein includes this variety of ways of forming complex propositions in his notion of logical form, but he also includes in it the forms of atomic propositions and even forms of (simple) objects. This is shown by the many passages in which he speaks of the forms of objects.

This emphasis by Wittgenstein on the form of simple objects is apparently unmotivated, and at the first sight self-contradictory. How can *simple* objects have a *form*? We saw in the preceding chapter that in the *Tractatus* they *can* have a structure or a form. But why should this form be as important as Wittgenstein clearly thinks it is?

Moreover, how can objects be at one and the same time content and form? We obviously have found here an additional interpretational problem. It is, moreover, a problem to which there is no simple solution in the existing literature. We shall solve it in sec. 6 below.

The complex of ideas we have discussed, which includes the transcendentality of objects, the ineffability and necessity of their existence, and the importance of their forms, was of central importance for Wittgenstein. One indication of this importance is that he retained some of these ideas for a long time after writing the *Tractatus*. This is in evidence in such passages as *Philosophical Investigations*, I, secs. 46–50 and *Philosophical Remarks*, III, sec. 36 (quoted below in sec. 8). These show clearly also that the reason that Wittgenstein thought of the existence of objects as being inexpressible was not a notional convention, but a deep and important feature of objects (simples), indeed their characteristic property, which he sought to put in a new perspective in his later philosophy.

4 INEFFABILITY OF OBJECTUAL EXISTENCE VS. THE INEFFABILITY OF SEMANTICS

We have tentatively suggested that the ineffability of objectual existence in the *Tractatus* might be a consequence of Wittgenstein's belief in what he has dubbed language as the universal medium, via the general ineffability of semantics. (Cf. chapter 1, sec. 4, above.) Purely historically, Wittgenstein might very well have been led to his thesis of inexpressibility of objectual existence through his belief in the general ineffability of semantics. It is also clear systematically that the two belong to one and the same group of ideas. Nevertheless there does not seem to be any inseparable link between the two.

What does follow from the assumption of language as the universal medium is the ineffability of the basic semantical relations between language and reality. In the case of the *Tractatus*, they are the name–object relations, which are admittedly inexpressible *par excellence* according to Wittgenstein. But this inexpressibility of name–object relations did not prevent one (according to the *Tractatus*) from using them in order to say what the object at the receiving end of the relation *is like*. Why can we not equally well use some one such relation to say that *there is* something at its receiving end? The mere ineffability of language–world relations does not imply that we cannot do so.

An analogy may be helpful here. Suppose one uses a pole to find out what a river bottom is like, e.g., whether it is sandy or muddy. We cannot use the pole in the same way to find out what the pole itself is like; we cannot use it to find out whether the unseen (underwater) part of the pole itself is hard or soft. But surely one can use the pole to decide whether there is any bottom reachable by the pole. The pole is here the analogue of a given name–object relation.

It can now be seen that an earlier claim in this chapter needs qualifications. (See the beginning of sec. 2 above.) In spite of the verbal similarity, 3.221 is *not* a sufficient basis of such propositions as 5.552 or 5.61. What is ineffable according to 3.221 is what it is which happens to be at the receiving end of a given naming relation. This is purely and simply the ineffability of naming relations. In contrast, what is ineffable according to 5.61 and 5.552 is what is, or perhaps whether there is anything at all that a given name stands for.

Thus, Wittgenstein's thesis of the ineffability of objectual existence is not explained either as a Fregean inheritance or as a corollary to the inexpressibility of name–object relations. The historical explanation of why Wittgenstein held this view must lie in the nature of the objects he postulated in the *Tractatus*.

The cutting edge of this problem can perhaps be illustrated by pointing out that while Wittgenstein's thesis in effect makes particular existential judgements necessary (as was observed above), in earlier philosophical literature these were frequently considered virtually paradigmatic examples of *contingent* judgements. For instance, all singular existential propositions were declared synthetic by Immanuel Kant.

5 THE OBJECTS OF THE *TRACTATUS* AS OBJECTS OF ACQUAINTANCE

The importance of Wittgenstein's ineffability thesis makes even more burning the question, What are the objects of the *Tractatus* really like, anyway? Perhaps one should here put an historian's cap on for a moment and ask: Where in Wittgenstein's background can one find a similar fusion or duality of the phenomenal and the objective? The most obvious answer lies in Bertrand Russell's work around 1913–14, the very years when the basic ideas of the *Tractatus* were crystallizing in Wittgenstein's mind. The sense-data out of which Russell constructs the external world exhibit a similarly perplexing ambivalence between the phenomenal and the objective. On the one hand, they are the data which senses give us, hence subject to all the illusions and other vagaries of sense-perception. On the other hand, they are not a part of one's psychological process of sense-perception, Russell and Moore insist very strongly. They are the *objects* of perception, part of the perceptual *contents*, not an aspect of the act of perceiving. Hence they exhibit the same ambivalence as do Wittgenstein's objects.

The anticipation is striking, and the intensive intellectual exchanges between Wittgenstein and Russell in the critical period 1913–14 make an influence, whether mutual or not, eminently likely. However, the hypothesis of a Russellian model for the objects of the *Tractatus* must be checked against hard historical data.

6 WITTGENSTEIN'S BACKGROUND IN RUSSELL

It is known that in 1913 Russell wrote a book entitled *Theory of Knowledge*, which he left largely unpublished because of Wittgenstein's criticisms. The unpublished part contains a theory of judgement, understanding, and logical truth. This book was eventually published in 1984 as volume 7 of Russell's collected papers.[3]

David Pears has aptly summarized his theory and shown how Wittgenstein both criticized it in detail in the *Tractatus* and modified it so as to arrive at his own picture theory of language.[4] The details need not detain us here. Suffice it to say that Russell's 1913 theory was an extension of his views on acquaintance as a basis both of knowledge and of meaning. Earlier, Russell had used the idea of acquaintance to explain where the simplest ingredients of our propositions came from. In *Theory of Knowledge*, Russell tries to evoke the same idea to account for logic and logical form, especially the logical forms of complex propositions. For instance, according to the earlier view, in order to understand a simple relational proposition, say 'aRb', one must be acquainted with the referents of 'a', 'R' and 'b'. Russell came to realize that this is not enough; something more is needed to distinguish, e.g., 'aRb' from 'bRa'. He identified this additional element with the *logical form* of the proposition, with which one must also be acquainted in order to understand the proposition. And this acquaintance Russell identified with knowledge of the corresponding existentially generalized proposition "$(\exists x)(\exists y)(\exists \phi).\, x\phi y$" and with knowledge of the logical truth of this generalized proposition. All such fully generalized propositions are hence necessarily, because logically, true.

The same account goes, according to Russell, for all propositions. For each structure which propositions can exhibit he likewise postulates an entity separate from its several ingredients, its logical form. This entity is also a potential object of acquaintance, of which one must have experience in order to understand the proposition.

In summary, we can thus say that in *Theory of Knowledge* Russell countenances two different classes of objects of acquaintance:

(i) Concrete objects of acquaintance, including both particulars and universals.
(ii) Logical forms.

The members of the class (i) are concrete 'Aristotelian' entities as distinguished from the abstract 'Platonic' entities (ii).

Pears describes aptly how Wittgenstein modified Russell's views so as to arrive at the doctrines displayed in the *Tractatus*. Very briefly, he eliminated Russell's second class (ii) of logical forms which Russell had used to accommodate logic and meaning within his theory of acquaintance. In particular, Wittgenstein eliminated Russell's free-floating forms expressed by completely general propositions, and *a fortiori* the need for acquaintance with such forms. It is for this reason that Wittgenstein can now say that we do not need any experience in logic (cf. 5.552).

What this change means is that the job that was earlier done by Russell's objects of acquaintance of the second kind (ii) will now have to be done by regular objects (i). But this job was primarily to account for the logical forms of complex propositions. So if these forms are not basic and irreducible, they must be built up of the other kinds of objects (i). In other words, all complex logical forms must be constructable from the forms of the simple concrete objects (i).

Here we suddenly have an explanation for one of the most fundamental and probably the strangest doctrines of the *Tractatus*. We found it puzzling, in sec. 3 above, that Wittgenstein not only countenanced logical forms of simple objects but placed a considerable emphasis on them. It was also striking that Wittgenstein should have treated his objects not only as the substance of the world but as constituting the form of the world. The full force – and full strangeness – of Wittgenstein's views was nevertheless brought out only incompletely in sec. 3. Not only were the logical forms of simple objects important for Wittgenstein; they were all-important. All logical forms can be constructed from them according to the *Tractatus*, because they now have to do the job which complex logical forms were performing for Russell.

To spell this out somewhat more fully, we can say that Wittgenstein thinks that the complex logical forms are all determined by the logical forms of elementary (atomic) propositions. Furthermore, the logical forms of atomic propositions are determined by the forms of objects. It is via this two-stage process that all logical forms can be reduced to the logical forms of simple objects. From them, all possible logical forms can be constructed. This view is so strange that it has demonstrably misled several competent commentators. We shall return to it in chapter 4 below. What we shall find there provides further evidence for the crucial importance of Wittgenstein's rejection of complex logical forms as independent objects for the doctrines of the *Tractatus*.

This puzzling but fundamental doctrine of the *Tractatus*, that all logical forms can be constructed from those of simple objects, is a consequence of Wittgenstein's rejection of complex logical forms as independent entities. Their job has to be done by something else, and the only candidates are the forms of simple objects (i). Hence we must be able, as it were, to assemble from them all logical forms, however complex. Thus the solution to our interpretational mystery is Wittgenstein's rejection of the second class (ii) of Russell's 1913 objects of acquaintance. Simple objects constitute the content of all conceivable states of affairs because they have to be dealt with as existing necessarily, and as being necessarily exhaustive of all that there is. This is due to their ineffability. The very same objects have to constitute, by being combined with each other, the form of any conceivable fact because logical forms do not exist as separate entities but have to be built up of the logical forms of simple objects. Thus Wittgenstein's simple objects are in a poignant sense at the same time both the form of the world and its substance (content).

There are good reasons to think that the way in which Wittgenstein actually arrived at his views was by starting out from views closely related to Russell's. In criticizing Russell's *Theory of Knowledge*, Wittgenstein is reported by Russell as saying that he had held the same (Russellian) view himself earlier, but had found it did not work.[5] Further reasons for believing in this line of development are provided by Pears, who shows in considerable detail how we can understand several different doctrines Wittgenstein puts forward in the *Tractatus* as having grown out of Wittgenstein's rejection of Russell's complex logical forms. An example of documentary evidence is, e.g., Wittgenstein's criticism in the *Tractatus* and in the *Notebooks 1914–1916* of the view that one needs experience in logic.[6]

In the *Tractatus*, the forms of simple objects govern the way in which these objects can be combined with each other. The form of an object is what is true of it a priori. This important role of the notion of logical form in the *Tractatus* provides indirect but instructive evidence for the proximity of Wittgenstein's views to those of Russell. This emphasis is not found in Frege or elsewhere in Wittgenstein's background, whereas it is (as we saw) a central feature of Russell's views in 1913.

The nice developmental story which Pears tells us and which we have elaborated makes little sense, however, unless Wittgenstein and Russell were talking about the same thing. And this can scarcely be the case, unless we assume that Wittgenstein retained the rest of Russell's view, at least in its main features. More specifically, it makes little sense to describe Wittgenstein as getting rid of the necessity of having acquaintance with complex logical forms unless we assume that he retained the idea that simples – the building-blocks of forms – are still objects of acquaintance. Even though Pears does not mention it, much less emphasize it, his discussion is tacitly predicated on the assumption that the objects of the *Tractatus* are essentially the same as Russell's objects of acquaintance.

We have thus found weighty reasons for thinking that Wittgenstein's objects postulated in the *Tractatus* coincided with the members of the class (i) of Russell's objects of acquaintance.

An intriguing historical question which arises here is the possibility of a Fregean influence on Wittgenstein in his venture beyond Russell. For the position to which Wittgenstein moved is firmly grounded in Frege's famous (or notorious) principle of compositionality (the functional principle, Davidson's 'Frege Principle'). It follows from that principle that the meanings of the component parts of a proposition – ultimately, of the simple sign it contains – completely determine its meaning. This is the linguistic counterpart to the idea that the forms of (simple) objects determine the forms of all propositions, a view which we saw Wittgenstein embracing. A partial bridge between the two principles is constituted by the connection which obtains between the concepts of logical form and sense in the *Tractatus*, as was seen in the preceding paragraph.

In the form of a slogan, we may thus characterize the leading ideas of the *Tractatus* as the result of imposing Frege's principle of compositionality on Russell's theory of acquaintance (as applied to logic and logical forms).

One problem we can now solve is the one that was left open in the preceding chapter. The reason why Wittgenstein had to ascribe a logical form to each of the simple objects is that he had no other materials from which to build the forms of atomic as well as complex sentences, having rejected Russell's logical forms as independent unanalysable entities. Thus what we have found in the present chapter meshes well with what we found in the preceding one.[7]

7 INTERPRETATIONAL AND TEXTUAL EVIDENCE

But what textual and doctrinal evidence is there for the outrageous-sounding identification of Russell's objects of acquaintance and

Wittgenstein's objects? A telling item of testimony is put forward by Wittgenstein himself when he writes in the *Philosophical Investigations*, I, sec. 46:

> What lies behind the idea that names really signify simples? Socrates says in the *Theaetetus*: ". . . there is no definition of the primary elements . . . out of which everything else is composed; for everything that exists in its own right can only be *named*, no other determination is possible, neither that it *is* nor that it *is not* . . . But what exists in its own right has to be . . . named without any other determination. In consequence, it is impossible to give an account of any primary element; for it, nothing is possible but the bare name; its name is all it has. But just as what consists of these primary elements is itself complex, so the names of the elements become descriptive language by being compounded together. For the essence of speech is the composition of names." *Both Russell's 'individuals' and my 'objects' (Tractatus Logico-Philosophicus) were such primary objects.* [Emphasis added in the last sentence.]

What is telling here is not only the bracketing together by Wittgenstein of Russell's individuals and the objects of the *Tractatus*, but the conjunction of this assimilation and the idea that the existence of any particular simple is inexpressible.[8]

All this is perhaps not very conclusive, for it does not contain any reference to the role of the objects of the *Tractatus* as objects of experience. Such a reference is to be found in the *Tractatus* itself, however:

> 5.552   The 'experience' that we need in order to understand logic is not that something or other is the state of things, but that something *is*; but that just is not an *experience*.
> Logic is *prior to* any experience – experience that something *is so*.
> It is prior to the How, not to the What. [We have modified the existing translations of this passage.]

This passage is especially significant for our interpretation, because it is obviously a direct comment by Wittgenstein on the ideas propounded in Russell's 1913 book *Theory of Knowledge*, which was briefly described above. Russell had suggested that we need acquaintance with the logical form of each proposition we are to understand. Wittgenstein denies this. For him, the possibility of all logical forms is packed into the objects.[9] All we need in order to grasp all the logical forms is to grasp the objects. But *with them we still have to be acquainted*. This is precisely what Wittgenstein says in the beginning of 5.552. It is particularly significant that the context shows that he is thinking of Russell's views in asserting that.

Admittedly, Wittgenstein goes on to say that 'experience' is here wrongly so-called. But the latter part of the quotation shows that what makes these experiences improper is precisely that they are about the existence of objects. (It is not the kind of experience which can be expressed in language.) Hence Wittgenstein's qualification does not reduce the evidential value of 5.552.

There are several passages in the *Tractatus* which are made more understandable by this interpretation of Tractarian objects, and hence support it, even though they can yield only indirect evidence for it. One of them is Wittgenstein's partial identification of myself and my world. In naïve thought, the two are juxtaposed; they are two contrasting poles. Yet Wittgenstein writes:

5.6   *The limits* of my language mean the limits of my world.

5.63   I am my world.

The basis of Wittgenstein's thesis is seen from the explanations he offers for his view. That the world is my world is shown, he says, by the fact that its limits are the same as the limits of my language. In 5.641 he even says that the philosophical 'I' is the limit of the world. Now it is clear that the limit he is talking about here is a limit determined by the totality of *objects*. In fact, in the very first elaboration of 5.6, quoted above, viz. in 5.61, Wittgenstein writes: '. . . we cannot say in logic: "this and this there is in the world, that there is not."'

But why should the dependence of the world on the totality of objects (which determines its limits) make it *my* world? This identification would be inexplicable if Wittgenstein's objects were merely physical atoms of some sort of other unrelated to myself. The real answer lies in the overall nature of Russell's and Wittgenstein's philosophical enterprise. They were both looking for what has to be given to me in order for me to understand my language. This is the role for which Russell's objects of acquaintance and Wittgenstein's simple objects are cast. What makes the two alike is precisely the requirement that they must be given to me in my experience in order to be able to serve their purpose.

But my experiences *are* my life. As Wittgenstein writes in *Philosophical Remarks*, VII, sec. 67:

Suppose I had such a good memory that I could remember all my sense impressions. In that case, there would, *prima facie*, be nothing to prevent me from describing them. This would be a biography.

For this reason, the limits of the totality of objects of my experiences *are* the limits of my world. Hence the identification of my life and the world is in the last analysis due to the world's consisting precisely of those objects that have to be given to me in *my* life experience in order for my language (and hence my thinking) to get started. It is not due to the metaphysical status of the objects as being phenomenal or anything like phenomenal. The real reason is that, whatever the metaphysical status of the ultimate objects is or may be, they will have to show up in my experience in order to be relevant to my language and thought. This requirement was not foreign to Russell and Moore, either, and explains some of the similarities between Wittgenstein and them. (Cf., e.g., notes 18, 20–22, below.)

In other words, the identity of the totality of my (simple) objects and my life is not due to the alleged fact that those objects are phenomenal or otherwise dependent on me. Rather, it is due to the fact (if Wittgenstein is right) that I depend on the basic objects given to me in my experience for my entire language and hence entire thinking. This is what Wittgenstein means when he says, as late as 1931–2:

> Sense-data are the source of our concepts. (*Wittgenstein's Lectures, Cambridge 1930–1932*, p. 81)

Hence the sense in which the objects are mine (and hence the world is mine) is that these objects have to be part of the content of *my* experience.

But why cannot I countenance objects entirely different from the ones given to me in experience? Wittgenstein does not formulate his answer in so many words, but it is nevertheless clear. Objects not given to me in experience are not objects that I can speak of in my actual language. They are objects of which I could say in my language that they do not exist or are not known to exist. But to say this would be to anticipate in my language what the language – the only language that I understand – would be if it were different. And this would, by Wittgenstein's token, violate the ineffability of semantics. Hence Wittgenstein's attitude to the basic objects of the *Tractatus* is heavily conditioned by his belief in language as the universal medium, studied above in chapter 1.[10]

We can now understand – at least understand better – why Wittgenstein should have identified the world and life:

> 5.621   The world and life are one and the same.

The objects which determine the world (in the sense in which he is speaking of the world here, not in the sense of 1.1) are the objects of one's immediate experience, and in a reasonably good sense they can be said to constitute one's life.[11]

Perhaps the most revealing propositions of the *Tractatus* are nevertheless some of Wittgenstein's comments, not about life, but about death:

> 6.431 Likewise the world does not change in death, but ceases to be.

This proposition fits in very well with the interpretation presented here, as does the following reason offered by Wittgenstein:

> 6.4311 Death is not an event in life. *One does not experience death.* [Emphasis added.]

By way of contrast, events of life are presumably experiences, and if the world and life are one, then the world consists of what is experienced.

Wittgenstein's remarks on the identity of the world and life in the *Tractatus* (5.621–5.63) are put into an interesting perspective by his later reiteration on the view we have ascribed to him recorded by Desmond Lee:[12]

> The world we live in is the world of sense-data . . .

A comparison with the *Tractatus* hence suggests very strongly that the world postulated there consists at least partly of something like sense-data.

The present interpretation is convincingly confirmed by the explanations of the first few propositions of the *Tractatus* which Wittgenstein offered during the academic year 1930–1 to Desmond Lee.[13] There Wittgenstein is reported to have said that, in the *Tractatus*,

> Objects etc. is here used for such things as a colour, a point in visual space etc. . . .

'Colour' could here be perhaps still taken to refer to physical colour, but points in a visual space are phenomenological, not physical.

Some indirect evidence for this interpretation of the objects of the *Tractatus* is also obtained from the status of the basic name–object relations in the *Tractatus*. They were left by Wittgenstein completely unanalysed and unexplained. This would be a very strange procedure if the objects were not given to us immediately in our experience.

Now 'Russell's account of . . . knowledge by acquaintance is primarily an attempt to trace back our understanding of the meanings of phrases to its source in our experience.'[14] The objects of acquaintance are precisely the end-points of this 'tracing back' procedure. Of such objects we do not any longer have to ask how they are named or how their names refer to them. Thus the interpretation defended here has the merit of helping to explain Wittgenstein's strange silence in the *Tractatus* on this crucial matter of naming relations. By the same token, language–world relations became a problem for Wittgenstein only later when he gave up the idea that objects are given to us in immediate experience. (Cf. chapter 8 below.)

8 THE PRIMARY LANGUAGE OF THE *TRACTATUS* IS PHENOMENOLOGICAL

The explanation Wittgenstein offered to Desmond Lee concerning the nature of objects of the *Tractatus* (quoted above) is also important here because it serves to confirm our interpretation of an interesting passage of his *Philosophical Remarks* (I, sec. 1):

> I do not now have phenomenological language, or 'primary language' as I used to call it, in mind as my goal.

According to *Philosophical Remarks*, such a 'primary' or 'phenomenological' language deals with 'data' (VI, sec. 57, p. 88), i.e., with 'what is immediate' (II, sec. 11, p. 88), i.e., with 'what is immediate' (II, sec. 11, p. 58). Similar statements are found elsewhere in Wittgenstein's middle-period writings. We shall return to them in chapter 6 below. They show that the logically and epistemologically correct language earlier envisaged by Wittgenstein dealt with *visual* space and other immediately given phenomena. Thus, if the passages quoted from *Philosophical Remarks* refer to the views Wittgenstein codified in the *Tractatus* (as we shall argue later), it follows that the primary (logically analysed) language postulated in the *Tractatus* was a *phenomenological* one, having as its objects the immediately given data.

From Wittgenstein's middle-period writings we can also see what he took the phenomenological character of his earlier basic language to entail concerning the objects he had postulated in the *Tractatus*. For instance, what were those earlier objects like? Wittgenstein once illustrates his point by saying:

The visual table is not composed of electrons. (*Philosophical Remarks*, III, sec. 36)

And in the next paragraph he writes:

> What if someone said to me 'I expect three knocks on the door' and I replied 'How do you know *three knocks* exist?' – Wouldn't that be just like the question 'How do you know six feet exist?' after someone has said 'I believe A is 6 feet high'?

These examples show unmistakably that the Tractarian objects Wittgenstein is discussing are phenomenological objects, such as *visual* tables or *expected* knocks.

There is other evidence for the phenomenological character of Wittgenstein's objects. For instance, there is his view, repeated in his middle-period writings, that logic (or 'grammar') and phenomenology are essentially one. (See below, chapter 6, sec. 4.) Why should Wittgenstein believe that logic and phenomenology are one? The missing link between the two is the concept of an object. Wittgenstein makes it clear that he thinks of the forms of simple objects as the rock bottom, the be-all and end-all of logic. This does not bring us any closer to the identification of logic and phenomenology, however, until it is realized that these fundamental building-blocks of all logical forms, the forms of simple objects, were phenomenological and that Wittgenstein's basic language in the *Tractatus* was therefore a phenomenological language.

We shall return to this point in chapter 6, sec. 4, below.

9   ACQUAINTANCE AND THE INEFFABILITY OF OBJECTUAL EXISTENCE

Other passages of the *Tractatus* which offer further indirect support to this interpretation will be introduced below. Meanwhile, it is important to point out one of the most striking links between the Russellian and Wittgensteinian views. It is the fact that Wittgenstein's thesis of the ineffability of the existence of objects has a perfect model in Russell. Indeed, on p. 138 of *Theory of Knowledge* Russell writes:

> Of an actually given *this*, an object of acquaintance, it is meaningless to say that it 'exists'.

Russell makes it clear that according to him this holds of all 'true proper names' in contradistinction to 'descriptions'.

Needless to say, if Russell's objects of acquaintance are identified with the objects of the *Tractatus*, Russell's view coincides perfectly with Wittgenstein's.

Similar, albeit somewhat less bold, statements are found in Russell's published writings. For instance, in 'The Relation of Sense-Data to Physics' he says that '*sense* gives acquaintance with particulars, and is thus a two-term relation in which the object can be *named* but not *asserted*, and is inherently incapable of truth and falsehood . . .'[15] This may be compared with 3.221, quoted above in sec. 2.

Nor is this doctrine of Russell's a passing fancy. It is merely one particular poignant consequence of his general idea that acquaintance supplies not only the building-blocks of our knowledge, but more importantly, the meanings (references) of our basic expressions.[16] Implicit in this view is the ineffability thesis which is being discussed in this chapter. For in order to say meaningfully of an object of immediate acquaintance that it exists, we must be able to refer to it meaningfully. But such a meaningful reference could be based on the actual existence of the object of acquaintance. Hence its existence cannot be expressed meaningfully (and non-trivially).

What we find in Russell is more than a mere anticipation of Wittgenstein's thesis of the ineffability of objectual existence. Above, we saw how one can arrive at the objects of the *Tractatus* by starting from Russell's objects of acquaintance and then transforming Russell's theory along the lines it is known that Wittgenstein transformed it. There is a related line of thought which shows how Wittgenstein was led to his ineffability thesis by starting from Russell's views and by making essentially the same changes in them as were indicated above. As we saw, Russell postulated complex logical forms as actually existing objects of acquaintance in order to account for logical truths within his theory of acquaintance. In effect, Wittgenstein replaced these actual forms by possible combinations of objects. But in order for these combinations of objects to be possible, the objects themselves must be actual.

This is Wittgenstein's concern in such statements as the following:

The logical combination between the things represented by names must of course be possible, and this will always be the case if the names really do stand for the things. (*Notebooks 1914–1916*, p. 26, on 11 November 1914)

There is thus an interesting historical connection between the two themes of this chapter, the interpretation of the objects of the *Tractatus* as Russellian objects of acquaintance and the ineffability of objectual existence in that work. One and the same insight solves both of the interpretational mysteries which form the dual theme of this chapter, at least as far as historical problems are concerned, viz. the insight that the objects Wittgenstein assumes in the *Tractatus* are phenomenological in nature. This is the reason that these two questions have been grouped together.

10 ACQUAINTANCE AND WITTGENSTEIN'S IDEA OF SHOWING

Here a reader is also likely to have a vivid experience of a terminological *déjà vu*. As we saw, Russell could not meaningfully say of an object of acquaintance that it exists or does not exist. But how can one then address Russellian objects of acquaintance? As we are reminded by Russell's formulation quoted above ('. . . an actually given *this* . . .'), their 'names', the only 'logically proper names' referring to external particulars, are 'this' and 'that'. Now how does Wittgenstein formulate *his* doctrine of the ineffability of objectual existence? By saying that

> 5.61 we . . . cannot say in logic: *this* and *this* there is in the world, *that* there isn't.

Wittgenstein is thus reproducing Russell's terminology almost *verbatim*. The same connection between the demonstrative 'this' and Wittgenstein's conception of object is emphatically asserted in the *Notebooks*, 16 June 1915 (p. 61):

> What seems to be given us *a priori* is the concept: *This* – Identical with the concept of the *object*.

Notice also what the view of simple objects is like that Wittgenstein criticizes in *Philosophical Investigations*, I, sec. 45:

> The demonstrative "this" can never be without a bearer . . . But this does not make the word into a name.

Now who was it that claimed that 'this' is a (logically proper) name? Russell in his theory of acquaintance. Yet it is ostensibly his own earlier views that Wittgenstein is criticizing in this part of the *Philosophical Investigations*.

These observations can be generalized. If Russellian objects of acquaintance cannot be said to exist, how can they be introduced?

According to Russell's sometime theory, there are in our language only two logically proper names for particular objects other than oneself, to wit, 'this' and 'that'. If so, Russellian objects of acquaintance are introduced by displaying them and pointing to them, that is, by showing them. This is a perfect precedent of Wittgenstein's mystical-sounding doctrine of *showing* in contradistinction to *saying*. It seems to us unmistakable that this Russellian idea was in fact one of the models on which Wittgenstein's notion of showing was based. On concrete Russellian objects of acquaintance it is literally true that they can only be named, that one can only speak about them, not express them in words. (Cf. 3.221.) It is undoubtedly also true in the literal sense of the word that what they are can only be *shown* but not *said*. Thus the gist of Wittgenstein's seemingly delphic doctrine of showing turns out to be a sober corollary to a semantics based on acquaintance.

This result explains certain peculiarities in the views represented in the *Tractatus* noted above in chapter 1. It was argued there that the reason why all the different things which, according to Wittgenstein, can be shown but not said is in the last analysis the ineffability (but 'showability') of simple objects. Now we can see why this reduction to simples should have been accepted by Wittgenstein. Not only do all semantical relations between language and the world reduce to relations between names and simple objects, according to Wittgenstein; all logical forms that there can be reduce to the logical forms of simple objects. Hence we reach an explanation of Wittgenstein's important idea that the formal properties of propositions, even though they cannot be stated in language, can always be shown. (See 4.12–4.1212.) They can be shown by displaying the simple objects of acquaintance out of whose forms the propositional form in question is constructed.

The ineffability of formal concepts follows from the general ineffability of semantics in general in Wittgenstein's eyes, but their showability follows only from the nature of Wittgenstein's simple objects of acquaintance. For showing was not in the *Tractatus* Wittgenstein's catch-all term for everything that cannot be stated in language but can be communicated in language. It is a specific term which has to be taken almost literally. (It is presumably for this reason that Wittgenstein stopped using it as soon as he gave up the assumption of a phenomenological language even though he continued to believe in the ineffability of semantics.)

11 WITTGENSTEIN'S SOLIPSISM

But when all is said and done, does this interpretation not still render Wittgenstein's objects and the world which they constitute hopelessly egocentric? After all, my sense-data are *my* sense data, and objects of my acquaintance are the objects *I* am acquainted with. Clearly, this question is related to the theme of section 7 above, where it was explained in what sense the world is *my* world for Wittgenstein.

It is not clear that the egocentricity of Wittgenstein's world is an objection to the historical accuracy of the interpretation defended here. On the contrary, on the basis of this interpretation we can understand what Wittgenstein actually says of this subject in the *Tractatus*. Indeed, it is hard to see how the way in which Wittgenstein introduces his remarks on solipsism in the *Tractatus* can make much sense except on some interpretation not unlike that being supported here. Wittgenstein's classic statement of how the totality of objects determines the limits of the world is 5.61:

> Logic pervades the world: the limits of the world are also its limits.
>
> So we cannot say in logic, the world has this in it, and this, but not that
>
> . . .

Immediately after 5.61 he goes on to introduce the subject of solipsism:

> 5.62   This remark provides the key to the problem, how much truth there is in solipsism.
>
> For what the solipsist *means* is quite correct; only it cannot be *said* but makes itself manifest.
>
> That the world is *my* world is shown by the fact that the limits of *the* language (the only language I understand) mean the limits of *my* world.[17]

Here the truth of what a solipsist means is presented as a consequence of the fact that the world is limited by the totality of objects. Why? The passage makes little sense unless it is the case that the objects are in some strong sense *mine*. Otherwise the fact that the world is determined by the totality of objects would not turn the world into *my* world. (Cf. 5.63: 'I am my world', and also 5.632 and 5.641.) It is indeed the case that such a relation to myself is intrinsic to objects on the interpretation defended here. If we construe Tractarian objects as objects of acquaintance, the only objects I have are the objects of *my* acquaintance. And if these objects define the world, then the world cannot but be my world. Hence Wittgenstein's qualified solipsism becomes not only understandable but positively predictable on this interpretation.

It is nevertheless important to note that on our interpretation Wittgenstein's solipsism is not predicated on any particular subjective (mind-dependent) status of the simple objects, for instance, on their being phenomenal in character. What matters is that they must be given to me in *my* experience in order to be the basic objects *my* language can refer to. Maybe this requirement of direct givenness entails further consequences concerning their metaphysical status, but even if that should turn out to be the case, Wittgenstein's solipsism is independent of those additional repercussions.

Even though Wittgenstein says blandly that 'what the solipsist means is quite correct', presumably intending solipsism to be understood in a traditional sense, what he counts as solipsism has a specific content. The background of his ideas seems to be a Russell-like project of constructing the physical (external) world out of *my* sense-data and other objects of acquaintance. Wittgenstein merely extends Russell's project by including also complex logical forms within its scope. For him, solipsism is right in emphasizing that the basic building-blocks of his construction must all be mine; realism is correct in maintaining that this 'reduction to acquaintance' does not reflect on the metaphysical reality of the rest of the world.

Thus Wittgenstein's semantical solipsism is but another facet of the all-important role of the objects of acquaintance in his ontology. For this reason, it manifests itself in the fact that the totality of my objects (my objects of acquaintance) determines the limits of my world. (Cf. 5.61.)

The peculiar sense in which my simple objects are mine and which colours his so-called solipsism is shown by his more explicit later comments, for instance, by *Philosophical Remarks*, VII, sec. 71:

> It could, e.g., be practical under certain conditions to give proper names to my hands and to those of other people, so that you wouldn't have to mention their relation to somebody when talking about them, since the relation isn't essential to the hands themselves; and the usual way of speaking could create the impression that its relation to its owner was something belonging to the essence of the hand itself.

Wittgenstein's point is that, even though the world is constructed of basic objects that as a matter of fact have a certain relation to myself, viz. being given to me, this relation does not belong to the essence of objects. This includes my empirical self. (See 5.63.) In this sense,

Wittgenstein says, solipsism 'coincides with pure realism'. (See 5.64.)

This is verified by the way Wittgenstein illustrates his thesis in *Philosophical Remarks*, VII, sec. 71:

> Let's assume that, with all the others, I can always see one particular object in visual space – viz. my nose –. Someone else naturally doesn't see this object in the same way. Doesn't that mean, then, that the visual space I'm talking about *belongs to me*? And so is subjective? No. It has only been construed subjectively here, and an objective space opposed to it, which is, however, only a construction with visual space as its basis. In the – secondary – language of 'objective' – physical – space, visual space is called subjective, or rather, whatever in this language corresponds directly with visual space is called subjective.

Wittgenstein's most general comment on the subject of solipsism is 5.62:

> For what the solipsist *means* is quite correct; only it cannot be *said*, but shows itself.

The interpretation adumbrated in this section shows in what sense this was in fact the case.

12 WITTGENSTEIN ON ETHICS AND AESTHETICS

From this perspective, one can also understand some of Wittgenstein's pronouncements on ethics and aesthetics in the *Tractatus*. For instance, consider the following:

> 6.43   If good or bad acts of will do alter the world, it can only be the limits of the world that they alter, not the facts, not what can be expressed by means of language.
> In short, their effect must be that it becomes an altogether different world. It must, so to speak, wax and wane as a whole.
> The world of the happy man is a different one from that of the unhappy man.

This can be understood on the basis of the idea that the objects of the *Tractatus* are objects of acquaintance in Russell's sense, conjoined with a theory of value not unlike what is expressed in the famous last chapter of Moore's *Principa Ethica*, 'The Ideal'. For Moore, the moral status of an act is determined by the value of its consequences, in the precise sense he spells out in *Ethics* and in *Principa Ethica*. Now where does the value of the consequences lie? What are the true unmixed goods? Moore's answer includes prominently 'aesthetic enjoyments' and 'pleasures of personal affection'[18] – truly a Bloomsbury answer. Both of these involve certain experiences. As does perception, these experiences have a certain immediate object. Had Moore not shown us in refuting idealism how to distinguish in general the experience of X from X itself? If these immediate objects of Moorean valuable experiences – the emotional cousins of Russell's and Moore's sense-data – are among Wittgenstein's objects in the *Tractatus*, it will be literally true that the world (the totality of objects) of a person who has valuable experiences is different from that of a person who does not. This is precisely what Wittgenstein says of the difference between a happy and an unhappy person.[19]

The upshot of this interpretation of Wittgenstein's remarks on ethics and aesthetics in the *Tractatus* is to see the young Wittgenstein much more as a Bloomsbury character, an Apostle, than as a future Tolstoyan mystic. There are reasons to think that this emphasis can be justified by further evidence.[20]

13 THE SUBSTANTIALITY OF OBJECTS

All this may still seem to contradict flatly what Wittgenstein says of the substantiality of objects in the *Tractatus*. In the beginning of this chapter, it was noted that Wittgenstein makes two different kinds of statements about Tractarian objects. The statements in which he speaks of them as phenomenological have been accounted for. But the other class of statements, those in which Wittgenstein emphasizes the substantiality of his objects, still remains to be explained. How can objects of acquaintance, which we can only point to, serve as the persisting, stable, unalterable form of the world? (Cf. 2.026–2.0271.) What can be less persisting, stable and unalterable than sense-data, which in Russell were the paradigmatic examples of the objects of acquaintance?

At first, this problem might seem to be due to a mere mistranslation. Wittgenstein's German word for what has here been translated as 'persisting' is *bestehend*. Elsewhere, this word and its cognate verb *bestehen* are frequently used by Wittgenstein to speak simply of the actual obtaining of states of affairs; witness especially 2.04–2.06, 2.11. Accordingly, in the crucial proposition 2.0271, *bestehend* is translated by Ogden as 'existent' and by Pears and McGuinness as 'subsistent'. Hence there might seem to be no problem present here, for Wittgenstein appears to claim merely that objects subsist, not that they are substantial.

Unfortunately (or fortunately), this attempted way out does not work. It leaves unexplained several other passages where Wittgenstein attributes substantiality and even persistence to objects. Even in 2.0271 objects are said to be determined (*das Feste*, translated by Pears and McGuinness as 'unalterable') in contrast to configurations, which are alterable (*das Wechselnde*) and inconstant (*Unbeständige*). Most importantly, it is simply a misrepresentation to assimilate the force of the word *Bestehende* in 2.0271 to its meaning in the propositions in which the obtaining states of affairs is being discussed. For in 2.0271 *objects* are contrasted to *configurations*, with the implication that the latter cannot in the sense relevant here be *bestehend*. Yet these configurations are but the states of affairs whose being Wittgenstein elsewhere expresses by means of the verb *bestehen*. Indeed, in the very next sentence (2.0272) Wittgenstein writes:

> The configuration of objects produces states of affairs.

Hence *bestehend* simply cannot mean the same in 2.0271 as it does in 2.04–2.06, and has to be translated in 2.0271 in its most common nontechnical sense by 'persisting' or 'stable', not 'existent' or 'subsistent'. Hence the substantiality problem remains.

The real solution to the problem posed by the substantiality of objects for the interpretation here supported is quite different. It can be reached by noting that all talk of persistence and stability is relative to some postulated change or variation. Now what is the relevant variation Wittgenstein has in mind here? An answer is given by 2.022–2.023, quoted above in sec. 3. They show beyond any doubt that the variation Wittgenstein is envisaging is a variation from one possible world to another. This has nothing to do with the persistence or alterability of objects in time. Wittgenstein's conception of existence is an atemporal one in that his existential quantifiers range over such objects as exist at some moment of time or other. This is seen, e.g., from 6.3611, where Wittgenstein says that 'there is no such thing' as the passage of time. This kind of existence has nothing to do with existence at some time but not at another. Wittgenstein's conception of existence amounts to momentary or, more accurately, atemporal being.[21] Because of their atemporality, the substantiality of simple objects is not affected by the alterability or even by the coming-to-be and disappearance of objects in time. These changes do not affect Wittgenstein's domain of quantification.

Rather, Wittgenstein's point is that this whole atemporal domain of individuals must remain constant when we move to consider other possible states of affairs. These other possible states have to built up (so to speak) from the objects which are given to us in *this* actual world.

But if so, the temporal ephemerality of sense-data and of many other objects of acquaintance does not disqualify them in the least from being substantial in Wittgenstein's sense. Wittgenstein is not talking about variation in time, but variation from one complete world history to another. In other words, Wittgenstein is concerned with the *logical* necessity of the existence of objects, not with a causal, physical, or temporal necessity. As he puts it in 6.37, 'The only necessity that exists is *logical* necessity.'

That this is Wittgenstein's meaning is vividly seen from his explanations of why objects are persistent. (Here what was found above in sec. 3 is highly relevant.) Wittgenstein's objects are substance-like, not because they are indestructible, but because they are the meanings of our simplest expressions, those expressions whose meanings cannot any longer be described but only displayed. In order to appreciate Wittgenstein's meaning, try to point and say, '*That* object does not exist.' This sentence is inevitably false, not because the object pointed to cannot cease to be, but for logical reasons which would make your speech-act self-defeating if the pointed object did not exist and which were Wittgenstein's reasons for maintaining that simple objects exist necessarily. Your utterance does not make sense unless you succeed in pointing to the object in question. But thn it is inevitably false. This is the reason that Wittgenstein relates the substantiality of objects, not to their immutability, but to their simplicity:

> 2.021   Objects make up the substance of the world. That is why they cannot be composite.

Our interpretation is conclusively confirmed by *Philosophical Remarks*, IX, sec. 95, where Wittgenstein writes:

> If someone says that substance is indestructible, then what he is really after is that it is senseless in any context to speak of the destruction of a substance – either affirm or deny it.

In other words, the alleged indestructibility of Wittgenstein substances is merely a corollary to the ineffability of objectual existence.

Rightly understood, Wittgenstein's doctrine of the substantiality and indestructibility of Tractarian objects supports our thesis of their phenomenological character. For where in the physical world do you find absolutely indestructible objects – objects which are *logically* impossible to destroy?

14 THE METAPHYSICAL STATUS OF THE OBJECTS OF WITTGENSTEIN'S *TRACTATUS*

The picture of the objects of the *Tractatus* which one is likely to form on the basis of most other expositions looks radically different from the one we have drawn here. Many commentators claim that Wittgenstein never made up his mind concerning the metaphysical status of the simple objects he was postulating there. This claim seems to be in a sharp conflict with our thesis that the objects of the *Tractatus* were Russellian objects of acquaintance. What are we to make of the majority view and of the prima facie evidence on which it is based?

It is important to realize that the two views, our thesis and the majority view, do not have to be as incompatible as they might first seem to be. What we have argued is that the (simple) objects Wittgenstein is talking about in the *Tractatus* are objects of immediate experience. They are the entities which have to be given to us in order for our propositions to have the meanings they have. This is a thesis about the *semantical* status of Tractarian objects. It does not yet determine the metaphysical status of these objects; it only determines their experiental and semantical status. Their metaphysical status depends on further assumptions; it is not yet fixed by their semantically and epistemologically privileged position.

This is seen clearly in Russell and Moore.[22] Basically, objects of acquaintance were for them defined as the objects of immediate experience. For instance, sense-data were for them initially the particulars which our judgements of immediate perception are about. As Russell puts it, 'logically, a sense-datum is an object, a particular of which the subject is aware.'[23] This does not yet prejudice their relation to the subject or to physical objects. It was only by means of further arguments, such as the different versions of the so-called argument from illusion, that Russell and Moore could conclude to their own satisfaction that the objects of immediate experience (acquaintance) could not be identified with physical objects. And even such arguments left several different answers open to the question of what the precise relation of sense-data to physical objects really is. Moore once went so far as to consider the possibility that some visual sense-data might be parts of the surfaces of physical objects. Russell argued in *Mysticism and Logic* that 'sense-data are physical.'[24] In particular, 'the existence of the sense-datum is therefore not logically dependent upon that of the subject'.

In view of this background, our identification of the objects of the *Tractatus* with Russellian objects of acquaintance does not by itself commit us to any particular view of their metaphysical status. For the same reason, there need not be any irreconcilable contradiction between our interpretation and the evidence that has prompted the idea that Wittgenstein left some of his metaphysical options open. By the same token, the interpretation of the objects of the *Tractatus* represented here is not incompatible with Wittgenstein's relative silence in the *Tractatus* concerning the precise nature of the objects he was postulating. They had to be given by experience (immediate experience) anyway, and hence cannot be anticipated a priori.

In particular, we are not committed to construing Tractarian simple objects as mental or otherwise phenomenalistic entities. In fact, evidence was adduced above in sec. 11 against such a construal.

However, it is not hard to see also that Wittgenstein could not very well accept Russell's physicalistic construal of sense-data, either. The likely reason is not that Wittgenstein had any deep misgivings about the physical world, but rather that he needed objects for semantical purposes that went beyond Russell's use of the objects of acquaintance as building-blocks of this one actual (presumably physical) world of ours. Wittgenstein's objects had to be also the building-blocks of all logical forms, and the substance of all the other possible states of affairs. For this reason, Russell's construction of our one and only external world from sense-data could not satisfy him, and for this reason he refused to commit himself to any one particular view on the metaphysical status of his objects, either.

Furthermore, Wittgenstein could not accept Russell's ideas about the subject (the I) and its relation to the objects of acquaintance, either. Such propositions of the *Tractatus* as 5.541–5.5421 show this amply. The subject is not one of the objects in the world. For this reason, too, Wittgenstein did not agree with Russell's views, and whatever alternatives to them he developed were based (so Wittgenstein thought) on the logical status of objects, not on their metaphysical character.

These facts are not changed by Wittgenstein's later (and admittedly oblique) characterization of the Tractarian objects as being 'phenomenological'. Phenomenological objects need not be phenomenalistic. Historically, Husserlian phenomenology was in fact sharply opposed to Machian phenomenalism. Husserl wanted to get '*zu Sachen selbst*', at things themselves. Notwithstanding popular prejudice, there is a sense in which he did not 'bracket' all ordinary objects, either, only those which were not given to us in immediate experience.[25] His subsequent slide to idealism – as uncharitable witnesses perceived it – was not a necessary consequence of his phenomenological posture alone. Later in this book, we shall argue that Wittgenstein's subsequent adoption of a physicalistic language as the only viable language of philosophy does not mean that he then denied the reality of merely phenomenological objects, e.g., private sensations. Vice versa, it is to be kept in mind that Wittgenstein's early preference for a phenomenological basic language does not necessarily imply that he did not believe in physical objects.

As an illustration of these general historical considerations, let us consider the one *obiter dictum* which probably has coloured, more than any other saying of Wittgenstein's, philosophers' views of the objects of the *Tractatus*. It is reported by Norman Malcolm.[26] This comment is often taken to constitute counter-evidence to any interpretation which, like ours, ascribes to the *Tractatus* a definite view as to what kind of entities the objects postulated there are, metaphysically speaking. This is nevertheless a wrong way of taking Malcolm's report, which runs as follows:

> I asked Wittgenstein whether, when he wrote the *Tractatus*, he had ever decided upon anything as an *example* of a 'simple object'. His reply was that at that time his thought had been that he was a *logician*; and that it was not his business, as a logician, to try to decide whether this thing or that was a simple thing or a complex thing, that being a purely *empirical* matter!

The crucial feature of this anecdote is that Malcolm did not ask Wittgenstein to explain the metaphysical status of objects postulated in the *Tractatus*. Malcolm asked him whether he had had in mind *particular examples* of Tractarian objects. In response to *this* question, Wittgenstein declares that it is an empirical matter what *particular instances* of simple objects might be available to us as examples. Now there is a perfectly good logical reason for the impossibility of giving particular examples of (simple) objects. Wittgenstein is obviously here alluding to the same reason as he had for denying that we can *say* that a particular simple object exists. (It has to exist in order for us to be able to speak of it.) As to which particular objects are known to us according to the *Tractatus*, we have seen above that they are just what is given to us in experience. We cannot anticipate a priori what they are. In this sense, what the simple objects are *is* a purely empirical matter according to the *Tractatus*.[27] In order to give you an object, we have seen, I ought to present you with an object of immediate acquaintance, point to it, and say 'this' or 'that'.

Hence Wittgenstein's answer to Malcolm's question does not constitute any reason for doubting our interpretation, but rather indirect evidence for it. We shall return to Malcolm's report below in the last section of this chapter.

The claim that Wittgenstein was not dealing in the *Tractatus* with the metaphysical status (phenomenological vs. physical) of his objects in any case is rebutted by his own explicit statement (in a letter to Schlick in 1932) that he had in the *Tractatus* been concerned with the problem of physicalism ('though not under this – horrible – name').[28]

15 FURTHER EVIDENCE

Even after all this has been said, part of our intial puzzle remains. If the objects of the *Tractatus* were objects of acquaintance (immediately experience), why did Wittgenstein not say so? Or, rather, why did he wait until the private query by Desmond Lee in 1930–1 to say so? Part of an answer is that it must have seemed fairly obvious to Wittgenstein, given his Russellian background. An analogous case is offered by passages like 5.552 (examined above in sec. 7) where Wittgenstein discusses such doctrines of Russell's as are expressed only in his *Theory of Knowledge*, which was not published in Wittgenstein's or Russell's lifetime. Notwithstanding the inaccessibility of Wittgenstein's subject matter, he never explained to his readers this aspect of the background of the *Tractatus*. It is likewise quite possible that Wittgenstein simply failed to call his reader's attention to other aspects of his Russellian heritage, including the role of acquaintance in his own thinking.[29]

Another partial explanation is that Wittgenstein might very well have thought that his purpose was made clear enough by his examples and other indirect 'elucidations'. Unfortunately, the testimony of Wittgenstein's examples has not as a matter of fact convinced all his readers. Some examples strongly support the kind of view we are arguing for here. The following example will have to represent this usage of Wittgenstein's:

> 2.0131   A spatial object must be situated in infinite space. (A spatial point is an argument-place.)
>
> A speck in the visual field, though it need not be red, must have some colour: it is, so to speak, surrounded by colour-space. Notes must have some pitch, objects of the sense of touch *some* degree of hardness, and so on.

Similar examples include 2.0251, 4.123 and 6.3751.

Some apparent counter-examples to the phenomenological character of simple objects are easy to explain away. It is, for instance, compatible with this character of *simple* objects that Wittgenstein should countenance *complex* physical objects. In order to see this, it suffices to recall Russell's project of interpreting objects of description, including physical objects, as logical constructs from objects of acquaintance. This 'reduction to acquaintance' was not calculated to reflect on the reality of physical objects as *complex* objects.

That this is Wittgenstein's view, too, is shown by 6.3431:[30]

> Through their whole logical apparatus the physical laws still speak of the objects of the world.

Wittgenstein's formulation ('through', in German *durch*) shows that the 'logical apparatus' of physics is for Wittgenstein analogous to Russell's 'logical constructions'.

That this is Wittgenstein's real meaning is demonstrated by a comparison with MS 105, p. 108, where Wittgenstein writes:

> Let us not forget that the language of physics, too, again describes only the primary [i.e., phenomenological] world and not a hypothetical world. The only hypothesis [of physics] is an assumption concerning the practical method of description.[31]

This is in fact closely similar to what Wittgenstein says in 6.341–6.342.

In spite of thus having the licence of acknowledging physical objects, Wittgenstein seems to use the term 'thing' (*Ding*) in this role fairly consistently; cf. e.g., 6.1231, 5.634, etc.

Apart from a few of passages which are hard to interpret, mainly 2.0232[32] and 2.02331,[33] Wittgenstein's use of the term 'object' thus strongly supports our interpretation.

In the *Tractatus*, there is nevertheless no unambiguous direct statement concerning the nature of the simple objects postulated there. In Wittgenstein's later writings there are plenty of pointers, however, in fact so many that we can here hope only to convey the reader their flavour rather than try to exhaust them.

For instance, in 'Some Remarks on Logical Form' Wittgenstein assumed that at least some attributions of degree to an experienced quality are atomic propositions. As examples of such attributions, Wittgenstein mentions those of a pitch to a given tone and a certain brightness or redness to a colour. This is strongly suggestive of the phenomenological character of the objects assumed there.

The Tractarian view is described vividly in *Wittgenstein's Lectures, Cambridge 1932–1935*, p. 7:

> Consider the reading Russell would give of his notation for 'There is a circle in the square': 'There is a thing which is a circle in the square'.

What is the thing? Some people might answer: the *patch* I am pointing to.

We have argued that the 'some people' Wittgenstein refers to include his own earlier self. Wittgenstein's own assimilation of Tractarian objects to Russell's individuals in *PI*, I, sec. 46, supports our interpretation.[34]

Wittgenstein goes on to criticize the idea of a phenomenological object, without using the term. He complains, among other things, that there is no 'substrate for the property of being a patch'.[35]

In the absence of any direct statement by Wittgenstein, where can we look for incontrovertible evidence? Clearly in the testimony of others. Now the two philosophers who were closest to Wittgenstein in the late twenties were Ramsey and Waismann. It is therefore especially significant that both of them agreed with our interpretation of the objects postulated by Wittgenstein and of the resulting nature of atomic propositions.

Sometime around 1929 Waismann compiled a number of 'Theses' which have been published as Appendix B to *Ludwig Wittgenstein and the Vienna Circle*. They seem to be intended as an aid in writing Waismann's *Logik, Sprache, Philosophie* which was announced in 1929 and which was described as an introduction to the ideas of the *Tractatus*. In his Introduction to *Ludwig Wittgenstein and Vienna Circle* (p. 18) Brian McGuinness describes the first draft of Waismann's work as not going beyond the *Tractatus*. Hence we can expect fairly direct evidence from Waismann's notes.

Waismann's 'Theses' contain unequivocal statements of what the elementary propositions of the *Tractatus* are like:

Phenomena (experiences) are what elementary propositions describe. (p. 249)

Elementary propositions describe the content[36] of our experience. All other propositions are merely an expansion of this content. (p. 254)

On p. 254 it is also implied that the purpose of Wittgenstein's language, unlike that of 'our ordinary language', is 'to reproduce the logical structure of phenomena'. Thus Waismann's 'Theses' yield suggestive evidence as to what the objects and elementary propositions of the *Tractatus* were like.

There is also strong evidence in Frank Ramsey's unpublished notes to the effect that something like our interpretation was accepted by him – and by Wittgenstein himself – as being the right way of reading the *Tractatus*. Here is an especially striking statement:

W says [it is] nonsense to believe in anything not given in experience
. . . For to be mine, *to be given in experience, is* [the] *formal property to
be a genuine entity.* [Emphasis added.] Other people's s.d. [= sense-
data] and my s.d. i.e. those attached to my body as other people's to
their bodies are logical constructions. For all we know does not involve
them; they simplify general laws but are not required by them any more
than m.o.'s [= material objects].

Take the criterion of what he sees to be the meaning of [what] he sees.
Similar I see – I see. Then I see is also connected with reality (visual
appearance) [in a way] other than how his seeing is, and this is [the
reason] that the world is my world.

Ramsey's telegraphic and at times ungrammatical language suggests
strongly that he is in this passage trying to write down what Wittgenstein
is saying to him there and then. We have tried to fill in the gaps the
best we can. The first paragraph shows that the 'genuine entities'
Wittgenstein is assuming are all given in experience. The second
paragraph suggests, through familiar ideas and locutions ('the world is
my world', cf. 5.62), that the views Wittgenstein is representing here
are indeed those of the *Tractatus*.[37] The quote is from item #004-21-
02 in the Pittsburgh Ramsey archives. If it is not the 'smoking gun'
that will clinch our case, it is hard to see what could be.

Again, in item #003-37-01 Ramsey writes:

Aquaintance – means fundamentally being able to judge about;
(1) individual acquaintance means being able to name.
(2) general acquaintance means being able to make general judgments
about . . .

Even though Ramsey's terminology is different from Wittgenstein's,
what he is saying here can be brought to bear on the *Tractatus*. There,
all simple objects are nameable; if one agrees with Ramsey, they must
therefore be objects of acquaintance.

Again, in item #002-25-10, Ramsey mentions phenomenalism as of
one of the levels of 'Ludwig's' thought.

Such cumulative evidence from Wittgenstein's closest associates
shows beyond reasonable doubt that the objects of the *Tractatus* were
indeed intended by Wittgenstein to be objects of acquaintance
(immediate awareness).

16 WITTGENSTEIN'S SILENCE – AND WHAT IT HIDES

The widespread view that Wittgenstein did not make up his mind as to
what the simple objects of the *Tractatus* are like has thus been shown

to be a myth. As many myths, it is nevertheless based on a partially correct perception. In the *Tractatus* Wittgenstein definitely was more secretive about his basic objects than he ought to have been, according to his own later standards. But the reason was not that he could not decide whether his *Gegenstände* were phenomenological or physical; it was that he could not decide what kinds of *phenomenological* entities they were.

In MS 115, pp. 55–6, Wittgenstein admits his own erstwhile indecision:

> It is of the greatest significance that we always think of logical calculus together with an example in which the calculus finds an application, and that we don't give examples and then say that they are not ideal ones, which we don't yet have. That is a sign of a misconception. (Russell and I have in different ways been afficted with it. Compare what I say in the *Tractatus* of elementary propositions and objects.)[38]

What prompted this comment were Wittgenstein's reflections on the undefinability of *red* and, in particular, the idea that 'here were an unanalysable *object* [*Gegenstand*] (like an element in chemistry).'

It is perhaps not immediately clear what all the failures were that Wittgenstein included in his self-indictment, but the first and foremost candidate surely is his hesitation as to how the basic units of our immediate experience, e.g., visual experience, are to be thought of. My visual field is complex, and even if I manage to single out a part of it, I still have something that is complex. Will such an analysis always terminate? And do its end-points, the true simples, have the same phenomenological reality as the original act of attending to the complex visual object?

> Is it imaginable that – e.g. – we should *see* that *all the points of a surface are yellow*, without seeing any *single* point of this surface? It almost seems to be so. (*Notebooks 1914–1916*, p. 50)

It was Wittgenstein's inability to reach a firm answer to such questions that barred him from giving unequivocal examples of his basic objects. Furthermore this problem is only a sample of an incredibly rich *fauna* of phenomenological questions Wittgenstein discusses in the *Notebooks 1914–1916* and often continues to discuss in his later philosophy but which he sweeps under the rug in the *Tractatus*. The notorious problem of colour incompatibility may be taken to be another case in point. In chapter 5, sec. 5, we shall find that Wittgenstein later confessed that in the *Tractatus* he merely believed that a satisfactory analysis of colour statements could be found, even though he did not have any particular analysis in mind. The nature of that very confession clearly suggests, however, that Wittgenstein thought of experienced colours as belonging to the phenomenological realm.

There is no need for us to examine the tortuous details of Wittgenstein's struggle with his phenomenological problems, beyond emphasizing that any solution, attempted or definite, that Wittgenstein might have adopted will obviously be compatible with our overall interpretation of the objects of the *Tractatus* as phenomenological objects.[39] We shall nevertheless commit the supererogatory act of returning briefly to Wittgenstein's problem concerning his phenomenological objects in chapter 5, sec. 6, below.

Even without any further inquiry, we can now see the real import of Wittgenstein's comment to Malcolm, quoted above in section 14, and in particular the import of his reference to the business of a logician as not involving a decision 'whether this thing or that was a simple thing or a complex thing'. This might seem to fly in the face of Wittgenstein's own view in the *Tractatus* according to which simple objects and their logical forms are precisely what a logician is in the last analysis dealing with. Why is Wittgenstein apologizing for the absence of particular examples qua logician and not qua phenomenologist? There is in reality no inconsistency here, however. Even though a logician traffics in the last analysis in the simple objects which a phenomenologist gives to him, he cannot anticipate the results of the earlier phenomenological analysis whose outcome tells a logician which phenomenological objects are simple and which ones are complex. Thus Wittgenstein's pronouncement is part and parcel of the point we are making in this section. It is another indication of the fact that Wittgenstein did not make up his mind in the *Tractatus* what kinds of phenomenological entities his simple objects of immediate acquaintance were.

Here we thus have the true explanation of Wittgenstein's silence in the *Tractatus* concerning the basic objects he hypostasized there. We began this chapter by noting this curious silence; we shall end it by stating the reason. Wittgenstein's uninformativeness was not due only to his belief in the ineffability of semantics. It was not only the case that according to his own doctrine he had to wait until immediate experience showed him which objects there are in the world, as he intimated to Malcolm. Most importantly, his silence was not due to his failure to decide the metaphysical nature of his objects. He had made up his mind in the *Tractatus* about the problem of physicalism vs. phenomenology, even though he later came to change it. His indecision was caused by his failure to carry to the bitter or sweet end his quest for unequivocal phenomenological atoms, the true basic

ingredients of immediate experience. Unfortunately this phenomenological uncertainty led Wittgenstein also to a decision not to say
anything about the relation of his objects to experience – that is, not
to do so until he bared his ontological soul to Frank Ramsey.

NOTES

1 One is easily tempted to go further and to suspect that the objects of the
Tractatus included *phenomenal* (*phenomenalistic*) ones. However, we do not
want to prejudge the question of the metaphysical status of the objects of
immediate experience. A philosopher like Russell may try to construct the
whole external world out of the objects of immediate experience, such as
sense-data, while denying that these objects are phenomenalistic or otherwise
subjective. Thus we have chosen the neutral term 'phenomenological', which
also turns out to have been used later by Wittgenstein himself. Cf. also
section 14.

2 It took logicians over thirty years to formalize Wittgenstein's treatment
of identity in the *Tractatus*. See Jaakko Hintikka, 'Identity, variables, and
impredicative definitions', *Journal of Symbolic Logic*, vol. 21 (1956),
pp. 225–45, and G. H. von Wright and Peter Geach, 'On an extended logic of
relations', *Societas Scientiarum Fennica, Comm. Phys.-Math.*, vol. 16, no. 1,
Helsinki, 1952.

3 Bertrand Russell, *Theory of Knowledge: The 1913 Manuscript* (The
Collected Papers of Bertrand Russell, vol. 7), edited by Elizabeth R. Eames
in collaboration with Kenneth Blackwell, Allen & Unwin, London, 1984.

4 David Pears, 'The relation between Wittgenstein's picture theory of
propositions and Russell's theories of judgment', *Philosophical Review*, vol.
86 (1977), pp. 177–96; reprinted in C. G. Luckhardt, editor, *Wittgenstein:
Sources and Perspectives*, Cornell University Press, Ithaca, N.Y., 1979,
pp. 190–212. Cf. also David Pears, 'Wittgenstein's picture theory and
Russell's theory of knowledge', in Hal Berghel et al., editors, *Wittgenstein,
The Vienna Circle, and Critical Rationalism, Proceedings of the Third
International Wittgenstein Symposium*, Hölder-Pichler-Tempsky, Vienna,
1979, pp. 101–7; 'The emergence of Wittgenstein's logical atomism', in E.
Morscher and R. Stranzinger, editors, *Ethics, Proceedings of the Fifth International Wittgenstein Symposium*, Hölder-Pichler-Tempsky, Vienna, 1981,
pp. 448–54.

5 See Russell's letter to Lady Ottoline Morrell, quoted in R. W. Clark,
The Life of Bertrand Russell, Cape, London, 1975, pp. 204–7.

6 See, e.g., 5.55–5.5561, *Notebooks 1914–1916*, pp. 3, 17, 21, 31, 99, etc.

7 Interesting light is shed on Wittgenstein's development by his letter to
Russell on 16 January 1913. (This letter also offers further evidence that
Wittgenstein included properties among his simples; cf. chapter 2 above.)
There he puts forward as a solution to his problems – and to those of Russell –
the idea that 'different kinds of things (individuals, qualities, relations, etc.)
are symbolized by different kinds of symbols which cannot possibly be

substituted in one another's place'. This is unmistakably a step towards the idea that the logical forms of simple entities (of different types) determine the way they can be combined with each other, which we have found to be one of the most characteristic tenets of the *Tractatus*.

Moreover, the specific way in which Wittgenstein expresses this idea is interesting. He analyses, e.g., the subject–predicate proposition 'Socrates is human' into 'Socrates' and 'something is human' (which, Wittgenstein says, 'I think is not complex'). What is interesting here is that '(∃x). x is human' is very closely related to the logical form (∃ɸ) (∃x). ɸx of the same proposition in Russell. Indeed, '(∃x). x is human' is naturally associated with the logical form of the quality of being human. Thus Wittgenstein's new idea in January 1913 is a step from the logical forms of propositions to the logical forms of different kinds of simple entities, precisely as we have suggested that Wittgenstein's development proceeded. In Wittgenstein's letter we can also see vividly how he arrived at his idea that the notion of logical form applies also, and indeed primarily, to simple objects (simple entities of different types), not merely to complexes (including propositions), as everybody else assumes. We can also see how Wittgenstein's idea of the logical forms of simple objects grew from the usual concept of logical form as the form of propositions rather than of objects.

8 It is prima facie a little surprising to find Wittgenstein speaking in the quoted passage (*PI*, I, sec. 46) of 'Russell's "individuals"' (the English word 'individuals' is used in Wittgenstein's original German text), for the term occurs rarely, if ever, in Russell's epistemological writings during the crucial pre-World War I period. Russell's favourite term is not 'individual' but 'particular'. However, the term 'individual' is used in the *Principia*. (Bertrand Russell and A. N. Whitehead, *Principia Mathematica I–III*, second edn, Cambridge University Press, Cambridge, 1925–7. See, e.g., Russell's Introduction to the second edn, vol. 1, p. xix.) There Russell and Whitehead identify in so many words individuals and particulars, and Wittgenstein undoubtedly has in mind early Russell's particulars. Now the paradigmatic examples of such particulars for Russell were sense-data, that is, individuals given to us in sense-perception. For instance, in *The Problems of Philosophy*, Home University Library, London, 1912 (reprinted Oxford University Press, Oxford, 1959, p. 93), Russell says that 'we speak of whatever is given in sensation, or is of the same nature as things given in sensation, as a *particular*'. Hence Wittgenstein's assimilation of the Tractarian objects to Russell's individuals amounts to assimilating them to something like sense-data.

9 Cf., e.g., 2.033 compared with 2.023.

10 For another explanation by Wittgenstein why 'the world is my world', see the statement recorded by Ramsey and quoted in sec. 15.

11 Further evidence for this identification of life and one's experiences is given in chapter 7, note 5, below.

12 See *Wittgenstein's Lectures, Cambridge 1930–32*, p. 82.

13 Ibid., p. 120.

14 David Pears, *Bertrand Russell and the British Tradition in Philosophy*, Collins (The Fontana Library), London, 1967, p. 97.

15 In Bertrand Russell, *Mysticism and Logic*, chapter 8, Longmans,

London, 1918; see p. 147. This article was first published in *Scientia*, no. 4, 1914. According to an unpublished biographical sketch of Wittgenstein by F. A. Hayek, a copy of this paper was one of the last philosophical communications from Russell which still reached Wittgenstein during World War I.

16 This has been spelled out aptly by David Pears; cf. his *Bertrand Russell and the British Tradition in Philosophy*, pp. 71–87, 97–115.

17 For the correct translation of this sentence, see Jaakko Hintikka, 'On Wittgenstein's "Solipsism",' *Mind*, vol. 67 (1958), pp. 88–91, challenged by G. E. M. Anscombe in *An Introduction to Wittgenstein's Tractatus*, Hutchinson, London, 1959, pp. 166–7, but vindicated by Wittgenstein himself, as reported by C. Lewy in *Mind*, vol. 67 (1958), pp. 416–23.

18 G. E. Moore, *Principia Ethica*, Cambridge University Press, 1903, p. 203.

19 This is supported further by Wittgenstein's entry in the *Notebooks 1914–1916* (p. 77, 24 July 1916): 'Ethics must be a condition of the world, like logic.' Of course the sense in which logic is a condition of the world is that of supplying to us its objects. (Cf., e.g., 5.552.)

20 Wittgenstein's idea that the objects of a person who has valuable experiences are different from those of a person who does not have them has in fact a close anticipation in Moore. In his Sunday Essay delivered on 24 November 1895 (quoted in Paul Levy, *Moore: G. E. Moore and the Cambridge Apostles*, Holt, Rinehart & Winston, New York, 1979, pp. 170–1) Moore discusses the nature of beauty and its objectivity:

> I would therefore try to define the beautiful as that with regard to which you have a specific emotion, the nature of which can only be discovered by looking into yourself, whenever you say that an object is beautiful, and finding what you mean thereby. But I must also maintain that this emotion is not merely yours, and capable of attaching itself to any object whatever but that some objects are by their very nature more capable than others of exciting it. When you say that a particular red is beautiful, you mean that you feel a pleasant emotion in contemplating it; and that emotion at once constitutes a different object: it is no longer a particular red, to be distinguished only by intellectual marks; it is no longer given you only as an object of knowledge, but actually given as an object of feeling.

If this is not close enough to Wittgenstein, witness Moore's application of his ideas to interpersonal comparisons:

> 'But different people think different things to be beautiful, and the same thing is thought ugly by one person and beautiful by another; how then can you say that that same thing *is* beautiful or ugly?' I must reply with a question: Is it the same thing? When the two people say "beautiful", they have to some extent the same notion: else the word "beauty" would be utterly without meaning . . . When, therefore, two people say of a thing, one that it is beautiful, and the other that it is ugly, the thing of which they are speaking is not the same thing.

This is not only a striking anticipation of one particular doctrine of the *Tractatus,* but represents an important aspect of the entire way of thinking on which Wittgenstein's work is based. Further specific evidence from Wittgenstein is found in the *Notebooks 1914–1916,* entry for 7 October 1916.

21 This atemporal character of the objects of the *Tractatus* is confirmed indirectly by the fact that when Wittgenstein later came to replace his earlier phenomenological objects by physical ones, the first step was to begin to worry about the temporality of the objects and their configurations that we actually speak of in our language. This will be discussed below in chapter 7, sec. 7. Wittgenstein's earlier conception is seen by contrast from his statements of the new position such as the following:

Wenn ich von den Wörtern und ihrer Syntax rede, so geschieht es "im II. System" [sc. im physikalischen System] und ebenso wenn ich von den symbolisierenden Beziehungen von Sätzen und Tatsachen rede. D.h. wir reden hier wieder von etwas in der Zeit ausgebreitetem und nicht momentanem. (MS 107, p. 232)

22 Cf., e.g., G. E. Moore, 'The status of sense-data', in *Philosophical Studies,* Routledge & Kegan Paul, London, 1922; Bertrand Russell, 'The relation of sense-data to physics', in *Mysticism and Logic*; Bertrand Russell, *Our Knowledge of the External World,* Allen & Unwin, London, 1914.
23 'The relation of sense-data to physics', sec. 4
24 'The relation of sense-data to physics', sec. 4.
25 Cf. here Jaakko Hintikka and Charles Harvey, review article on David W. Smith and Ronald McIntyre, *Husserl and Intentionality, Husserl Studies,* vol. 1 (1984), pp. 201–12.
26 Norman Malcolm, *Ludwig Wittgenstein: A Memoir,* Clarendon Press, Oxford, 1958, p. 86.
27 Wittgenstein makes essentially the same point in *Letters to Russell, Keynes and Moore,* p. 39 (translation, pp. 41–2):

A proposition such as '$(\exists x). x=x$', for example, is really a proposition of *physics.* The proposition

$$'(x): x=x. \supset .(\exists y). y=y'$$

is a proposition of logic and it is then for *physics* to say *whether any thing* exists.

28 This letter has been published in Michael Nedo and Michele Ranchetti, editors, *Wittgenstein: Sein Leben in Bildern und Texten,* Suhrkamp, Frankfurt am Main, 1983, pp. 254–5.
29 If Wittgenstein does not point out explicitly in the *Tractatus* that the objects he is dealing with there are objects of acquaintance, he is merely following Russell's example. Perhaps the most surprising peculiarity of Russell's early thought is his unstated and indeed obviously unwitting assumption that the real objects which he has to handle and which can serve as values of bound variables are all of them objects of immediate acquaint-

ance. This assumption is betrayed, e.g., by Russell's near-incredible assertion at the end of 'On Denoting' that his theory of definite descriptions implies that 'in every proposition that we can apprehend . . . all the constituents are really entities with which we have immediate acquaintance.' All that Russell's theory entails in this direction is of course that all constituents of our propositions are values of the quantificational variables by means of which he analyses definite descriptions. Hence Russell is here assuming that their values are all objects of acquaintance.

The same assumption is in operation when Russell offers earlier in 'On Denoting' as an example of what now would be called a *de re* construal of the proposition 'George IV wished to know whether Scott was the author of *Waverley*' a situation in which 'George IV had seen Scott at a distance, and had asked "Is that Scott?".' In other words; the *res* in question is assumed by Russell without any further argument to be an object of acquaintance.

If Russell thus failed to signal one of the most important assumptions he made in 'On Denoting', it ought not to be surprising if Wittgenstein does not explicitly mention the very same assumption in the *Tractatus*, either.

30 We are using here the Ogden translation, which here reproduces Wittgenstein's intentions more faithfully than the Pears–McGuinness one. The Ogden translation was approved by Wittgenstein himself, except that it was Wittgenstein who put in the telltale particle 'still'. See *Letters to C. K. Ogden*, p. 53.

31 The German text reads: 'Vergessen wir nicht daß die physikalische Sprache auch wieder nur die primäre Welt beschreibt und nicht etwa eine hypothetische Welt. Die Hypothese ist nur eine Annahme über die praktische Art der Darstellung.'

32 This proposition is not intended to be taken literally in any case, as is signalled by Wittgenstein's words 'in a manner of speaking' and confirmed by a comparison with 2.0251.

33 This proposition reads:

2.02331   Either a thing has properties that nothing else has, in which case we can immediately use a description to distinguish it from the others and refer to it; or, on the other hand, there are several things that have the whole set of their properties in common, in which case it is quite impossible to indicate one of them.

For if there is nothing to distinguish a thing, I cannot distinguish it, since otherwise it would be distinguished after all.

This statement cannot be taken literally, either, for in the *Prototractatus* it is prefaced by the idiomatic warning 'beiläufig gesprochen'. The fact that Wittgenstein there relies on showing (*zeigen*) as the paradigmatic way of telling two objects apart supports our interpretation. However, it seems impossible to draw definite conclusions from this passage, which (in conjunction with 2.0233) is best understood as a metaphysical underpinning to Wittgenstein's treatment of identity, explained by Wittgenstein in 5.5302–5.5303. Also, 2.02331 is a comment on 2.0233, which shows that Wittgenstein is here discussing the internal properties of objects. Hence the problem in 2.02331 is what can be expressed *in language*, for it is the internal properties of objects that can be mirrored in language by its formal properties. It is therefore scarcely relevant here.

34 In G. E. Moore, *Some Main Problems of Philosophy*, Allen & Unwin, London, 1953 (consisting of lectures originally given in 1910–11), p. 30, a patch in one's visual field is presented as a paradigmatic example of sense-data. More specifically, Moore distinguishes the patch from its colour, size, and shape, including only the patch among sense-data.

35 In MS 106, p. 75, Wittgenstein offers as examples of elementary propositions the following: 'For instance, if I say, "here's red" and "here's green".' This is precisely what elementary propositions ought to be like on our interpretation. The German text reads: 'Z.B. wenn ich sage: "hier ist rot" und "hier is grün".'

36 Not 'context', as a Freudian misprint makes the English translation read.

37 That we are here dealing with Wittgenstein's early views is also suggested by his way of using the term 'sense-datum'. Later he identifies a sense-datum with 'the private object that is there before my mind' (*Zettel*, sec. 498). This usage prevails as early as in *Wittgenstein's Lectures, Cambridge 1930–1932*, pp. 69, 71, 81, and 109. If this were the meaning of the term, Wittgenstein ought to identify in the quoted passage sense-data with 'genuine entities', for they are precisely what is supposed to be given in experience. In contrast to Wittgenstein's later usage, we find a close connection between different people's sense-data and their bodies in Russell; witness, e.g., Russell's admission that sense-data are 'physiologically subjective'. Hence the remarks recorded by Ramsey seem to pertain to an early stage of the development of Wittgenstein's ideas.

38 The German text read as follows:

Es ist von der größten Bedeutung, daß wir uns zu einem Kalkül der Logik immer ein Beispiel denken, auf welches der Kalkül eine Anwendung findet, und daß wir nicht Beispiele geben und sagen, sie seien eigentlich nicht die idealen, diese aber hätten wir noch nicht. Das ist das Zeichen einer falschen Auffassung. (Russell & ich haben, in verschiedener Weise an ihr laboriert. Vergleiche was ich in der "Log. phil. Abh." über Elementarsätze & Gegenstände sage.)

39 Abstracted from the context provided by proximate entries, the following passage might appear to present evidence against our interpretation:

But it also seems certain that we do not infer the existence of simple objects from the existence of particular simple objects, but rather know [*kennen*] them – by description, as it were – as the end-product of analysis, by means of a process that leads to them. (*Notebooks 1914–1916*, p. 50, dated 23 May 1915)

(We are grateful to Ian Hacking for calling our attention to the need to address this passage.) It is easily seen, however, that Wittgenstein's use of the term 'description' in connection with our knowledge of simple objects is nonliteral and not in conflict with our interpretation. For one thing,

Wittgenstein indicates by his words 'as it were' that he is speaking of description in an unusual sense. Second, *kennen* is the German expression for knowledge by acquaintance. Third, the context of the quote shows clearly that the issue occupying Wittgenstein's attention in late May of 1915 was the difficulty incumbent in the contrast between simples and complexes, not the contrast between acquaintance and description. Three days earlier, he writes, 'A complex just is [*ist eben*] a thing!' (*Notebooks 1914–1916*). And on 24 May, having mentioned several disparate complexes, he writes (ibid.):

> Even if we don't know [*kennen*) simple objects from intuition [*Anschauung*], we do know [*kennen*] complex objects from intuition, we know [*wissen*] from intuition that they are complex.– And that they must ultimately consist of simple things?

We have given here our own translation rather than the standard one, in order to bring out better what we think is Wittgenstein's meaning. G. E. M. Anscombe translates 'aus der Anschauung . . . kennen' as 'have . . . acquaintance with', which is linguistically possible. It is scarcely in keeping with Russell's and Wittgenstein's terminology, however, in which intuition (*Anschauung*) was a much narrower term than acquaintance. When Russell thought in 1913 that all logical forms are obtained from acquaintance, he definitely did not thereby assume that they are obtained from intuition. (Cf. also 6.233–6.2331). Thus Wittgenstein is not contemplating, not even counterfactually, the possibility that simple objects are not given by acquaintance. Apart from the translation, it is in any case unmistakable that in the quoted passages Wittgenstein is discussing the relation between simple and complex phenomenological objects, not one between phenomenological and physical objects.

4

What is the Logic of the
Tractatus Logico-Philosophicus?

1 WITTGENSTEIN AS AN HEIR TO FREGE

What has been found in the earlier chapters helps us to put into perspective Wittgenstein's ideas about logic in the *Tractatus*. In that book, Wittgenstein makes contributions to formal logic, puts forward and discusses an abundance of ideas in the philosophy of logic, and uses them as an important ingredient in his overall philosophical system. What are we to think of his ideas about logic? First, what precisely are Wittgenstein's logical ideas? This is not an occasion to launch an exhaustive examination. Wittgenstein's leading ideas are nevertheless easily identified. It is sometimes said that the two fundaments of the logic of the *Tractatus* are the so-called picture theory and the theory of truth-functions. We shall begin here by arguing that both these ideas are integral parts of one and the same tradition.

What is this tradition? One historically natural – and illuminating – perspective is to consider Wittgenstein's *Tractatus* as a part of the tradition in logic and logically based philosophy which was begun by Frege and which was continued later by, among others, Russell, Tarski, Carnap, and the rest of the Vienna Circle, as well as their numerous followers among logicians and analytically oriented philosophers.[1]

As van Heijenoort has aptly spelled out,[2] Frege's first and foremost achievement was not his theory of sense and reference, but the interrelated conceptions of logical language ('Begriffsschrift') and logical system. The basic features of the Fregean conception of a logical language have been accepted by most subsequent logicians and analytic philosophers, even though they were apparently accepted by virtually no earlier ones.[3] In this sense, the Fregean idea of a logical language has been one of the greatest success stories in the history of philosophy. Frege's conception of logical language has in fact dominated the subsequent discussion to a much higher degree than is being acknowledged by contemporary philosophers and to a higher degree than has been entirely healthy for them.

Wittgenstein is in many respects an integral part of this Fregean tradition, to the extent that his overall philosophy in the *Tractatus* could almost be described as the metaphysics that naturally accompanies the Fregean conception of logical language. Even though this viewpoint is not exhaustive, it helps us to appreciate several aspects of Wittgenstein's views in the *Tractatus*.

What is a Fregean language like?[4] With some amount of oversimplification, it can be described as follows: it can be used to speak of a universe of discourse (domain of individuals) D on which a number of properties and relations have been defined. Individuals are called by Frege *objects,* properties and relations *functions.* The former are described by Frege as being saturated; they are represented in language by proper names. The latter, i.e., properties and relations, are said by Frege to be unsaturated. They are represented in language by symbols (function symbols) which have one or more argument-places associated with them. By plugging names of objects (individuals) for all the argument-places (of a first-order function symbol – we shall disregard the others for the time being), we can form (i) an atomic proposition (associated with that function symbol). From atomic propositions and other propositions already formed, we can form new ones in two ways: (ii) by means of propositional connectives and (iii) by means of quantification. In the latter procedure, the name of an object in a proposition is replaced by a new variable of the appropriate kind which is then bound to an initial quantifier.

Two other formation procedures can also be considered as being an integral part of the Fregean conception of logical language: (iv) we can form identity statements by inserting '=' between two names; (v) we may also introduce higher-order predicates and higher-order quantifiers.

Most of these features of Fregean languages are also found in the basic language of the *Tractatus,* with the same intended semantics as in Frege. We shall review briefly the different types of propositions.

(i) What was found in chapter 2 above shows that Wittgenstein's basic ontology was the same as Frege's. It included not only individuals (Frege's 'objects'), but also properties and relations. The chief difference is a terminological one in that Wittgenstein also called properties and relations 'objects'. This ontology is reflected in the atomic propositions postulated by Wittgenstein in the *Tractatus.* (He called them elementary propositions, *Elementarsätze.*) Their general structure is the same as in Frege. Their truth-conditions are discussed in sections 3–5 of this chapter.

(ii) As far as propositional connectives are concerned, there apparently is a complete agreement between Frege and Wittgenstein. (But cf. sec. 8 below.) Wittgenstein is sometimes said to have invented the truth-function theory. A closer examination of Frege's work quickly shows, however, that he was perfectly well aware of the truth-functional characterizations of the propositional connectives, and thought of them as giving the meaning of these connectives.[5] Moreover, Wittgenstein indicates clearly that he was aware of following Frege's informal ideas in developing his truth-function theory:

> 4.431 The expression of agreement and disagreement with the truth-possibilities of elementary propositions expresses the truth-conditions of a proposition.
>
> A proposition is the expression of its truth-conditions.
>
> (Thus Frege was quite right to use them as a preliminary explanation of his conceptual notation . . .)

However, since Frege did not believe in the expressibility of semantics in language, he did not develop systematically the theory of truth-functions, nor even formulate the truth-function theory 'officially'. Even though Wittgenstein likewise believed in the ineffability of semantics, he was more willing to break his self-imposed rules, and to break them much more radically, than Frege. This is what enabled him to formulate for the first time explicitly the basic ideas of truth-function theory.

(iii) As far as quantifiers are concerned, the main difference between Frege and Wittgenstein is that Wittgenstein tried to reduce them to truth-functions. We shall discuss this attempt below in section 9 of this chapter. Wittgenstein's attempt is based on certain non-Fregean assumptions underlying his logic.

(iv) The same assumptions affected Wittgenstein's treatment of identity. To some extent the problems which led Wittgenstein to his ideas about identity and its proper treatment in logical symbolism were present in Frege.

(v) There does not seem to have been any major differences between Frege and Wittgenstein as far as their basic attitude to higher-order quantifiers is concerned. Both accepted them without any qualms.

Wittgenstein acknowledges himself that he is following the Fregean tradition. After having described his own ideal language – 'a sign-language that is governed by *logical* grammar – by logical syntax', he says (in 3.325):

> The conceptual notation of Frege and Russell is such a language, though, it is true, it fails to exclude all mistakes.

The fact that Wittgenstein tried to correct several alleged mistakes in the logical languages of both Frege and Russell has led many philosophers to overlook the high degree to which his 'sign-language . . . governed by *logical* grammar' agrees with Frege's, especially in its leading ideas. Occasionally Wittgenstein even praises Russell's notation; see, e.g., 3.318, 4.012, 5.513, etc.

2 THE FREGE PRINCIPLES IN WITTGENSTEIN

Thus the conception of a basic language represented in the *Tractatus* is in many ways very close to Frege's ideas, as far as the customary ingredients of contemporary logic are concerned. A more detailed examination would strengthen this impression of overall similarity. The similarity is not accidental, either. It is based on the fact that Frege and Wittgenstein both accepted the same leading principles on which their respective logical languages were largely based. The most important of those principles are probably the following:

(a) The ineffability of semantics.
(b) The multiple ambiguity of 'is' and its cognates between the 'is' of identity, the 'is' of predication, the 'is' of existence, and the 'is' of class-inclusion.
(c) The principle of compositionality, also known as the functional principle or the Frege principle. According to it, the meaning of a complex expression is a function of the meanings of its constituent expressions.
(d) The contextual principle, according to which 'only a proposition has sense; only in the context of a proposition does a name have a meaning'. (3.3)

We shall discuss these four briefly in order.

(a) Wittgenstein's belief in the ineffability of semantics was discussed and documented in chapter 1 above. The presence of the same assumption in Frege has been shown convincingly by van Heijenoort.[6]

(b) The Fregean doctrine that 'is' is ambiguous[7] is asserted in so many words by Wittgenstein in 3.323:

> In everyday language it very frequently happens that the same word has different modes of signification – and so belongs to different symbols – or that two words that have different modes of signification are employed in propositions in what is superficially the same way.
>
> Thus the word 'is' figures as the copula, as a sign for identity, and as an expression for existence; 'exist' figures as an intransitive verb like 'go', and 'identical' as an adjective; we speak of *something,* but also of *something's* happening.[8]

He also practises what he preaches in his own logical notation, even though in his treatment some of the different senses of 'is' fare differently from what happens to them in Frege. In Wittgenstein's logical language, the 'is' of predication is treated mainly in the same way as in Frege and Russell, while the 'is' of identity disappears, and the 'is' of existential quantifier is reduced to truth-functions. More accurately expressed, the existence of kinds of objects is expressed in the *Tractatus* by existential quantification, which is then reduced to disjunction. The existence of a particular object, in contrast, is inexpressible according to the *Tractatus,* as we saw in chapter 3 above.

This shows that the Frege–Russell ambiguity thesis was not a mere ornament in the edifice of the *Tractatus.* Without the distinction, he could not have treated the allegedly different senses of 'is' differently. This would have made a tremendous difference in his overall doctrine.

(c) Compositionality is asserted explicitly by Wittgenstein in 3.318 (with an acknowledgment to his predecessors):

> Like Frege and Russell I construe a proposition as a function of the expressions contained in it.

One aspect of the importance of this principle for Wittgenstein was discussed above in section 6 of chapter 3. This importance is also reflected by such theses of the *Tractatus* as 3.2–3.21.

(d) As was already mentioned, the contextual principle is asserted by Wittgenstein in 3.3.

The importance of these principles for Frege's thought has not been spelled out fully in the literature. It seems to us immensely important. Some of the detailed evidence for this belief is found in Jean van Heijenoort,[9] Jaakko Hintikka,[10] and Leila Haaparanta.[11] Because of their importance for Frege, Wittgenstein's acceptance of these principles constitutes a significant link between the two.

3 WITTGENSTEIN'S SO-CALLED PICTURE THEORY

Perhaps the most dramatic link between Wittgenstein and the Fregean tradition is his so-called picture theory of language.[12] It is often thought of as an original and mysterious creation of Wittgenstein's. In reality it can be considered (subject to a number of qualifications) as being little more than a dramatization of certain Fregean ideas which Tarski later built into his truth-conditions for atomic propositions.

A starting-point is offered here by chapter 2, where it was seen that the elementary (atomic) propositions of the *Tractatus* were like the simplest sentences in Frege – or, for that matter, in almost anywhere else in recent logic. An elementary proposition did not consist of a number of names of particulars strung together by some additional 'logical tie' or 'copula'; it consisted of a number of 'names' of objects belonging to different but matching logical types. These objects could, for instance, be a property and a particular; a two-place relation and two particulars, etc. Because their types complement each other, they can 'hang together like the links in a chain'.

Hence many similar things can be said of the *Elementarsätze* of the *Tractatus* as can be said of other logicians' atomic sentences. Naturally, the most important thing that can be said of them are their truth-conditions. When is an elementary proposition true? How does it express what it expresses? Again, what we found above in chapter 2 will help us here. One of Wittgenstein's most explicit answers is as follows (addressed to a special case):

> 3.1432   Instead of, 'The complex sign "*aRb*" says that *a* stands to *b* in the relation R', we ought to put, '*That "a"* stands to "*b*" in a certain relation says *that aRb*.'

This passage was discussed in chapter 2 above. There it was shown that part of Wittgenstein's point is that the relation R is represented in language, not by the *letter* 'R', but by the (linguistic) *relation* of flanking the letter in a certain order. This is the 'certain relation' Wittgenstein mentions.

If so, we can read from 3.1432 a truth-condition for the proposition in question. The proposition expressed by the propositional sign '*aRb*' is true if and only if the relation in the world that corresponds to 'R' (in the sense Wittgenstein explains) obtains between the objects named by '*a*' and '*b*' *(in this order), i.e., if and only if the complex formed by the three linguistic entities, 'a', 'b', and the relation of* flanking 'R', matches the configuration of the objects these three linguistic entities represent (name). This account can obviously be extended to all elementary propositions.

The generalization is formulated by Wittgenstein himself in more abstract terms in 3.21:

> The configuration of objects in a situation corresponds to the configuration of simple signs in the propositional sign.

That this correspondence or matching is what constitutes truth is shown, e.g., by 4.024:

> To understand a proposition means to know what is the case if it is true.

This account is (given the results of chapter 2 above) so natural, not to say obvious, that very little seems to hang on it. In reality, however, this point gives rise to several highly interesting observations.

First, Wittgenstein has another term for the relation between an elementary proposition and the state of affairs it represents. It is precisely what Wittgenstein means by the former's being a *picture* of the latter. 'A proposition is a picture of reality. A proposition is a model of reality as we imagine it,' Wittgenstein says (in 4.01), and explains this idea as follows:

> 4.021   A proposition is a picture of reality: for I know the situation it represents if I understand the proposition.

The way I know the represented situation on the basis of the proposition is precisely by heeding the matching relation which Wittgenstein calls 'picturing'. This is verified by a comparison between 4.021 and 4.024. It shows that the picture relation, which enables one to understand an elementary proposition, is precisely the same as the relation which makes the proposition true.

Second, Wittgenstein's 'pictures' in the *Tractatus* are in reality not very pictorial. The crucial idea in Wittgenstein's view is precisely what mathematicians mean by an isomorphic representation or isomorphic mapping. This is spelled out by Wittgenstein himself on pp. 36–7 of *The Blue Book* where he speaks of pictures which are not 'pictures by similarity'. He makes it clear there that the sense in which a proposition is a picture according to him is not a picture by similarity.

From this it follows that Wittgenstein's 'theory' applies more obviously and more perspicuously to a non-picturesque logical symbolism than to real pictures or natural-language sentences. Indeed, the fact that his account can be explained especially happily by means of the logical notation is noted by Wittgenstein himself:

4.012   It is obvious that a proposition of the form '*aRb*' strikes us as a picture. In this case the sign is obviously a likeness of what is signified.

It may even be that Wittgenstein's entire picture theory was largely inspired by the notation of *Principia Mathematica* and modelled on it. It is, for instance, significant that the ideas of *logical* portrayal and of a representation of *logical* properties play an important role in Wittgenstein's very first remarks on his 'picture theory', as shown by pp. 7–8 of Wittgenstein's *Notebooks 1914–1916*. 'Logical pictures' are repeatedly mentioned also in the *Tractatus*; see 2.18–2.19, 3, 4.03. It does not seem misleading to think of them as propositions represented in a logical notation. The enormous influence of Russell's and Whitehead's work on Wittgenstein is easily obscured by his criticisms in the *Tractatus* of several different details of the *Principia* notation. These criticisms nevertheless concern other features than the basic parts of logic, with the sole exception of Russell's treatment of identity. They hide the large area of agreement between Russell and Wittgenstein, as far as the structure of the basic logical language is concerned.

Third, it can be seen that the isomorphism requirement makes little sense unless entities of different logical types (logical categories), such as individuals (i.e., particulars), properties, and relations are represented in language by expressions of the same type, that is to say, individuals by individuals, relations by relations, etc. This important principle of categorial analogy was discussed briefly in chapter 2, sec. 5, above. It has been appropriately spelled out and emphasized by Erik Stenius, who also notes the minor qualifications it needs. (See *Wittgenstein's 'Tractatus', passim.*)

4 PICTURE THEORY VS. TRUTH-DEFINITIONS

It is even more interesting to note that the correspondence relation, which, according to this analysis, constitutes the truth of an elementary proposition, is essentially the same relation which makes such a proposition true according to the truth-definitions codified in logical semantics. In such a truth-definition, we are typically considering an evaluation which assigns to each name of a particular object, e.g., to each of '*a*' and '*b*', a member of the domain D. We may call them $v(a)$ and $v(b)$. Likewise, $v(R)$ is a class of ordered pairs of members of D, if '*R*' is a two-place relation symbol. Then '*aRb*' is defined to be true if and only if the pair $<v(a), v(b)>$ is a member of $v(R)$.

The evaluation function is obviously closely related to the naming relations of the *Tractatus,* although not in a uniform way. The individuals (members of the domain of individuals) $v(a)$ and $v(b)$ are obviously intended to be the objects which '*a*' and '*b*' stand for (name). The interpretation of $v(R)$ is only slightly more complicated, and is still quite obvious. The members of $v(R)$ are intended to be those pairs of objects between which the relation obtains which is represented by '*R*'. But this implies that '*aRb*' is true according to the semantical (Tarski-type) truth-definition described above precisely when the 'pictorial' matching relation obtains between the atomic (elementary) proposition in question and the state of affairs. In brief, as far as atomic propositions are concerned, *the so-called picture theory is equivalent with the clause for atomic sentences in a Tarski-type truth-definition.* The famous picture relation is nothing but the self-same isomorphism relation which in logical semantics defines the truth of atomic sentences. The mislabelled 'picture theory of language' is nothing but Wittgenstein's anticipation of the first clause of a Tarski-type truth-definition.

This is verified by a comparison between 4.021 and 4.024. It shows that the picture relation in which one's understanding of an elementary proposition is based is precisely the same as the relation which makes the proposition true.

Such truth-conditions of elementary propositions constitute an important part of the conception of elementary logic which is here being ascribed to Frege. Historically speaking, it was of course formulated much later than Frege and somewhat later than Wittgenstein's *Tractatus.* There is nevertheless little doubt that Frege was familiar with the idea, even though his allegiance to the conception of language as the universal medium prevented him from putting it forward 'officially', that is, as an explicitly formulated doctrine. Hence we have discovered here an especially striking sense in which Wittgenstein is providing in the *Tractatus* a metaphysics to go together with the Fregean conception of elementary logic.

These observations also serve to de-mystify Wittgenstein's picture view by showing precisely where its very simple logical gist lies.

This bland identification of Wittgenstein's 'picture theory' and an element of Tarski-type logical semantics requires certain qualifications and explanations. There are important differences between Wittgenstein's picture ideas and the Tarski–Carnap semantics for atomic sentences. Even if these differences do not excuse philosophers' failure to point out the connection, they may help to explain it.

There are differences of at least three different types: first, in logical semantics, Wittgensteinian objects are not all treated in the same way, not even *mutatis mutandis*; second, the picture idea is used in logical semantics only in connection with atomic sentences; third, from a Wittgensteinian vantage point, there cannot be any *theory* like the picture theory or logical semantics, for what they are trying to express is ineffable.

We shall discuss these points in what follows.

The first main discrepancy is that different Tractarian objects are treated differently in logical semantics. The names of particulars (individuals), say 'a' and 'b', have indeed as their values $v(a)$ and $v(b)$ the objects named by them. However, an n-place predicate sign, say 'R', is assigned a set of n-tuples of individuals as its value $v(R)$. This differs in several ways from Wittgenstein's procedures, and is in certain respects unsatisfactory for his purposes. What represents according to Wittgenstein is not the predicate symbol, for instance our two-place relation symbol 'R', but the linguistic relation associated with it, in our example, the relation of flanking the letter 'R'. And what this linguistic relation stands for is not a class of pairs of individuals (call it C), but a certain actual relation obtaining between some individuals. The class C is, in Fregean terms, merely the value-range (*Wertverlauf*) of the relation.[13] Hence the procedure of logical semanticists differs from Wittgenstein's, and is bound to appear to a faithful Tractarian somewhat uneven and therefore misleading. For one thing, the treatment offered by logical semantics violates the categorial analogy principle mentioned above.

But does this difference matter? At first sight it does not. For it apparently comes down pretty much to the same whether one speaks of value-ranges of functions or functions themselves. Frege drew the distinction, but it makes so little difference for him that subsequent philosophers have sometimes overlooked the distinction.

Yet for Wittgenstein it does make a difference. It is conspicuous (on the basis of such statements of Wittgenstein's as 2.022–2.023) that he is effect considers his objects as potential members of several different possible facts and states of affairs. In this respect, he differs sharply from Frege. In different states of affairs a relation may obtain between different individuals. Hence it does not suffice, for the purpose of interpreting a relation symbol 'R', to give the value-range of the correlated relation in the actual world. One has to give it in all different possible worlds. This separates Wittgenstein's picture idea from Tarski-type truth-definitions.

This is not the end of the story, however. It may be argued that to specify *all* these value-ranges *is* precisely to specify the relation represented by the linguistic flanking relation. (This assumption is what the so-called possible-words semantics is predicated on.) But if this is recognized, the difference between the picture theory of the *Tractatus* and logical semantics (when it is extended to modal logic) turns out to be largely an illusion. It is due to the fact that in the discussion above Wittgenstein's views were compared with a truth-definition in non-modal first-order logic, whereas in the *Tractatus* Wittgenstein is considering a multitude of possible facts and hence in effect is involved in modal logic. Once this fact is recognized, the apparent difference largely disappears.

The second asymmetry between Wittgenstein's picture idea and Tarski-type truth-definitions will be discussed in sections 6–8 below.

The third and most important difference between Wittgenstein's ill-named 'picture theory of language' and the views of subsequent logical semanticists is that Wittgenstein's view was not, and could not be for him, a *theory*, or a part of a theory. It could not be, because it was inexpressible. Here we meet one of the most striking consequences of Wittgenstein's adherence to the idea of language as the universal medium, discussed in chapter 1 above. The basic identity of Wittgenstein's picture view and an important part of subsequent logical semantics has been hidden by the fact that Wittgenstein rejected (or, rather, would have rejected) the ideas of logical semantics lock, stock, and barrel. The reason for the rejection is not that this theory is mistaken according to Wittgenstein's lights, but rather that it deals with those basic language–world relations which according to the view of language as the universal medium are ineffable.

In spite of these three significant differences, there is an important connection between Wittgenstein's picturing idea and Tarski-type truth-definitions for atomic sentences.

In sum, Wittgenstein's 'picture theory of language' was somewhat like the old Holy Roman Empire, which was neither holy, Roman, nor much of an empire. In Wittgenstein's theory, it was structural identity (isomorphism), not the relation of picturing in any vivid sense, that played the crucial role. It was not a theory, for it could not be expressed in language. Finally, it was not a theory of language, either, but rather a picture theory of truth. For we can of course form any number of meaningful propositions *à la Tractatus* which do not 'picture' in the sense of not being isomorphic with any actual facts at all. It is only when a proposition is true that it is a 'picture' (isomorph) of an actual fact.

It thus turns out that the two most prominent logical theories of Wittgenstein, the 'picture theory' and the theory of truth-functions, are part and parcel of the Fregean tradition. Moreover, by and large the two theories are but dramatizations of the two aspects of a Tarski-type truth-theory (subject to the qualifications mentioned in the next section.) The picture theory serves the same purpose as the clause or clauses in a Tarskian truth-definition which deal with atomic propositions, and is in fact closely related to them. Truth-function theory is apparently calculated to serve the same purpose as the recursive clauses of the same truth-definitions: they extend the notions of truth and falsity from atomic propositions to all others.

All this is true, and important, for the purpose of understanding the overall systematic structure of the *Tractatus* as well as its historical position. Alas, it turns out to be only a part of the story. There is another streak in the logical theory of the *Tractatus* so unexpected that many commentators have missed it altogether. We shall return to it in sec. 6 below.

5 DIFFERENT ASPECTS OF THE 'PICTURE THEORY'

Meanwhile, however, Wittgenstein's so-called picture theory needs a few more words, not so much for the sake of understanding what Wittgenstein says, as for the purpose of putting into perspective philosophers' comments on his views. These have often been vitiated by a failure to distinguish from each other the different ideas which are typically discussed together under the heading of Wittgenstein's 'picture theory'. What we have so far concentrated on almost exclusively is the idea of isomorphism as a truth-condition of elementary propositions. The reason for this concentration is that this truth-conditional relation is what Wittgenstein means by a proposition's being a picture. This is shown, among other things, by 4.021 and 4.024, discussed above.

In spite of such strong textual support, our interpretation of Wittgenstein's picture idea as being little more than an especially vivid formulation of the same idea as underlies the usual truth-conditions for atomic propositions, will strike many readers as strange and perhaps even distorted.

This reaction is unjustified, however. What has happened in most discussions of the so-called picture theory is that it is taken to be an *exhaustive* theory of language understanding. At first sight, this is not so far from what we are saying. As the quotations just given show, language understanding is for Wittgenstein based on those very truth-conditions that we have emphasized. What makes a difference here is the exhaustiveness claim attributed to Wittgenstein. It makes a difference because the status of the picture (isomorphism) relation as the *sole* basis of language understanding in the *Tractatus* is based on other assumptions which have nothing to do with the idea which we have called the picture idea, i.e., with the thesis that structural identity is a truth-condition of elementary propositions. One cannot hope to achieve any clarity in discussing Wittgenstein's views in the *Tractatus* and their subsequent fate in his later thought without distinguishing these collateral assumptions from the picture idea proper.

What has to be the case if the 'pictorial' isomorphism relation is to be an exhaustive account of language understanding? At least two further assumptions have to be made.

(i) First, it has to be assumed that no separate account needs to be given of the name–object relations which are presupposed in the isomorphism ('picturing') relation between a proposition and the corresponding fact. If these name–object relations are not simple two-place relations but require to be grasped before the holding of the isomorphism relation can be ascertained, picturing cannot be the be-all and end-all of language understanding.

(ii) Second, the range of all admissible combinations of names must match the entire range of possible configurations of their objects. For if not, one has to decide first, upon being given a proposition, whether the combination of names it is really represents a possible state of affairs, in order to understand what (if anything) it means.

It is clear that Wittgenstein makes both assumptions in the *Tractatus*. It is equally clear that they are both independent of the isomorphism idea. For this reason, it is unfortunate all these three ideas are in effect lumped together in the usual discussions of Wittgenstein's 'picture theory' in the literature. Furthermore, there is no evidence that Wittgenstein himself intends to refer to either assumption (i) or (ii) when he speaks of propositions as pictures of facts. We shall return to the simplicity assumption (i) in chapter 8 below and to the exhaustiveness assumption (ii) in chapter 5. The realization that both these assumptions are independent of the isomorphism idea is especially important for the purpose of understanding the later development of Wittgenstein's philosophical ideas. For if the picture idea proper (isomorphism as constituting truth-conditions) is independent of (i) and (ii), Wittgenstein could have continued to believe in the picture idea while giving up these other assumptions (i) and (ii). If the three were assimilated to each other, as often happens in the literature, it would not make sense to ask whether Wittgenstein later gave up 'the picture theory of language' or not.

6 COMPLEX PROPOSITIONS VS. SIMPLE OBJECTS

If one approaches the logical doctrines codified in Wittgenstein's *Tractatus* by the sole means of the observations so far made, in other words, as a link in the tradition Frege launched, one is nevertheless in for a rude surprise. There are views expressed there which are simply incomprehensible on that basis.

First and foremost, logic is in the Frege tradition thought of as a theory of *complex* propositions. It is a theory of how the truth or falsity of a complex proposition depends on the truth and falsity of its constituent propositions and eventually on the references of the simplest symbols it contains. The different ways of constructing complex propositions go hand in hand with the different branches of logic: propositional connectives with propositional logic (including the theory of truth-functions), quantifiers with quantification theory (predicate calculus), intensional operators with intensional logic, etc. Wittgenstein's theory of truth-functions seems to be in agreement with this conception, and so seems to be Wittgenstein's acceptance of the contextual principle. (See sec. 2 above.)

However, Wittgenstein makes it unmistakably clear in the *Tractatus* that on his view logic is in the last analysis a study of the simplest ingredients of the world and of their linguistic representatives, not of complexes or of their representatives, complex propositions. The logic of Wittgenstein's *Tractatus* is a logic of simple objects and names, not of facts and complex propositions. For instance, in 4.0312 Wittgenstein writes:

> The possibility of propositions is based on the principle that objects have signs as their representatives.

That for Wittgenstein all logic is essentially logic of objects is also shown by his statement in 5.552 that logic is prior to the question 'How?' (e.g., how different objects are related to each other), but not prior to the question 'What?' (i.e., what objects there are in the world).

In so far as logic is the study of logical forms, it is basically a study of the forms of (simple) objects, not of the forms of complex propositions. In the *Notebooks 1914–1916* Wittgenstein writes (p. 23, dated 1 November 1914):

> The logical form of the proposition must already be given by the forms of its component parts.

The component parts meant here must be names, as a comparison of passages like 3.2–3.22 shows.

Another way of putting the same idea of Wittgenstein's is to say that the structural elements, often called logical constants, which are usually thought of as the main means of building complex propositions out of simple ones, are not needed for this job. Wittgenstein emphasizes that this idea is exceptionally important for him. Indeed, 4.0312 continues as follows:

> My *fundamental idea* [emphasis added] is that the 'logical constants' do not represent anything; that the *logic* of facts cannot be represented. [14]

It is also highly relevant here that Wittgenstein claims that the forms of *all* propositions are given as soon as the elementary ones are given:

> 5.47   It is clear that whatever we can say *in advance* about the form of all propositions, we must be able to say *all at once*. In fact elementary propositions themselves contain all logical operations. For '*fa*' says the same thing as
>
> '$(\exists x).fx. x=a$'.
>
> Wherever there is compositeness, argument and function are already present, and where these are present, we already have all the logical constants.

The point Wittgenstein is making here about quantified propositions is analogous to what he says in 5.4–5.41 about truth-functions (cf. also 5.441):

> At this point it becomes manifest that there are no 'logical objects' or 'logical constants' (in Frege's and Russell's sense).
>
> The reason is that the results of truth-operations on truth-functions are always identical whenever they are one and the same truth-function of elementary propositions.

In other words, according to Wittgenstein the logical operations one performs on elementary propositions are not genuine functional operations because they can yield identical results in some cases and can even lead back to elementary propositions. However, it is hard to see the force of the 'because' here. Why should the occasional reducibility of the outcomes of logical proposition-forming operations back to elementary propositions show that they are not representing genuine functional relationships? We do not think that Wittgenstein's best reasons for his position are in evidence here. We shall try to find better ones in the next few sections. [15]

The most telling way of putting Wittgenstein's paradoxical-sounding doctrine is to say that according to him *all* propositions, not just elementary ones, are pictures in the sense explained in sections 3–4 above. This constitutes in fact another important difference between Wittgenstein's picture theory in the *Tractatus* and truth-clauses for atomic sentences in logical semantics *à la* Carnap. The best evidence for this claim is probably the fact that Wittgenstein introduces the 'picture theory' in the *Tractatus* in completely general terms, without any special reference to elementary propositions. (See especially 2.1–3.) The generality of the picture idea likewise seems to be presupposed in several specific propositions; witness, e.g., 2.1:

> We picture facts to ourselves.

As *Tractatus* 2 shows, a 'fact' (*Tatsache*) is complex, consisting in the existence of (possibly several) states of affairs.[16]

Max Black and others have taken Wittgenstein's picture theory to apply primarily to atomic propositions. Black writes that 'the picture theory therefore needs to be supplemented by an account of the function of logical signs which Wittgenstein's discussion of truth-functions will attempt to provide.'[17] The truth seems to be, however, that Wittgenstein is not thinking of the truth-function theory as much as a supplement to the 'picture theory' as an aspect of it. Wittgenstein is not only striving to supplement the picture theory by the theory of truth-functions (and by his reduction of quantifiers to truth-functions) so as to be able to define the logical forms of complex propositions; he is also thinking of this process as a reduction of the logical forms of complex propositions to those of simple ones; as an extension of the picture theory to complex propositions; and as an elimination of logical constants.[18]

7 WITTGENSTEIN'S REJECTION OF COMPLEX LOGICAL FORMS AS OBJECTS OF ACQUAINTANCE

Wittgenstein's emphasis on simple objects and on their forms is completely predictable on the basis of what was found in chapter 3. It was argued there that Wittgenstein's overall philosophical position in the *Tractatus* was the outcome of a radical modification of an earlier view of his which largely coincided with Russell's position in his 1913 book *Theory of Knowledge*. As was mentioned in chapter 3, sec. 6, there are according to Russell's view two kinds of irreducible objects of acquaintance: (i) sense-data, ordinary universals and other concrete objects of acquaintance; (ii) logical forms. The latter class of objects of acquaintance was evoked by Russell for the purpose of explaining our knowledge of logical truths and logical forms and, more generally, our understanding of complex propositions. Accordingly, a realm of special nonsensuous Platonic objects of acquaintance, viz. the logical forms, is postulated by Russell for the purpose of dealing with logical complexity and logical truth.

As was indicated in chapter 3, what Wittgenstein did was to dispense with the second class (ii) of objects of acquaintance altogether. Hence their job, too, had to be done by the remaining objects of acquaintance (i). The main task of (ii) had been to constitute all the forms of all (complex as well as elementary) propositions. This task now had to be accomplished by the forms of simple objects. Out of these forms, and solely out of them, we must be able to assemble each and every form of a complex proposition, which reflects the form of a number of objects combined into a fact.

The problem is epitomized by Wittgenstein's central term 'logical form'. Russell had used it to cover both the forms of atomic propositions and the forms of complex propositions, defined linguistically by logical signs (propositional connectives, quantifiers, etc.). The thrust of Wittgenstein's ideas in moving away from Russell was, as was shown in chapter 3, following David Pears,[19] an attempt to eliminate complex logical forms, including the logical forms of propositions, as independent abstract entities and to analyse them in terms of objects and their logical forms:

> 2.0123   If I know an object I also know all its possible occurrences in states of affairs. (Every one of these possibilities must be part of the nature of the object.)

Pears considers the picture theory as the crucial ingredient of Wittgenstein's explanation of how the logical forms can be constructed out of objects. What Pears does not emphasize is that the picture idea takes care of only a part of the task. It is not enough for Wittgenstein to explain how the logical forms of elementary propositions can be built up of objects; he has to account also for the logical forms of complex propositions by the sole means of the forms of simple objects. This additional task is obviously what Wittgenstein's treatment of truth-functions, plus his attempted reduction of quantified propositions to truth-functions, is calculated to accomplish. What is most remarkable is that Wittgenstein apparently thought that the picture idea can somehow be extended to complex propositions and used to explain their logical forms, too.[20]

We can now see that Wittgenstein's attempted elimination of logical constants is in reality but a particular (albeit particularly important) aspect of his general elimination of logical forms as independent objects of acquaintance – and, indeed, as independent entities in any sense. The importance Wittgenstein attributes to this point, calling it 'my fundamental idea', is eloquent testimony to the role of Wittgenstein's Russellian background in the formation of the views he expresses in the *Tractatus.*

Unawareness of this background has led many philosophers to misinterpret the Tractarian passages quoted in the preceding section and others like them. It has not been realized how radical they are in reality. They do not assert merely that logical constants are not names of objects. Wittgenstein is also saying that all the so-called logical constants disappear from the last and final logical representation of every meaningful proposition. How extreme Wittgenstein's view is can be seen from his claim that 'all logical constants must already occur in the simple proposition' (*Notebooks 1914–1916*, p. 29). This contradicts diametrically the usual view according to which logical constants are our means of constructing complex propositions from simple ones. Wittgenstein continues to contradict the usual view in the *Tractatus*. Admittedly, in the most obvious formulation of his doctrine in 5.47 (quoted above) Wittgenstein merely says that 'an elementary proposition really contains all logical *operations* in itself' (emphasis added) instead of saying that it contains all logical constants. However, he clearly means logical *constants*. In the very same section 5.47 Wittgenstein says that 'one could say that the sole logical *constant* [emphasis added] was what *all* propositions . . . had in common with one another'. And in making a point in 5.441, which closely parallels 5.47, Wittgenstein speaks in so many words of logical constants:

> This vanishing of the apparent logical constants also occurs in the case of . . . '$(\exists x).\mathrm{f}x. \; x=a$', which says the same as '$\mathrm{f}a$'.

In the preceding section Wittgenstein discusses propositional connectives and argues that they 'are not material functions'. Hence they are clearly thought of by Wittgenstein as being among the (apparent) logical constants that vanish from the right notation.

The reason why Wittgenstein does not say in 5.47 that elementary propositions contain all logical constants is clearly not that he did not think so, but that he was emphasizing in the *Tractatus* that the so-called logical constants, obviously including propositional constants, disappear altogether by the time a full logical analysis of our propositions is accomplished. This is what we saw him asserting in 5.4. His reasons for this claim will be discussed in the next section.

In view of Wittgenstein's background, it is of interest to note that there is a close connection, perhaps a near-identity, in Wittgenstein's mind between the various logical forms which Russell postulated as objects of acquaintance in 1913 and the meanings of logical constants. As we saw, he writes in 5.47:

> Wherever there is compositeness, argument and function are present, and where these are present, we already have all the logical constants.

Hence the elimination of complex logical forms as separate objects easily became for Wittgenstein tantamount to an elimination of logical constants.

Now we can also appreciate fully the point of the notorious 'links in a chain' proposition which has occasioned so much interpretational confusion. (Cf. chapter 2, sec. 8, above.) The proposition reads, in its context:

> 2.0272   The configuration of objects produces states of affairs.

> 2.03   In a state of affairs objects fit into one another like the links of a chain.

> 2.031   In a state of affairs objects stand in a determinate relation to one another.

We saw in chapter 2 above that Wittgenstein is not here illustrating the absence of properties and relations from his ontology, as Copi thought.[21] What he is exorcising are logical constants. He is saying, as Copi et al. correctly saw, that no extra 'logical glue' is needed to combine objects into a state of affairs. However, for the author of the *Tractatus* this dispensable glue does not consist of relations, but of logical constants (complex logical forms). The point Wittgenstein is making here could also be expressed by amplifying 2.0272 as follows:

> A configuration of objects (and nothing but objects) forms a state of affairs (without any outside help).[22]

Even though Wittgenstein's view that all complex logical forms are built up of the logical forms of simple objects is thus predictable, given his historical background, it is nevertheless quite striking. At first sight, it seems to be in conflict with his own theory of truth-functions developed in the very same work. As we shall argue in the next section, however, Wittgenstein's truth-function theory was philosophically speaking designed to be self-destructive. The ultimate aim of his theory of truth-functional connectives was to show that they are strictly speaking dispensable, and that there is nothing in the world that in any way corresponds to them. Hence they cannot be genuine ingredients of any 'logical picture' of states of affairs.

That Wittgenstein really thought of his truth-function theory as an *elimination* of propositional connectives is confirmed conclusively by a footnote on p. 106 of *Wittgenstein's Lectures, Cambridge 1932–1935:*

> . . . we could do away with *negation, disjunction, conjunction*, etc. and use *true* and *false*, making up a notation containing only the words 'true' and 'false'. I once did that, with the notation for truth-functions.

Admittedly Wittgenstein in 4.21–4.26 makes a number of statements which apparently restrict the scope of the picture theory (and related conceptions) to elementary propositions. If this is Wittgenstein's intention, then perhaps he did not see any problem in reconciling with each other the picture theory and the truth-function theory. But propositions 4.21–4.26 are not conclusive. They do not solve our problem, but acerbate it. For all that they say, by and large, of elementary propositions are the same things as Wittgenstein had said earlier about propositions in general. This is readily seen by comparing, e.g., 4.21 with 4.031 and 4.0311 (especially the second sentence), 4.22 with 4.0311 (first sentence), 4.33 with 3.3, 4.26 with 1.11 and 4.1, etc.

The overall structure of Wittgenstein's argument in the *Tractatus* shows what the function of 4.21–4.26 really is. They do not present Wittgenstein's considered opinion; they present his problem. In 4.21–4.26, Wittgenstein notes that many of the things he had said earlier of propositions in general apply unproblematically only to elementary propositions, but not to complex ones. This forces him to analyse the logical structures of complex propositions so as to show that in the relevant respects (especially with respect to his picture theory) they are on a par with elementary propositions. In the next section we shall argue that this is what Wittgenstein attempts to do in arguing first for his proposition 5 and then for his proposition 6.

8 WITTGENSTEIN'S ARGUMENT

All that has been said so far does not yet help one to understand how Wittgenstein proposed to extend his picture idea from elementary propositions to all propositions so as to dispense with logical constants altogether. How could he have thought that such an extension is even possible?

An answer to this question is found in the *Tractatus*. What is needed is a firm look at the structure of Wittgenstein's argument there. How, according to him, are all other propositions obtained from elementary ones? The answer is given by one of the main theses of the *Tractatus*, viz. his proposition 5:

A proposition is a truth-function of elementary propositions.

Hence what Wittgenstein has to show in order to demonstrate the pictorial character of all propositions is to show that this character is not affected by truth-functional operations (i.e., truth-functional ways of constructing complex propositions from atomic ones). For he had argued earlier that each elementary proposition, being a concatenation of names, is a picture. (Cf., e.g., 4.22 and 4.26.)

This preservation of the picture idea by truth-functional combinations of simpler propositions might seem hopeless to defend, so hopeless, indeed, that it does not seem to have occurred to most interpreters of the *Tractatus* that it is what he is maintaining there. How can he do that? How can anyone try to do so?

Clearly, by examining the nature of truth-functions. This is precisely what Wittgenstein does. What is the outcome of his analysis? It is given by the next main thesis of the *Tractatus*, that is, by proposition 6. At first sight, this thesis seems to differ from the other main propositions of the book by being much less general, much less philosophical, and much more arbitrary in that it presents only one of many possible ways of expressing any truth-function of given elementary ones. In reality, it is an integral part of Wittgenstein's overall argument. For what thesis 6 of the *Tractatus* says is that an arbitrary truth-function of elementary propositions can be represented as the result of the repeated use of one particular truth-function, which is the simultaneous denial of a number given propositions. 'Simultaneous denial' of course means here the conjunction of the negations of all the given (argument) propositions.

But how could such a representation possibly help Wittgenstein to maintain his picture idea? It helps him if he can argue that the two components of the only requisite operation, negation and conjunction, preserve the pictorial character of propositions. Now one half of this double task is easy. A conjunction of pictures is clearly interpretable as a single larger composite picture. But this idea seems impossible to extend from conjunctions to other truth-functions.

What Wittgenstein's representation of all truth-functions thus shows is that he has to argue for the preservation of the pictorial character of propositions only in the case of one other truth-function, the negation. Now it is unmistakable that Wittgenstein in fact argued that negating a proposition, say *p*, does not change its pictorial character – and also unmistakable how he sought to argue his point. He does so by means of his theory of the sense (polarity) of propositions. For instance, in 5.2341 he says that 'negation reverses the sense of a proposition'. What he has in mind is shown more explicitly by his pre-*Tractatus* notes. The following is a case in point:

> Names are points, propositions arrows – they have *sense*. The sense of a proposition is determined by the two poles *true* and *false*. (*Notebooks 1914–1916*, pp. 101–2; cf. *Tractatus* 3.144)

> What we know when we understand a proposition is this: We know what is the case if the proposition is true, and what is the case if it is false. (*Notebooks 1914–1916*, p. 98)

What these claims amount to is that we understand *p* and ~*p* by means of the *same* representative or 'pictorial' relationship. The only difference is that the two 'poles', true and false, are reversed. These two 'poles' are mentioned explicitly in Wittgenstein's analysis of truth-functions in the *Tractatus*; see 6.1203. The same point is made in the *Tractatus*:

> 4.0621   The propositions 'p' and '~p' have opposite sense, but there corresponds to them one and the same reality.

For this reason,

> 5.5151   The positive *proposition* necessarily presupposes the existence of the negative *proposition* and *vice versa*.

It is significant that this thesis occurs as an explication of 5.51, which is where Wittgenstein explains the nature of his one and only basic truth-function forming operation.

Hence, according to Wittgenstein in the *Tractatus*, not only is ~*p* a 'picture' if *p* is; it is *the same picture*, but with its 'sense' (its 'logical polarity') reversed.[23]

This means of course that negation is in a sense ultimately eliminated from the semantics and ontology of the *Tractatus*. Predicate negation was dispensed with in the earlier symbolic languages of Frege and Russell in favour of propositional negation. Now Wittgenstein strives to eliminate propositional negation, too, by means of the idea of picture polarity.

This completes Wittgenstein's tacit argument for the generalization of the picture idea to all propositions. By thus uncovering his implicit line of thought, we have not only found support for our overall interpretation. We can now see how Wittgenstein's truth-function theory serves as an integral part of the architectonic of the *Tractatus*. Even such idiosyncratic-looking details as his use of only one of the two possible Sheffer primitives (cf. *Tractatus*, p. xiv) turns out to be tailored precisely to his purported philosophical conclusion, as does his prima facie quaint idea of the sense (polarity) of proposition. More generally, Wittgenstein's theory of truth-functions is not a meta-physician's excursion into pure logic, but a link in Wittgenstein's chain of reasons for his overall view of language and its connection with the world. Among other things, we can see why theses 5 and 6 are included by Wittgenstein among the major propositions of the *Tractatus*.

A *fortiori*, Wittgenstein's attempted reduction of quantifiers to truth-functions serves the same purpose in the same way. In the next section, we are going to show that this purported reduction is connected in other ways, too, with the central ideas of his philosophy in the *Tractatus*.

Meanwhile, it may be noted that Wittgenstein's extension of the picture idea from elementary propositions to all their truth-functions ipso facto shows in what sense he thought of the logical constants representing truth-functions as being dispensable in the last analysis. They are eliminable in terms of the two ideas of (i) compound pictures (doing the job of conjunction) and of (ii) the polarity of pictures (doing the job of negation). These ideas belong according to Wittgenstein to the picture theory rather than to the theory of truth-functions. They bring to light a facet of Wittgenstein's picture view of truth which we have not previously registered, supplementing what was said of his picture idea in secs. 4–5 above.

9 WITTGENSTEIN'S TREATMENT OF QUANTIFIERS

The influence of Wittgenstein's conception of the nature of simple objects on his logical theory is not limited to the features of this theory so far noted. The insights into this conception reached above in chapter 3 make it possible to understand better another aspect of his logical doctrines, viz. his treatment of quantifiers. Prima facie, there seems to be little connection between Wittgenstein's notion of an object and his reduction of quantifiers to truth-functions. There is nevertheless an extremely important link.

Wittgenstein's treatment of quantifiers marks a major difference between his language in the *Tractatus* and the usual first-order languages. Wittgenstein's basic notation does not include quantifiers; he construes quantified sentences as conjunctions and disjunctions. The sense in which he does so can be seen from 5.52 (which presupposes for its notation 5.502 and 5.501). For a blunter and therefore more useful formulation, we can turn to G. E. Moore's account of Wittgenstein's lectures:[24]

> [Wittgenstein] said [in 1930–33] that there was a temptation, to which he had yielded in the *Tractatus*, to say that $(x) .fx$ is identical with the logical product
> '$fa . fb . fc . . .$',
> and $(\exists x). fx$. identical with the logical sum
> '$fa \lor fb \lor fc \lor . . .$';
> but that this was in both cases a mistake.

It is often thought that Wittgenstein's early treatment does not work because it cannot be assumed that all objects have names. (They may be too numerous for this purpose, e.g., of a non-denumerable cardinality.) If so, it should be the case that the infinitary logics which have been developed in the last twenty years could be expected to vindicate Wittgenstein's approach, for in them all the limitations on the length of disjunctions and conjunctions and on the cardinality of names can be removed.[25] Yet these infinitary logics do not help Wittgenstein in any obvious way in this department, even though there are of course interesting connections between quantifiers and infinite conjunctions and disjunctions.

The really interesting presuppositions of Wittgenstein's procedure lie elsewhere. If (say) $a, b, c . . .$ were not all the objects there actually are, *or* if they did not all exist *necessarily, or* if they did not *necessarily* exhaust all the objects there *can* be, the equivalence

$$(*) \, (\exists x) f(x) \longleftrightarrow (f(a) \lor f(b) \lor f(c) \lor . . .)$$

would not be logically true. In brief, Wittgenstein's treatment of quantifiers depends crucially on his assumption that there is a unique set of objects, each of which exists necessarily and which collectively exhaust all the individuals that can possibly exist.

As Wittgenstein later put it, as reported by G. E. Moore,[26]

> In order to make clear exactly where the mistake lay, he [Wittgenstein] first said that in the case of such a universal proposition as 'Everybody in this room has a hat' (which I will call 'A'), he had known and actually

said in the *Tractatus*, that, even if Smith, Jones, and Robinson are the only people in the room, the logical product 'Smith has a hat, Jones has a hat and Robinson has a hat' cannot possibly be identical with A, because in order to get a proposition which entails A, you obviously have to add 'and Smith, Jones, and Robinson are the only people in the room'.

This diagnosis is not quite complete. Wittgenstein needs for the 'identity' he talks about also the assumption, 'Smith, Jones, and Robinson exist, and are all in the room.'

Moore does not make really clear in what way Wittgenstein's cozy little lecture room is doing duty for our whole big universe. For instance, it is not made clear that for the two propositions to be identical, the presence of Smith, Jones, and Robinson in the room has to be a logical necessity, and so has the impossibility that anybody else should be present. It can nevertheless be shown that for the entire world the assumptions that would vindicate the equivalence (*) are in effect made in the *Tractatus*. According to what Wittgenstein is presupposing there, if Smith, Jones, and Robinson exist and are simple objects, they are *necessarily* in the enormous room called the world, and if they should be the only objects there, they *necessarily* are the only objects in the world. In fact, it was argued above in chapter 3 that Wittgenstein makes these assumptions in the *Tractatus*. They constitute his thesis of the substantiality of objects.

But why should Wittgenstein have adopted a view as outrageous as this? He is in effect claiming it to be logically impossible that there should be fewer or more objects in the world than there in fact are. Why should Wittgenstein believe anything as strange as this? An answer is implicit in what was found above in chapter 3, secs. 9 and 13. It is the ineffability of the existence of particular objects discussed there that provides Wittgenstein with what he takes to be a justification of the assumptions on which we saw his treatment of quantifiers, exemplified by (*), as resting. For this ineffability, Wittgenstein thought, implies that we have to treat the existence of actually existing individuals as being a priori. Logic is a priori, he says. (Another formulation Wittgenstein uses is to say that logic is transcendental.) And logic in the sense relevant here is for him determined by the totality of objects.

Thus Wittgenstein took this a priori status of objects to mean that we have to treat each of the actually existing objects as existing necessarily, and to treat their totality as necessarily exhausting all the objects that can exist. Whatever possible states of affairs there could possibly be must consist of the same objects as the actual world. This is just what he asserts in 2.022–2.023 (quoted in chapter 3 above).

Hence Wittgenstein's 'transcendental' treatment of the existence of objects provides the foundation for his theory of quantifiers in the *Tractatus*. His theory of quantification stands or falls with the idea that we cannot say in language of a particular object that it exists.

Wittgenstein's later (1930–3) diagnosis of his 'mistake', as reported by G. E. Moore and quoted above, is highly interesting because it shows that he *never gave up his old mistake.* Wittgenstein's definitive objection to his earlier view is *not* the dependence of the identity (*) on the assumptions just mentioned, but the infinite (indefinite?) character of the second member of the equivalence. He thinks of the class of disjuncts in the second member as 'defined by grammar', i.e., determined logically, while the real criticism is precisely the opposite one, i.e., that it is not. This is shown by his arguments as reported by Moore:

> . . . if we are talking of 'individuals' in Russell's sense (in contradistinction to people in this room) . . ., the case is different, because, in that case, there is no proposition analogous to 'Smith, Jones and Robinson are the only people in the room'. The class of things in question, if we are talking of 'individuals', is . . ., in this case, determined not by a proposition but by our 'dictionary': it is 'defined by grammar'.

Here we thus have a striking example of the continuity of Wittgenstein's thought from the *Tractatus* to his later thought. Apparently Wittgenstein never fully recanted his real reason to think that quantified sentences are like long truth-functions. The only trouble he found with this idea later was, roughly speaking, that the disjunctions and conjunctions needed to accommodate quantifiers became infinite (or otherwise too long).

To sum up the main thrust of this chapter, we find it truly remarkable that the distinctive characteristics of the logic of the *Tractatus* – that is, those strange-looking views that separate Wittgenstein's early views on logic from the rest of the Frege–Russell tradition – can be understood as from the very same line of development which led Wittgenstein to his conception of the simple objects, as explained in the preceeding chapter. Both doctrines were outcomes of Wittgenstein's rejection of logical forms as independent objects of acquaintance together with his acceptance of the rest of Russell's theory of acquaintance. The different facets of the *Tractatus* have much more in common historically than first meets the eye.

NOTES

1 The unity of this tradition lies much more in the logical tools employed by its members than in any doctrinal continuity. The main ideas out of which these logico-linguistic tools have been forged will be discussed here.
2 Jean van Heijenoort, 'Logic as calculus and logic as language', *Synthese*, vol. 17 (1967), pp. 324–30.
3 See Jaakko Hintikka, 'Semantics: a revolt against Frege' in G. Flöistad, editor, *Contemporary Philosophy: A New Survey*, vol. 1, Martinus Nijhoff, The Hague, 1981, pp. 57–82; '"Is", semantical games, and semantical relativity', *Journal of Philosophical Logic*, vol. 8 (1979), pp. 433–68.
4 The best concise exposition of Frege's logical ideas is probably Montgomery Furth's Introduction to his translation of Frege's *Grundgesetze* (*The Basic Laws of Arithmetic*), University of California Press, Berkeley and Los Angeles 1967, pp. v–lxiii). Cf. also Jaakko Hintikka, 'Frege's hidden semantics', *Revue internationale de philosophie*, vol. 33 (1979), pp. 716–22.
5 Cf. the references in notes 2 and 4 above.
6 See note 2 above.
7 Cf. Jaakko Hintikka, note 3 above; Leila Haaparanta, 'On Frege's concept of being', in Simo Knuuttila and Jaakko Hintikka, editors, *The Logic of Being: Historical Studies*, D. Reidel, Dordrecht, 1986; Leila Haaparanta, *Frege's Doctrine of Being* (*Acta Philosophica Fennica*, vol. 39), Societas Philosophica Fennica, Helsinki, 1985.
8 In a review of an obscure logic book, published in the *Cambridge Review* on 6 March 1913, Wittgenstein lists as one of its author's mistakes that 'he confounds the copula "is" with the word "is" in expressing identity . . .' (See Eric Homberger et al., editors, *The Cambridge Mind*, Little, Brown, Boston, 1970 pp. 127–9.) According to Lee's notes (*Wittgenstein's Lectures, Cambridge 1930–1932*), Wittgenstein relied on the alleged ambiguity of 'is' during his early middle period. See p. 4, Lecture A II 1.
9 See note 2 above.
10 See note 3 above.
11 See note 7 above.
12 Concerning this 'theory', see Erik Stenius, *Wittgenstein's 'Tractatus'*, Basil Blackwell, Oxford, 1960; Jaakko Hintikka, *Logic, Language-Games and Information*, Clarendon Press, Oxford, 1973, chapter 2.
13 See Furth, note 4 above.
14 Pears and McGuinness translate Wittgenstein's words more cautiously and render 'daβ die "logischen Konstanten" nicht vertreten' by 'that the "logical constants" are not representatives'. This is unexceptional, but we are arguing that Wittgenstein's real purpose was to make a much stronger statement.
15 Wittgenstein's problems in this direction are illustrated by the fact that his own example in 5.47 (quoted above) is fallacious or, more charitably speaking, rests on certain assumptions which Wittgenstein makes in the *Tractatus* but which by hindsight are hard to defend. The equivalence of '*Fa*' and '($\exists x$). *Fx*. *x=a*' depends entirely on the tacit assumption that the term '*a*' is not empty. This assumption is in fact made in almost all well-known

formulations of quantification theory. However, this is little more than an historical accident. When the assumption is discarded, as is done in the so-called 'free logics' (see Jaakko Hintikka, 'Existential presuppositions and existential commitments', *Journal of Philosophy*, vol. 56 (1959), pp. 125–37; Hugues Leblanc and T. Hailperin, 'Non-designating singular terms', *Philosophical Review*, vol. 68 (1959), pp. 239–43), this equivalence becomes invalid. Hence Wittgenstein's own example tells against, not for, his claim. Ironically, even though Wittgenstein's example is thus useless for his avowed purpose of arguing that the logical operations of conjunction and existential quantification are already 'contained' in elementary propositions, it can be used for another purpose close to Wittgenstein's heart. This purpose is to argue that the notion of identity is dispensable. Even though Wittgenstein did not put it in quite this way, he could have said that this notion is already 'contained in' the other elementary propositions. His equivalence in 5.47 illustrates this, for it can be used (in an appropriately generalized form) as the one and only assumption that characterizes the notion of identity. See Jaakko Hintikka, *Distributive Normal Forms in the Calculus of Predicates* (*Acta Philosophica Fennica*, vol. 6), Helsinki, 1953, last chapter. Hence Wittgenstein is using an interesting observation for a wrong purpose.

16 See also *Notebooks 1914–1916*, p. 130, paragraph 1 of the letter dated 19 August 1919. Or witness 2.182: 'Every picture is *at the same time* a logical one.'

17 Max Black, *A Companion to Wittgenstein's 'Tractatus'*, Cornell University Press, Ithaca, N.Y., 1964, p. 220.

18 In an earlier paper, Jaakko Hintikka has argued (*Logic, Language-Games and Information*, Clarendon Press, Oxford, 1974, chapter 2) that if one seriously attempts to extend the picture view to all complex propositions (without the restrictive assumptions made in the *Tractatus*), sentences can no longer be construed as pictures. They have to be thought of as recipes for picture construction. In this extended sense, the picture idea is applicable to complex and not only to atomic propositions. This view is apparently foreign to the *Tractatus*, even though it makes a brief appearance in *Philosophical Remarks* (see II, sec. 10). Indeed, Wittgenstein would have had to revise his treatments of logical truth radically if he had adopted this recipe-idea in the *Tractatus*. For if all sentences are recipes for picture construction, rather than ready-made pictures, there is no longer any reason to think that the special status that some that them have (that of being logically true) can be immediately recognized from their syntactical form, even in principle. Logically true propositions could no longer be construed as their own proofs (cf. 6.1265); there could be surprises in logic (cf. 6.1261).

19 'The relation between Wittgenstein's picture theory of propositions and Russell's theories of judgment', *Philosophical Review*, vol. 86 (1977), pp. 177–96; reprinted in C. G. Luckhardt, editor, *Wittgenstein: Sources and Perspectives*, Cornell University Press, 1979, pp. 190–212.

20 It is also apparent from 4.466 that Wittgenstein thinks of complex propositions (truth-functions) as being built up out of simple signs in the same way as elementary propositions:

What corresponds to a determinate logical combination of signs is a determinate logical combination of their meanings. It is only to the uncombined signs that *absolutely any* combination corresponds.

In other words, propositions that are true for every situation cannot be combinations of signs at all . . .

21 Irving Copi, 'Objects, properties, and relations in the *Tractatus*', *Mind*, vol. 67 (1958), pp. 145–65.
22 Indeed, Wittgenstein makes the point we are attributing to him in 4.0311–4.0312.

One name stands for one thing, another for another thing, and they are combined with one another. In this way the whole group – like a *tableau vivant* – presents a state of affairs.

The possibility of propositions is based on the principle that objects have signs as their representatives.

23 This idea is reasserted by Wittgenstein as late as MS 109, p. 101: 'In a negative sentence, the picture (the plan) is used in a way different from a positive one, in that it is used to exclude, to hinder.'

The German reads: 'Im negativen Satz wird das Bild (der Plan) anders gebraucht, als im positiven, dadurch daß es ausschließend, hindernd gebraucht wird.'
24 See 'Wittgenstein's lectures in 1930–33', in G. E. Moore, *Philosophical Papers*, Allen & Unwin, London, 1959, pp. 252–324.
25 Cf., e.g., Carol Karp, *Language with Expressions of Infinite Length*, North-Holland, Amsterdam, 1964; H. J. Keisler, *Model Theory for Infinitary Logic*, North-Holland, Amsterdam, 1971.
26 MS 109, p. 297.

5

Some Remarks on (Wittgensteinian) Logical Form

1 THE CONCEPT OF LOGICAL FORM

In chapter 3 above it was argued that the objects postulated in Wittgenstein's *Tractatus* were Russellian objects of acquaintance, except that Wittgenstein tried to eliminate all complex objects of acquaintance as independent primitives and proposed to build, as it were, all their forms out of the forms of simple objects.[1] However, a major prima facie objection to this interpretation still remains to be discussed. This discussion will lead us to take up another main theme of the *Tractatus,* the concept of logical form.

The problem is this: It is often thought, and said, that a phenomenalistic or a phenomenological interpretation of the *Tractatus* is made impossible by the phenomenon of *colour incompatibility* and indeed by any other similar prima facie dependence between simple phenomenological predicates. On this view, 'red' and 'green' cannot refer to simple objects, for then the two elementary sentences 'this is red' and 'this is green' would not be independent, since they are mutually exclusive. This would contradict what Wittgenstein says in so many words in 2.062. ('From the existence or nonexistence of one state of affairs it is impossible to infer the existence or nonexistence of another.') Hence, it is claimed, phenomenological predicates like 'red' and 'green' cannot represent Tractarian objects. The best-known example of an argument of this kind occurs in the first few pages of G. E. M. Anscombe's book *An Introduction to Wittgenstein's Tractatus.*[2] Such arguments seem to be widely accepted.

Moreover, there are reasons why this objection is to be taken seriously other than its extensive circulation. It must be realized that the objection touches one of the most central ideas of the whole *Tractatus.* We might call it the idea of *logical form.* It makes an appearance here because logical dependencies between atomic propositions would violate Wittgenstein's important general principle that the only necessities are logical necessities. According to Wittgenstein, such logical necessities can always be seen from the logical form of the propositions in question. This logical form is displayed by the purely notational features of the sentence in a logically correct language. Wittgenstein formulates this idea (among other places) in 2.203:

A picture contains the possibility of the situation that it represents.

Or, as Wittgenstein puts a closely related point in 6.113:

It is the peculiar mark of logical propositions that one can recognize that they are true from the symbol alone, and this fact contains in itself the whole philosophy of logic.

The notion of logical form is one of the most important ideas of the *Tractatus*, as was aptly emphasized as early as 1923 by Frank Ramsey. One thing that is important about it is that it defines the aim of all philosophical analysis of particular concepts. What one has to do in such an analysis is to develop a notation for the concepts in question in such a way that all necessary connections between them become logical truths, ultimately truth-functional tautologies, which can be recognized from the purely notational features of our sentences.

The importance of this idea can be gauged from the fact that it puts in a new light Wittgenstein's comments on the pictorial character of language in the *Tractatus* discussed above in chapter 4. There we emphasized that for Wittgenstein a true elementary (atomic) sentence is a picture of the corresponding fact in a sense closely related to Tarski-type truth-conditions for such sentences.[3] Now we can see that there is a different sense in which a sentence reflects the logical form of reality.

In the former sense, the sense in which elementary sentences are compared to 'pictures' by Wittgenstein, an elementary sentence is a model of reality as it would have to be in order for the sentence to be true. It depicts one particular configuration of objects by displaying an analogous configuration of names. As Wittgenstein expresses this in 2.15:

The fact that the elements of a picture are related to one another in a determinate way represents that things are related to one another in the same way.

In this latter sense, the sense in which sentences represent the form of the world, a sentence reflects the logical form of reality in that all the *possible* combinations of its constituent symbols represent *possible* complexes of the corresponding entities in reality, and vice versa, i.e., every possible configuration of these entities must be matched by some possible (correctly formed) combination of symbols. The notion of logical form is therefore in a sense a *modal* notion. This is illustrated in the *Tractatus* by such propositions as the following:

> 2.151   Pictorial form is the *possibility* that things are related to one another in the same way as the elements of the picture. [Emphasis added.]

Propositions 2.18–2.181 show the connection between 2.151 and the following propositions:

> 2.202   A picture represents a possible situation in logical space.
>
> 2.203   A picture contains the possibility of the situation that it represents.
>
> 3.4   A proposition determines a place in logical space . . .
>
> 3.411   In geometry and logic alike a place is a possibility: something can exist in it.

The requirement that the combinatorial possibilities of names must match the totality of potential configurations of their objects imposes important restraints on the correct symbolism (correct language). It is illustrated by such sections of the *Tractatus* as the following:

> 2.18   What any picture, of whatever form, must have in common with reality, in order to be able to depict it – correctly or incorrectly – in any way at all, is logical form, i.e. the form of reality.
>
> 4.121   Propositions *show* the logical form of reality. They display it.
>
> 4.1211   Thus one proposition '*fa*' shows that the object *a* occurs in its sense, two propositions '*fa*' and '*ga*' show that the same object is mentioned in both of them.
> If two propositions contradict one another, then their structure shows it; the same is true if one of them follows from the other. And so on.

2 PICTURING VS. MIRRORING

This idea that the structural properties of language must reflect the structural properties of the world is the basis of Wittgenstein's notion of *internal property,* developed primarily in 4.122–4.128. It is often assimilated to Wittgenstein's 'picture theory of language'. The two ideas are nevertheless different, and should be distinguished sharply from each other. The distinction is also marked quite clearly by Wittgenstein terminologically. He restricts the term 'picture' (*Bild*) to the sense in which sentences are isomorphic replicas of possible states of affairs. He is in fact remarkably consistent in this usage. In contrast, when he speaks of the way the logical form of a sentence matches the internal form of reality, he uses such terms as 'mirrors' (*spiegelt*) or 'shows' (*zeigt*), as in 4.121, or 'displays' (*weist . . . auf*), as in 2.172. Hence it can only lead to confusion to refer to this idea of logical form by speaking of picturing or picture theory. In order to mark the distinction terminologically, we shall speak of *mirroring* rather than *picturing* in connection with the idea that the totality of admissible combinations of names reflects the totality of possible combinations of their objects in reality. This seems to be in keeping with Wittgenstein's terminology.

In order to appreciate the difference between picturing and mirroring, it may be helpful to recall that the narrower picturing idea is essentially what underlies the first clause in a Tarski-type recursive truth-definition, viz. the truth-clause for atomic sentences. (See chapter 4, sec. 3, above.) For such a truth-clause, of course, it does not matter whether the totality of admissible atomic sentences and their combinations matches the totality of possible configurations of the individuals and their predicates in reality. Later philosophers have discussed the question whether the admissible combinations of atomic propositions ought to be restrained in some cases by means of certain 'meaning postulates'. Resorting to such restraints would amount to a failure of one's notation to reflect fully the logical form of reality. Wittgenstein in effect rules them out in 5.473 by writing, 'Whatever is possible in logic is also permitted.' Now no one has taken the discussion of meaning postulates to be relevant to the correctness of Tarski-type truth-definitions, i.e., to the picture idea in its narrower sense. By the same token, the picture idea in its strict Tractarian sense can be unproblematically true even when the mirroring requirement is not satisfied.

To be explicit, we must nevertheless point out that the picturing idea and the mirroring idea are to some extent interdependent. The mirroring idea makes no sense without the picturing idea, for what it says is that each admissible combination of names pictures (*not* 'mirrors'!) a state of affairs which obtains in some possible world (and vice versa). In that possible world, this combination of names would be a true sentence. Hence mirroring presupposes picturing.

Conversely, suppose that we agree that a true sentence pictures a state of affairs in the sense that its structure (as a combination of names) matches the structure of the corresponding objects (the ones its constituent names stand for) in the world. To be able to speak of this structure presupposes that we know how the sentence is to be parsed, that is, which parts can vary independently of which others. As Wittgenstein puts it, 'form is the possibility of structure' (2.033), *form* being the modal idea that governs the way an object can occur in different configurations. (Cf. 2.0141.) Ultimately, this means for Wittgenstein that we know the structure of a sentence only if we know what the names are of which it consists and what their respective logical forms are. (Our point here should be compared with Wittgenstein's description of how the logical form of a sentence is uncovered by replacing names by variables; see 3.315.) But knowing this makes little sense unless the replacement of a name in the sentence by another one results in a new sentence which pictures another (possible) state of affairs, obtained by the analogous change in the objects named. In other words, the viability of the picturing idea presupposes some amount of mirroring. (This dependence is in effect asserted by Wittgenstein in 2.22.) That is, it presupposes that *some* of the admissible combinations of names represent *some* of the possible configurations of objects. To this extent, the picture idea and the mirror idea go together. However, there is nothing in the picture idea that implies that the mirroring relation has to be *complete*, i.e., that *every* admissible concatenation of names has to match a possible state of affairs, and vice versa. In this sense, the picture idea can be valid even though the perfect language postulated by the mirror idea has not been reached.

This independence of the picture idea from the mirror idea is significant, for it is only from the mirroring assumption that Wittgenstein obtains some of his most sweeping theses in the *Tractatus*. They include the claim that the logical form is the form of reality (2.18, 4.121), that all logical propositions ('logical truths') can be recognized from the symbolism alone (6.113), that we cannot think of anything illogical (3.03, cf. also 5.473), etc. All these theses become suspect as soon as the completeness of the mirroring relation is given up, even though such a step will not affect the picturing idea at all.

The distinction between picturing and mirroring is not without important further consequences. For instance, it has been claimed that Wittgenstein's picture theory was independent of the meta-physical absolutism and atomism of the *Tractatus*.[4] This claim is correct, if picture theory is understood in the same way as we have done. If it extended to include what we have called the mirroring idea, the claim is entirely false.

Another difference between the ideas of picturing and mirroring is that the latter notion, but not the former, can be applied to names. A name is not in any sense a picture of its object, according to Wittgenstein. However, a name can mirror its object in the sense that the possibilities of the name's being combined with other names match the possibilities of its objects being combined with the corresponding objects.[5]

In the jargon of the *Tractatus*, we might say that picturing in the proper Wittgensteinian sense is a relation between a *true* sentence and a *subsistent* (*bestehend*) state of affairs. Strictly speaking, it is therefore a solecism to speak of a picture theory of *language* in the *Tractatus*. What we might find there is a picture theory of *truth*. (Of course, it could not have been a *theory* for Wittgenstein, but we are letting that point pass here.) As far as *language* is concerned, one should speak of *mirroring* or *reflecting* rather than of *picturing*. What is being mirrored by our sentences are not states of affairs, either, but the logical form of the world. (Cf. 4.121.) And the mirroring is done by the logical form of a sentence, not by the sentence as a picture. Hence it would be much more appropriate to speak of the *mirror theory of language* than of a picture theory of language. Perhaps even more appropriately one might speak of the mirror theory of the logic of a correct language. The contrast we are describing can be epitomized by saying that in the *Tractatus* the sentences of a logically correct language are *pictures* of possible facts while its logic is a *mirror-image* (*Spiegelbild*) of reality.

Here we can see clearly how tempting it is to include the mirroring idea in the alleged Wittgensteinian 'picture theory of language' and even to give it pride of place there. We registered this temptation above in chapter 4, sec. 5. We can now see that the exhaustiveness assumption (ii) which was mentioned there and which is codified in the mirroring idea is closely related to other important Wittgensteinian ideas, especially to that of logical form.

Thus the problem of colour incompatibility is not just an interesting interpretational puzzle in its own right, but is an essential part of the much wider problem of understanding Wittgenstein's ideas of logical form and of logic as mirroring the world. This problem threatens to force Wittgenstein to introduce in effect such 'meaning postulates' as are ruled out by his ideas of mirroring and logical form.

3 TRACTARIAN OBJECTS AND THE PROBLEM OF COLOR INCOMPATIBILITY

The problem posed by the phenomenon of colour incompatibility is nevertheless solvable. Arguments of the general type instantiated by Anscombe depend, no matter how their details are formulated, on an important presupposition which is not accepted by Wittgenstein. It is assumed in these arguments that, if *red* and *green* are objects, we know what their logical type must be. The objection assumes, in effect, not only that the natural-language propositions 'This patch is red' and (pointing to the same patch) 'This patch is green' are incompatible, but also that they are subject–predicate propositions, to be represented in the correct notation as something like '*R(a)*' and '*G(a)*'. The problem that ensues lies in the fact that although the two propositions are incompatible, this incompatibility is not logical in the sense of being shown by the notation used. In particular, the incompatibility in question does not reduce to a truth-functional contradiction. A contradiction for Wittgenstein is a precisely defined notion of truth-function theory (see 4.46), which lends a sharp edge to his claim that colour incompatibilities can be thought of as such contradictions. This is shown by 6.3751:

> For example, the simultaneous presence of two colours at the same place in the visual field is impossible, in fact logically impossible, since it is ruled out by the logical structure of colour . . .

> (It is clear that the logical product of two elementary propositions can neither be a tautology nor a contradiction. The statement that a point in the visual field has two different colours at the same time is a contradiction.)

What directly follows from this (cf. 6.375) is nevertheless not a corollary concerning the status of colours as purported objects, but a corollary concerning the status of colour attributions: they are not of the simple subject–predicate form. Thus it seems to us that Anscombe is foisting on the philosophers she is criticizing an assumption which they do not have to make and which is in fact mistaken. There is no reason to think that Wittgenstein ever thought of colour attributions of the form 'this is red' as being of the subject–predicate form. Here the warnings Wittgenstein issued at the end of the second paragraph of 'Some Remarks on Logical Form' are especially timely. He speaks there of how 'ever so many different logical forms' are projected (translated) 'in ever so many different ways' into ordinary language with its characteristic 'norms'. 'And for this very reason we can draw no conclusions . . . from the use of these norms as to the actual logical form of the phenomena described. Such forms as "This paper is boring", "The weather is fine", "I am lazy", which have nothing whatever in common with one another, present themselves as subject–predicte propositions, i.e. apparently as propositions of the same form.' Wittgenstein clearly could have added 'This patch is red' to his list.

Much of the force of Anscombe's argument is thus lost when we notice its dependence on her attribution to her opponents of an assumption concerning the logical form of colour ascriptions. For on alternative assumptions the situation is quite different. For instance, we may assume, as a thought-experiment, that the general concept of colour is to be represented in language, not by a class of colour-predicates, but by a function c which maps points in visual space into a colour space. Then the respective logical forms of 'this patch is red' and 'this patch is green' would be $c(a) = r$ and $c(a) = g$, where r and g are the two separate objects *red* and *green*, respectively. The logical incompatibility of the two colour ascriptions would then be reflected by the fact that the colours *red* and *green* are represented by different names. And if so, the two propositions are *logically* incompatible after all. Their incompatibility is shown by their logical representation in the usual logical notation: a function cannot have two different values for the same argument because of its 'logical form', i.e., because of its logical type. That attributions of different perceptual qualities are intrinsically single-valued, i.e., represented logically speaking by genuine functions, is in fact forcefully asserted by Wittgenstein in 2.0131, quoted below.

Our observations thus put in a new light the question whether colour incompatibility violates Wittgenstein's idea that the only necessities are purely logical necessities. The answer to this question depends on what we take the logical form of colour concepts to be, in other words, what we take to be the right notation for colour concepts. If each individual colour is represented by a one-place predicate, we obtain necessities that are not logical; if we construe the general concept of colour as a mapping of points into a colour-space,[6] colour incompatibilities do not create nonlogical necessities (according to our usual conception of logic). G. E. M. Anscombe in effect assumes that the people she is criticizing have to opt for the former alternative. This alternative is certainly foreign to Wittgenstein, however, as is shown inter alia by his lifelong preoccupation with the space of colours. (Cf., e.g., *Philosophical Remarks*, XXI, sec. 221.) One simply cannot do justice to this idea of colour-space by treating particular colour-words as primitive predicates, quite independently of the problem of colour incompatibility.

Did Wittgenstein actually construe colour discourse in the way our thought-experiment prescribes? From an ahistoric, systematic viewpoint it looks as if Wittgenstein were committed to such a construal of the general concept of colour and of the individual colour terms by his frequent references to the *space* of colours. For if colours form a space, the attribution of some particular colour to an object does not mean merely to ascribe an unanalysable one-place predicate to it. One also has to indicate the location of this colour in colour-space in order to bring out the logical complexity of the colour attribution. But this in effect means for a contemporary logician that colour attributions amount to a mapping of such objects as can be coloured into the colour-space. Hence it is not misleading to discuss Wittgenstein's views by reference to the mapping idea.

Yet the historical truth seems to be that Wittgenstein never spelled out the mapping construal of colours. We do not know for sure why he failed to do so. He may have been uncomfortable with functions as primitive objects, for the logical laws holding of them are not as easily thought of as being reducible to tautologies as most other analytic truths. Be this as it may, the most we can claim here is that the construal of colour as a function mapping points in visual space into the colour-space is in keeping with the spirit of Wittgenstein's thinking, even though it may very well turn out that he never assented to it verbally.

4 AN ANALOGY BETWEEN SPATIAL AND COLOUR CONCEPTS

Something close to our mapping idea is also suggested by the analogy of spatial concepts and colour concepts which Wittgenstein relies on in the *Tractatus*. This analogy plays an important role in Wittgenstein's discussion of colours in the *Tractatus*. One reason for its importance is that the same incompatibility problem as is exhibited by colour concepts is also posed to us by spatial concepts. For instance, one and the same spot of colour cannot be located in two different parts of space. Wittgenstein does not see any problem in such spatial incompatibility, however. He obviously thinks that by using a suitable spatial notation such incompatibilities can be accounted for. As he puts it, space is a form of spatial objects. For instance, in 2.0251 we read:

Space [and] time . . . are forms of objects.

Hence spatial relations can be pictured by suitable spatial relations:

2.171   A picture can depict any reality whose form it has. A spatial picture can depict anything spatial, a coloured one anything coloured, etc.

Now Wittgenstein clearly thinks that he can treat colours on a par with space and time. In fact, the last but one quote runs in its entirety as follows:

2.0251   Space, time and colour (being coloured) are forms of objects.

The parallelism of 2.171 and 2.0251 shows how Wittgenstein thought that he could solve the problem of colour incompatibility by treating colours in the same way as spatial concepts. He thought that it is possible to devise a notation which reflects the necessary inter-relations of colour concepts and thereby to show how the appropriate structures (forms) are built into the objects we are dealing with in colour attributions.

That this is the general direction of Wittgenstein's thought is shown by 6.3751, the one section of the *Tractatus* where Wittgenstein comes closest to facing squarely the problem of colour incompatibility. The first paragraph presents the problem:

For example, the simultaneous presence of two colours at the same place in the visual field is impossible, in fact logically impossible, since it is ruled out by the logical structure of colour.

The second paragraph shows how Wittgenstein thinks the problem can be solved:

Let us think how this contradiction appears in physics: more or less as follows – a particle cannot have two velocities at the same time; that is to say, it cannot be in two places at the same time; that is to say, particles that are in different places at the same time cannot be identical.

Here Wittgenstein's reference to 'this contradiction' (*dieser Wider-spruch*) cannot mean colour incompatibility, but the much more general problem of apparent incompatibilities between the atomic proposition of a notation, which in physics can be attributions of a velocity, or of a location in space, to a point mass. In other words, the middle paragraph of 6.3751 is not an explanation of the *physical basis* of colour incompatibility, as many interpreters have taken it to be.[7] Instead, it presents (Wittgenstein thinks) a solvable *analogue* to the problem from the field of particle mechanics. Wittgenstein in effect assumes that the incompatibility problem can be solved in the case of particle mechanics by the simple expedient of a suitable kinematic notation, and claims that an analogous solution is possible in the case of colours.[8] Admittedly, it is not indicated by him how this is done, but at least we an see what it is that Wittgenstein thinks can be done here.

Wittgenstein discusses the same subject matter somewhat more fully in *Notebooks 1914–1916* on 16 August 1916:

> A point cannot be red and green at the same time: at first sight there seems no need for this to be a logical impossibility. But the very language of physics reduces it to a kinetic impossibility. We see that there is a difference of structure between red and green.
>
> And then physics arranges them in a series. And then we see how here the true structure of the objects is brought to light.
>
> The fact that a particle cannot be in two places at the same time does look more like a logical impossibility.
>
> If we ask why, for example, then straight away comes the thought: Well, we should call particles that were in two places different, and this in turn all seems to follow from the structure of space and of particles.

Here essentially the same point as was in 6.3751 apparently given as an *explanation* of colour incompatibility (cf. '*this* contradiction') is presented as an *object of comparison* ('does look more like'), thus verifying our surmise concerning the status of the middle paragraph of 6.3751. In the first paragraph of the *Notebooks* passage, Wittgenstein admittedly refers to the physical nature of colour. But it is not clear that the analysis of colour Wittgenstein has in mind is an analysis of the physical constitution of colour, e.g., as electromagnetic radiation of a certain frequency. In the light of Wittgenstein's later self-criticism, it seems likeliest that what he means is a phenomenological analysis which lies 'midway between science and logic' (*Remarks on Colour,* II, sec. 3) and which he later rejected. This is strongly suggested by the fact that Wittgenstein's concern is merely the '*language* of physics'. The quoted *Notebooks* entry thus strengthens our interpretation further.

The importance of the parallelism between colour and space is also in evidence in Wittgenstein's later writings. In them, logical connections between geometrical concepts are compared to the theorems of geometry. Wittgenstein even speaks of 'colour geometry'.[9]

If the gist of Wittgenstein's treatment of colour incompatibility is an analogy between colour and space, why did Wittgenstein not tell us that this is how he proposed to solve the problem? Why did he not tell us what the logical structure of colour concepts really is? The answer is that according to Wittgenstein it cannot be told a priori. As we saw earlier, by *form* Wittgenstein means something that a suitable logical notation can bring out. For instance, the difference between a one-place predicate and a two-place predicate is a difference in form. Now such differences in form cannot be anticipated a priori, Wittgenstein argues in 5.55–5.5542 (cf. also 4.1274). Especially clear is Wittgenstein's statement in 5.555:

> It is clear that we have a concept of an elementary proposition *apart from its particular logical form.* [Emphasis added.]

Hence the question of the correct form (representation) of colour propositions must be left to be gathered from our use of colour concepts (cf. 4.002, 4.011). No wonder, therefore, that Wittgenstein did not feel called upon to explain it to us.[10]

5 THE LOGICAL FORM OF COLOUR ASCRIPTIONS

Certain objections can be made to what has been said. First, the analysis of the concept of colour which turns it into a function from points in space to colours does not do the whole job. It presents to us an analysis of colour concepts which turns colour incompatibilities into logical truths in the conventional sense of truths that can be seen from the mere notation. But this conventional sense need not be Wittgenstein's. In particular, it is hard to see how this notation could transform colour incompatibilities into truth-functional contradictions in Wittgenstein's precise sense.

This objection is well taken, but it does not cut much ice. It is admittedly hard to see how precisely Wittgenstein could have tried to transform colour incompatibilities into the truth-functional contradictions of the *Tractatus*. This was Wittgenstein's problem at the time, however, not ours. It is not very hard to argue that Wittgenstein believed that the missing transformation could somehow be carried out within a language of pure experience. All we need to explain here is how Wittgenstein might have thought that he could reconcile the status of colours as objects with the mutual independence of atomic propositions. The analysis we mentioned is enough to show that such an explanation can in principle be quite straightforward.

The difficulty of reducing logical truths of relational logic to truth-functional tautologies need not be insuperable, either, in Wittgenstein's view. This is shown by the observations made above in chapter 4. There it was pointed out that truth-functional dependencies did not constitute for Wittgenstein the rock bottom layer of logical relationships. This role he assigned to the 'logic' of combinations of objects and of their 'pictorial' representation in language. Hence the analysis of colour as a mapping from points into a colour-space does not, according to Wittgenstein's ultimate views in the *Tractatus*, need any particular reduction to a truth-functional form. What is needed is the general reduction of all logical forms to the forms of simple objects. Here we have in fact an example of the tension in the *Tractatus* between logic in the ordinary sense (requirement of tautologicity) and Wittgenstein's phenomeno-logic, i.e., the idea that all logical forms are built up from the forms of simple objects of acquaintance.

A second objection is that Wittgenstein's ontology in the *Tractatus* did not include functions (as distinguished from properties and relations) as primitives, insofar as we can lift the self-imposed veil of silence which Wittgenstein maintains. This was probably due to his treatment of identity in the *Tractatus*, which made it awkward for him to characterize functions in the usual way as relations for which the last *relatum* is uniquely determined by the choice of the other terms. This objection is likewise well taken, but the difficulty it points out is again Wittgenstein's rather than ours.

But what *was* the logical form of colours according to Wittgenstein? It is in any case clear that Wittgenstein is adamant that colour ascriptions are not of the subject–predicate form:

> When Frege and Russell spoke of objects they always had in mind things that are, in language, represented by nouns, that is to say bodies like chairs and tables. The whole conception of objects is hence very closely connected with the subject–predicate form of propositions. It is clear that where there is no subject–predicate form it is also impossible to speak of objects in this sense. Now I can describe this room in an entirely different way, e.g. by describing the surface of the room analytically by means of an equation and stating the distribution of colours on this surface.[11]

Here we can have a glimpse of how Wittgenstein thought we can then colour incompatibilities into logical impossibilities. If the equation he mentions is one which specifies the colour of the different points of the surface, then his solution is to all practical purposes the one we have suggested earlier in this section.

The same point is made by Wittgenstein also in *Ludwig Wittgenstein and the Vienna Circle*, pp. 74–5.

Wittgenstein thus came close to the functional analysis of colour that we have outlined. We are tempted to say that it expresses what Wittgenstein really meant but that his preferred modes on conceptualization were different. They were much closer to home – 'home-baked' was one of his favourite words – than the abstract construal of the general concept of colour as amounting to a mapping from visual space to a colour-space. For this reason, Wittgenstein approached the functional analysis as an explicit doctrine only at the very end of his quest of the logical form of colour attributions, and never accepted it as an explicit thesis.

In any case, the last word must be left to Wittgenstein. He describes the development of his own views on colour incompatibility in MS 112, pp. 249–53, dated 26 November 1931. The line of thought he discusses there is also in evidence in 'Some Remarks on Logical Form' and in MS 105, pp. 82–90 (even numbered pages). Even though Wittgenstein is not always a completely reliable witness concerning his own earlier views, we have to take his words very seriously. On p. 251 he writes:

> When I wrote the *Tractatus* (and even later) I believed that fa = fa. ~fb [i.e., a logical incompatibility between ascriptions of different colours to the same thing] would be possible only if fa were a logical product of another sentence and ~fb – hence fa = p. ~fb – and I was of the opinion that fa [i.e. a colour ascription] could be split up into such a [logical] product. At the time I did not have any clear idea of how I thought that such an analysis could be found. Or, rather: I thought of constructing a notation, which would serve to express the right grammatical use in every context through its nature (i.e., its rules would be very simply formulated and would in a certain sense already carry in themselves [this use], as any perspicuous notation would do); but I forgot that, if this reformulation of the sentence f(a) were to consist in its being replaced by a logical product, then the factors of this product must have an independent sense already known to us.[12]

Whatever there is to be said of this self-description, one thing is totally clear. *Wittgenstein's attempted explanation of colour incompatibilities in the* Tractatus *is compatible with a phenomenological interpretation of his basic language* in that work, and in fact supports it. For in the analysis of fa that Wittgenstein mentions, ~fb occurs as one of the conjuncts. Hence the phenomenological quality *the absence of b* (and, by the same token, the experiential property of lacking any one given colour) survives Wittgenstein's analysis in spite of its phenomenological nature. Moreover, Wittgenstein's dissatisfaction with the sense of the unknown conjunct p is due to its not being *bekannt*, which most likely means its not being given in acquaintance. In general, one looks in vain for any non-phenomenological objects in Wittgenstein's proposed analysis.

Even more clearly, Wittgenstein is not relying on any physical analysis of colour in terms of electromagnetic waves (or whatever), confirming our conclusion in sec. 4 above.

These observations are supported in addition by Wittgenstein's descriptions of his further development. First, he says that in carrying out the *Tractatus* approach he was led to construe the analysed form of a colour ascription as a conjunction which expresses which colours are partly present in a given location, to be followed of course by a statement saying that they are all the ingredients of the given colour. All such component statements are fully as phenomenological as the unanalysed colour ascription. But even this does not give the right 'grammar' either. Why? In MS 112, pp. 253–3 Wittgenstein writes:

> But this does not give the right grammar: the presence of a red tinge without any other tinge should mean that this location has a pure red colour. That seems to us nonsense, and the mistake can be cleared up as follows: It must lie in the grammar of this red tinge that it comes in degrees; a reddish blue can be closer or less close to the pure red and hence, in this sense, contain more or less red. The proposition which specifies that red is present here as an ingredient of a colour should therefore *specify* somehow a quantity of red; but then this proposition must have a sense also outside the logical product, and it must hence make sense to say that this location is coloured pure red and *contains* such-and-such quantity of red, and this makes no sense.[13]

Wittgenstein plays here with the idea of interpreting colour attributions as assignments of a certain degree or intensity of colour to an object. This idea occurs as early as in 'Some Remarks on Logical Form'. It makes positive colour attributions compatible with each other, for 'red is present to degree q_1', in brief q_1r, and 'red is present to degree q_2', in short q_2r, can be both true even when $q_1 \neq q_2$, as long as as there is no tacit qualifier 'only' lurking in these statements. (Just as, Wittgenstein says, 'there are 4 apples in this basket' and 'there are 3 apples in this basket' can both be true.) This does not make basic colour attributes logically independent, however, for if $q_2 \geq q_1$, q_2r implies q_1r. Hence Wittgenstein in the end gives up the quest for logical independence of what he once would have called atomic propositions, without putting forward any definitive doctrine. Thus Wittgenstein's search for the definitive logical form of colour ascriptions literally ends in a failure here.

It also appears from Wittgenstein's later remarks on colour that even his 1931 views could not in any case satisfy him in the long run. Perhaps a pure colour can be described by specifying the degrees of basic colours in it, but that does not do justice to such things as impure colours, transparent vs. opaque colours, etc., commented on extensively by Wittgenstein in his *Remarks on Colour*. As Wittgenstein puts a part of his programme in MS 105, p. 88:

The right representation of colour does not only have to show that when a is red, it cannot also be green, but all the internal properties must show up which we know when we know the colours. Hence everything which pertains to the kinship of particular colours to each other and their relation to black and white.[14]

It seems to us that such aims of the latter-day Wittgenstein would have been served better by an analysis of colour as a mapping from visual space to a colour-space than by the degrees-of-intensity analysis Wittgenstein once attempted. In general, the conceptual problems Wittgenstein raises concerning colours are naturally construed as questions concerning the structure of the colour-space into which coloured objects are mapped in colour attributions. This is the underlying reason why many of Wittgenstein's remarks are suggestive of our analysis, even though he seems never to have embraced it in so many words.

Another important change took place during Wittgenstein's early middle period concerning colour attributions and indeed atomic propositions in general. From Waismann's notes we see how Wittgenstein gave up the idea that atomic propositions are compared with facts one by one and opted for a 'holistic' view according to which entire *systems of propositions* are compared with the reality.[15] Wittgenstein's reported words show that he was pushed to this conclusion precisely by the problem of colour incompatibility:

Once I wrote: 'A proposition is laid against reality like a ruler. Only the end-points of the graduation lines actually touch the object that is to be measured.' I now prefer to say that *a system of propositions* is laid against reality like a ruler. What I mean by this is the following: If I lay a ruler against a spatial object, I lay *all the graduation lines* against it at the same time. It is not the individual graduation lines that are laid against it, but the entire scale. The statements describing for me the length of an object form a system of propositions. Now it is such an entire system of propositions that is compared with reality, not a single proposition. If I say, for example, that this or that point in the visual field is *blue*, then I know not merely that but also that this point is not green, not red, not yellow, etc. I have laid the entire colour-scale against it at one go. This is also the reason why a point cannot have different colours at the same time. For when I lay a *system* of propositions against reality, this means that in each case there is only *one* state of affairs that can exist, not several – just as in the spatial case.

We shall return to this matter from a different perspective in chapter 8, sec. 6. Here we only note that the quotation vividly shows that a large part of the difficulties which confront us in trying to make coherent sense of Wittgenstein's views of colours in the *Tractatus* is an intrinsic difficulty in Wittgenstein's views, not an interpreter's problem. It is no wonder that we could not come up with an explicit detailed notation which would vindicate the logical independence of colour attributions in the teeth of his other theses, for when Wittgenstein tried to produce one himself, he failed in the end. For the earlier quotations from MS 112 show that he soon found fault with the details of the account he had offered earlier but that he could not produce a completely satisfactory corrected account later, either. Without false modesty we therefore suggest that our functional analysis of colour would have solved Wittgenstein's problem in Wittgenstein's own spirit, while admitting that this analysis apparently cannot be pinned on him as an overt tenet.

At the same time, Wittgenstein's difficulties with the colour incompatability problem illustrate the phenomenological issues which we mentioned in chapter 3, sec. 16, and which caused him not to try to specify the precise phenomenological nature of his simple objects in the *Tractatus*.

6 THE ABSOLUTENESS OF VISUAL SPACE

A few supplementary remarks may help to round out our discussion. Wittgenstein's procedure of packing the logical structure of such notions as space, time, and colour into the forms of particular objects may seem to be wrong-headed already in the case of space. If we are right – and if Wittgenstein was right in his explanations to Desmond Lee in 1930–1[16] – space means here essentially *visual* space. But how can a point in visual space possibly have a form of its own? And how can such a point be one particular entity with an identity of its own? How is it distinguished from all the other points of my visual space? Wittgenstein raises this question in so many words in *Philosophical Remarks*, XX, sec. 206:

> Whether it makes sense to say 'This part of a red patch (which isn't demarcated by any visible boundary) is red' depends on whether there is absolute position. For if we can speak of an absolute location in visual space, I can then also ascribe a colour to this absolute location even if its surroundings are the same colour.

This problem is obviously part and parcel of the difficulties which beset Wittgenstein's quest for the true phenomenological simples in the *Tractatus* and which were mentioned at the end of chapter 3 above. Wittgenstein continued his work on these problems well after the *Tractatus*. In *Philosophical Remarks*, Wittgenstein is still wrestling with them (see XX, sec. 205):

> Can we say a patch is simpler than a larger one?
> Let's suppose they are uniformly coloured circles: what is supposed to constitute the greater simplicity of the smaller circle? . . .
> And so it seems to me that the smaller patch is not simpler than the larger one.

> It seems as if it is impossible to see a uniformly coloured patch as composite, unless you imagine it as *not* uniformly coloured. The image of the dissecting line gives the patch more than one colour, since the dissecting line must have a different colour from the rest of the patch.

One crucial question here is whether individual points in visual space have a reality of their own independently of their qualities and their relations to other points in a visual space. For instance, can a point in the middle of a uniformly coloured patch have an independent existence as a 'simple', i.e., as an ultimate ingredient of one's visual space? Wittgenstein opts for an affirmative answer (ibid., sec. 206):

> It's obviously possible to establish the identity of a position in the visual field, since we would otherwise be unable to distinguish whether a patch always stays in the same place or whether it changes its place.

This view is called by Wittgenstein the *absoluteness* of visual space. It is precisely what he needs in order to defend the idea that points in a visual space have a logical form and hence can be Tractarian objects. It also suggests a reason why Wittgenstein did not let the problems he worried about in the *Notebooks 1914–1916* deter him from considering points in a visual space as examples of simple objects in the *Tractatus*.

Wittgenstein defends the absoluteness of visual space at length in *Philosophical Remarks*, XX, sec. 206.[17] The details of Wittgenstein's discussion do not matter here. What is crucial is the aim of Wittgenstein's attempt. He formulates his own point by saying that 'in the visual space there is absolute position' (ibid.). Likewise he asserts in MS 112, p. 241 (25 November 1931) that we can speak of points in a visual space in an absolute sense. This absoluteness of the visual space with its locations is what enables us to individuate its several points.

Even though Wittgenstein never solved to his own satisfaction the problem of colour representation (of the logical form of colour ascriptions), he did thus solve, at least for his own benefit, the problem of the simple constituents of the visual space. Yet this solution, such as it was, came more than ten years after he had finished the *Tractatus,* and hence could not alleviate the intellectual discomfort which led Wittgenstein to gloss over the problem of phenomenological simples in the *Tractatus.*

7 WITTGENSTEIN VS. RUSSELL ON SIMPLES

We have relied heavily in our discussion on the idea that each simple object has a logical form. This idea can be challenged, if only prima facie. For, it may be asked, how can *simples* like objects have forms? It is true that Wittgenstein labels the objects of the *Tractatus* 'simples'. Indeed, this attribute of objects is closely related to the ineffability of their existence. However, this objection can be met. It was shown above in chapter 2 that the Wittgensteinian notion of simplicity did not exclude the possibility that a simple object can be said to have a form.[18] This result is all the more remarkable because the same cannot be said without qualifications of Russellian objects of acquaintance, e.g., sense-data. According to David Pears,[19] Russell failed 'to maintain a strict distinction between a sense-datum treated as a bare particular in abstraction from whatever properties and relations it may possess and a sense-datum treated as a complex object which includes its properties and relations'. Pears also registers a tendency in Russell to consider sense-data as formless 'bare particulars'. In this chapter, we have been emphasizing the connections and similarities between the objects of the *Tractatus* and Russell's objects of acquaintance. The time has now come to point out also a major discrepancy between Wittgenstein's simple objects and at least one important class of entities we can be acquainted with according to Russell, viz. sense-data. As was shown in chapter 2 above, even the simplest Wittgensteinian objects are fully structured. They are therefore radically different from such 'bare particulars' as Russell's sense-data were sometimes taken to be by their postulator.

This does not invalidate the link we have found between Wittgenstein and Russell. Admittedly, this difference between Russell and Wittgenstein survived Russell's theories of knowledge by acquaintance. Russell tended to consider a sense-datum, no matter of what vintage, simply as the unanalysable, bare bearer of certain perceptual properties. But this difference is explainable in developmental terms. In the historical perspective sketched in chapter 3 above, Wittgenstein's objects are as much heirs of *complex* objects of acquaintance in Russell as of his simples. By definition, such objects can have structure, and (being forms of *complex* propositions) can introduce dependencies between different propositions.

NOTES

1 The development of Wittgenstein's position in the *Tractatus* from Russell's position in his 1913 book *Theory of Knowledge* was analysed above in chapter 3. Our discussion is based on earlier work by David Pears summarized in 'The relation between Wittgenstein's picture theory of propositions and Russell's theories of judgment', *Philosophical Review* vol. 86 (1977), pp. 177–96. Cf. also David Pears, 'The emergence of Wittgenstein's logical atomism', in E. Morscher and R. Stranzinger, editors, *Ethics, Proceedings of the Fifth International Wittgenstein Symposium*, Hölder-Pichler-Tempsky, Vienna, 1981, pp. 448–54.

2 Hutchinson, London, 1959, pp. 25–8.

3 See above, chapter 4, sec. 4, and Jaakko Hintikka, 'Language-games' in Jaakko Hintikka et al., editors, *Essays on Wittgenstein in Honour of G. H. von Wright* (*Acta Philosophica Fennica*, vol. 28, nos. 1–3), North-Holland, Amsterdam, 1976, pp. 105–25.

4 Erik Stenius, *Wittgenstein's 'Tractatus'*, Basil Blackwell, Oxford, 1960.

5 This implies that, according to Wittgenstein, the choice of names for simple objects is not arbitrary in an important respect.

6 We are grateful for discussions with Dr Liselotte Wiesenthal, whose emphasis on the concept of colour-space in Wittgenstein led us to realize its importance.

7 For example see Max Black, *A Companion to Wittgenstein's 'Tractatus'*, Cornell University Press, Ithaca, New York, 1964, ad loc.

8 Rush Rhees is right here; see his review of Maslow in *Philosophical Review*, vol. 72 (1963), pp. 213–20, especially p. 216.

9 See here, inter alia, *Zettel*, secs. 346–7; *Remarks on the Philosophy of Psychology*, II, sec. 421; *Remarks on Colour*, III, secs. 3, 9–10. In other passages, an appeal to physical considerations is even more clearly ruled out than in the *Tractatus*; cf., e.g., *Remarks on Colour*, III, secs. 232–4.

10 Wittgenstein even seems to think of the impossibility of anticipating the logical forms of objects as a consequence of this ineffability of objectual existence; cf. chapter 1 above.

11 See *Ludwig Wittgenstein and the Vienna Circle*, p. 41.

12 The German original reads: 'Ich glaubte als ich die "Abhandlung" schrieb (und auch später noch), daß fa = fa. ~fb nur möglich wäre, wenn fa das logische Produkt aus irgendeinem andern Satz und ~fb – also fa = p. ~fb – wäre, und war der Meinung fa werde sich in ein solches Produkt zerlegen lassen. Dabei hatte ich keine klare Vorstellung davon, wie ich mir die Auffindung einer solchen Zerlegung dachte. Oder vielmehr: ich dachte wohl an die Konstruktion eines Zeichens, das die richtige grammatische Verwendung in jedem Zusammenhang durch seine Beschaffenheit zum Ausdruck brächte (d.h. seine Regeln auf einfach gestaltete und in gewissen Sinne schon in sich trüge, wie jede übersichtliche Notation); aber ich übersah, daß, wenn diese Umgestaltung des Satzes f(a) in seiner Ersetzung durch ein logisches Produkt bestehen sollte, dann die Faktoren dieses Produkts einen unabhängigen und bereits bekannten Sinn haben mußten.'

13 The German original reads: 'Aber dies gibt nicht die rechte Grammatik: Es mußte das Vorhandensein eines roten Stiches ohne irgend eines

anderen Stiches die rein rote Färbung dieses Orts bedeuten; das scheint uns unsinnig & der Fehler klärt sich so auf: Es muß im Wesen (in der Grammatik) dieses roten Stiches liegen, daß ein mehr oder weniger von ihm möglich ist; ein rötliches Blau kann dem reinem Rot näher & weniger nahe [p. 253] liegen also, in diesem Sinne, mehr oder weniger Rot enhalten. Der Satz welcher angibt daß Rot als Ingrediens einer Farbe hier vorhanden ist müßte also irgendwie eine Quantität von Rot *angeben* (nennen); dann aber muß dieser Satz auch außerhalb des logischen Produktes Sinn haben, & es müßte also Sinn haben zu sagen daß dieser Ort rein Rot gefärbt ist und die & die Quantität von Rot *enthalte*, und das hat keinen Sinn.'

14 The German original reads: 'In der richtigen Darstellung der Farbe muß sich nicht nur zeigen daß wenn a rot ist es nicht zugleich grün sein kann, sondern alle jene internen Eigenschaften müßen sich zeigen, die wir kennen wenn wir die Farben kennen. Also alles was sich auf die Verwandschaft der einzelnen Farben zu einander und ihr Verhältnis zu Schwarz und Weiß bezieht.'

15 See his discussion with Wittgenstein on 25 December 1929, published in *Ludwig Wittgenstein and the Vienna Circle*, pp. 63–4, and also as the second Appendix to *Philosophical Remarks*.

16 See chapter 3 above and cf. Desmond Lee, editor, *Wittgenstein's Lectures, Cambridge 1930–32*, p. 120, where Wittgenstein explains what the objects of the *Tractatus* were like.

17 We are thankful to Dr Liselotte Wiesenthal for calling our attention to the importance of this passage.

18 See above chapter 2, sec. 6.

19 David Pears, *Bertrand Russell and the British Tradition in Philosophy*, Collins (The Fontana Library), London, 1967, pp. 162–3.

6
Wittgenstein in Transition

1 HOW MANY WITTGENSTEINS WERE THERE?

What we have found in the previous chapters of this book about Wittgenstein's early philosophy also helps us to solve a major problem concerning the subsequent development of his views. This problem is: What was the change that took place in Wittgenstein's thinking when he moved away from his early philosophy to his later ideas? It is known that the first and foremost change took place sometime in 1928–9. But what is this change? It is a sad comment on the standards of current Wittgensteinian scholarship that the urgency of this question has been realized only by a few of the most perceptive Wittgensteinians. One of them is G. H. von Wright, who writes that 'it will probably remain a matter of future debate to what extent there is continuity between the "early" Wittgenstein of the *Tractatus* and the "later" Wittgenstein of the *Investigations*.'[1] Another one is Anthony Kenny, who once gave a talk entitled 'How many Wittgensteins were there?'[2] His intriguing answer was that there may have been only one, or maybe three, but certainly not just two, as the facile popular view has it. The plot is thickened by the reports according to which Wittgenstein himself spoke to his friends in a way which emphasized the contrast between the *Tractatus* and his later philosophy.[3]

We do think that there is a sense in which there were just two Wittgensteins, Kenny notwithstanding, and we would like to end the debate von Wright predicted. However, we recognize that this is no mean task. For one thing, all the answers to the question concerning Wittgenstein's first and decisive change of heart in 1929 that one can find in the literature are mistaken or misleading. For instance, it is often said that he gave up the 'picture theory of language'. It will be argued later in this book, however, that in the most literal sense Wittgenstein never gave up the picture idea. (See chapter 9 below.) Likewise, it is sometimes said that Wittgenstein gave up the idea that language operates with precise rules. Yet this idea was not explicitly rejected by Wittgenstein till considerably after 1929, if he had ever held it. For he had written in the *Tractatus* 4.002 that everyday language is a part of the human organism and is no less complicated than it.[4]

It has been argued that the eventual decisive difference between Wittgenstein's theory of language in the *Tractatus* and in the *Philosophical Investigations* is the role language-games play in the latter as the semantical links between language and reality.[5] We shall reach the same conclusion. But, as we shall ourselves spell out in some detail, the concept of language-game gained a prominent place in Wittgenstein's thinking no earlier than in 1934–5, that is, at least five years after his initial 'conversion'. Wittgenstein's adoption of this concept therefore cannot explain his earlier change of mind.

Similar criticisms can easily be levelled at each and every explanation that can be found in the literature of what happened to Wittgenstein in 1929.

Wittgenstein's writings around this time show that he had become restless with several doctrines of the *Tractatus,* including the mirroring idea, which he criticizes in his 1929 paper 'Some Remarks on Logical Form'. However, there were precious few new constructive ideas in that lone published paper, and whatever there were, he quickly rejected again. The crucial change was not just his disenchantment with some particular ideas of the *Tractatus,* but finding in at least one important respect an alternative new leading idea.

2 TWO LANGUAGES – TWO WITTGENSTEINS

What, then, was this new idea that came to Wittgenstein in 1929? The answer turns out to be surprisingly simple. It is based on our interpretation, argued for in chapter 3 above, of the language assumed in the *Tractatus* as a language of immediate experience. It is our thesis in this chapter that the decisive turning-point in Wittgenstein's philosophical development in 1929 was *the replacement of this phenomenological language by an everyday physicalistic language* as his operative language, and, indeed, as the only viable basic language in philosophy. Moreover, we shall argue that this was the *only* clear-cut initial change in Wittgenstein's views and that the other developments of his philosophical ideas during his so-called middle period can be viewed, at least genetically, as further consequences of this first new step. Among other things, this means that the problems he was struggling with were by and large the same as before.

Why do we want to put forward this thesis, which will undoubtedly strike some readers so far-fetched? Because Wittgenstein asserts it himself. The first book-length exposition of his new views that he wrote is *Philosophical Remarks*. In the very first section of that book Wittgenstein writes:

> I do not now have phenomenological language, or 'primary language' as I used to call it, in mind as my goal. I no longer hold it to be necessary.

And it is not merely the case that a purely phenomenological language is not necessary; it is not possible, either. For Wittgenstein continues:

> What is possible and necessary is to separate what is essential in *our* language from the unessential.

Similar statements are found elsewhere.[6] The formulation used in F. Waismann, *Ludwig Wittgenstein and the Vienna Circle*, p. 45, is quite striking:

> I used to believe that there was the everyday language that we all usually spoke and a primary language that expressed what we really knew, namely phenomena. I also spoke of a first system and a second system. Now I wish to explain why I do not adhere to that conception anymore. I think that essentially we have only one language, everyday language.

By calling (in our quote from *Philosophical Remarks*) the basic language he is discarding 'phenomenological', Wittgenstein undoubtedly means just that it is deals with phenomena, i.e., with 'what is immediate'.

It is our thesis that in so far as there were just two Wittgensteins, it is the change of his language paradigm that marks the watershed between the two genetically and systematically.

3 FURTHER EXPLANATIONS

Even though the quotations just given are unequivocal and indeed quite emphatic, they call for further explanations and comments.

First, even though in the quotations so far given Wittgenstein only speaks of his new basic language as *everyday* language, his statements elsewhere show clearly that he thought of it as a *physicalistic* language. This is shown, e.g., by *Philosophical Remarks*, II, sec. 11:

> The propositions of our grammar are always of the same sort as propositions of physics and not of the same sort as the 'primary' propositions which treat of what is immediate.[7]

Second, the first passage we quoted from *Philosophical Remarks*, I, sec. 1, p. 51, may seem to be weaker than we need. It says that Wittgenstein no longer held a phenomenological language to be *necessary*. What we are claiming is that Wittgenstein no longer considered it *possible*. It was pointed out above that collateral evidence (including the very next sentence) shows that this is what Wittgenstein presumably meant. It turns out that this is in fact what Wittgenstein originally said himself. The quoted passage occurred originally in Wittgenstein's notebooks (MS 107, p. 205, written in the autumn of 1929). There is an interesting difference, however, between the original entry and the current edited version of *Philosophical Remarks*. In the notebooks Wittgenstein says that he does not any longer consider a phenomenological language *possible,* not just not necessary, as the edited text says. His words are:

> Ich halte sie [sc. die phänomenologische Sprache] jetzt nicht mehr für möglich.

Since this is in any case what Wittgenstein clearly intends, one is tempted to suspect a slip on the part of some editor or other, be it that the careless editor in question might have been Wittgenstein himself. There is more than this to Wittgenstein's formulation, however. Wittgenstein's change of wording probably reflects a genuine hesitation on his part, not concerning what he believed, but concerning what he thought he could prove.[8]

Likewise, in an important entry in his notebooks (MS 107, p. 176),[9] Wittgenstein writes that

> the assumption that a phenomenological language were possible and that only it would properly speaking say what we must want to express in philosophy is, I believe, absurd.

Third, even though Wittgenstein changed his basic philosophical language, he did not change the aims of his philosophical enterprise. This is shown by the way our quotation from *Philosophical Remarks,* I, sec. 1, continues:

> That is, if we so to speak describe the class of languages which serve their purpose, then in so doing we have shown what is essential to them and given an immediate representation of immediate experience. Each time I say that, instead of such and such a representation, you could also use this other one, we take a further step towards the goal of grasping the essence of what is represented.
>
> A recognition of what is essential and what is inessential in our

language if it is to represent . . . does the same job as the construction of a phenomenological language.[10]

Wittgenstein's continued interest in the given (the phenomena) is strikingly shown also by MS 107, pp. 223–4 (dated 1 December 1929):[11]

> A phenomenon is not a symptom of something else but is the reality.
>
> A phenomenon is not a symptom of something else which then makes a sentence true or false but it is itself what verifies the sentence.

Thus one of Wittgenstein's main philosophical aims is still to understand immediate experience.[12] The outcome of the language switch therefore is, in Wittgenstein's memorable words, that 'the world we live in is the world of sense-data; but the world we talk about is the world of physical objects.'[13]

As far as Wittgenstein's words in *Philosophical Remarks,* I, sec. 1, are concerned, we still have a few interpretational questions on our hands. For one thing, what is the address of Wittgenstein's words 'I used to believe' and similar back references? The editor of *Ludwig Wittgenstein and Vienna Circle* surmises (p. 51) that 'here Wittgenstein no doubt refers to earlier manuscript volumes in which some of the PR may have occurred for the first time'. It is true that the idea of phenomenological language is mentioned in some of them; cf., e.g., MS 105, pp. 1–5, 122. However, a comparison with the *Tractatus* shows very little difference between the views expressed in these early notebooks and the *Tractatus.* It seems to us inconceivable that Wittgenstein could have adopted a major new doctrine, as the idea of phenomenological basis language would have been, without the slightest indication that it was for him a new departure. Instead of postulating a separate phase of Wittgenstein's thought for which there is absolutely no direct evidence, it is much more natural to take him to be referring to the views expressed in the *Tractatus,* albeit in a somewhat different terminology. We argued above in chapter 3 that this is how we have to understand the basic language postulated in the *Tractatus,* anyway. Hence he must be taken to be referring to the *Tractatus.*

However, a terminological problem still remains, in that Wittgenstein does not speak anywhere in the *Tractatus* or in the *Notebooks 1914–1916* of a 'primary system' or a 'primary language' ('as I used to call it') or a 'first language' in connection with his phenomenological basic language. The former term (or its counterpart 'second system') is used by Wittgenstein, e.g., in *Philosophical Remarks,* VII, sec. 68

and in MS 107, p. 232. The term 'primary language' or the term or 'secondary language' occurs in *Philosophical Remarks*, V, sec. 53, and VII, secs. 69, 71. The two pairs of terms are obviously taken by Wittgenstein to be synonymous.

Wittgenstein's words 'as I used to call it' must indeed refer to something he did earlier in the twenties. We do not know where and when. It may be surmised, none the less, that Wittgenstein is referring to discussions with Ramsey or with members of the Vienna Circle. Indeed, Carnap frequently calls a phenomenalistic language *erste Sprache* ('primary or first language').[14] And in his paper 'Theories' Ramsey speaks of 'the primary system' in a way closely reminiscent of Wittgenstein's usage.[15] Hence Wittgenstein's terminology is compatible with our interpretation, even if it does not directly support it.

4 WITTGENSTEIN'S OWN TESTIMONY

Our interpretation of Wittgenstein's transition from his early views to his later philosophy is confirmed in a variety of ways by what he says himself. Instructive evidence is, for instance, found in the so-called *Big Typescript* (no. 213 in von Wright's catalogue,[16] probably 1933), pp. 437–40. Indirectly, this passage also supports our interpretation of the notion of object in the *Tractatus*. Its interest is largely due to the fact that it is one of the few middle-period occasions on which Wittgenstein comments fairly directly on his earlier notion of object (*Gegenstand*).

The very title of this passage, whose original text is given in an appendix to this chapter (see below), is fascinating. This passage is the beginning of the section entitled 'Phänomenologie ist Grammatik' ('Phenomenology Is Grammar') of the chapter 'Phenomenology'. Wittgenstein might as well have used as the title of this section 'grammar serves the same purpose as phenomenology', for he begins by saying that 'the examination of the rules according to which we use our language . . . amounts to, i.e., accomplishes the same as, the construction of a phenomenological language . . .' This shows again the identity of Wittgenstein's philosophical aims before and after his 'conversion'. It also shows that Wittgenstein is no longer engaged in a 'construction of a phenomenological language', even though he is concerned with the same phenomenological problems as before.

We can also see what Wittgenstein means by his often repeated assertion that 'phenomenology is grammar' or that phenomenological analysis is conceptual analysis (see, e.g., *Remarks on Colour*, II, sec. 16). His point could almost be expressed by saying that 'grammar (i.e., semantics) replaces phenomenology', in other words, Wittgenstein's new philosophy replaces his old one, except for the fact that even in his later philosophy he obviously thought of immediate experience as only *one* source of 'grammatical' insights.

In the second paragraph Wittgenstein applies this idea to the concept of object.

> Assume that there are in my visual field two red circles of equal size on a blue background. What is it that is present here in duplicate and what is present only once? . . . One could say: we have here *one* colour but two locations. But it was said that redness and circularity are properties of two objects [*Gegenstände*] which one could call patches and which have certain spatial relations to each other. The explanation 'there are here two objects – patches – which . . .' sounds like a physical explanation. Like somebody's asking 'what are the red circles that I see over there?' and my answering 'They are two red lanterns, etc.' Such an explanation is nevertheless not required here. (To want to resolve our dissatisfaction by means of an explanation is the mistake of metaphysics.) What worries us here is the unclarity of the grammar of the sentence 'I see two red circles on a blue background', especially its relation to the grammar of the sentences 'There are two red balls on the table', and again 'I see two colours in this picture'. I can naturally say, instead of the former sentence, 'I see two patches with the properties Red and Circular in [this] spatial relation to each other' – and equally well 'I see the colour red on two circular locations next to each other' – if I stipulate that this sentence is to mean the same as the sentence above. Then the grammar of the words 'patch', 'location', 'colour', etc. must adjust to the [grammar] of the words in the former sentence. The confusion arises here because we believe that we have to decide about the presence or absence of an object (thing), viz. the patch, in the same way as one decides whether what I see is (in a physical sense) red paint or a reflection. (This passage occurs for the first time in MS 112, pp. 240–1, dated 24 November 1931.)

Perhaps the most interesting aspect of the quoted passage is that Wittgenstein there raises explicitly the question of what the objects are that are involved in the perceptual situation he has described. He first considers two possibilities: either the objects involved are colours and we are ascribing to them certain spatial attributes, or else the objects we are dealing with are patches and colours are their attributes. In both of these alternatives, objects are phenomenological in nature (experienced colours, locations in the visual field, etc.). What Wittgenstein eventually argues is that *both* these ways of talking are secondary in relation to our language of physical objects and their properties. Indeed, the very question as to what the objects present are arises, according to Wittgenstein, from a false analogy with questions concerning the nature of the physical objects present in a given situation. This rejection of both types of phenomenological objects is obviously predicated on the primacy of physicalistic languages. Wittgenstein is rejecting a language which posits irreducible phenomenological objects because such a language is secondary in relation to a physicalistic language. Hence the passage in question shows, on the one hand, what the objects were that Wittgenstein had postulated earlier and, on the other hand, that he had changed his standpoint so as to make a physicalistic language and physical objects primary in relation to a phenomenological language and phenomenological objects.

Wittgenstein is diagnosing the tendency to postulate phenomenological objects as being due to an illicit transfer of physicalistic concepts to the phenomenological realm. (Cf. here especially the last sentence, 'The confusion arises here . . .') This shows especially clearly the sense in which Wittgenstein is changing his basis language from a phenomenological language to a physicalistic one.

This evidence for Wittgenstein's transition from a phenomenological basic language to a physicalistic one is reinforced by other evidence. In fact, the quoted passage continues as follows:

> Mistaken application of our ways of expressing ourselves physicalistically to sense-data. 'Objects', i.e., things, bodies in the space of a room – and 'objects' in a visual field.

In *Remarks on Colour*, III, sec. 127, Wittgenstein writes (undoubtedly in criticism of his earlier views):

> Colours are not objects with definite properties which we could without further ado look for, and imagine colours which we are not yet familiar with.[17]

It is important to realize that Wittgenstein is not arguing in the long quoted passage that the choice of the locutions we employ is arbitrary, e.g., whether or not we countenance phenomenological objects. The only conventionalism Wittgenstein allows is the choice between different phenomenological entities, and this conventionalism is based on his claim that both kinds of phenomenological entities he mentions are secondary in relation to physical objects. Although Wittgenstein says that one can for instance introduce the locution 'I see two patches with the properties Red and Circular,' this sentence can only serve as a paraphrase of the corresponding physicalistic sentence. What is more, and indeed crucial here, the 'grammar' (i.e., the logic) of the phenomenological sentence must adjust itself to the logic of the physicalistic one.

Here we can see also a nice illustration of how insights into 'grammatical' (logical and semantical) relationships can according to Wittgenstein serve to clarify the logic and semantics of our ways of speaking of phenomenological matters. It is in this sense that phenomenology indeed amounts to 'grammar' for Wittgenstein.

All told, we have here strong evidence for our interpretation of Wittgenstein's change of mind about the philosophically basic language and about the objects it deals with.

Another passage where Wittgenstein criticizes his own earlier conception of object (*Gegenstand*) occurs in *Philosophical Remarks*, IX, sec. 95:

> I see three circles in certain positions; I close my eyes, open them again and see three circles of the same size in different positions. Does it make sense to ask whether these are the same circles and which is which? Surely not. However, while I can see them, I can identify them (even if they move before my eyes, I can identify the circles in the new places with those that were in the earlier ones). If I give them names, close my eyes, open them again and see that the circles are in the same places, I can give to each its name once more. (I could still do this even if they had moved so as to exchange places.) In any case, I always name (directly or indirectly) a location.

This passage is a part of a series of comments on the nature of objects. It is of a somewhat tentative nature, and bears the character of Wittgenstein in transition. Wittgenstein is there partly anticipating his later criticism of ostension. (Cf. chapter 8 below.) Ostension cannot in the case Wittgenstein describes give us a criterion of continued identity. Hence not everything we can point to and name is a bona fide object. All this foreshadows Wittgenstein's later views. However, he still thinks that we can name locations in visual space – a doctrine deemed worthy by Wittgenstein of an extended discussion in the same book (cf. chapter 5, sec. 6 above) and a doctrine firmly within the Tractarian ambit of ideas.[18]

5 WITTGENSTEIN AND CARNAP ON '*DIE PHYSIKALISCHE SPRACHE ALS UNIVERSALSPRACHE*'

Indirect but striking evidence for our interpretation of Wittgenstein's new position is also forthcoming from Wittgenstein's correspondence.[19] To put the main point bluntly, Wittgenstein accused Carnap of using his (Wittgenstein's) idea of physicalistic basis language without permission and without proper acknowledgement. This shows vividly that Wittgenstein thought that the idea of physicalistic language was an important idea, a new idea, and *his* idea.

The details, such as we have been able to ascertain them, are as follows: On 6 May 1932, Wittgenstein received an offprint by Carnap from *Erkenntnis,* which prompted him to write to Schlick several letters, the first on the same day as his receipt of the offprint.[20] The content of the letter strongly suggests that the offprint was Carnap's 'Die physikalische Sprache als Universalsprache der Wissenschaft'. One of the relevant statements in the letter is that Wittgenstein is afraid that 'my own work will be considered merely as a reheated version (*zweiter Aufguβ*) or plagiarism of Carnap'. The preceding sentence shows also that Wittgenstein is thinking of the content of the new, as yet unpublished, ideas which he had developed in the preceding four years.

Now what are the new ideas in which Wittgenstein had anticipated Carnap or arrived at the same results independently? The most important of them seems to have been the idea of physicalism. On a request by Neurath himself, Carnap had included in 'Die physikalische Sprache' an acknowledgement to Neurath:

> Neurath has been the first one to require, in the discussion of the Vienna Circle and in the paper referred to, that one should no longer speak of 'contents of experiences' [or 'sense-data', *Erlebnisinhalten*] and of comparisons between a proposition and 'reality', only of propositions; furthermore, he has put forward the thesis of physicalism in its most radical form. I thank him for many valuable impulses.[21]
> [Translation by Jaakko Hintikka]

Wittgenstein took this acknowledgement to Neurath to reflect Carnap's obliviousness to Wittgenstein's introduction of, and emphasis on, a physicalistic basis language.

Unfortunately, this central issue quickly got enmeshed with others. The quoted pasage shows that the ideas of physicalism and physicalistic language had in Carnap's and Neurath's thinking got entangled with the idea of the ineffability of semantics. This was, of course, one of Wittgenstein's most central ideas in the *Tractatus.* For this reason, Wittgenstein referred to the *Tractatus* after Schlick had talked to Carnap and reported back to Wittgenstein Carnap's claim that Wittgenstein 'sich mit der Frage des Physikalismus nicht befasst hat'. Wittgenstein wrote:

> Secondly, it is false that I have not dealt with the problem of 'physicalism' (albeit not under this – horrible – name and with the same brevity with which the entire *Tractatus* is written) . . .

We have changed the punctuation (including bracketing) in order to bring out Wittgenstein's sense.[22] A later part of the same letter, dealing with the idea of 'formal mode of speech' was quoted above in chapter 1, sec. 5. This letter is somewhat confusing in that Wittgenstein here lumps together his new ideas and the ideas he had put forward in the *Tractatus*. He also deals at the same time with two apparently different matters, viz. his new idea of the primacy of physicalistic languages and his old idea of the ineffability of semantics. It is true that Wittgenstein deals in effect with both of them in the *Tractatus*, but in an entirely different manner. He embraces whole-heartedly the 'formal mode of speech', albeit not under this name, as we saw in chapter 1. He deals with physicalism and physicalistic language implicitly by rejecting them in favour of a phenomenological language, as we saw in chapter 3. In view of this multiplicity of issues Wittgenstein compresses in a couple of sentences, it is small wonder that Carnap never understood what precisely Wittgenstein had in mind, and was reduced to saying (in a letter to Schlick on 28 September 1932): 'I don't find in the *Tractatus* any clear statement of physicalism,' which of course is not what Wittgenstein had claimed. It is in any case unmistakable (especially on the basis of the letter to Schlick on 6 May 1932) what Wittgenstein's main concern was. It was Carnap's appropriation of Wittgenstein's idea of physicalistic language as the basic and, indeed, universal language. Clearly Wittgenstein thought of this as *his* new idea and attached to it a tremendous significance.

If the issue had been anything less important than the first and foremost idea of Wittgenstein's new philosophy, his reaction to Carnap's paper would seem petty. In the light of our discovery of the significance of physicalistic language for the born-again Wittgenstein, his concern becomes much more understandable.

6 THE CONTINUITY OF WITTGENSTEIN'S PHILOSOPHY

One of the theses of this chapter is that Wittgenstein's switch from a phenomenological to a physicalistic language was the *only* initial change in his philosophical position. If correct, this thesis implies a major change in the way many philosophers have looked upon Wittgenstein's writings during what would conventionally be called his middle period (roughly 1929–36). This way is represented by the seriously misleading title Rush Rhees gave to *The Blue and Brown Books*: 'Preliminary Studies for the "Philosophical Investigations"'. If we are right, *The Blue Book* is in most respects still very much within the Tractarian ambit of ideas. No wonder von Wright says that 'I myself find it difficult to fit the Blue Book into the development of Wittgenstein's thought.'[23] Thus a great deal of light can be thrown on the *Tractatus* by attending to Wittgenstein's writings during the early middle period and also by attending to Waismann's book *The Principles of Linguistic Philosophy*, which was begun as a statement of Wittgenstein's philosophy and which has many points of contact with *Philosophical Remarks*.

Some consequences of this overall view will be presented in later parts of this book. Likewise, further evidence for it will be marshalled as we go along. It may nevertheless be noted here that, for instance, a detailed examination of *Philosophical Remarks* betrays in fact a wealth of specific doctrines which the author of that book shares with the Wittgenstein of the *Tractatus*. We have registered some of them in earlier chapters. Cases in point are language as the universal medium (cf. chapter 1 above), the precise character of the substantiality of objects (IX, sec. 95), the identity of my experiences with my life (VII, sec. 67), and many others.

In the rest of this chapter, we shall argue for our overall view of the nature of Wittgenstein's change of position by examining two themes which are prominent in Wittgenstein's thinking during his early middle period and which present especially intriguing interpretational problems. They are Wittgenstein's references to phenomenology and his reliance on ostensive definitions.

7 WITTGENSTEIN AND PHENOMENOLOGY

It was found in chapter 3 above that, according to Wittgenstein's views in the *Tractatus,* all logical forms – including the entire logical structure of our conceptual framework – are determined by the logical forms of simple objects (*Gegenstände*). These objects are given us as the objects of *immediate experience*. The entire 'logical structure of the world' can thus be read off from immediately given data.

This conception may seem weird and its attribution to Wittgenstein therefore questionable. This appearance of strangeness may be reduced by comparing Wittgenstein's views with those of other philosophers. Wittgenstein's conception turns out to be closely similar to those of phenomenologists. Their basic idea is precisely the same as Wittgensteinian doctrine just mentioned, viz. that we can uncover the conceptual structure of the world by attending to our immediate experience. Hence, if Wittgenstein's view is deemed absurd, then so must be deemed the whole Husserlian project. Wittgenstein himself expresses his phenomenological viewpoint as late as 1931–2 by saying that 'sense-data are the source of our concepts.'[24]

This important connection between Wittgenstein's *Tractatus* and phenomenology has escaped the attention of even those philosohers (especially Herbert Spiegelberg and Nicholas F. Gier)[25] who have emphasized the points of contact between the later Wittgenstein and phenomenology. It is nevertheless very real indeed. It is illustrated among other things by Wittgenstein's strong emphasis throughout his career on his aim to understand our immediate experience. Even when he gives up the primacy of a language of acquaintance, he sees this change merely as a way of reaching the same goal, as was pointed out earlier in this chapter (pp. 140–1).

The similarities which Spiegelberg and Gier have noted between Wittgenstein's middle-period views and phenomenology are really only relics of this much more fundamental kinship between Wittgenstein's ideas in the *Tractatus* and those of Husserlian phenomenology. Here we see once again how many of Wittgenstein's early 'middle-period' views were merely Tractarian doctrines in a new garb. For instance, Spiegelberg aptly notes that Wittgenstein often discussed in his later philosophy under the heading of 'grammar' matters which might as well be – and indeed more naturally – called phenomenological.[26] This is nevertheless only a pale shadow of the similarity between the Husserlian idea of phenomenology and what is called 'logic' in the *Tractatus*. In the light of this comparison we can among other things understand considerably better than before how Wittgenstein could in the *Tractatus* think, e.g., of colour incompatibility as a matter of logic, for this 'logic' is now seen to bear a distinct similarity to what might be called the phenomenology of colour. (No one would be surprised by the idea that colour incompatibilities are a matter of the phenomenology of colour.) We can now also see how deeply 'phenomenological' Wittgenstein's idea in the *Tractatus* is that we need experience in logic, albeit not experience (in the usual sense) of *how* the objects are, but experience in the sense of experience of *what* objects there are. (This is shown by the famous proposition 5.552 of the *Tractatus*.) As Gier points out,[27] this logical or 'grammatical' character of Wittgenstein's phenomenology is one of the things that distinguishes it from Machian phenomenalism. It has its roots in Wittgenstein's view in the *Tractatus* that all logic (all logical forms) can be built up from the logical forms of simple objects given to us in immediate experience. This is the ultimate source of Wittgenstein's idea that 'phenomenology is grammar'. The background of Wittgenstein's views on phenomenology is shown vividly by his insistence, well before he even reached any of his characteristic middle-period views, that it is phenomenology that supplies the 'grammar' of the language of physics and that phenomenology, unlike physics, represents only possibilities, not laws.[28] This is of course but another version of the Tractarian ideas that all logical forms go back to the logical forms of immediately given ('phenomenological', Wittgenstein could have said) objects and that the logical form of an object governs the possibilities of its being combined with other objects. Hence Wittgenstein could say, 'Phenomenology is Grammar', as he does in a section title in the *Big Typescript*. In *Remarks on Colour*, II, sec. 16, Wittgenstein likewise says that phenomenological analysis is conceptual analysis.

In view of such deep connections between Wittgenstein's ideas and phenomenology it is not entirely surprising to see him going as far as to say, 'You could say of my work that it is "phenomenology".'[29]

Wittgenstein is nevertheless clearer than the phenomenologists as to what the 'logic' really is like that we can lift from our immediate experience. Such a logic deals only with meanings, not with facts. And, what is at least a prima facie difference as compared with Husserl, these meanings concern principally the range of possibilities that an object of experience allows. As Wittgenstein says in the *Tractatus* of the objects which are (cf. 3.203) the meanings of names:

> 2.0141   The possibility of its occurring in states of affairs is the form of an object.

> 2.013   Each thing is, as it were, in a space of possible states of affairs.

Now this aspect of Wittgenstein's views is stated forcefully by him in *Ludwig Wittgenstein and the Vienna Circle*, p. 63:

> Physics wants to determine regularities; it does not set its sights on what is possible. For this reason physics does not yield a description of the phenomenological states of affairs. In phenomenology it is always a matter of possibility, i.e. of sense, not of truth and falsity.

This Wittgensteinian improvement on Husserl's views resembles Jaakko Hintikka's suggested replacement of Husserl's conception of 'intentionality as directedness' by a deeper conception of intentionality as being an intrinsically modal ideal ('intentionality as intensionality'), i.e., as involving always a range of alternative possibilities.[30]

Now we can see why the career of the term 'phenomenology' was relatively brief in Wittgenstein. As was noted, he used it repeatedly during his early middle period, but gave it up to some extent later. Spiegelberg speaks in the title of one of his papers of 'Wittgenstein's *Phänomenologie* (1929–?)'. In the light of what we have found about the substance of Wittgenstein's doctrine (disregarding his terminology), a more appropriate time reference would be '(1913–29)'. He gave up partly the term 'phenomenology' because there was no longer the same analogy between his new project and phenomenology as there was between his earlier views and those of phenomenologists. A more pertinent question than why he only spoke of phenomenology in connection with his early views is why he went on using it at all during his middle period. The answer is that Wittgenstein used the term as long as he did because his aim still was to understand 'phenomena', i.e., what is immediately given to us in our experience. This aim survived the change of his basic language. It is Wittgenstein's rejection of phenomenological language as an independent basis language, combined with his continued interest in phenomenological problems (problems concerning 'the given' or immediate experience) that lends its characteristic flavour to his later use of the terms 'phenomenology' and 'phenomenological'. Since there is no pure phenomenological language, there cannot be any systematic science of phenomenology of the kind that, e.g., Husserl attempted to build, but there are phenomenological problems. This is what Wittgenstein says in a more cryptic form in *Remarks on Colour,* I, sec. 53, and III, sec. 248:

> There is no phenomenology, but there are phenomenological problems.

The solution of these problems lies according to Wittgenstein in the clarification of the way our language of immediate experience operates.

Thus our results concerning Wittgenstein's change of mind in 1929 concerning his basic language enable us to understand the way he uses the term 'phenomenology' and his relation to phenomenologists like Husserl.

8 WITTGENSTEIN, CARNAP, SCHLICK, AND HUSSERL

Another part of the background of Wittgenstein's use of the term 'phenomenology' is Carnap's *The Logical Structure of the World,*[31] which appeared in 1928. Carnap's programme there is to construct the structure in question from the 'given', which according to Carnap is to be understood as a sequence of elementary experiences (ibid., sec. 64). This is in a rough agreement with the *Tractatus,* as we have interpreted it. Now Carnap repeatedly compared his programme with Husserl's phenomenology.[32] Hence it may very well have been Carnap's references to phenomenology which first alerted Wittgenstein to the similarities between his own erstwhile views and Husserl's project.

There is an interesting difference between Carnap's *Aufbau* and Wittgenstein's *Tractatus*, however. The basis of the ontology of the *Tractatus* is a class of objects of acquaintance of different logical types. In contrast, the basis of Carnap's construction is a sequence of momentary total experiences. Out of these, qualities are constructed. But not even qualities are like particular sense-data in Russell's sense. On one occasion Carnap writes:

> If we wish to differentiate ... two like constituents of the two elementary experiences, then it does not suffice just to characterize them as to quality, but we must, in addition, identify the elementary experience to which they belong. Only a constituent which is so identified is an individual, strictly unique constituent in the proper sense. In contrast to a constituent which is characterized only as to its quality, we wish to call it a 'sensation'. (Ibid., sec. 93)

These 'sensations' are thus analogous to Wittgenstein's 'objects'. But for Carnap, they are subjective, ephemeral and temporal, whereas the objects of the *Tractatus* constitute the atemporal, 'objective' substance of the world. Thus Carnap writes:

> Sensations properly belong to the object domain of psychology; qualities, on the other hand, belong to the domain of phenomenology or the theory of objects. (Ibid.)

Thus in Carnap's usage 'phenomenology' is restricted to a holistic analysis of experience, in contradistinction to such atomistic theories as we have attributed to the *Tractatus*.[33] This prompts the interesting question, which we cannot answer here, whether Wittgenstein's somewhat belated-looking adoption of the term 'phenomenology' was connected with his roughly simultaneous adoption of a holistic view of the connections between language and experience.

Wittgenstein's use of the term 'phenomenology' and the relation of his ideas to Husserl's is put into an interesting perspective by his discussion with Schlick about Husserl on 25 December 1929, recorded in *Ludwig Wittgenstein and the Vienna Circle*, pp. 67–8. His remarks show that he had acquired, presumably from Schlick and Carnap, some knowledge of Husserl's ideas, at least enough to refer to him by name. Schlick raises the question as to what one can say to 'a philosopher who believes that the statements of phenomenology are synthetic *a priori* judgements'. The example Wittgenstein discusses in his reply is the good old chestnut, 'An object is not red and green at the same time.' What he emphasizes is that this proposition is true for what he calls grammatical (logical) reasons; it is not a material truth.

If one said, 'An object *cannot* be red and green at the same time,' this would be true in the sense of a *logical* 'cannot'. Wittgenstein sees Husserl as declaring that there is a third possibility besides logical and material (a posteriori) truth. 'To that I would reply that it is indeed possible to make up words, but I cannot associate a thought with them.' This is not unlike Schlick's objections to Husserl.

In fact, several different remarks of Wittgenstein's on phenomenology echo Schlick's criticisms of Husserl's belief in the synthetic a priori:

> But what kind of a proposition is that, that blending in white removes the colouredness from the colour?
>
> As I mean it, it can't be a proposition of physics.
>
> Here the temptation to believe in a phenomenology, something midway between science and logic, is very great.

This quote is from *Remarks on Colour,* II, sec. 3. Similar remarks are found elsewhere. For Wittgenstein, there is no synthetic a priori, nothing 'between science and logic'.

However, it is remarkable that Wittgenstein is like Husserl in that for him, too, the allegedly synthetic truths a priori are all obtained from experience, and refer to possible experiences. Indeed, Wittgenstein formulates his objection to an object of this kin by saying, 'I cannot see such an object' (*Ludwig Wittgenstein and the Vienna Circle,* p. 67). In ibid., p. 77, Wittgenstein in fact acknowledges that the proposition (or pseudo-proposition), 'An object is not red and green at the same time', is based on experience, although not on the kind of experience which can be expressed by means of a proposition. 'If you wish, I could just as well say, logic is empirical – if *that* is what you call empirical.'

Here Wittgenstein is in effect granting his imaginary interlocutor the luxury of an option he denied Husserl. Hence it might seem that the difference between Wittgenstein and Husserl is much smaller than first meets the eye. What separates the two is not their respective conceptions of phenomenology, but their conceptions of logic. Now Wittgenstein's conception of logic has been found to be idiosyncratic anyway. No one else has ever thought that all that there is to logic in the fullest sense of the word are in the last analysis the forms of the simple objects which experience gives to us. Could it be that Wittgenstein is merely *calling* those truths 'logical' that Husserl *calls* synthetic a priori? No, the matter is not as simple as that. What distinguishes these two philosophers is that Wittgenstein is thinking of what immediate experience gives us as *logic* whereas Husserl thinks of it as synthetic truths a priori. For Wittgenstein logical truths are not nonvacuous, assertable truths. As he thought of them, they were for him mere tautologies, 'grammatical' truths. (Thus Wittgenstein's slogan, 'phenomenology is grammar', is partly directed against Husserl.) We cannot even say that Husserlian synthetic truths a priori are for Wittgenstein logical *truths*. In the strict sense of the word, there are no logical truths for Wittgenstein. Such alleged truths cannot be said, i.e., formulated as meaningful propositions. They can only be shown. Their only reflections in language are grammatical observations. For Husserl, what phenomenological reflection yields is not a matter of logic only. For instance, he did not take the possibilities that manifest themselves in experience to be purely logical possibilities. They are 'motivated' possibilities determined partly by one's background beliefs and background knowledge.

It nevertheless seems that Wittgenstein's views on this topic mellowed over the years. In some of his later remarks Wittgenstein in fact came close to retracting the basic assumption of his earlier criticism of Husserl's idea of synthetic a priori:

> There seem to be propositions that have the character of experiential propositions, but whose truth is for me unassailable. That is to say, if I assume that they are false, I must mistrust all my judgments. (*Remarks on Colour*, III, sec. 348)

Here we see vividly at one and the same time how very close Husserl and Wittgenstein (the Wittgenstein of the *Tractatus* – for it is the early Wittgenstein that we have been speaking of in the last few paragraphs) are in certain respects and also that there nevertheless are significant differences between the two, differences of which Wittgenstein was aware.

9 OSTENSION AND SHOWING

The most striking link between Wittgenstein's early middle-period thinking and the *Tractatus* remains to be discussed. Once again, our results reached in chapter 3 above provide a starting-point. It was found there that Wittgenstein's mysterious-sounding idea of *showing* has to be understood in an almost literal sense. Since the simple objects of the *Tractatus* have to be given to us for our language to make sense, we cannot say in language that some particular simple object exists. Nor can its essence be expressed in language, because that would enable us to get around the impossibility of expressing its existence.[34] For we could then say that it exists by saying that these essential properties are in fact exemplified. As Wittgenstein puts it in *Philosophical Remarks*, IX, sec. 94:

There is a sense in which an object may not be described.

That is, the description may ascribe to it no property whose absence would reduce the existence of the object to nothing, i.e. the description may not express what would be essential to the existence of the object.

How, then, can we introduce a simple object into our discourse? Wittgenstein's answer is: by showing it. What he means by this is brought out by his background in Russell as was spelled out in chapter 3, sec. 10. Russellian objects of acquaintance are introduced by exhibiting them, i.e., by pointing to one of them and saying 'this' or 'that'. Likewise, for the young Wittgenstein the concept of a simple object is identical with the concept of 'this'. In other words, a simple object can only be introduced into the language Wittgenstein postulates in the *Tractatus* by showing it in an almost literal sense and by pointing to it.

Now, in the critical daylight of a Vienna Circle discussion, what can we call such an introduction of a new name into one's language and what can we say about it? Obviously, it is precisely what is known as an *ostensive definition*. As a matter of fact, ostensive definitions play a major role in Wittgenstein's middle-period writings. This role of ostensive defining is clearly a heritage of the role of showing in the *Tractatus*.[35]

This historical connection can be spelled out in a variety of ways. One prominent occasion on which showing makes it appearance is the first page of *The Blue Book*, where all non-verbal explanations of meaning are said to be (admittedly 'very roughly') ostensive definitions. This dichotomy between verbal and ostensive definitions is nothing but the saying–showing contrast in a new garb. The same claim for the generality of ostensive definitions is made by Wittgenstein in *Philosophical Grammar*, II, sec. 24 (p. 60). Another formulation of essentially the same point is found in ibid., IV, sec. 56. This formulation is especially interesting because it is related closely to Wittgenstein's ideas in the *Tractatus*.

The correlation of an object and a name is generated by nothing but a table, by *ostensive gestures* [emphasis added] at the same time as the name is uttered, or by something similar.

It follows from the semantical role of ostensive definitions that they are inexpressible in language, for Wittgenstein believed throughout his philosophical life in the ineffability of semantics. Ostensive definitions are showings; what they convey to the recipient cannot be said in language. It is therefore a fundamental misunderstanding of Wittgenstein to try to construe the verbal *Erläuterungen* ('clarifications') of the *Tractatus* 3.263 as ostensive definitions, as some commentators have sought to do.[36]

Even when Wittgenstein begins to doubt the conception of language understanding and language learning on which ostensive defining is the end-all and be-all, he is explicit about what he is rejecting:

> The concept of meaning I adopted in my philosophical discussions originates in a primitive philosophy of language.
>
> The German word for 'meaning' [*Bedeutung*] is derived from the German word for 'pointing' [*deuten*]. (*Philosophical Grammar*, II, sec. 19)

This role of ostensive definitions in Wittgenstein's early middle-period philosophy shows the deep roots of this philosophy in the ideas of the *Tractatus*.

These observations also help to understand better the background of Wittgenstein's criticism of ostensive definitions in *PI*, I, secs. 26–30, 45, etc. In his preface to the *Philosophical Investigations*, Wittgenstein informs us that his views are best understood by contrasting them to those expressed in the *Tractatus*. Yet he does not seem to be concerned with ostensive definitions at all in his early work. The solution to this puzzle is that, although the term 'ostensive definition' does not occur in the *Tractatus*, the idea can be found there under the guise of the idea of 'showing' and indeed plays a major role in the *Tractatus*. By criticizing what look like his own middle-period views Wittgenstein is in effect criticizing the *Tractatus*.

It turns out, however, that Wittgenstein's ideas of ostensive definitions were less unequivocal and less stable than we have so far indicated. We shall accordingly return to this subject in chapter 8, sec. 4, below.

NOTES

1 G. H. von Wright, *Wittgenstein*, Basil Blackwell, Oxford, 1982, p. 27.
2 Cf. Anthony Kenny, *The Legacy of Wittgenstein*, Basil Blackwell, Oxford, 1984, p. viii.
3 In their book *Essays in the Unknown Wittgenstein*, Prometheus Press, Buffalo, N.Y., 1984, Morris Lazerowitz and Alice Ambrose claim that everybody else has failed to realize that 'Wittgenstein's middle period

represents a fundamental breakthrough in the history of philosophical thought'. For reasons evolving in the course of this chapter and its successors, we do not subscribe to this view, either.

4 The reason why this statement has not been taken to be a genuine anticipation of Wittgenstein's later views is the assumption that he distinguished in the *Tractatus* between a complicated everyday language and a clear ideal language, which is supposed to be what most of his remarks pertain to. This contrast, which seems to be due to Russell, is firmly denied by Frank Ramsey in his unpublished notes. (See, e.g., item # 002-29-01 of the Frank Ramsey Archives at the University of Pittsburgh, first two lines: 'Wittgenstein [not dealing with a perfect language but any language Russell wrong].') (The brackets are Ramsey's.) If Ramsey is right, then the entire contrast between the early Wittgenstein, who believed in sharp rules of language, and the later one who did not, is a myth.

5 Jaakko Hintikka, 'Language-games' in Jaakko Hintikka et al., editors, *Essays on Wittgenstein in Honour of G. H. von Wright* (*Acta Philosophica Fennica*, vol. 28, nos. 1–3). North-Holland, Amsterdam, 1976, pp. 105–25.

6 See *Philosophical Remarks*, secs. 12, 53, 57, 71, 75, and 213.

7 Similar testimony is found in *Philosophical Remarks*, VI, sec. 57 and VII, secs. 68–9, 71. Further evidence is forthcoming in sec. 4 of the present chapter.

8 Cf. chapter 10, sec. 1, below.

9 The German text reads: 'Die Annahme daß eine phänomenologische Sprache möglich wäre und die eigentlich erst das sagen würde was wir in der Philosophie ausdrücken müssen [wollen] ist – glaube ich – absurd. Wir müssen mit unserer gewöhnlichen Sprache auskommen und sie nur richtig verstehen.' Cf. appendix to the present chapter.

10 The last clause reads in German 'kommt auf die Konstruktion einer phänomenologischen Sprache hinaus', which is rendered in the English translation as 'amounts to the construction of a phenomenological language'. Both translations, ours and that of the Rush Rhees edition, are linguistically viable. However, in view of collateral content evidence, our translation appears preferable.

11 The German text reads:

Das Phänomen ist nicht Symptom für etwas anderes sondern ist die Realität.

Das Phänomen ist nicht Symptom für etwas anderes was den Satz erst wahr oder falsch macht sondern ist selbst das was ihn verifiziert.

12 On at least one later occasion (MS 113, pp. 514–15, dated 19 May 1932) Wittgenstein even played with the idea that there could be a phenomenological *language* in the form of painted pictures or suchlike representing one's immediate experiences.

13 See *Wittgenstein's Lectures, Cambridge 1930–1932*, p. 82. That this was indeed Wittgenstein's view is confirmed, e.g., by *Philosophical Remarks*, VII, sec. 67 (first paragraph). See also what Wittgenstein says in MS 113, p. 465 (9 May 1932):

Was wir im physikalischen Raum denken, ist nicht das Primäre, das wir nur mehr oder weniger erkennen können; sondern was vom physikalischen Raum wir erkennen können, zeigt uns wie weit das Primäre reicht und wie wir den physikalischen Raum zu denken haben.

14 Rudolf Carnap, 'Die physikalische Sprache als Universalsprache der Wissenschaft', *Erkenntnis*, vol. 2, nos. 5–6 (1932), pp. 432–65. Arthur Benson writes in his bibliography of Carnap in the Library of Living Philosophers volume on Carnap that nos. 5–6 of vol. 2 'appeared in 1932, although the title page of Bd. 2 is dated "1931"'.

15 Frank Ramsey, *The Foundations of Mathematics*, Routledge & Kegan Paul, London, 1931, pp. 212–36, especially pp. 212–13.

16 G. H. von Wright, *Wittgenstein*, pp. 43–57.

17 Similar pronouncements are made by Wittgenstein elsewhere; see, e.g., *Philosophical Remarks*, VI, sec. 57; VII, secs. 68–9; XX, sec. 213. In these other passages Wittgenstein nevertheless does not bring his new physicalistic viewpoint (or language) to bear on the status of objects as clearly as he does in the quoted passage.

18 It is known that of the main purposes for which Wittgenstein returned to Cambridge in 1929 one was to 'work on visual space' (*Ludwig Wittgenstein and the Vienna Circle*, p. 17).

19 In writing this section we have used information made available to us by Prof. G. H. von Wright and by Prof. Rudolf Haller.

20 A copy of the text of this letter has kindly been provided to us by Prof. G. H. von Wright. The whereabouts of the original letter is not known to us.

21 Note 14 above, p. 452. Notice that Carnap here in effect attributes also the idea that semantics is ineffable to Neurath. This is undoubtedly the reason why the paternity of this idea, too, became an issue in Wittgenstein's complaints about Carnap's unauthorized use of his ideas.

22 The original has appeared in Michael Nedo and Michele Ranchetti, editors, *Wittgenstein: Sein Leben in Bildern und Texten*, Suhrkamp, Frankfurt am Main, 1983, pp. 254–5.

23 G. H. von Wright, *Wittgenstein*, p. 27.

24 Lee, op. cit. (note 13 above), p. 81.

25 See Herbert Spiegelberg, 'The puzzle of Wittgenstein's *Phänomenologie* (1929–?) (with supplement 1979)' in Herbert Spiegelberg, *The Context of the Phenomenological Movement*, Martinus Nijhoff, The Hague, 1981, pp. 202–28; 'Wittgenstein calls his philosophy "phenomenology": one more supplement to "The puzzle of Wittgenstein's "Phänomenologie"'', *Journal of the British Society for Phenomenology*, vol. 13 (1982), pp. 296–9; Nicholas F. Gier, *Wittgenstein and Phenomenology*, SUNY Press, Albany, N.Y., 1981.

26 For the motivation of Wittgenstein's wide sense of the term 'grammar', see chapter 1, sec. 6, above.

27 *Wittgenstein and Phenomenology*, pp. 93–4.

28 See MS 105, pp. 3, 5.

29 M. O'C. Drury, 'Conversations with Wittgenstein', in Rush Rhees, editor, *Personal Recollections of Ludwig Wittgenstein*, Basil Blackwell, Oxford, 1981, p. 131.

30 See Jaakko Hintikka, *The Intentions of Intentionality and Other New Models for Modalities*, D. Reidel, Dordrecht, 1973, title essay.

31 Rudolf Carnap, *Der logische Aufbau der Welt*, Weltkreis-Verlag, Berlin, 1928.
32 Ibid., e.g., secs. 3, 64, 65, 93, 106, 124, 150, 152, and 164.
33 We are grateful to Prof. Robert Beard for calling our attention to this fact.
34 There is of course another, trivial, sense in which objects can be described. (This is what elementary propositions do.) Wittgenstein is perfectly well aware of it, too; see *Philosophical Grammar*, Appendix, p. 208.
35 Ostensive definitions are in fact related in so many words to the idea of showing by Moritz Schlick: 'The business of defining cannot go on indefinitely, so eventually we come to words whose meaning cannot again be described in a proposition; it has to be pointed out [*aufgewiesen*]; the meaning of the word must ultimately be *shown* [*gezeigt*], it has to be *given*.' This quote is from Moritz Schlick, *Philosophical Papers*, D. Reidel, Dordrecht, 1979, vol. 2, p. 264. Similar pronouncements are found in ibid., pp. 220, 310, 458.
36 P. M. S. Hacker, 'Frege and Wittgenstein on elucidations', *Mind*, vol. 84 (1975), pp. 601–9. But see chapter 8, sec. 4 below, for a description of an interlude in Wittgenstein's development during which he could briefly have assimilated ostensions to *Erläuterungen*.

APPENDIX
THE BIG TYPESCRIPT, pp. 437–8

Phänomenologie ist Grammatik

Die Untersuchung der Regeln des Gebrauchs unserer Sprache, die Erkenntnis dieser Regeln und übersichtliche Darstellung, läuft auf das hinaus, d.h. leistet dasselbe, was man oft durch die Konstruktion einer phänomenologischen Sprache leisten [erzielen] will.

Jedesmal, wenn wir erkennen, daß die und die Darstellungsweise auch durch eine andre ersetzt werden kann, machen wir einen Schritt zu diesem Ziel.

"Angenommen, mein Gesichtsbild wären zwei gleichgroße rote Kreise auf blauem Grund: was ist hier in zweifacher Zahl vorhanden, und was einmal? (Und was bedeutet diese Frage überhaupt?) – Man könnte sagen: wir haben hier *eine* Farbe, aber zwei Oertlichkeiten. Es wurde aber auch gesagt, rot und kreisförmig seien Eigenschaften von zwei Gegenständen, die man Flecke nennen könnte, und die in gewissen räumlichen Beziehungen zueinander stehen." Die Erklärung 'es sind hier zwei Gegenstände – Flecke – die . . .' klingt wie eine Erklärung der Physik. Wie wenn Einer fragt 'was sind das für rote Kreise, die ich dort sehe' und [p. 438] ich antworte 'das sind zwei rote Laternen, etc.' Eine Erklärung wird aber hier nicht gefordert (unsere Unbefriedigung durch eine Erklärung lösen zu wollen ist der Fehler der Metaphysik). Was uns beunruhigt, ist die Unklarheit über die Grammatik des Satzes 'ich sehe zwei rote Kreise auf blauem Grund';

insbesondere die Beziehungen zur Grammatik der Sätze [*eines Satzes*] wie 'auf dem Tisch liegen zwei rote Kugeln'; und wieder 'auf diesem Bild sehe ich zwei Farben'. Ich kann [darf] natürlich statt des ersten Satzes sagen: 'ich sehe zwei Flecken mit [von] den Eigenschaften Rot und kreisförming und in der räumlichen Beziehung Nebeneinander' – und ebensowohl: 'ich sehe die Farbe rot an zwei kreisförmigen Oertlichkeiten nebeneinander' – wenn ich bestimme, daß diese Ausdrücke das gleiche bedeuten sollen, wie der obige Satz. Es wird sich dann einfach die Grammatik der Wörter 'Fleck', 'Oertlichkeit', 'Farbe', etc. nach der (*Grammatik*) der Wörter des ersten Satzes richten müssen. Die Konfusion entsteht hier dadurch, daß wir glauben, über das Vorhandensein oder Nichtvorhandensein eines Gegenstands (Dinges) – des Flecks – entscheiden zu müssen; wie wenn man entscheidet, ob, was ich sehe (im physikalischen Sinn) ein roter Anstrich oder ein Reflex ist.

Irrtümliche Anwendung unserer physikalischen Ausdrucksweise auf Sinnesdaten. 'Gegenstände', d.h. Dinge, Körper im Raum des Zimmers – und 'Gegenstände' im Gesichtsfeld; der Schatten eines Körpers an der Wand als Gegenstand! Wenn man gefragt wird: 'existiert der Kasten noch, wenn ich ihn nicht anschaue', so ist die korrekte Antwort: 'ich glaube nicht, daß ihn jemand gerade dann wegtragen wird, oder zerstören'. Die Sprachform 'ich nehme x wahr' bezieht sich ursprünglich auf ein Phänomen (als Argument) im physikalischen Raum (ich meine hier: im 'Raum' der alltäglichen Ausdrucksweise). Ich kann diese Form daher nicht unbedenklich auf das anwenden, was man Sinnesdatum nennt, etwa auf ein optisches Nachbild.

Note: We have reproduced here the typescript text of MS 213 as it stands, without much editing. Brackets in the text (other than page numbers) are Wittgenstein's own. The double quotes on p. 437 (beginning of the third paragraph) indicate a near-quote from Wittgenstein's own MS 105, p. 15. It is highly significant that Wittgenstein raised the question he is dealing with here at an early stage of his transition from the *Tractatus* position to his middle-period philosophy.

In MS 105, loc. cit., Wittgenstein rejects likewise his experimental proposal, but without any diagnosis of what is wrong with it:

> Ein scheinbarer Ausweg wäre natürlich der, zu sagen, rot und kreis-förmig sind Eigenschaften (externe) von zwei Gegenständen die man etwa Flecken nennen könnte und diese Flecken stehen in gewissen räumlichen Beziehungen zu einander; aber das ist Unsinn.

Thus Wittgenstein clearly has not yet in MS 105 reached a stable theoretical position.

7
How Did Wittgenstein Come to Change his Mind?

1 WITNESSING WITTGENSTEIN AT WORK

In the preceding chapter we saw what the first and foremost change in Wittgenstein's philosophical views is that launched his development away from his early philosophy towards the position he eventually reached in the *Philosophical Investigations*. It consisted in Wittgenstein's replacing a phenomenological language by a physicalistic one as his basic language. We have not yet raised the question: Why did Wittgenstein change his language paradigm? How did he come to reject the language of the given in favour of everyday public language?

Wittgenstein's development from the earlier position to the later one is seen vividly, sometimes dramatically, in his unpublished notebooks. In them, we can witness in considerable detail how Wittgenstein worked his way to clarity concerning the impossibility of a phenomenological basis language. Apart from thus allowing us to have a rare close look at a great philosophical mind at work, a study of the way Wittgenstein came to change his mind about his preferred language in philosophy is instructive in that it shows how the seeds of his further development were contained in the line of thought he carried out in the autumn of 1929.

The decisive steps were taken by Wittgenstein in October 1929, and they are reflected in MS 107. The early entries in it are undated, but from p. 153 on most of the entries are dated, the first recorded date being 6 October 1929. In the early pages of this MS a phenomenological language is repeatedly mentioned as a realistic possibility (p. 3):[1]

> And yet there can be a phenomenological language . . . Or is it so: Our ordinary language is also phenomenological . . .[2]

Earlier in the same year Wittgenstein had likewise written:

> From the above it is seen – as is otherwise obvious – that the phenomenological language represents the same as our ordinary

physical mode of expression and has only the advantage that many things can be said in it more concisely and with less danger of misunderstanding. (MS 105, p. 122)[3]

Yet in MS 107, p. 176 (dated 22 October 1929), Wittgenstein calls (as we saw in chapter 6, sec. 3) a phenomenological language 'absurd' and adds:

> We must get along by means of our usual language and only understand it correctly. [For the German text, see note 9 to chapter 6 above.]

This idea quickly stabilized in Wittgenstein's mind as a firm thesis. For instance, the last long quote in chapter 6, sec. 2, above is from a discussion with Schlick and others only two months later (22 December 1929).

What happened that changed Wittgenstein's mind so radically – and apparently so quickly?

2 WITTGENSTEIN'S GROWING DOUBTS

Wittgenstein's philosophical crisis in October 1929 was in reality a culmination of a longer process that came to a head then. This entire development can be followed in Wittgenstein's notebooks.

Wittgenstein's doubts about phenomenological languages began early. In February 1929, he writes (MS 105, p. 3):[4]

> Much seems to speak for thinking that a description of the visual space by means of physics is really the simplest one. That is, that physics is the true phenomenology.

But he hastens to retract this idea:

> But against this one can make an objection: physics aims at truth, i.e., at correct predictions of events, while phenomenology doesn't do that. It aims at *meaning*, not at *truth*.
> But one can say: physics has a language and uses this language to express propositions. These propositions can be true or false. These propositions constitute physics and the grammar [constitutes] phenomenology (or whatever one wants to call it).

Here Wittgenstein does not even set up any contrast between a physicalistic and a phenomenological language.

On pp. 108–10 of MS 105 he does present a contrast between the two kinds of languages and ponders upon their relationship. It is significant that the idea of verification plays a special role in his thoughts about this matter:[5]

> Phenomenological language describes precisely the same as the usual physical one. Only it must restrict itself to what is verifiable.
>
> Is that possible in the first place?
>
> Let's not forget that the physical language again also describes only the primary world and not a hypothetical one. The hypothesis [of a physical world] is merely an assumption concerning the practical [correct] way of representation.
>
> Now is this hypothetical element essential for every representation of the world?
>
> Suppose I had such a good a memory that I could remember all my sense impressions. In that case there would, prima *facie*, be nothing to prevent me from describing them. This would be a biography. And why shouldn't I be able to leave everything hypothetical out of this description?

A phenomenological language thus still seems to reign supreme in the end. However, Wittgenstein goes on to discuss the pros and cons of such languages, concluding with the rhetorical question concerning a phenomenological description of one's past experiences:[6]

> Isn't it clear that this is the most immediate description that can be thought of?

A few pages later (p. 122) Wittgenstein likewise appears to be entirely happy with a phenomenological language. (Cf. our quote above in sec. 1.)

From Wittgenstein's notes it is seen that it was his investigation of the nature of perceptual space and of its relation to physical space that gradually forced him to focus his attention to the contrast between phenomenological and physical languages. In the course of his investigations he finds more and more differences between the two kinds of space.

This contrast did not come about at once, however, On p. 1 of MS 107 Wittgenstein still countenances an independent phenomenological description of the visual space:[7]

> The visual space has its independent reality as it is.
>
> It does not itself contain any autonomous subject.
>
> It can be described immediately (though we are far from knowing a mode of expression which does describe it). The usual physical language is related to it in a *very* complicated way instinctively known to us.

The problem concerning the interrelations of phenomenological and physical languages continued to bother Wittgenstein, undoubtedly largely because of his preoccupation with visual space. In the midst of notes on problems in the foundations of mathematics, Wittgenstein suddenly writes in MS 106, pp. 102–4:[8]

> The description of phenomena by means of the hypothesis of a material world [*Körperwelt*] is indispensable because of its simplicity, compared with the incomprehensibly complicated phenomenological description. If I see various detached parts of a circle [Wittgenstein draws a picture], then an accurate direct description of them is perhaps impossible, but the specification that they are parts of a circle . . . is simple.

3 LANGUAGE HAS TO BE COMPARED WITH THE WORLD

It seems to us that the crucial question in Wittgenstein's thinking nevertheless did not concern the contrast between the phenomenological and the physical as much as the problem of language–world relations, culminating in the problem of verification. Wittgenstein at first continues to think that the language–world links, which he at this time identifies with verification, must operate through direct experience. On p. 142 of MS 107 he still writes:[9]

> What the immediate datum is to the proposition which it verifies, that a seen relation between structures is to the equation which it verifies.

Here verification is still assumed to take place via immediate experience. Likewise on p. 142 of MS 107 (that is to say, in late September or early October) he still happily speaking of how 'an immediate *datum*' can verify a sentence of the ordinary language. But on p. 152 he writes:[10]

> You cannot compare a picture with reality unless you can set it against it as a yardstick.
> You must be able to fit the proposition on to reality.

Thus he has moved from the idea that a reception of a datum is enough to verify a sentence to the idea that an an actual comparison of a sentence with reality must be performed by the language user. Not any indirect comparison will suffice, either; the comparison must be a veritable juxtaposition.

Moreover, this requirement of actual confrontation is not merely one of many important problem about language. It was *the* problem of semantics. As Wittgenstein puts it,

> Verification is not just *one* indication of truth but *the* sense of a proposition. (MS 107, p. 143)[11]

As we saw, this verification means actual comparison:[12]

> I must really *compare* reality with a proposition.

4 LANGUAGE IS A PART OF THE PHYSICAL WORLD

It is not hard to see how the requirement of direct comparability leads Wittgenstein to the thesis that only a physicalistic language is possible. Wittgenstein needed a supplementary assumption, however, in order to draw his conclusion. This extra premise was the idea that *language itself is a part of the physical world*. As Wittgenstein himself expresses this thesis in *Philosophical Remarks*, VII, sec. 68:

> The language itself belongs in the second [i.e., physicalistic] system. If I describe a language, I am essentially describing something that belongs to physics. But how can a physical language describe the phenomenal?

That this idea was in Wittgenstein's mind at the crucial time is shown by the fact that this passage occurs in a slightly earlier notebook, viz. in MS 105, p. 114. The same idea occurs also in MS 107, p. 232, where Wittgenstein says in so many words that not only does the syntax belong to the physicalistic system but that so do 'the symbolizing relations between sentences and facts'. We shall return to this assumption in section 6 below.

It was only when Wittgenstein was hit by the full force of the idea that language itself belongs to the physical world and that the process of the verification of a proposition, which amounts to a comparison between language and the world, therefore must take place in the same world, that he came to be ready to draw the right conclusion from premises to which he had subscribed for weeks and months. That is what happened in October 1929.

5 WITTGENSTEIN DRAWS THE CONCLUSION

The line of reasoning that slowly crystallized in Wittgenstein's mind in the autumn of 1929 was in its gist the following: If language itself belongs to the realm of physical objects, its sentences can be compared in the intended strong sense only with what is also physical. As Wittgenstein expressed his point in a lecture on 2 February 1930, 'the measuring-rod must . . . be in the same space as the thing measured . . .' Hence only a physicalistic language is possible, because only the sentences of a physicalistic language can be compared with facts and hence can represent them.

This conclusion seems to have dawned on Wittgenstein for the first time on 11 October 1929. On pp. 159–60 of MS 107 he still tries at first to say something about the immediately given:

> The immediately given is caught in a constant flux. (It has in fact the form of a river.)

He nevertheless realizes at once that he is trying to say the unsayable:

> It is quite clear that if one wants to say here the ultimate, one must instead come to the limit of the language which expresses it.[13]

Wittgenstein also realizes at once the implications of what he is saying:

> The worst philosophical errors always arise when we try to apply our ordinary – physical – language in the area of the immediately given.

This passage is from MS 107, p. 160 (dated 11 October 1929) and occurs also in *Philosophical Remarks,* VI, sec. 57.

In briefest possible terms, Wittgenstein's 'deduction' thus ran as follows: the basic sentences of our language must be compared directly with (virtually, superimposed on) the facts they represent. But since language itself belongs to the physical world (cf. preceding section), such comparisons must take place in the physical world. Hence only what there is in the physical world can be represented directly in language.

Wittgenstein does not yet trust his new insight, however, but goes on to discuss the question whether – and, if so, how – the phenomena of visual space can be expressed in a physicalistic language, which in this case means the language of Euclidean geometrical space. He formulates his problem as follows (p. 165):

> But the great question is: Can one translate the "blurredness" of a phenomenon by means of an imprecise drawing?[14]

In a few days he nevertheless finds a solution to the particular problem he is worried about. (See MS 107, pp. 164ff., especially pp. 172–4.)

And as soon as he has done so, Wittgenstein is ready to brand phenomenological language as 'absurd' (MS 107, p. 176).

Thus the change we claim took place in Wittgenstein's views in 1929 can be followed almost from day to day in his notebooks from that year.

6 WITTGENSTEIN'S CONVERSION AND THE PUBLICITY OF LANGUAGE

Undoubtedly other currents of thought than the one we have described were running through Wittgenstein's mind. However, the one line we have diagnosed was clearly crucial for him. This line of thought is interesting also because it is connected with other themes in Wittgenstein's thought. For one thing, why should he have thought that language itself was part of the 'second [i.e., physicalistic] system'? An answer, or at least part of an answer, is easily available. As was mentioned in chapter 1, sec. 9, it was the idea of language as the universal medium that encouraged Wittgenstein's belief in the publicity of language. In the *Tractatus*, Wittgenstein had in a similar way been led to the view that all that we can meaningfully express in language about language are its purely formal features. In contrast, the semantics of any language is inevitably inexpressible in that language. When Wittgenstein broadened his interests to questions of language use, language teaching and language learning, the same assumption led him to a somewhat more liberal but still quite striking view that all that can be involved in language teaching and language learning are the publicly observable aspects of the relevant occasions, including both the signs involved (as in the *Tractatus*) and also the accompanying behaviour. On one occasion (MS 108, p. 277) Wittgenstein writes:

> But if one says "How am I supposed to know what he means, all I can see are merely his symbols," then I say: "How is *he* supposed to know what he means, all that he has are merely his symbols."[15]

The context shows that Wittgenstein is there discussing the ineffability of semantics. But if the symbols are everything that is involved in an act of language learning, then what is being learned can scarcely be anything but a part of a public (physicalistic) language. Thus it seems likely that Wittgenstein's assumption that language learning must be about public (physicalistic) objects was promoted by his belief in language as the universal medium.

168 _Wittgenstein's change of mind_

The line of thought just sketched is embraced almost in so many words in the passage we quoted above from _Philosophical Remarks,_ VII, sec. 68. A little later (ibid., sec. 69, paragraphs 2–3) Wittgenstein likewise writes:

> What we understand by the word 'language' unwinds in physical time. (As is made perfectly clear by the comparison with a mechanism.) Only what corresponds to this mechanism in the primary world could be the primary language.

And in his lectures in Cambridge Wittgenstein says on 27 January 1930:

> We learn/teach language by using it. The linguistic convention is conveyed by linking the proposition to its verification.

The same exclusive concentration on the public aspects of language by Wittgenstein in 1929–30 is witnessed by his frequent use of the term 'grammar' where one would normally expect 'logic' or 'semantics'. This revealing tendency in Wittgenstein was commented on in chapter 1, sec. 6, above, and it is instantiated among other occasions in _Wittgenstein's Lectures, Cambridge 1930–32,_ pp. 8–17, 46–9, etc., in MS 105, pp. 3, 5, etc.

Even though the details of Wittgenstein's argument are perhaps less than completely clear, it is obvious that he is in the quoted passages moving from the public (physicalistic) character of _language_ to conclusions concerning of the nature of the _objects_ that can be represented in language.

It may also be significant that in Wittgenstein's complaints about Carnap's use of his ideas (see chapter 6, sec. 5, above) the two ideas of physicalism and 'the formal mode of speech' got entangled with each other. If our interpretation is right, the latter idea provided Wittgenstein with a reason to adopt the former.

The grounds of Wittgenstein's newly acquired belief in the publicity of language are nevertheless not entirely clear. It seems that they were not wholly transparent in Wittgenstein's own mind, either, nor completely trusted by him. We shall resume this important sub-plot of our story in chapter 10, secs. 1–2 and 12, below.

7 OTHER LINES OF THOUGHT

Other, converging, lines of thought contributed to this conclusion. It is, for instance, revealing to note Wittgenstein's preoccupations with another corollary to the need of language–world confrontations taken together with the assumptions that language itself belongs to the physical world. Because of these two assumptions, language–world comparisons must take place *in time*. This makes the status of Wittgenstein's objects in the *Tractatus,* which were atemporal entities, extremely dubious. For if these objects are atemporal, complexes of such objects are presumably also atemporal. But, if so, these atemporal facts will be impossible to compare with the propositions of our language, which belong to the world of physical time. This matter occupies Wittgenstein intensively in *Philosophical Remarks:*

> If the world of sense-data is timeless, how can we speak of it at all? . . .
> Our propositions are only verified by the present. (Ibid., V, sec. 48)

> If, now, phenomenological language isolates visual space and what goes on in it from everything else, how does it treat time? Is the time of 'visual' phenomena the time of our ordinary idioms of physics? (Ibid., VII, sec. 75)[16]

Thus considerations pertaining to the relation of language to time were also instrumental in alienating Wittgenstein from the atemporal phenomenological objects of the *Tractatus.*

It appears that Wittgenstein's growing doubts about phenomeno-logical objects in 1929 had still other sources. The more closely he examined these alleged objects, the less they seemed to exhibit the kind of logical behaviour genuine objects should conform to. They do not even seem to be capable of serving as values of quantifiers. For instance, in MS 107, pp. 10–12 Wittgenstein criticizes the Fregean conception of the logical form of number attributions.[17] They do not presuppose that the entities counted are members of some general range of all quantifiers.

> Not even a certain generality is essential to numerical statements. E.g., if I say "I see three equally large circles situated at equal distances" . . .
> If I give a correct description of the visual space in which 3 red circles are located on a blue background, then certainly there will not occur the expression "($\exists$x,y,z): x ε circular and red. y ε circular and red, etc." (pp. 11–12)

The objects Wittgenstein contemplates here are clearly phenom-enological. However, the arguments he presents in the quote tend to show that they are not only incapable of being cast into the usual logical notation; they are not really genuine objects of knowledge. Wittgenstein continues in fact:

> Admittedly one could write this: There are three circles, which have the property of being red. But here comes to light a difference between

improper objects; patches of colour in visual space, tones, etc., etc. and the elements of knowledge, the proper objects.

Here Wittgenstein in effect rejects phenomenological objects in favour of physicalistic ones. He fails to follow up on his result, however, and the passage therefore remains merely as anticipation of the change which took place in his thinking a couple of months later. There is nevertheless a striking contrast in emphasis between Wittgenstein's words here and his comments only ten notebook pages earlier on the independent reality of the visual space (see sec. 2 above). Surely such an independence should imply that visual objects can be proper objects in the sense of being genuine objects of knowledge.

The quoted passages are especially interesting for us here in that they are addressed to the same problem and virtually to the same example as the long passage from the *Big Typescript* (MS 213) quoted and analysed above in sec. 4 of chapter 6. A comparison between the two shows vividly how Wittgenstein's thinking developed from 1929 to 1933.

8 WITTGENSTEIN'S OWN TESTIMONY

It also appears from Wittgenstein's notebook entries in October 1929 that he himself experienced this period as a severe crisis in his philosophical work. Time and again he complains about not being able to think clearly. Thus on 8 October he writes:

> The philosophical region of my brain is still in the dark. And it's only when a light is again lit there that the work will go on. (MS 107, pp. 155–6)[18]

And on 9 October he writes:

> The problem of the truth of a sentence eludes me. I am aware that the most magnificent problems lie next to me. But I don't see them or cannot grasp them. (MS 107, p. 156)[19]

And on the threshold of his breakthrough Wittgenstein writes on 11 October:

> Today I feel a very special dearth of problems around me; which is a sure sign that the most important and hardest problems are *in front of me*. (MS 107, p. 158)[20]

After his breakthrough Wittgenstein writes (MS 107, p. 179):

Today I could do a little more philosophy, thank God.
[Könnte heute etwas mehr philosophieren, Gott sei dank.]

Thus we clearly have to date the decisive turn in Wittgenstein's thinking in October 1929.

9 CLUES TO WITTGENSTEIN'S DEVELOPMENT

What we have found also provides a foundation for understanding Wittgenstein's philosophical development from 1929 on. This development will be studied in the next few chapters. A few observations can nevertheless be made here.

First, Wittgenstein's change of mind was not in the least a result of, or the reason for, a shift in his attention from language–world relations to speech-acts or other similar matters of language usage. On the contrary, Wittgenstein's dramatic breakthrough was prompted by a keener awareness of the problem of language–world comparisons. In fact, our observations, especially the last few quotes of sec. 3, show that Wittgenstein's change of language paradigm was closely connected with his idea that the meaning of a sentence is shown by its method of verification. This connection is also shown by Wittgenstein's discussion with Schlick and others on 22 December 1929. Wittgenstein says there that he wants to explain why he no longer believes in a phenomenological language and ultimately gives as his reason that 'the meaning of a sentence consists in its verification'. And on 25 October 1929 (MS 107, p. 177) Wittgenstein writes of a particular sentence:

Its only relation to reality is the way it is verified.[21]

However, the verification of propositions in a physicalistic language is a many-splendoured thing, unlike the direct verification of a phenomenological proposition by a given *datum*. In the next few chapters, we shall suggest that Wittgenstein's interest in the procedures of verification was the first step in the development of his later idea of language-game.

The other main idea which helped to lead Wittgenstein to his new position was that language itself is a part of the physical world. It was noted that this idea was inspired by Wittgenstein's belief in language as the universal medium, which remained operative in his later

thought. What is especially interesting, in view of his later development, is that Wittgenstein takes the physicalistic character of language
to imply its *public* character. His rejection of phenomenological
languages is thus in effect a rejection of private languages, and as such
the germ of his famous but ill-named 'private language argument' in
the *Philosophical Investigations*, especially in *PI*, I, secs. 243–315.
This argument therefore has to be viewed against the background of
Wittgenstein's change of mind in October 1929. We shall take up this
aspect of the story again in chapter 10 below.

Thus the seeds of much of Wittgenstein's later philosophy were
sown in the autumn of 1929.

Some light can also be thrown on Wittgenstein's earlier development by what we have found. An observation which a scrutiny of
Wittgenstein's middle-period notebooks enables us to make is that
they contain absolutely no evidence indicating that a belief in a
phenomenological basis language had not been an integral part of his
philosophical stance all through his career until 1929. (Cf. chapter 3,
sec. 8, and chapter 6, sec. 4, para. (iv), above.) This supports what
was said in chapter 3 above about the nature of the objects Wittgenstein
postulated in the *Tractatus*.

NOTES

1 This entry in MS 107 is undated. It was made sometime in the summer
of 1929. Another reference to phenomenological languages is found in ibid.,
p. 4.

2 The German text reads: 'Und doch kann es eine phänomenologische
Sprache geben . . . Oder ist es so: Unsere gewöhnliche Sprache ist auch
phänomenologisch . . .'

The context of this quote is interesting, and shows that the problem of
phenomenological language was for Wittgenstein intimately related to the
problem of the limits of language. The German reads (MS 107, pp. 2–3):

Was ich nicht denken darf, kann die Sprache nicht ausdrücken. Das ist
unsere Beruhigung. Wenn mann aber sagt: Der Philosoph muß
aber eben in diesen Kessel hinuntersteigen und die reine Realität selbst
erfassen und ins Tageslicht ziehen, so lautet die Antwort daß er
dabei die Sprache hinten lassen müßte und daher unverrichteter
Dinge wieder heraufkommt. [Text unclear.] *Und doch kann es eine
phänomenologische Sprache geben.* [Emphasis added.]

3 The German text reads: 'Aus dem vorigen geht hervor – was übrigens
selbstverständlich ist – daß die phänomenologische Sprache das selbe
darstellt wie unsere gewöhnliche physikalische Ausdrucksweise – und nur

den Vorteil hat, daß man mit ihr manches kürzer und mit geringerer Gefahr des Mißverständnisses ausdrücken kann.
4 The German original reads:

Es scheint viel dafür sprechen daß die Abbildung des Gesichtsraums durch die Physik wirklich die einfachste ist. D. h. daß die Physik die wahre Phänomenologie wäre.

Aber dagegen läßt sich etwas einwenden: Die Physik strebt nämlich Wahrheit d.h. richtige Voraussagungen der Ereignisse an während das die Phänomenologie nicht tut; sie strebt *Sinn* nicht *Wahrheit* an.

Aber man kann sagen: Die Physik hat eine Sprache und in dieser Sprache sagt sie Sätze. Diese Sätze können wahr oder falsch sein. Diese Sätze bilden die Physik und die Grammatik die Phänomenologie (oder wie man es nennen will).

5 The original reads as follows:

Die phänomenologische Sprache beschreibt genau dasgleiche wie die gewöhnliche, physikalische. Sie muß sich nur auf das beschränken was verifizierbar ist.

Ist das überhaupt möglich?

Vergessen wir nicht daß die physikalische Sprache auch wieder nur die primäre Welt beschreibt und nicht etwa eine hypothetische Welt. Die Hypothese ist nur eine Annahme über die (richtige) praktische Art der Darstellung.

Ist nun dieses Hypothetische jeder Darstellung der Welt wesentlich?

Angenommen ich hätte ein so gutes Gedächtnis daß ich mich meiner sämtlichen Sinneseindrücke erinnern könnte. Dann spricht nichts dagegen daß ich sie beschriebe. Es wäre das eine Lebensbeschreibung. Und warum sollte ich nicht alles Hypothetische aus dieser Beschreibung fortlassen können?

The last paragraph makes a guest appearance in *Philosophical Remarks*, VII, sec. 67.
6 The original reads: 'Ist es nicht klar, daß das die unmittelbarste Beschreibung wäre, die sich denken läßt?'
7 The original reads:

. . . Der Gesichtsraum so wie er ist hat seine selbständige Realität.

Er selbst enthält kein Subjekt. Er ist autonom.

Er läßt sich unmittelbar beschreiben (aber wir sind weit davon entfernt eine Ausdrucksweise zu kennen die ihn beschreibt). Die gewöhnliche physikalische Sprache bezieht sich auf ihn in einer *sehr* komplizierten und uns instinktiv bekannten Weise.

8 The original reads: 'Die Beschreibung der Phänomene mittels der Hypothese der Körperwelt ist unumgänglich durch ihre Einfachkeit verglichen mit der unfaßbar komplizierten phänomenologischen Beschreibung. Wenn ich verschiedene zerstreute Stücke eines Kreises sehe . . . so ist ihre genaue direkte Beschreibung vielleicht unmöglich aber die Angabe daß es diese Stücke eines Kreises sind . . . ist einfach.'

9 The original reads: 'Was das unmittelbare Datum zu einem Satz der gewöhnlichen Sprache ist den es verifiziert, das ist die gesehene arithmetische Beziehung der Strukturen zu der Gleichung die sie verifiziert.'

10 These sentences appear later in *Philosophical Remarks*, IV, sec. 43. The original German of the latter has the following variant: 'Man muß den Satz mit der Wirklichkeit *zur Deckung bringen* können.'

11 The original reads: 'Die Verification ist nicht *ein* Anzeichen der Wahrheit sondern *der* Sinn des Satzes.'

12 The original is in MS 107, p. 153, and reads: 'Ich muß die Wirklichkeit ja tatsächlich mit dem Satz *vergleichen* können.'

13 The German text of these two quotes reads:

Das unmittelbare ist in ständigem Fluß begriffen. (Es hat tatsächlich die Form eines Stromes.) . . .

Es ist ganz klar, daß wenn man hier das Letzte sagen will man eher auf die Grenze der Sprache kommen muß, die es ausdrückt.

14 The German text reads (p. 165): 'Die große Frage aber ist: kann man die "Verschwommenheit" des Phänomens in eine Ungenauigkeit der Zeichnung übersetzen?'

15 The German text is given in Appendix to chapter 1 above.

16 Cf. here also *Philosophical Remarks*, V, secs. 49–52; VII, sec. 67–72.

17 The German original reads:

Nicht einmal eine gewisse Allgemeinheit ist der Zahlangabe wesentlich. Wenn ich z.B. sage "ich sehe drei gleichgroße Kreise in gleichen Abständen angeordnet".

[Wittgenstein draws a picture]

Wenn ich eine richtige Beschreibung des Gesichtfeldes gebe in dem 3 rote Kreise auf blauem Grund stehen, so wird da gewiß nicht der Ausdruck vorkommen "($\exists$x,y,z): x ε kreisförmig und rot. y ε kreisförmig und rot, etc." . . .

Freilich könnte man so schreiben: Es gibt drei Kreise, die die Eigenschaft haben rot zu sein. Aber hier tritt der Unterschied zu Tage zwischen uneigentlichen Gegenständen, Farbflecken im Gesichtsfeld, Tönen, etc. etc. und den Elementen der Erkenntnis, den eigentlichen Gegenständen.

18 The original reads: 'Die philosophische Gegend meines Gehirns liegt noch immer im Dunkeln. Und erst wenn da wieder das Licht angezündet wird geht die Arbeit wieder an.'

19 The German reads: 'Das Problem der Wahrheit eines Satzes ent-schlüpft mir. Ich bin nur bewußt daß die herrlichsten Probleme in meinen nächsten Nähe liegen. Aber ich sehe sie nicht oder kann sie nicht fassen.

20 The German reads: 'Ich fühle heute eine so besondere Armut an Problemen um mich; ein sicheres Zeichen daß *vor mir* die wichtigsten und härtesten Probleme liegen.'

21 The German reads: 'seine einzige Beziehung zur Wirklichkeit ist die Art seiner Verification'.

8

From Ostension to Language-games

1 THE LIMITS OF OSTENSION

If we are right, the shift in Wittgenstein's language paradigm discussed in the preceding two chapters was the only important initial
novelty in his early middle-period thought.[1] It is nevertheless clear
that it could not remain the only change in Wittgenstein's philosophy.
This initial change soon inspired and necessitated others. What
happened in Wittgenstein's thinking in (roughly) 1929–36 was that he
gradually worked his way to clarity as to what else he had to modify in
his earlier philosophy. For this reason, it is crucial to understand what
Wittgenstein did in 1929 in order to understand his entire subsequent
philosophy.

The basic facts of the case are clear enough. In chapter 7, secs. 3–5,
above, we saw that Wittgenstein's change of his basic language was
motivated by the requirement that language must be capable of being
compared with reality *directly*. But, since the sentences of a language
belong to the physical 'system', they can be compared only with the
physical reality. Hence they can directly speak only of the physical
world, i.e., the languge must be physicalistic. But this was not the end
of the story. As Wittgenstein gradually came to appreciate, not all
propositions dealing with physical reality can be compared with their
subject matter without further ado, either. He originally required that
a proposition must be capable of being 'fitted on to reality' (cf.
Philosophical Remarks, V, sec. 54), but soon he is worried as to how
the language–world links really operate. In *Philosophical Remarks*,
III, sec. 32, he asks:

Where does the sign link up with the world?

In that book, Wittgenstein never really answers his own question.

When Wittgenstein traded his onetime phenomenological basis
language for an everyday physicalistic one, he thereby acquired a new
set of problems. As long as he thought that ultimate objects are given

to us by direct acquaintance, there was no problem as to how the names of these objects are taught and learned or what the basic language–world links are. The basic language–world links are established by direct confrontations with the objects that one's language speaks of, and they are simple two-place relations between a name and the corresponding object of acquaintance. But in a physicalistic language the intricate web of language–world relations becomes a problem. Many physical objects are too large, too small, too distant, or otherwise too inaccessible to our senses to allow us to confront them directly in our experience. There is no reason, either, that this should not be the case with the objects which physically speaking are the most basic ones, e.g., atoms. Thus Wittgenstein's change of his language paradigm meant that language–world relations became a problem for him, whether they are considered from the vantage point of name–object relations, language teaching and language learning, or from the vantage point of comparisons between a proposition and reality. It is ironic that the new position to which Wittgenstein was led by emphasizing the importance and the immediacy of language–world comparisons had the consequence of making those very same comparisons a serious problem from him.

Initially, Wittgenstein probably thought that the character of his new basic language as an *everyday* language dealing with medium-sized perceptible physical objects was enough to avoid most of the problems. Of course, this assumption presupposed some sort of reduction of the inaccessible part of the world of mathematical physics to the world of everyday physical objects and to this behaviour. This idea would have been as natural for Wittgenstein (cf., e.g., *PI*, I, sec. 116) as it was for Russell, as witnessed, e.g., by *The Problems of Philosophy*.[2] But gradually it became clear to Wittgenstein that not all important problems about language–world relations could be dismissed in this way.

The 1929 change of basic language thus contains the seeds of Wittgenstein's further development. This can be seen especially vividly by considering language learning and language teaching. Ostension, that heir of Wittgenstein's all-important idea of 'showing' in the *Tractatus*, can happily serve as the one and only way that is needed to define sense-data (or other objects of immediate experience) or otherwise to introduce them into one's discourse. But when the language of such immediately given objects was replaced by an everyday physicalistic language, ostension could no longer do the whole job or even the main job. The variety and variability of everyday physical objects, even apart from the vagaries of the more esoteric entities populating the world of sciences, are simply too radical to enable us to define them ostensively. How do you point to the State of California?; to objects you do not know by acquaintance in Russell's sense? How do you define ostensively entities of other logical types than individuals? All through his middle period, Wittgenstein repeatedly expresses his worries about ostension and assembles an impressive collection of reminders of its failures.

For instance, even when Wittgenstein claims on p. 1 of *The Blue Book* that ostensive definitions comprise all nonverbal definitions, he immediately qualifies his statement by saying that this holds only 'very roughly' and asks:

> Need the ostensive definition itself be understood? Can't the ostensive definition be misunderstood?

The most telling criticism Wittgenstein makes is probably that in order to understand what the teacher is pointing to in ostensive defining, the hearer must know the logical status of the entity defined. Thus, if you point to two red square pieces of paper and utter a word (in a definitory context), are you defining a particular (this pair of objects), a material (paper), a form (square), a colour (red), or a number (two)?[3] The basic difficulty here is due to the multiplicity of logically different kinds of basic entities to be defined, which goes way beyond the multiplicity we would have to cope with if we only had objects of immediate experience to define in the last analysis. Thus one cannot, e.g., define ostensively absent objects, even if one is speaking over the phone to someone who sees them (MS 116, sec. 377). And the same goes even for other people's immediate experiences. Moreover, if the very words 'there' and 'this' used in ostensive defining are thought of as being themselves introduced ostensively, this ostension would have to be quite different from ordinary ostensive teaching (*PI*, I, secs. 9, 38).

In view of this plethora of indictments against ostensive defining, it is striking that Wittgenstein nevertheless still considered it as the paradigm case of nonverbal explanation of meaning in 1933–34, when he dictated *The Blue Book*. (It is also curious that he later put forward in the *Philosophical Investigations* as criticisms of ostensive definitions many of the same ideas which he had held during his middle period while he had assigned to ostensive definitions an extremely important place in language understanding.) We shall return to the role of ostension in Wittgenstein's middle-period philosophy in sec. 4 below. Wittgenstein's persistence in emphasizing ostension is in any case a vivid testimony to his deep commitment to the ideas of showing and ostension. At the same time, Wittgenstein's tardiness in discarding the idea of ostensive definition is also due to his difficulties in finding a viable alternative account of meaning and meaning-giving. One of the most fascinating facets of Wittgenstein's philosophical career is the way he gradually fought his way to clarity in this crucial matter. His struggle is witnessed by his middle-period writings, perhaps most dramatically by *The Blue and Brown Books*. Before discussing these developments, we nevertheless have to put the issues in a somewhat more general perspective.

2 OSTENSION AND NAMING

The idea that ostension is the prime vehicle of language teaching and language learning has a meaning-theoretical counterpart. It is the idea that the basic links between language and the world are simple two-place relations of naming. This idea is embraced by Wittgenstein in the *Tractatus*. If it is correct, it implies the possibility of using ostension as the typical medium of meaning-giving. For all we then have to do in order to assign a language its meaning is to establish the requisite basic naming (world–object) relations. And what could be a simpler way of doing that than exhibiting each object and assigning a name to it in an act of ostensive defining? The attractions of this view are illustrated by the recent popularity of Kripke's so-called causal theory of naming,[4] which is of course nothing but a variant of Wittgenstein's sometime doctrine.

Wittgenstein's eventual disenchantment with ostension went hand in hand with his growing criticism of simple two-place relations of naming as the paradigm case of language–world connections. This simple model was made impossible by Wittgenstein's adoption of a physicalistic basis language. Like Wittgenstein's criticisms of ostension, his doubts in this department began early and gradually escalated to a frontal attack. From the time of *Philosophical Grammar* on, Wittgenstein habitually illustrates the view he is criticizing by a quote from St Augustine and formulates his criticisms by reference to it.[5] Wittgenstein describes the conception he is abandoning by saying that on it, naming is the end-all and be-all of language understanding and that on it you understand a word completely as soon as you know what it stands for (*PI*, I, sec. 264). We shall later find that in the *Philosophical Investigations* Wittgenstein distinguishes this mistaken conception of word–object relationships even terminologically in the *PI* from a correct (or at least neutral) way of thinking about those relationships.[6]

3 OSTENSION AND RULES

Why, then, did Wittgenstein stake so much on ostensive definitions during his middle period if he was well aware of the problems besetting them? Why did he continue to rely on these definitions after he realized that the simple two-place relations they can establish are insufficient as a basis of semantics? In spite of some hesitation on Wittgenstein's part, the main answer to these questions is fairly clear. Wittgenstein thought that a successful ostensive definition could give to the recipient the *rule* for the use of the word to be defined, or at least an important part of such a rule.[7] For this reason, Wittgenstein could continue to emphasize the importance of ostensive definitions even after he began to hold that it is the use of a word (its 'grammar') that characterizes its meaning. If this use is governed by a rule and if this rule can be conveyed to a learner in an ostensive definition, such a definition can still serve as a typical way of meaning-giving. This, by and large, was Wittgenstein's position during his middle period.

That this was Wittgenstein's view is shown among other things by *Philosophical Grammar,* II, sec. 24:

> By "explanation of the meaning of a sign" we mean other rules for use but above all *definitions.* The distinction between verbal definitions and ostensive definitions gives a rough division of these types of explanation.
>
> It may seem to us as if the other *grammatical rules* for a word had to follow from its ostensive definition, since after all an ostensive definition, e.g. "that is called 'red'" determines the meaning of the word "red". [Emphasis added in the last sentence.]

Wittgenstein goes on to point out that other rules are needed in language over and above those that are conveyed to the learner in an ostensive definition. However, he sees the role of ostensive definitions as the one and only nonverbal way of giving to the learner certain crucial rules governing the word to be learned.

Perhaps the clearest statement of Wittgenstein's emphasis on rules in his middle-period philosophy of language is the following:[8]

> To explain a word such as "red" by pointing to something gives but one rule for its use, and in cases where one cannot point, rules of a different sort are given. All the rules together give the meaning . . .
> The rules constitute the meaning, and are not responsible for it.

The idea of rule colours Wittgenstein's whole conception (at the time) of his philosophical enterprise. A little later (*Philosophical Grammar,* II, sec. 32) he writes:[9]

> We are interested in language as a process in accordance with explicit rules. For philosophical problems are misunderstandings which must be removed by clarifying the rules according to which we are inclined to use words.

It is, furthermore, instructive to see that during his middle period Wittgenstein gives a different twist to the thought-experiment of a jungle-linguist (cf. *PI,* I, sec. 206) from the one he gives to it later, in that he emphasizes the role of rules in the learning of the unknown language. In the *Big Typescript* (MS 213), p. 426 he writes:[10]

> The savages have games (or at least we call them games) for which they possess no written rules, no compendium of rules. Let's consider now the activity of an explorer who visits the country of these people and devises lists of rules for these games. That is precisely analogous to what a philosopher does.

It is also interesting to see that Wittgenstein does not yet at this point have a full-fledged notion of language-game, even though he is groping towards it, for he continues:

> (But why don't I say: "The savages have languages (or at least . . .) for which they don't possess any written grammar . . ."?)

It is likewise highly significant to see that, whereas in the *Philosophical Investigations* language-games will later be the rock bottom of semantics, in *Philosophical Grammar,* II, p. 244, rules have the same exalted status:

> You can't get behind the rules, because there isn't any behind.

If there is a distinctive position that characterizes Wittgenstein's middle period, here it is: it is the role of rules in language use and language understanding. Some consequences of this general position deserve special mention. First, learning the meaning of a word will consist in the acquisition of a rule (or a complex of rules) governing its use. This is in contrast both to his earlier view, according to which the meaning of a word is learned by grasping a simple two-place relation, and to his later views, according to which what is acquired in learning a new meaning is the mastery of a technique, not the knowledge of a rule.

This interpretation of Wittgenstein's middle period might seem to involve a serious problem, however. We said that Wittgenstein went on to rely on ostensive definitions ('showings') because he thought that they can give the learner the rule which governs the use of the word to be learned. But how can they possibly do this? How can one single ostensive confrontation with the object to be defined give me the rule for using the name of this object?

There is a genuine difficulty here, but it is Wittgenstein's sometime problem, not a difficulty for our interpretation. In fact, an analogous problem besets Wittgenstein's early philosophy of language. In the *Tractatus* it is an ostension-like showing that gives me an object, and not just the existence of the object, but also its logical form. Now this logical form goes way beyond what can be immediately witnessed. It governs among other things the way in which the object can or cannot enter into different possible states of affairs. (Cf. 2.012–2.0141.) How can immediate acquaintance with the object give one such a form? Wittgenstein never tells us, and we believe that this failure shows that there is a serious difficulty in his early philosophy.

The problems as to how ostension can give us the rule which governs the use of the *definiendum* is merely a new form of this older problem. This problem was eventually instrumental in forcing Wittgenstein out of his middle-period position. However, the presence of this problem in Wittgenstein's middle-period philosophy is no surprise and no objection to our interpretation. For the purpose of confirming this interpretation, it suffices to show that Wittgenstein in fact believed that an ostensive definition can give the learner a rule for the use of the defined word; and this we showed earlier in this section.

4 OSTENSION AND CONNECTIONS BETWEEN LANGUAGE AND REALITY

What was said in secs. 1–3 above of Wittgenstein's development nevertheless leaves a gap in his chronology. What we have said applies to Wittgenstein's position roughly in 1933–4. In 1929–33 he explored a different avenue which nevertheless did not lead to a satisfactory philosophical position. It is not our aim to explore this Wittgensteinian byway in detail. However, the line of thought which Wittgenstein adopted for a while colours strongly everything Wittgenstein said about ostension in 1930–2 and is closely connected with other important Wittgensteinian ideas. It is therefore in order to discuss it briefly. The concept of ostension again serves as a useful focal point. Wittgenstein does not use the term 'ostensive definition' in the

Tractatus, and ostensive definitions do not seem to play any role there. Yet he is on the record as confessing that 'in the *Tractatus* logical analysis and ostensive definition were unclear' to him. Wittgenstein's self-confessed mistake was that he 'thought that there was "a connexion between language and reality"'. (*Ludwig Wittgenstein and the Vienna Circle,* pp. 209–10. Wittgenstein made these remarks on 1 July 1932.) This statement shows two remarkable things. First, it suggests that, appearances notwithstanding, ostension was taken by Wittgenstein in the *Tractatus* to be *the* connection between language and the world. It is *the* way in which the basic unanalysable links between language and reality, viz. the name–object relations are established. Ostension *is* showing in the sense in which Wittgenstein uses this term. This is of course precisely what we argued above in chapter 3, sec. 10. This way of looking at the *Tractatus* is confirmed further by Waismann's 'Theses' (unpublished as Appendix B to *Ludwig Wittgenstein and Vienna Circle*) in which he tried to capture the philosophy of the *Tractatus.* There we read (p. 246):

> There are two ways of giving a sign meaning: 1. By means of *ostension* . . . 2. By means of *definition.* In this case the meaning of a sign is explained by means of signs that already have a meaning.
>
> A definition remains within language. Ostension steps outside language and connects signs with reality.

Second, the quoted statement shows that in 1932 Wittgenstein rejected this view lock, stock, and barrel.

Why the rejection? What happened seems to have been this: Wittgenstein's physicalistic turn in October 1929 was prompted (among other things) by his belief in language as the universal medium and in the consequent ineffability of all semantics, i.e., the ineffability of all connections between language and reality. This led him to suspect everything that is not reflected in the purely formal aspects of language. But in 1929–33 Wittgenstein pushed the idea of the ineffability of semantics even further than in the *Tractatus.* The idea of 'showing', reformulated as the notion of ostensive defining, was among the most prominent victims of this sweeping rejection. In rejecting all matters semantical, Wittgenstein was not only in tune with the Vienna Circle and its self-imposed restriction to the 'formal mode' of language use. Wittgenstein accused Carnap in so many words (as we saw above in chapter 1, sec. 5) for borrowing the idea of the ineffability of semantics from him without proper acknowledgement.

But even though the inexpressibility of semantics is the ostensible reason why Wittgenstein rejected ostensive definitions for a while, the deeper reasons were somewhat different. After all, the ineffability of semantics did not prevent Wittgenstein from emphasizing the role of ostension under the guise of showing in the *Tractatus*. Wittgenstein's real reasons were the ones indicated in sec. 1 above. His switch from a phenomenological language to a physicalistic one made it impossible for him to define all his irreducible objects ostensively. It was pointed out above in sec. 1 that one of Wittgenstein's major objections to ostensive definitions was their dependence on the logical status of the entity to be defined, which the learner therefore must know independently. Now many of such logical differences between different kinds of entities are due largely to Wittgenstein's recently acquired physicalistic semantics and logic. This point can be illustrated, e.g., by recalling Wittgenstein's saying in *PI*, I, sec. 28, that the same gesture may be part of an ostensive definition of 'the name of a person, as that of a colour, of a race, or even of a point of the compass'. The differences between those options clearly belong to the ontology of everyday objects rather than to the phenomenological realm.

For a mixture of such reasons Wittgenstein rejected for a while the idea that ostensive definitions can serve as language–world links. According to Wittgenstein's new wider conception of what is included in language, ostensive definitions do not enable us to step outside language, nor do they establish connections between language and reality. This belittling view of ostension dominates for instance *Wittgenstein's Lectures, Cambridge 1930–32*. There we find near-dismissals of ostensive definitions like the following:

> The ostensive definition does not get us away from symbolism . . . All we can do in an ostensive definition is to replace one set of symbols by another. The result is a proposition, which can be true or false. (p. 23, and cf. p. 43 for a similar statement)

This may seem to be blatantly wrong, for surely gesture of pointing can take us out of the sphere of mere language – or so it seems. Wittgenstein denies this, and explains that what we establish in an ostensive definition is not a link between language and reality, but a link between written or spoken language and *the language of gestures*.

> One of the implements of our language is ostensive definition. But with such ostensive signs we have only a mere calculus.

> What we call a connection between language and reality is the connection between spoken language and, for example, the language of gestures. (Ibid., p. 102)[11]

Thus ostensive definitions temporarily lose their central role in language teaching and language learning for Wittgenstein. The same emphasis on the ineffability of semantics which propelled the ideas of showing and ostension to prominence in Wittgenstein's thinking thus later prompted their near-downfall. Consequently, ostensive definitions are not mentioned at all (as far as we have ascertained) in *Philosophical Remarks*. This view persists still in parts of *Philosophical Grammar*:

> The ostensive definition may be regarded as a rule for translating from gesture language into a word langue. (See IV, sec. 45.)

The occurrence of the term 'rule' in this quotation nevertheless foreshadows Wittgenstein's next move.

In more general terms, Wittgenstein's treatment of ostension as amounting merely to a translation from gesture language to word language is part and parcel of his explanatory strategy in 1930–2. He is trying to get rid of all semantical problems, i.e., all problems concerning language–world relations, by pointing out that they cannot be expressed in language. This idea is not entirely new, and it echoes partly the last proposition of the *Tractatus*. (It is also remarkably similar to the stance adopted by the Vienna Circle at the same time.) However, in 1930–2 Wittgenstein pushed it further than in the *Tractatus* or, perhaps more appropriate expressed, he took a dimmer view than he had earlier done of what can be shown. A characteristic statement expressing this line of thought is found in MS 108, p. 196 (dated 28 June 1930):[12]

> The thought 'that such and such is the case (p)' is made true by the fact that the case is such and such (p). That the connection between thoughts and the world cannot be represented (for this representation doesn't say anything at all) must be the answer to my problems.

Wittgenstein's self-comparison with Kant quoted in chapter 1, sec. 3, above, is another expression of the same explanatory strategy. It was penned by Wittgenstein on 10 February 1931 (MS 110, p. 61). That Wittgenstein's statement on 28 June 1930 pertains also to language and not merely to thinking is confirmed by what Wittgenstein says one day and two pages later: 'The thought is a symbol.' ('Der Gedanke ist ein Symbol.')

Similar ideas are aired by Wittgenstein in MS 108, pp. 193–6, where he goes so far as to suggest that his leading ideas are based on the insight that one cannot transcend language in language or transcend one's thoughts in thinking. His denial on 1 July 1932 (quoted above)

of 'a connexion between language and reality' is but another manifestation of the same syndrome. In general, Wittgenstein seems to
have thought during this phase of his philosophical quest that his most
important problems would be dissolved as soon as one realized the
ineffability of semantics.

However, in the long run – a run of about three years – this attempt
to dismiss all semantical problems because they are ineffable did not
satisfy Wittgenstein. When we open *The Blue Book, Wittgenstein's
Lectures, Cambridge 1932–35,* or even *Philosophical Grammar,* we
find not only a wealth of references to ostensive definitions but a
renewed emphasis on their role. What has happened? What happened
meanwhile is that a new concept entered the centre stage of
Wittgenstein's thought: the concept of *rule.* Wittgenstein no longer
thinks that he can get rid of language–world links by sending them to
Coventry. Now he acknowledges rules as constituting the bridge
between the two.[13] Accordingly, Wittgenstein sees rules as the end-all
and be-all of language, or at least of his chosen way of looking at
language. This also enables Wittgenstein again to assign pride of place
to ostensive definitions – because and in so far as they convey to the
learner the *rule* which is to be obeyed by the *definiendum.* Even
though this vindication of ostensive definitions is not without qualifications, it is unmistakable. What strong emphasis Wittgenstein puts
on ostensive definitions in *The Blue Book* is shown for instance by his
use of them as the prime example of meaning-giving on p. 37:

> We need only ask ourselves: "How should we explain what the sentence
> means?" Such an explanation might consist of *ostensive definitions.* We
> should say, e.g., "this is King's College" (pointing to the building),
> "this is fire" (pointing to a fire). *This shews you the way in which words
> and things are connected.* [Emphasis added.]

Likewise, in MS 114 (begun on 27 May 1932), p. 168, Wittgenstein
says without hesitation that 'an ostensive definition establishes [*stellt
her*] a connection [*Verbindung*] between a word and "a thing" ["*einer
Sache*"]'. This connection is calculated to enable the mechanism of
which our language is a part to function in a certain way.[14]

It is likewise instructive to see that even Wittgenstein's growing
doubts about ostensive definitions are now couched in terms of rules:

> "Ostensive definition" is used in many senses. The ostensive definition
> of "I" involves a different sort of pointing than the ostensive definition
> of "object", though one might point to the same thing in both cases. An
> ostensive definition is not really a definition at all. *Ostensive definition
> is only one rule for the use of a word.* [Emphasis added. From
> *Wittgenstein's Lectures, Cambridge 1932–1935,* p. 45][15]

It is this second wind of ostensive definitions in Wittgenstein's philosophy that carries them to their prominent position on the first page of *The Blue Book* as the only form of nonverbal definitions. Later, ostensive definitions lose their privileged position again, this time because they (and the rules they were supposed to give to the learner) lose their primacy in relation to language-games. But before that could happen, Wittgenstein had to develop a full-fledged notion of language-game and to assign to language-games the role ostensive definitions had held in the *Tractatus*, viz. the role of connecting language and the world. We shall witness this process in the next few sections of this chapter.

5 FROM RULES TO LANGUAGE-GAMES

Wittgenstein's heavy reliance on rules soon posed serious problems for him. In the long haul, not even rules could do the job of saving ostensive definitions. In the *Tractatus*, the naming relations are absolutely simple. The only thing you can say of the relation of a name to its object is that the name stands for the object. There is nothing that constitutes or mediates this relation. Now Wittgenstein introduces for the first time such an intermediary in the form of the rule which governs the application of a name to its objects. But the postulation of such an intermediary does not end the questions that one can – and must – raise here. For instance, what is the conceptual status of this intermediate entity, the rule? How precisely does it accomplish its mediating task? What does it mean to follow such a rule? Here we can see the germ of one of the major themes of Wittgenstein's later philosophy, the problem of rule-following.

The nature of rules was an urgent problem for Wittgenstein for a variety of reasons. If there was anything that went against his grain, it was the postulation of obscure intermediate entities (*Mittelwesen*, as he sometimes called them) between our language and the world.[16] And yet at this stage of his thinking rules threatened to become for him such intermediaries. What can we say about them? What is the mode of existence of these abstract rules? What role do they play in the actual understanding of language, anyway? The introduction of rules and criteria does not seem to clarify the relation of a name to its object but to introduce a further mystery into the picture. As Wittgenstein himself later put it,

Naming appears as a *queer* connection of a word with an object. (*PI*, I, sec. 38)

To express the problem in Wittgenstein's own terms, what does it mean to follow a rule? Wittgenstein discusses this question, or closely related questions, several times during his middle period and later most extensively in the *Philosophical Investigations*, I, secs. 143–242. One possible attempted answer is that to follow a rule is merely to act in accordance with it. Wittgenstein initially rejects this view sharply. In *The Blue Book*, pp. 12–13, Wittgenstein rejects the view that the teaching of language is a mere drill whose function is to make sure that the learner in fact follows the rules. He complains that in this way you can only understand the causal antecedents of language use, not its real nature. In logically informed language use (fully understood observance of a rule) 'the rule is *involved* in the understanding, obeying, etc.', in other words, 'as I should like to express it, the symbol of the rule forms part of the calculation.'

But this view did not satisfy Wittgenstein in the long run. For one thing, it leads to a regress. If to follow a rule is to apply a symbolic expression for it, as a formula in calculation, how do we know that we follow the symbol correctly? What is it to follow the symbolic expression of a rule? In the *Philosophical Investigations*, Wittgenstein later spells out at length the reasons why he had rejected his own earlier attempted solution to the rule-following problem.

What, then, does rule-following – at least the kind of rule-following involved in the use of language – consist in? How do we decide when a rule is being followed? When does a rule exist that can mediate a word–object relation? Here is what Wittgenstein says of the matter, toward the end of his famous rule-following discussion (*PI*, I, secs. 143–242):

> Following a rule is analogous to obeying an order. We are trained [*aberichtet*] to do so; we react to an order in a particular way. But what if one person reacts in one way and another in another to the order and the training? Which one is right?

> Suppose you come as an explorer into an unknown country with a language quite strange to you. In what circumstances would you say that the people there gave orders, understood them, obeyed them, rebelled against them, and so on?

> People's shared way of acting [or, more literally: 'The shared human way of acting'] is the frame of reference by means of which we interpret an unknown language. (*PI*, I, sec. 206)[17]

What Wittgenstein's point in *PI*, I, sec. 206, amounts to is an entirely different answer to the question of rule-following from what he had said himself in *The Blue Book*, in *Philosophical Remarks*, and other middle-period writings. If you suspect that someone is merely acting in accordance with a rule but not really following it, the question Wittgenstein later wants to raise is not whether the agent has some particular symbolic formulation in his mind when he follows the rule or what role some particular codification of the rule plays in his process of rule-following. As Wittgenstein later (*PI*, II, xi, p. 217) put this point,

> If God had looked into our minds he would not be able to see there whom we are speaking of.

The thing to do in investigating whether someone is following the rule, and not merely acting in accordance with it, is to explore the broader behavioural and conceptual context in which the alleged rule-following takes place. Suppose that I give an order to someone and he acts in accordance with it. Suppose further that I suspect that he did not really obey my order, e.g., that his action was prompted by a conscious decision independent of my order or perhaps by a panic reaction. How (in principle) do I decide? Wittgenstein answers: Not by looking inside his mind, but by raising such questions as, e.g., 'Has he been trained to obey orders in the first place?'; 'What similar practices has he been taught?'; etc. In the last analysis, it is only the common framework of modes of behaviour which he and I share that can provide the answer.

Wittgenstein calls this wider horizon of related rule-governed activities, which is needed to answer questions of rule-following, a *language-game*. Indeed, it is only against the backdrop of some particular language-game that questions of rule-following can be meaningfully asked in the first place. This explains the crucial role of language-games in Wittgenstein's mature philosophy. Even though the term appears informal and even playful, the notion of language-game has a sharply defined function in Wittgenstein's late philosophy. It is an answer to an important specific question to which he had himself given a different answer earlier. Its primary function is theoretical, not therapeutical.

The job of actually played language-games cannot be done by rules in any sense in which their linguistic or symbolic expressions are involved. For instance, with a side glance at the role he had assigned to the symbolic expression of a rule in following it in *The Blue Book*, Wittgenstein writes in *PI*, I, sec. 221:

> My symbolic expression was really a mythological description of the use of a rule.

A closely similar point is made by Wittgenstein in *PI*, I, sec. 183.

Thus Wittgenstein was gradually led from an emphasis on rules as mediating the language–world connections to a position that it is entire language-games that serve in this all-important mediating role. The end-point of this development is seen from passages like *PI*, I, secs. 82–6. This development marks the transition from Wittgenstein's middle-period thinking to his mature philosophy in the *Philosophical Investigations*. The slow transition is seen in different ways in Wittgenstein's writings, and it has several interesting repercussions.

One consequence is that ostensive definitions lose their crucial importance. They are replaced by language-games as the central concept in Wittgenstein's theory of language. The end point of this development is seen from the *Philosophical Investigations*. After having argued that an ostensive definition alone will not explain the meaning (use) of a name, he writes in the same spirit:

> One has already to know (or to be able to do) something in order to be capable of asking a thing's name. But what does one have to know? (I, sec. 30)

It is clear that Wittgenstein does not any longer accept rules as an answer to his own question. Wittgenstein answers his own question a little later (sec. 37):

> What is the relation between name and thing named? – Well, what *is* it? Look at language-game (2) [explained earlier by Wittgenstein] or another one: There you can see what this relation can consist in.[18]

So it is the entire language-game that constitutes the name–object relation, not a particular rule or criterion.

Thus it is the idea of language-game that in Wittgenstein's later philosophy replaces the role of rules that he relied on during his middle period. Language-games are Wittgenstein's definitive solution to the problems he could not handle by means of the concept of rule. They are characteristic of Wittgenstein's last period in contradistinction to his middle period, in so far as the two can really be told apart.

6 LANGUAGE-GAMES AS CONSTITUTING NAMING RELATIONS

This gradual genesis of the concept of language-game is so important as to deserve some additional discussion. From the beginning of Wittgenstein's new interest in philosophy, he had emphasized the *use* of language as a key to its meaning. However, at the early stages of the new approach Wittgenstein's conception of use was rather undifferentiated. Ostension was prominently connected with it, and is conception of use had also frequent overtones of mere usage. In crystallizing his views, Wittgenstein came to put more and more weight on the complex nonverbal activities which we associate with different words and phrases. For these Wittgenstein used the term *language-game*. In *The Blue and Brown Books* (plus to some extent in the other works from the same period) one can follow almost step by step the process by means of which Wittgenstein came to his mature view of language-games as constituting the basic relations between language and the world.

When Wittgenstein first introduces the idea of a game into his discussions of how language operates, its function is different from the role which it in the end assumes. His initial point is merely to highlight the central role of rules in his approach to language.

> Grammar describes the use of words in the language. So it has somewhat the same relation to language as the description of a game, *the rules of the game* [emphasis added], have to the game.

> But we look at games and language from the viewpoint of a game played according to rules. That is, we always *compare* language with a procedure of that kind. (*Philosophical Grammar*, II, sec. 26; the standard translation has been modified)

Far from thinking of the role of games as constituting language–world relationships, Wittgenstein was thus glorifying the role of rules in the use of language. Games were a suitable object of comparison for a philosophical student of language because they were rule-governed activities. In *Philosophical Grammar*, III, sec. 77, Wittgenstein describes his strategy by saying:

> When we study language we envisage it as a game with fixed rules. We compare it with, and measure it against, a game of that kind.

This was the early use of the idea of game in Wittgenstein: a means of highlighting the role of rules in the use of language. The games Wittgenstein has in mind are artifically constructed objects of comparison for the actual use of language. They serve the same purpose as the idea of calculus in much of Wittgenstein's middle-period philosophy.[19]

It is crucial for the purpose of understanding Wittgenstein's thinking to realize what his problems were. He is asking certain questions that were made urgent for him by his change of language paradigm, first and foremost the questions: How is our language connected wit the world? What is the relation of a name to the object named? An early stage of Wittgenstein's quest is illustrated by *Philosophical Remarks,* III, sec. 32. Wittgenstein raises there once again the paramount question, '. . . what is the connection between signs and world?' He offers no clear-cut answer, and merely says: 'Perhaps we have to say that the phrase "interpretation of signs" is misleading and instead we ought to say "the use of signs".' Wittgenstein does not take this idea to be a full answer to his own question. He does not yet think of the use of a sign as constituting the very 'connection between sign and world' he is looking for.

Characteristically, only the use of language is mentioned here by Wittgenstein, not language-games. Their role in *Philosophical Grammar* and in *The Blue Book* is still a modest one. For instance, in the former (see II, sec. 26, and cf. X, sec. 134) Wittgenstein notes that 'studying the nature of the rules of games must be useful for the study of grammatical rules, since it is beyond doubt that there is some sort of similarity between them'. There is no indication here that this similarity might be deepened into a veritable identity.

In *The Blue Book,* language-games still play a minor role even when they are explicitly mentioned. They are thought of merely as artifically constructed simplified models which are useful as objects of comparison with natural languages (p. 17). The acquisition of new meanings is thought of by Wittgenstein in terms of ostensive definitions, not in terms of learning new games (p. 37).[20]

The dramatic change comes in *The Brown Book.* One of the germs of Wittgenstein's late ideas about language-games is his observation that language-games play a crucial role in *language learning.* (Cf. *Philosophical Grammar,* IV, sec. 56: 'The connection between words and things is set up by the teaching of language.') In *The Brown Book* Wittgenstein writes: 'Children are taught their native language by means of such games.' And 'when the boy or grown-up learns what one might call special technical languages . . . he learns more language-games.'[21] In view of Wittgenstein's general assumption that one of the keys to language understanding lies in the processes of language learning, this suggests to Wittgenstein a new way of looking upon language-games. He is no longer looking at them as useful objects of comparison in the study of language or even as parts of a language, 'but as languages complete in themselves, as complete systems of human communication' (ibid.). The idea that language-games are the general link between language and reality is very close to the surface here, but is not yet put forward explicitly by Wittgenstein. Nor is there any hint here of the later idea that language-games might be conceptually prior to their rules. (Cf. section 8 below.) On the contrary, in *The Brown Book* Wittgenstein in effect keeps on introducing new language-games by means of their rules.

The breakthrough comes when Wittgenstein returns to the problem of the nature of the basic naming relations, the crucial links between language and the world in *The Brown Book*, p. 172. He asks there:

> What is the relation between a name and the object named, say, the house and its name?

He answers the question himself in a most significant way which highlights the contrast between the earlier idea of basic meaning relations as simple two-place relations and the less restrictive model on which the basic meaning (naming) relations are constituted by language-games:

> I suppose we could give either of two answers. The one is that the relation consists in certain strokes having been painted on the door of the house. The second I meant is that *the relation* we are concerned with *is established*, not just by painting these strokes on the door, but *by the particular role which they play in the practice of our language* as we have been sketching it. [Emphasis added.]

The latter answer is precisely the one that we suggested is characteristic of Wittgenstein's mature philosophy. It is the one that Wittgenstein embraces in the *Philosophical Investigations*. Most importantly, it is the answer that commits Wittgenstein to maintaining that the basic semantical relations (naming relations) have their mode of existence in different language-games. A little later in *The Brown Book* (p. 173) Wittgenstein in fact calls the practices he is discussing 'games'.

Wittgenstein goes on to diagnose the temptation to accept the first answer, that is, to postulate 'the mysterious relation of the object and its name', and to defuse this temptation. He concludes that

> . . . we might use the expression "The relation of name and object does not merely consist in this kind of trivial, 'purely external', connection", meaning that *what we call the relation of name and object is characterized by the entire usage of the name*; but then it is clear that there is no one relation of name to object, but as many as there are uses of sounds and scribbles which we call names. (p. 173; emphasis added again)

Wittgenstein's comment that there is a legitimate use of the notion of the naming relation (provided that we remember that is not a primitive relation and that it is not the same relation in all cases) is reminiscent of what will be argued below in chapter 10, sec. 9, about

Wittgenstein's own usage of *Name* and *benennen* in the *Philosophical Investigations* in contradistinction to *Bezeichnung* and *bezeichnen*. In order to appreciate Wittgenstein's point, it is important to realize that he is not in the least denying the *reality* of naming relations or replacing them by sundry speech acts and their interrelations. Language-games do not *replace* naming relations according to later Wittgenstein; they *constitute* them.

The criticism of the 'mysterious relation' view is clearly closely connected with Wittgenstein's criticisms of ostensive definitions.

In sum, Wittgenstein's crucial doctrine that language-games serve as links between language and reality makes its first full-scale appearance in *The Brown Book*.

7 AMPLIFICATIONS AND IMPLICATIONS

As usual, Wittgenstein's philosophical thought nevertheless turns out to be so protean that it is impossible to split it into neatly compartmentalized periods. Prima facie, *The Brown Book* passage just commented on seems to have a striking anticipation in *The Blue Book,* p. 69:

> We are inclined to forget that it is the particular use of a word only which gives a word its meaning. Let us think of our old example for the use of words: Someone is sent to the grocer with a slip of paper with the words "five apples" written on it. The use of the word *in practice* [Wittgenstein's italics] is its meaning. Imagine it were the usual thing that the objects around us carried labels with words on them by means of which our speech referred to objects. Some of those words would be proper names of the objects, other generic names (like table, chair, etc.), others again, names of colours, names of shapes, etc. That is to say, *a label would only have a meaning to us in so far as we made a particular use of it.* [Emphasis added.] Now we could easily imagine ourselves to be impressed by merely seeing a label on a thing, and to forget that what makes these labels important is their use.

Wittgenstein goes on to say that emphasis on ostensive definitions is a case in point:

> In this way we sometimes believe that we have named when we make the gesture of pointing and utter words like "This is . . ." (the formula of the ostensive definition).

This passage in fact comes close to expressing the gist of Wittgenstein's later position. It is remarkable to find the contrast between the idea of words as mere labels and the idea of words receiving their meanings from their use in practice (and not merely their use in language) clearly expressed as early as in *The Blue Book.* The criticism of ostensive definitions and the idea of meaning as use are also noteworthy. However, Wittgenstein is not yet saying that the naming (labelling) relation *consists in* language-games; he merely says that it is the use of the labels that makes them *important.* Likewise, it is a letdown to find that at this stage of his development Wittgenstein applies the idea of language-game merely to one special case, viz. to the first-person pronoun 'I'. Textually, the passage quoted from *The Blue Book,* p. 69, is in fact sandwiched in as a part of his discussion of the use of the first person singular pronoun in such sentences as 'I have a pain'. Even though the germ of his full later position is clearly present here, Wittgenstein drew the major conclusions from his ideas only later.

This, incidentally, seems to be characteristic of Wittgenstein's development in general. He repeatedly came upon new insights by considering first specific problems, and realized only later their whole applicability. Another case in point is his discussion of rule-following in the *Philosophical Investigations,* which can be thought of as a generalization of his earlier comments on reading.

The quoted passage is nevertheless striking for two other reasons. First, it shows how Wittgenstein's ideas about privacy and the self developed in inseparable connection with his ideas about the way our language operates in general. It constitutes excellent evidence for the interpretation of Wittgenstein's views on privacy and publicity which will be put forward in chapter 10 below.

Second, it shows that the uses of language (the language-games) which Wittgenstein has in mind are not primarily intralinguistic activities. They are uses *in practice,* i.e., they are rule-governed interactions with our nonlinguistic environment. This point will be discussed more fully below in chapter 9, sec. 4.

In general, it must be emphasized that the central role of language-games in Wittgenstein's philosophy did not come about at once. Indeed, he used the notion of language-game with a remarkable frequency as early as in the *Big Typescript* (MS 213) in 1933. But his use of this notion there is different from its later functions, and there is a sense in which it did not yet hold the centre stage at all. Wittgenstein's early use of the term 'language-game' is merely another way of emphasizing the importance, not of language-games themselves, but of their rules. This is expressed concisely by Wittgenstein in the title of section 48 (p. 196) of the *Big Typescript*: 'language functions as language only through rules, which guide us in their use, as a game is a game only in virtue of its rules.' Language-games became the focal point of Wittgenstein's philosophy of language only later, when they were declared primary with respect to their rules by Wittgenstein.

8 THE PRIMACY OF LANGUAGE-GAMES

This new role of language-games as mediating the basic language–world connections requires a number of comments. At first sight, the idea that it is language-games that constitute name–object relations appears to mark little progress and no fundamental change in Wittgenstein's views as compared with the role of rules as playing the crucial role in language understanding and language acquisition. For surely, it may be alleged, language-games must be grasped and learned by means of their rules. Hence the new role of language-games seems to do little to shake the hegemony of rules in Wittgenstein's philosophy.

Indeed, much of what Wittgenstein does in *The Brown Book* is precisely to introduce a large number of interesting language-games by indicating what their rules are, and then exploiting them for philosophical purposes.

Wittgenstein recognizes that there is a close connection between the concept of language-game and the concept of rule. However, he inverts their relative priority from what we usually take it to be and thereby saves, to his own satisfaction, the primacy of language-games. It is obvious that he has to do this, for without such a reversal of priorities rules would indeed continue to rule supreme, as they did in his middle-period thought.

In this way Wittgenstein is led to one of the most characteristic theses of his later philosophy of language, viz. to the primacy of language-games. He tells us in so many words to 'look on the language-game as the *primary* thing' (*PI*, I, sec. 656). Or, as he says in *PI*, I, sec. 654:

> Our mistake is to look for an explanation where we ought to look at what happens as a 'proto-phenomenon'. That is, where we ought to have said: *this language-game is played.*[22]

In later Wittgenstein, language-games are truly the measure of all things.

It is clear that Wittgenstein's views flies in the face of many generally accepted opinions. Hence it might be expected that he will argue for the primacy of language-games over their rules at some length.

This expectation is amply fulfilled by Wittgenstein's famous (or notorious) discussion of rule-following in *PI*, I, secs. 143–242. Commentators have often been puzzled by the rationale of this extended analysis. Typical of the frustrated attempts to understand it is the following:

> The maximum of seamlessness in the web of Wittgenstein's argument is obtained by treating sections 143–242 [of *PI*, I] as a criticism of the notion that anyone who utters a sentence and *means* or *understands* it is operating a calculus according to definite rules (sec. 81).[23]

This explanation is inadequate in several respects. On the one hand, the idea of language as being like a calculus with sharp rules was given short shrift by Wittgenstein almost twenty pages before the discussion of rule-following even begins. On the other hand, most of Wittgenstein's discussion of rule-following is formulated so as to apply also to sharp, calculus-like rules.[24] Indeed, in several passages he deals, in so many words, with the rules for calculating (see, e.g., secs. 233–6). Thus Baker's interpretation waters down Wittgenstein's point. Far from trying to eliminate from his discussion the sharp, calculus-like cases, he is facing them squarely and arguing that *even in such paradigmatic cases of exact calculating as in following an algebraic formula,* understanding the rule is not identical with knowing a formula or following the rule identical with using the formula. (Cf. especially secs. 151–2.) Wittgenstein cannot make his point without comparing ordinary language constructively with a calculus, not just critically.

The other critical points which Wittgenstein is sometimes supposed to be making in the rule-following discussion are not to be found there, either. For instance, Wittgenstein is supposed to deny that a rule determines its applications, e.g., that an algebraic formula determines the steps of calculation.[25] (Cf. *PI*, I, secs. 189–90.) In reality, Wittgenstein does not argue that a rule does this or that it does not. Rather, he argues that the question makes sense only in certain language-games; and then it may sometimes have to be answered affirmatively:

> "But *are* the steps then *not* determined by the algebraic formula?" – The question contains a mistake.

(See also the rest of sec. 189.) Likewise, Wittgenstein is not arguing that the rules of our language-games are inexact. Rather, he remarks that the very question of inexactness vs. exactness arises only against the background of suitable language-games (see, e.g., *PI*, I, sec. 88).

Notwithstanding widespread misinterpretations, one can understand perfectly well what Wittgenstein was up to in his discussion of rule-following. Indeed, once one realizes how important it was for Wittgenstein to establish the logical (conceptual) primacy of language-games over their rules, it is not hard to see that this is precisely what he is arguing for in *PI*, I, secs. 143–242.[26]

This primacy is, for instance, what Wittgenstein highlights by saying that rules are obeyed *blindly* (*PI*, I, sec. 219). He does not mean, of course, that a rule-follower is not often, perhaps usually, aware of what she or he is doing. He does not mean, either, that we do not often use formulas, recipes, or other symbolic codifications of a rule in following it. Wittgenstein's point is a conceptual one. (Cf. *PI*, I, sec. 217.) What goes on in one's mind is not a criterion of whether a rule is being followed, he is saying. Ergo, the presence of a formula in one's mind is not what it *means* to follow the rule expressed by the formula. Nor does the use of a formula do more than push the problem of rule-following from one place to another, for now it becomes a problem as to how the formula is followed. Eventually, according to Wittgenstein, we will come in any case to a place where all we can say is 'this complex of rules is being followed'. And such complexes of rules are precisely what Wittgenstein calls language-games. Hence his point about rules being followed blindly amounts to saying that inquiring into what goes into rule-following does not help us to understand what it means to play a language-game. On the contrary, rule-following has to be understood by reference to language-games.

There are many other indications that the primacy of language-games over their rules is an important part of what Wittgenstein is arguing for in the rule-following discussion. Here is one of them:

> Where the connection effected between the sense of the words "Let's play a game of chess" and all the rules of the game? Well, in the game's rule-list; in the teaching of chess; in the daily practice of playing. (*PI*, I, sec. 197)

Thus the entire extensive rule-following discussion in the *Philosophical Investigations* occupies a natural and important niche in the total structure of Wittgenstein's overall argument. In the same way as Wittgenstein is exorcising ostensive definitions from his philosophy in many of the early sections of the *Philosophical Investigations* in his discussion of rule-following he is exorcising rules from a place of honour in his philosophy of language and subordinating them to those language-games they are ingredients of.[27]

Wittgenstein did not reach his thesis of the conceptual supremacy of language-games over their rules in one fell swoop. It was the result of a long process of development whose details remain to be investigated.[28] The fact that readers have not paid more attention to Wittgenstein's thesis may even testify to the fact that the development was never quite completed, that Wittgenstein never reached complete clarity in the matter. It is nevertheless fairly clear to any perceptive reader of Wittgenstein's unpublished notebooks that his views in the matter of the relative priority of language-games with respect to their rules were developed first by reference to arithmetical rules and logical rules of infererence. This is also suggested by the way in which Wittgenstein argues for his thesis in the *Philosophical Investigations*.

9 TRAINING VS. RULE-LEARNING

Wittgenstein's switch of primacies from rules to language-games had drastic consequences for his ideas of language learning. If language-games are the last court of semantical appeal, then strictly speaking you do not learn new language-games by learning their rules; you learn new rules by mastering the language-games of which they are a part. And in principle language-games are not *taught* to a student in a normal narrow sense of the word. Rather, a student is *trained* to master the language-game. This is in fact strongly emphasized by Wittgenstein in the rule-following discussion; witness, e.g., *PI*, I, sec. 206, quoted above in sec. 5.

The new primacy Wittgenstein claims for his language-games is reflected on the level of language-learning by his point that language can be learned without learning rules. In *PI*, I, sec. 31, Wittgenstein expresses this point by reference to the game of chess:

> One can . . . imagine someone's having learned the game without ever learning or formulating the rules.

What Wittgenstein argues in the rule-following discussion is that this possibility represents conceptually speaking the paradigm case of language-learning.

It is this same point that Wittgenstein is making by identifying the teaching of a language-game with training rather than with propositional learning. As pointed out by C. J. B Macmillan,[29] the current English translation does not do full justice to this point of Wittgenstein's. The point is made by Wittgenstein, e.g., in *PI*, I, sec. 198:

Let me ask this: what has the expression of a rule – let's say, a sign-post – to do with my actions? What sort of connection obtains there? Well, perhaps this: I have been trained [*abgerichtet*] to react to this sign in a particular way, and I do so react to it.

"But by that you have only indicated the causal connection, explained only how we came to take our directions from the sign-post, but not what this following-of-the-sign really consists in." No, I have also indicated that one takes one's directions from the sign-post only in so far as there exists an established use, a custom [to do so].

A pair of obviously intended double quotes has been supplied here. We have also made some other changes in the translation. The second paragraph shows especially vividly how the 'mere training' idea is in Wittgenstein calculated to establish the primacy of language-games.

With respect to language-learning, too, the contrast between Wittgenstein's middle-period and later works is striking. An instructive passage, which incidentally also illustrates several other themes of this chapter, is found in *The Blue Book*, pp. 12–13. It was mentioned in sec. 5 above, but it is worth quoting more fully. Wittgenstein is there discussing the nature and preconditions of ostensive learning.

If we are taught the meaning of the word "yellow" by being given some sort of ostensive definition (a rule of the usage of the word) this teaching can be looked at in two different ways.

A. The teaching is a drill . . .

B. The teaching may have supplied us with a rule which is itself involved in the process of understanding, obeying, etc., "involved", however, meaning that the expression of this rule forms part of these processes.

We must distinguish between what one might call "a process being *in accordance with* a rule", and "a process involving a rule" . . . We shall say that the rule is *involved* in the understanding, obeying, etc., if, as I should like to express it, the symbol of the rule forms part of the calculation . . .

Here, especially in the case B, we can see the close connection that there was for Wittgenstein during his early middle period between ostensive languge learning and the acquisition of the rules that govern the use of the word to be learned.

What makes the quoted passage especially instructive is that Wittgenstein is there (i.e., at the time of *The Blue Book*) still rejecting totally the idea of language learning by means of mere drill (case A):

This drill causes us to associate a yellow image, yellow things, with the word 'yellow' . . .

In so far as the teaching brings about the association . . . it is the *cause* of the phenomena of understanding, obeying, etc.

The rule which has been taught and is subsequently applied interests us only in so far as it is involved in the application. A rule, so far as it interests us, does not act at a distance.

This contradicts diametrically Wittgenstein's later views, according to which language learning is in the last analysis assimilated to a drill in contrast to the acquisition of some particular rules. We have here a vivid example of the change which took place in Wittgenstein's views in 1933–6.

10 WITTGENSTEIN VS. CRITERIA

An important conclusion concerning Wittgenstein's later philosophy is now possible. The 'logic' of the *Philosophical Investigations* is not only not a logic of rules. Wittgenstein is there rejecting outright the primacy of rules. The logic of Wittgenstein's mature philosophy is a logic of language-games. These language-games are conceptually prior to their rules. They do not replace name–object relations; they constitute these relations.

There is another idea which has played an important role in many discussions of Witrtgenstein's later philosophy and which is in many ways closely related to the concept of rule. It is the notion of *criterion*. This notion has probably prompted more discussion than any other Wittgensteinian concept. It turns out in fact to be a sensitive index of the development of his views, albeit in a different way than many philosophers have thought. At the same time, the force of the term 'criterion' turns out to be peculiarly subtle and elusive in Wittgenstein's mature writings. Its import can be fully understood only later, after we have examined more closely some of Wittgenstein's other central ideas. A preliminary discussion is nevertheless appropriate here.

Prima facie, it might seem that the two notions of *rule* and *criterion* must go together. A criterion for a phenomenon seems to provide the speaker with a rule for the use of a word referring to this phenomenon, and a rule for the use of an expression apparently yields a criterion for its correct use.

In his middle-period writings, Wittgenstein does in fact relate criteria and rules to each other rather closely. In the simplest cases at least, the actually formulated rule gives us a criterion for the correct application of a word. For instance, in *The Blue Book*, pp. 24–6 criteria and rules are assimilated to each other very closely. (See below, this section.) Furthermore, in *Philosophical Grammar*, II, sec. 26, there is likewise little to choose between the two notions.

Because of this onetime close connection between the notions of *criterion* and *rule*, and because of the eclipse of rules in Wittgenstein's mature philosophy, one is led to expect a similar decline of the role of criteria in his philosophy as expressed in such late works as the *Philosophical Investigations*. It is in fact the case that in so far as Wittgenstein abides by the sense of 'criterion' which assimilates rules and criteria to each other, criteria play only a subordinate role in the *Philosophical Investigations*.

There are several indications of the unimportant role of this sense of 'criterion' in the *Philosophical Investigations*. A comparison between *The Blue Book*, pp. 24–6, and *PI*, I, secs. 288–90, is instructive here. In both passages, Wittgenstein is concerned with the identification of pains, in *The Blue Book* admittedly in the special case of toothache. In *The Blue Book*, Wittgenstein acknowledges in so many words that 'to explain my criterion for another person's having a toothache is to give a grammatical explanation about the word "toothache" and, in this sense, an explanation of the meaning of the word "toothache"'. What will such an explanation look like?

> When we learnt the use of the phrase 'so-and-so has toothache' we were pointed out certain kinds of behaviour of those who were said to have toothache. As an instance of these kinds of behaviour let us take holding your cheek.

In the next sentence Wittgenstein calls these characteristic modes of behaviour 'criteria'. In order to explain his point, he embarks on a thought-experiment:

> Suppose that by observation I found that in certain cases whenever these criteria told me that a person had a toothache, a red patch appeared on the person's cheek.

Somebody might now ask Wittgenstein,

> "How do you know A has toothache when you see a red patch?" I should then point out that certain phenomena had always coincided with the appearance of the red patch.

> Now one may go on and ask "How do you know that he has got toothache when he holds his cheek?" . . . You will be at a loss to answer this question, and find that here we strike rock bottom, that is we have come down to conventions.

These 'conventions' are just what Wittgenstein elsewhere in the same discussion calls 'criteria'. They are here the 'rock bottom' of the semantics of 'toothache'.

Wittgenstein goes on to distinguish criteria and symptoms and to admit that 'in practice if you were asked which phenomenon is the defining criterion and which is a symptom, you would in most cases be unable to answer this question'. He equates languages operating by means of sharp criteria with languages that obey strict rules, thereby incidentally showing how closely the two notions are related to each other in his mind.

In *PI*, I, secs. 288–90, the very same behaviour which in *The Blue Book* served as a criterion of toothache is now said *not* to depend on criteria. Only 'if we cut out human behaviour, which is the expression of sensation . . . [do] I need a criterion of identity for the sensation . . .' (*PI*, I, sec. 288.) In the same spirit Wittgenstein says in secs. 289–90:

> To use a word without justification does not mean to use it without right.

> What I do is not, of course, to identify my sensation by criteria: but to repeat an expression.

In general, the basic language-games which give our sensation-vocabulary its meaning do not operate according to the *Philosophical Investigations* by means of criteria. These language-games will be discussed more closely in chapter 10 below. Suffice it therefore to give only a few indications here.

In *PI*, I, sec. 244 Wittgenstein says that to teach a child the word 'pain' is to 'teach the child new pain-behaviour'. In other words, 'the verbal expression of pain replaces crying and does not describe it'. But if so, the use of the word 'pain' cannot be connected with criteria, as little as a child's crying is based on criteria.

In *PI*, I, sec. 270 Wittgenstein presents a thought-experiment of how a sensation-word might be introduced into language. There is no need to analyse this thought-experiment in detail here, for Anselm Müller has done it for us.[30] Müller aptly sums up a part of his conclusions by saying that, according to Wittgenstein,

> We can imagine the use of an expression which resembles the use of names of sensations in a number of ways *without being connected with a criterion*. [Emphasis added.]

In so far as Wittgenstein in his mature writings uses the term 'criterion' in the narrow sense in which a criterion is closely related to the notion of rule, Wittgenstein thus downgrades criteria in his later philosophy. The 'logic' of the *Philosophical Investigations* is neither a logic of rules nor a logic of criteria in this sense of 'criterion'. Logically speaking language-games are primary with respect to rules and criteria.

11 CRITERIA AND LANGUAGE-GAMES

However, this is not the end of the story of Wittgenstein's use of the term 'criterion'. What happens in his mature philosophy is that the meaning of this word shifts. It is given a partly new use by Wittgenstein, even though he still occasionally uses it in the older sense.[31] This new use is less clear-cut than the older one. We shall return to it below in chapter 11. Here we shall give only preliminary indications of what this new use amounts to.

On the basis of what has been said, it is perhaps not difficult to appreciate the point of Wittgenstein's new use of the term 'criterion'. If language-games are prior to their rules, as Wittgenstein was seen to hold, then the only criterion for the use of a word is in the last analysis the entire language-game in which it plays a role or, as Wittgenstein sometimes expresses his point, the only criterion is the *application* of the word. Wittgenstein expresses this almost in so many words by saying in the middle of his discussions of rule-following, that 'the application is still a criterion of understanding' (*PI*, I, sec. 146). Likewise Wittgenstein writes in *PI*, I, sec. 190:

> It may now be said: "The way the formula is meant determines which steps are to be taken". What is the criterion for the way the formula is meant? It is, for example, the kind of way we always use it, the way we are taught to use it.

Hence it is natural for Wittgenstein to employ in his latest works the term 'criterion' to call attention to the entire language-game in which a word plays a role, or to some characteristic features of this game. This is the new use just mentioned. One is tempted to say that in this usage the words 'criterion' and 'language-game' are correlative terms. The vaunted 'need for criteria' for the use of a word which Wittgenstein is supposed to have emphasized in reality means need for a public language-game in which the word plays a role. As we might also put the point, the term 'criterion' suffered the same fate as 'calculus' and partly even 'grammar' in Wittgenstein's later philosophy: it became dependent on the term 'language-game' and at times almost synonymous with it.

We can now see that it is a fundamental mistake to think that Wittgenstein operated with a single 'criteriological relation' which connects the meaning of a word and the 'criterion' or 'criteria' of what the word represents, e.g., pain and the 'criteria' of pain.[32] In the old, narrow sense of criterion, there simply is according to the later Wittgenstein no criterion of pain; our pain-vocabulary just does not operate by means of well-defined criteria. But in the new, more flexible sense there is no genuine 'criteriological relation', either. One can often speak of criteria in a useful way, and Wittgenstein avails himself liberally of such locutions. But 'criteria' in this wider sense – e.g., the various manifestations of pain Wittgenstein countenances – cannot be terms of a 'criteriological relation', either, for they are criteria only by courtesy of a language-game in which they are 'moves'. A grimace is a 'criterion' of pain only in a language-game of spontaneous expressions of pain; a lookalike grimace is not a criterion of pain when it occurs on the face of an actor in a play. Language-games are conceptually prior to such quasi-criteria, just as they are conceptually prior to their rules. Hence the real point of Wittgenstein's new use of the term 'criterion' is not to mark by its means a special relation which a criterial sign bears to what it is usually thought to be a criterion of. The real point of the term is to call attention to the language-game which is being played (or being presupposed).

On the basis of what has been said, many uses which Wittgenstein makes of the term 'criterion' in the *Philosophical Investigations* are given a sharper profile.

The most straightforward occurrences of the word 'criterion' in the *Philosophical Investigations* are perhaps those that are found in Wittgenstein's discussion of rule-following (*PI*, I, secs. 143–242). As was in effect pointed out above, a large part of the upshot of this whole discussion is that rule-following is not based on criteria. It is the entire language-game that determines – in so far as a determination is possible – whether or not a rule is followed. And a language-game is not learned by learning criteria; it is taught by training and inculcation. Against this background and in the context of Wittgenstein's discussion, several occurrences of 'criterion' all can serve the purpose of showing that language use in general, and rule-following in particular, do *not* turn on criteria. Cases in point include secs. 146, 149, 159–60, 164, 182, 185, 190, 238. These call for few comments.

The most characteristic, and probably most frequent, uses of the term 'criterion' in the *Philosophical Investigations* are those in which Wittgenstein is merely calling the reader's attention to the characteristic public moves in the language-game by means of which we can speak of a certain entity or phenomenon. These uses instantiate what was referred to in the beginning of this section as Wittgenstein's new, broader sense of 'criterion'.[33] Sometimes Wittgenstein is not so much calling our attention to the moves one makes in certain language-games as to the objective preconditions of such moves; see, e.g., *PI*, I, sec. 253.

The other side of the same coin is in evidence when Wittgenstein wants to point out that we have not (not yet) been given any language-game which would give a certain linguistic expression its meaning. What *is* this language-game? Wittgenstein typically expresses this question by asking: What are the *criteria* on the basis of which this expression is used? This usage is in fact also frequent in the *Philosophical Investigations*.[34]

In order to gain a feeling for Wittgenstein's way of using the word 'criterion', we may consider the first two occurrences of the term listed in note 34, viz. *PI*, I, secs. 51 and 56. They deal with colour recognition, especially with correctness and mistakes in connection with colour recognition. In sec. 51, Wittgenstein is discussing a language-game which relies essentially on a correlation between certain colours and our words for them. Assuming a discrepancy in the use of the correlation, he asks: 'What is the criterion by which this is a mistake?' He discusses the possibility that the correspondence, and *a fortiori* the criterion of mistake, might consist in the correlated colour's always coming before the language users' minds when a colour-word is uttered. Even though Wittgenstein does not want to rule out in principle such uses of colour-images, he ends up saying that that is not what the correspondence consists in. What it does consist in are the rules of the entire game. It is especially important here that these rules have to be understood in a sense in which 'an observer can read these rules off from the practice of the game'.[35] These rules plus the accompanying behaviour distinguish what is a mistake and what is correct. 'But how does the observer distinguish . . . between players' mistakes and correct play? There are characteristic signs of it in the players' behaviour. Think of the behaviour characteristic of correcting a slip of the tongue' (sec. 54).

What this means is of course that the 'criterion' mentioned in sec. 51 is not really a criterion in any strict sense, and certainly not in the sense in which Wittgenstein's late philosophy is supposed to be based on 'the logic of criteria'. The clues that one uses to spot slips of the tongue are not criteria in the sense of neo-Wittgensteinian philosophers. The way in which we actually recognize slips of the tongue is not by means of criteria or rules. It is a language-game of its own that has to be learned or otherwise acquired. Hence it is clear that Wittgenstein is here using the word 'criterion' simply and solely to call attention to a certain language-game.

The same applies to Wittgenstein's use of the word 'criterion' in sec. 56:

> But what if . . . we *bear in mind* the colour (for instance) that a word stands for? . . . But what do we regard as the criterion for remembering it right?

Wittgenstein's answer is:

> If we had no memory we should be at the mercy of a sample.

Of course we are not at the mercy of a sample. What the real criteria of remembering correctly are, is explained by Wittgenstein elsewhere. Once again, they are not 'criteria' in any strict sense, but turn in principle on the whole practice of a language-game.

Thus our observations throw light on a number of uses of the term 'criterion' in the *Philosophical Investigations*. We shall return to a number of others in chapter 11. There we shall also discuss further the force of the term 'criterion' in Wittgenstein's later philosophy.

NOTES

1 This statement needs some qualification, however. For one thing, Wittgenstein had independently arrived at his 'holistic' view of the connections between language and the world. (See chapter 9, sec. 6, below.) This change in his views is nevertheless unconnected with the developments discussed in the present chapter.

2 Bertrand Russell, *The Problems of Philosophy*, Home University Library, London, 1912.

3 Cf. *PI*, I, secs. 27–35; *The Blue and Brown Books*, pp. 130–1; *Philosophical Remarks*, I, 6; *Philosophical Grammar*, I, 19; II, 24, 25; IV, 45.

4 Saul Kripke, *Naming and Necessity*, Harvard University Press, Cambridge, Mass., 1980.

5 See *Philosophical Grammar*, I, sec. 19; *The Blue and Brown Books*, pp. 77–9, *PI*, I, secs. 1–19, 30–3.

6 See chapter 10, secs. 8–9, below.

7 From *The Blue Book*, pp. 12–14, it is seen that Wittgenstein intended the rule thus conveyed to the learner to be taken in a strong sense, so strong, indeed, that the learner could thereafter use the rule as a reason for acting in a certain way and that the actual formulation of the rule could be involved in following the rule. Wittgenstein did not mean merely a capacity to act in accordance with the rule. For this – somewhat surprising – point, see sec. 9 below.

8 See *Wittgenstein's Lectures, Cambridge 1932–35*, pp. 3–4.

9 The crucial role of rules in the *Philosophical Grammar* is also vividly shown by X, sec. 133, where Wittgenstein says in so many words that it is rules 'that determine a meaning'. And in MS 109, p. 284, Wittgenstein writes:

'That is, language functions as a language only through the rules which we observe in using it. (As a game functions as a game only through rules.)' The German reads: 'D.h. die Sprache funktioniert als Sprache nur durch die Regeln nach denen wir uns in ihrem Gebrauch richten. (Wie das Spiel nur durch Regeln als Spiel funktioniert.)'

10 The German text reads: 'Die Wilden haben Spiele (oder wir nennen es doch so), für die sie keine geschriebenen Regeln, kein Regelverzeichnis besitzen. Denken wir uns nun die Tätigkeit *eines Forschers,* die Länder dieser Völker zu bereisen und Regelverzeichnisse für ihre Spiele anzulegen. Das ist das ganze Analogon zu dem, was der Philosoph tut. [Warum sage ich aber nicht: "Die Wilden haben Sprachen (oder wir . . .) . . . keine geschriebene Grammatik haben . . ."?]'

11 Cf. here also MS 109, p. 288, MS 110, p. 185, and MS 302 ('Diktat für Schlick'), pp. 2–3, 10. Wittgenstein's half-hearted assimilation of ostensive definitions to the 'elucidations' of the *Tractatus* (see note 36 to chapter 6, above) is likewise restricted to this episode (1929–33) in the development of his views.

12 The German reads: 'Der Gedanke "daß es sich so verhält (p)" wird durch die Tatsache daß es sich so verhält (p) wahrgemacht. Daß sich der Zusammenhang zwischen Gedanken und Welt so nicht darstellen läßt (denn diese Darstellung sagt gar nichts) muß die Antwort auf meine Probleme sein.'

13 A curious twist is given to the concept of rule in Wittgenstein by the fact that he first tried to interpret the relevant rules as intralinguistic rules, i.e., as rules that serve the purposes of translation from one language to another rather than rules that serve language–world correlations. For this reason Wittgenstein can employ the term before he had again admitted that he is discussing world–language links. The ambivalence of the terms is illustrated by passages like the following: '"Wissen was der Fall ist, wenn der Satz wahr ist" kann nur heißen, die Regel kennen nach der er zu kontrollieren ist.' (MS 109, p. 78.)

And on p. 80 Wittgenstein writes: 'Einem Plan folgen ist wesentlich dieselbe Tätigkeit wie eine Projection [*Übersetzung,* Wittgenstein's alternative] nach einer bestimmten Regel zu kontrollieren.' Wittgenstein tries to avoid committing himself to language–world comparisons by suggesting that the rules which can be embodied in language serve to prepare us for the actual use of language, but that the actual application is not a part of language. In MS 109, p. 77, Wittgenstein writes: 'Darum kann die Sprache nur den Plan ausdrücken, nicht seine Anwendung. Und die Logik nur den Plan untersuchen.' We have here a sharp contrast to Wittgenstein's later thought, according to which the use (application) of language is an integral part of the language-games which constitute the projective relations between language and reality. Cf. chapter 9, sec. 9, below.

14 The kinship of ostensive definitions and rules is vividly shown by *Philosophical Grammar,* III, sec. 39, where Wittgenstein relates his problem to that of rule-following, which later become a major preoccupation for him.

15 Similar statements are found elsewhere; cf., e.g., *Philosophical Grammar,* X, sec. 133.

16 Cf. here *PI,* I, sec. 94; MS 108, p. 7.

17 Here G. E. M. Anscombe translates 'die gemeinsame menschliche Handlungsweise' as 'the common behaviour of mankind'. However, there is in Wittgenstein's writings no evidence that he believed in a way of behaviour common to the entirety of mankind, and plenty of evidence that he believed on the contrary in cultural and linguistic relativism. For instance, in *PI*, I, sec. 240 Wittgenstein says that 'the working of our language' is based on a 'framework'. It is obviously language-games which according to him constitute these frameworks. (See also chapter 1, sec. 11, above, for further evidence.) Hence our translation 'people's shared way of acting' seems preferable as a translation of Wittgenstein's German words.

18 The translation of sec. 37 requires a comment. G. E. M. Anscombe translates 'worin diese Beziehung etwa besteht' as 'the sort of thing this relation consists in'. This misses Wittgenstein's precise point, however, because he is not trying to convey a rough idea of the kind of thing the naming relation *is*. He is giving sharp examples of what it *can be*. Both ways of taking the passage are linguistically possible interpretations of the operative German word *etwa*. However, ours is confirmed by the way the passage continues: 'This relation may also consist, among many other things, in the fact that hearing the name calls before our mind the picture of what is named . . .' This is not an approximate explanation of what the naming relation consists in in general; it is an explicit example of what it *can* consist in. This line of thought establishes a kind of superiority of the game over its rules, even though Wittgenstein does not seem to have been inclined to stake his entire philosophical fortune on it.

19 It looks likely that Wittgenstein first came to compare mathematical activity (calculating) with games. Thus he writes in MS 112, p. 1 (5 October 1931): 'But an arithmetical game is very well thinkable . . . A game in contradistinction to what?'

The German text reads: 'Wohl aber ist ein arithmetisches Spiel denkbar . . . Ein Spiel im Gegensatz wozu?'

In autumn 1931 Wittgenstein in fact compares mathematical activity repeatedly with playing a game. Gradually he seems to have extended the comparison so as to apply also to nonmathematical uses of language.

20 Likewise, the analogy between inventing a language and inventing a game which Wittgenstein puts forward in *Philosophical Grammar*, X, sec. 140, remains a mere analogy, and the contrast Wittgenstein there draws between inventing a game and inventing a tool indicates that he has not yet realized that language-games can themselves serve precisely as tools in dealing with the world by means of language.

21 *The Blue and Brown Books*, p. 81.

22 This passage occurs earlier in MS 116.

23 Gordon Baker, 'Following Wittgenstein: some signposts for *Philosophical Investigations* §§143–242', in Steven H. Holtzman and Christopher M. Leich, editors, *Wittgenstein: To Follow a Rule*, Routledge & Kegan Paul, London, 1981, pp. 31–71.

24 See secs. 143–5, 146, 151–2, 179–80, 185–93, 197 – the rules of chess are not indefinite or fuzzy! –, 214, 226, etc.

25 G. P. Baker and P. M. S. Hacker, *Wittgenstein: Understanding and Meaning*, Basil Blackwell, Oxford, 1980, pp. 91–2.

26 This is not to say that the discussion of rule-following does not have other purposes in Wittgenstein than to show the conceptual primacy of language-games over their rules. On the contrary, it seems clear that the famous discussion serves the same general purpose as some of the later passages of the *Philosophical Investigations* in which Wittgenstein argues that certain psychological words do not express mental occurrences or mental states. 'Understanding' in understanding a rule will be a case in point. This purpose of Wittgenstein will be discussed briefly in a later chapter. (See chapter 11, sec. 10 below.) This point is undoubtedly important for Wittgenstein, although not nearly as central as has been generally assumed by philosophers.

27 Wittgenstein put forward at different times also another, weaker, argument for the primacy of language-games over their rules. If one says that a language-game is defined by its rules, Wittgenstein says in *PI*, I, secs. 561–9, we have to distinguish between essential and inessential rules. And this distinction does not turn on the list of rules for a game, but on the *point* of the entire game.

28 Our way of looking at Wittgenstein's discussion of rule-following in the context of the overall development of his views receives some indirect support from the fact that, according to G. H. von Wright's lists of the origins of the different sections of the *PI*, all of this discussion is of a relatively late origin. Most of the earliest are dated 1936 or 1937; they include sections 151, 156–78, 189–97, 215–16. A single section (sec. 239) is dated in 1934; it deals with the special case of the use of the colour word 'red', not with the general problem of rule-following. Of the relatively early sections, 158–171 likewise deal with a special case of rule-following, viz. the rule-following involved in reading. One section (sec. 182) is dated 1938, and all the rest are either dated 1944–5 or do not have any anticipations in the surviving manuscripts and typescripts. In particular, most of the crucial sections 198–242 date from the years 1944–5. This agrees well with our view that the rule-following discussion is an important step in Wittgenstein's transition from his middle period to the late one. We are grateful to Professor von Wright for making this unpublished list available to us. Cf. also G. H. von Wright, 'The origin and composition of the *Philosophical Investigations*' in his book *Wittgenstein*, Basil Blackwell, Oxford, 1982, pp. 111–36.

29 C. J. B. Macmillan, 'Wittgenstein and the problems of teaching and learning', in Werner Leinfellner et al., editors, *Language and Ontology, Proceedings of the Sixth International Wittgenstein Symposium*, Hölder-Pichler-Tempsky, Vienna, 1982, pp. 483–6.

30 Anselm Müller, 'No need for criteria?', in E. Leinfellner et al., editors, *Wittgenstein and His Impact on Contemporary Thought, Proceedings of the Second International Wittgenstein Symposium*, Hölder-Pichler-Tempsky, Vienna, 1978, pp. 306–9.

31 It is highly significant that the only occurrence of a contrast between criteria and symptoms in the *Philosophical Investigations* is in a passage (I, sec. 354) which Wittgenstein wrote at a relatively early stage of his quest. It occurs in MS 115, pp. 73–4 and was probably written in the early months of 1934. It seems that Wittgenstein never again used the contrast between criteria and symptoms or the notion of symptom in his latest writings (after 1944).

32 Cf., e.g., Gordon Baker, 'Criteria: a new foundation for semantics', *Ratio*, vol. 16 (1974), pp. 156–89.

33 Among these uses there are the following occurrences of 'criterion': *PI*, I, secs. 238, 542; II, vi, p. 181, xi, pp. 198, 203, 222 (last three occurrences).

34 Witness, e.g., *PI*, I, secs. 51, 56, 258, 509 (the 'criterion' missed there is found in *PI*, II, xi, p. 198), 580; II, xi, p. 222 (first occurrence of 'criterion').

35 See op. cit., sec. 54, and *Philosophical Grammar*, II, sec. 24.

9
Language-games in Wittgenstein's Later Thought

1 LANGUAGE-GAMES AS CONSTITUTING THE BASIC LANGUAGE–WORLD LINK

In the preceding chapter, we reached a vantage point from which we can see in a sharper relief much of Wittgenstein's mature philosophy, represented prominently by the *Philosophical Investigations*. The main insight we have gained is the *role of language-games as the basic semantical links between language and reality* in Wittgenstein's mature philosophy. This observation is so important that it deserves a number of supplementary explanations and comments.

First, it is important to be clear what our thesis is. In the preceding chapter, language-games were considered in different perspectives. One of them is as Wittgenstein's last and final answer to the question as to what it is that one learns in learning a language. However, language-games can be viewed in many other perspectives. One of them (also considered in the preceding chapter) is offered by a different but interrelated problem which also interested Wittgenstein intensively during his middle period, 1929–35. Already in the *Tractatus* Wittgenstein spoke of the basic 'projective' relations between language and the world. The problem as to what these relations are occupied Wittgenstein in 1929–35. It represents in fact one of his main preoccupations during this period, as witnessed, e.g., by his paper 'Some Remarks on Logical Form' (1929). Numerous other expressions of the same interest are found in his middle-period writings. It was only when he reached his thesis of language-games as constituting the basic name–object relations that he was able to tell us definitely what the projective relations are that connect words and sentences on the one hand, and objects and facts on the other.

It is useful to give Wittgenstein's problem a quasi-epistemological reformulation and to ask: How can an observer recognize the basic semantical links between language and reality? How are they taught and learned? What does a jungle-linguist have to witness to ascertain that such a relationship holds? These all boil down to the question:

What is the mode of existence of the basic semantical relations between language and the world? It is the central thesis of the preceding chapter, and one of the central theses of the present work, that this question admits of a simple answer according to the Wittgenstein of the *Philosophical Investigations*. This blunt answer is: *language-games*.[1] The 'missing links' between the expressions of our language and the reality with which the language helps us to deal are recognized by observing certain rule-governed human activities ('institutions' in a wide sense of the word). The learning of language does not consist, St Augustine and the author of the *Tractatus* notwithstanding, in a series of acquisitions of sundry names for different entities. It consists in learning those language-games that serve to mediate the word–object reltions. The teaching of these games is logically speaking more like training the learner in a new skill than conveying to him definitions of words and expressions, no matter whether or not these definitions are verbal. What a jungle-linguist has to witness in order to figure out the meanings of the words of an unknown language are the language-games which the speakers of the language engage in and through which their basic language–world relations are revealed – revealed, because that is wherein they consist.

2 AGAINST THE RECEIVED VIEW OF LANGUAGE-GAMES

The interpretation defended here differs sharply from a widespread way of looking at Wittgenstein's later philosophy of language. For brevity, this influential interpretation will be called the 'received view'. According to this popular view, in his later philosophy Wittgenstein gave up all attempts to show how language is tied to reality in any direct way. As one writer has expressed this view, the later Wittgenstein tells us not to attend to the meaning of our expressions, but to the way these expressions are used.[2] What is important (on this allegedly Wittgensteinian idea) are not any 'vertical' links that would relate our words to objects and our sentences to facts, but 'horizontal' links between different moves in our language-games. This interpretational strategy, which depends on a particular way of looking at Wittgenstein's concept of language-game, is based on ascribing to Wittgenstein the idea that to understand language amounts to understanding the role in our lives played by different kinds of utterances in different circumstances.

When applied to declarative sentences, it follows from this interpretation of Wittgenstein that, according to him, not even the ordinary descriptive meaning is based on truth-conditions. One possible Wittgensteinian counterpart to truth-conditions may on this view be found in assertability or justifiability conditions. On such a variant of the view under scrutiny, a statement might be justified, not when there is a fact corresponding to it, but when its assertion is justified by the role it plays in our language-related activities, ultimately in our lives.

Admittedly, this 'received view' of Wittgenstein's later philosophy of language is not always formulated explicitly, but either taken for granted or – typically – buried under Wittgenstein's ambiguous identification of meaning with use or else under his treacherous term 'grammar'. It is not a part of our argument to show that this 'received view' is widespread or influential. We are using it simply as an object of comparison for the purpose of bringing our own interpretation into a sharper focus. However, one should not underestimate the hold of this view on philosophers. In order to make it clear that we are not fighting windmills, we have compiled a sample list of a number of passages from the literature in which this view is put forward in some variant or other. They are listed in note 3 below.[3] Even though the received view is typically assumed unreflectively and not asserted as an explicit interpretational thesis, these references demonstrate that it is indeed an important aspect of the way in which many influential philosophers have looked at Wittgenstein's later philosophy.

What we are arguing for in this book is an interpretation of Wittgenstein's later philosophy of language which is almost diametrically opposed to what we have labelled the received view. Far from trying to get rid of vertical links between language and reality, the later Wittgenstein emphasized them. On this new interpretation, the first and foremost function (although not the only one) of Wittgenstein's language-games is to serve as such links. It is about the nature of just those representative relationships (generalized so as to dispense with any sharp dichotomy between simple and complex signs) that Wittgenstein wants to tell us something in such later writings as the *Philosophical Investigations*. He even speaks of these representative relations as relations of naming.[4] But while these naming relations had been left completely unanalysed in the *Tractatus*, Wittgenstein is now telling us – at least by means of examples – in what these relations consist. They are established and maintained by language-games of different kinds. The vital importance of the concept of language-game in Wittgenstein's later philosophy shows dramatically how misleading the received interpretation of this philosophy is. Far from denying the existence, or the crucial role, of vertical relationships between language and reality, Wittgenstein is on the contrary emphasizing their significance by making his vitally important language-games the very heart of these relationships. If there was a period when Wittgenstein was reticent about the semantical relationships between words and things, it was not his later period but the time of the *Tractatus*.

Some evidence for the role of language-games as establishing the basic language–world links was presented in the preceding chapter, especially in sec. 6. Further evidence will also be presented below in connection with the examination of the fate of the picture theory.[5]

3 LANGUAGE-GAMES AND THE INEFFABILITY OF SEMANTICS

Our thesis here is, it was said, that one of the main functions of language-games in Wittgenstein's later philosophy is to serve as the connecting links between language and reality. If this is Wittgenstein's point in his later philosophy of language, why does he not say so? Wittgenstein's silence has misled the majority of subsequent philosophers. We have argued that he does in fact sometimes say what we claim he means, but even if this is right, the question can legitimately be raised, and raised as a prima facie objection to the present interpretation, as to why he does not emphasize it much more. Wittgenstein simply does not underline the semantical role of language-games nearly as strongly as the interpretation here defended suggests that he should have. Why does Wittgenstein not come out and *say* in so many words that it is language-games that mediate between language and the world?

The answer is that he did not think it was sayable. Here the results reached above in chapter 1 offer important indirect support for the present interpretation. There it was found that for Wittgenstein semantical relations were ineffable. From this it follows that the role of language-games as a semantical link between language and reality is likewise ineffable. Hence the only aspects of language-games one can meaningfully speak of, according to the view of language as the universal medium, are its external, nonsemantical features such as the relationships between different language-acts, the relation of such acts to their context, etc. This is why Wittgenstein easily gives the impression of dealing almost exclusively with speech-acts and other intralinguistic phenomena in discussing language-games. As we have seen, Wittgenstein maintains in the *Tractatus* that all the rules of logic have to be formulated purely formally (syntactically), because these formal properties of our sentences are all that is expressible in language. In an analogous way, in the *Philosophical Investigations* he concentrates on the external 'grammar' of language-games because this is the only aspect of these games which can be expressed in language. All use of language presupposes certain language-games, and is a move in some language-game. These games are presupposed when any use is made of language. Hence, we cannot in our language theoretically discuss the language-games which this language pre-supposes, or say what would happen if, e.g., their rules were varied. *Semantics is ineffable* in Wittgenstein's later philosophy quite as much as in his earlier philosophy.

Thus Wittgenstein's apparent emphasis on horizontal relations between utterances and contexts, as well as between different contexts of utterance, is based on an optical illusion. These horizontal connections are important in displaying and instantiating the language-games which give our sentences their meanings, that is, their various connections with reality. They are the game counterparts to the 'elucidations' mentioned in the *Tractatus* 3.263. Moreover, such horizontal moves in language-games are *all* we can strictly speaking convey to the next person about these familiar but theoretically elusive language-games by means of the literal meaning of our words, for we cannot *say* what these games are like, we cannot describe them, nor can we formulate a systematic theory about them in language. But the main function of language-games themselves is to establish such vertical connections. Ironically, the impossibility (for Wittgenstein) of saying anything about language-games in language stems from this very semantical function they perform.

Moreover, it was pointed out in chapter 1, sec. 13, that the old Wittgenstein practised far stricter semantical abstinence than did the young philosopher. In his early work, Wittgenstein had spoken freely of many subjects which he acknowledged to be unspeakable in the final analysis. He climbed up on a ladder that later he discarded – or perhaps transformed into the slippery rope of showing, as distinguished from the measured progress of saying. (Cf. *Tractatus* 6.54.) In contrast, it seems that the later Wittgenstein deprived himself quite deliberately of the corresponding opportunity, and that this procedure has made his philosophy unnecessarily mystifying to many commentators. The unassisted climb has proved precarious to an overwhelming majority of authors of papers on the so-called private language argument and on related topics. Combined with Wittgenstein's view of language as the universal medium, his reluctance to use heuristic devices as freely as he did in the *Tractatus* has led several commentators to think that Wittgenstein denied what in fact he firmly believed, including the role of language-games as linking language and the world to each other.

The main conclusion of this section is therefore this: It lies in the nature of Wittgenstein's assumptions that much of the evidence for the thesis of the semantical role of language-games has to be indirect. Some such evidence was given in the preceding chapter, and some more evidence will be found in the later sections of the present one. However, an important part of the total evidence must consist in showing how this thesis helps us to understand other features of Wittgenstein's late philosophy. This task will be undertaken in the next two chapters. They are thus not merely applications of insights definitely established; whatever success they have will reflect back and yield further credibility to the main thesis of this chapter.

4 LANGUAGE-GAMES VS. GAMES IN LANGUAGE

The main rival interpretation of Wittgenstein's late philosophy of language is the view that we have dubbed the received interpretation. It is sometimes formulated by saying that Wittgenstein gave up asking questions concerning the meaning of our expressions and instead asked about their use. This way of putting Wittgenstein's point seems to be based on his own pronouncements. However, this formulation is misleadingly ambiguous. On one of its readings it agrees with the interpretation advocated here. This reading means to understand the 'use' of an expression that Wittgenstein intends as the language-game which is its 'logical home'. However, this is not the reading presupposed by the received interpretation. Instead of taking Wittgenstein at his word when he says that the meaning of a word *is* typically its use in language (cf. *PI*, I, sec. 43), the representatives of the received view think that Wittgenstein looked away from questions of truth-conditional meaning entirely, in the sense of not being interested in the language–world relationships. Rather, Wittgenstein is perceived as concentrating on the different utterances or other languge-acts, their interrelations, their contexts, and their nature, according to this received view.

There are several facets to this contrast between the new interpretation presented here and the received one. On the received view, Wittgenstein means by the *use* of an expression something not unlike usage. Is this what Wittgenstein really intends? In the famous identification of meaning and use in *PI*, I, sec. 43, the German word used is *Gebrauch*. This word has two essentially different senses. It can serve to emphasize that something is *customary*. This is the sense the received view relies on. However, the word can also signal that something is being *utilized* or *put to use*. (This use is reflected by such idioms as *Gebrauchsanweisung*, 'direction for use'.) This use squares very well with Wittgenstein's comparison between words and tools, and is strongly suggestive of the new interpretation.

That this is Wittgenstein's intended meaning is shown, over and above the tool-analogy, by Wittgenstein's parallel use of the words *Verwendung* and *Anwendung*, which do not mean primarily linguistic *usage* but use in the sense of *utilization* and *application*. Another clear proof that Wittgenstein is not looking away in the *Philosophical Investigations* from the word–world links but rather is asking what these links consist in is found in *PI*, I, sec. 10:

> Now what do the words of this language signify? What is supposed to show what they signify, if not the kind of use [*Gebrauch*] they have? And we have already described that . . . Of course, one can abbreviate the description of the use of the word . . . to the statement that this word signifies this object . . .

If the use of a word did not serve as a link between language and the world, it could not be abbreviated in this way.[6]

Thus the received view is fallacious. It involves the mistake of understanding Wittgenstein's language-games as predominantly intra-lingual (verbal) games, games whose moves consist typically of speech-acts. By contrast, on the interpretation advocated here the 'moves' consist of transitions in which utterances can play a role but normally not the only role; on the contrary, many moves need not involve any verbal utterances. Let us call this mistake of the received interpretation the *fallacy of verbal language-games*. It is one of the most widespread misunderstandings of Wittgenstein's late philosophy.

There is an implicit warning against the fallacy of verbal language-games in the very way in which Wittgenstein explains the term 'language-game' in the *Philosophical Investigations*:

> The word "language-*game*" is here meant to emphasize that the *speaking* of language is *part of* [emphasis added] an activity or a form of life. (*PI*, I, sec. 23)

On the received interpretation, the speaking of a language is not *a part of* a language-game; it would be all of it.

A further warning is built into another famous passage of the same work. It is the very passage in which the term 'language-game' is introduced:

I shall also call the whole, consisting of language and the actions with which it is interwoven, the "language-game". (*PI*, I, sec. 7.)[7]

Here language-game is said to consist not just of language or language use, but also of certain actions. The contrast Wittgenstein draws indicates that the actions or activities in question are *not* linguistic.

Perhaps the clearest evidence for our interpretation comes from *On Certainty*, sec. 229, where what obviously are language-games are contrasted to talking:

Our talk gets its meaning from the rest of our proceedings

Here we have an explicit contrast between speaking a language and using it in the way that gives it its meaning.

The fallacy of verbal language-games has a subtle corollary which, by way of contrast, throws interesting light on Wittgenstein's real meaning. This equally fallacious corollary says that the language-game which is the logical home of a word or an expression is one in which this word or expression is uttered. (This fallacy is a cornerstone of the theory of so-called speech-acts.) It is fallacious, for the only hope there is of maintaining the language-game view is by distinguishing in principle the different games which are played by uttering a given word on different occasions from the games which give this word its meaning. Of course, moves made in the two games *may* coincide in certain cases. Those rare cases are what Austin called the performatory uses of language. Their unusual status makes them exceptionally interesting. From a Wittgensteinian perspective, they nevertheless must be considered exceptions rather than typical cases.

Examples are not hard to find. If I say, 'Jack promised to marry Jill', *I* am not engaged in the language-game of promising, even though it is true that that 'game' (the institution of 'promising') is what gives the verb 'to promise' its meaning (use). Or we can take an example from Jaakko Hintikka's theory of semantical games,[8] according to which the logical homes of quantifier words is a language-game of seeking and finding. If I say, 'For each flowering plant there exists an insect that pollinates it,' I am not engaging in a game of flower-gathering and insect-seeking, although I must in principle master such games in order to understand the sentence.

On at least one occasion, Wittgenstein explicitly makes a distinction between the two kinds of language-games, viz. a distinction between, on the one hand, the language-game which gives a certain word its meaning (and through which we learn this meaning), and, on the other hand, the language-game in which we utter the word:

> The word 'lying' was taught to us in a particular way in which it was fastened to a certain behaviour, to the use of certain expressions under certain circumstances. Then we use it, saying that we have been lying, when our behaviour was not like the one which first constituted the meaning. ('Notes for Lectures on "Private Experience" and "Sense Data"', p. 252 of the reprint)

The distinction is not only clear here; it is dramatic, even though Wittgenstein does not use the term 'language-game' here. It is dramatic, because to utter the words 'I am lying' would defeat the very purpose of the language-game of lying.[9] Hence there is no doubt that Wittgenstein was prepared to make the distinction with which we are concerned here. It is not clear, however, to what extent Wittgenstein explicitly acknowledged the distinction in its full generality.

5 VARIETY OF LANGUAGE-GAMES

Perhaps the most important reason why the nature of language-games in later Wittgenstein has been misunderstood is what Wittgenstein uses this term to highlight two entirely different (although compatible) ideas. On the one hand, Wittgenstein employs it to emphasize the role of rule-governed human activities in constituting the basic representative relationships between language and reality. On the other hand, the term serves in Wittgenstein to highlight the fact that language can be used in many different ways, not just descriptively. As Wittgenstein could have said (and in effect said), there are many, many different language-games besides the descriptive (fact-stating) ones. This is what Wittgenstein is emphasizing, for instance, in *PI*, I, secs. 23–4, 27. Witness, e.g., sec. 23:

> But how many kinds of sentence are there? Say assertion, question, and command? – There are *countless* kinds: countless different kinds of use of what we call "symbols", "words", "sentences". And this multiplicity is not something fixed, given once for all; but new types of language, new language-games, as we may say, come into existence, and others become obsolete and get forgotten.
>
> (We can get a *rough picture* of this from the changes in mathematics.)

The received view arises when the main function of the idea of language-game in later Wittgenstein is taken to be to illustrate this multiplicity of uses of language. There is no need to deny the reality or the importance of Wittgenstein's emphasis on the nondescriptive uses of language. In fact, this emphasis is here taken for granted, in part

precisely because it has received so much attention in recent literature. The one-sided attention to nondescriptive language-games has
nevertheless led to the mistakes of the 'received view' described
earlier. That Wittgenstein extended his attention over and above the
purely descriptive uses of language is taken to show that he lost
interest in the language–world links whose role is seen most clearly in
descriptive uses of language. This leads to the view that Wittgenstein
in effect rejected the whole idea of descriptive (truth-conditional)
meaning. This step is fallacious, however, and sufficient evidence has
been marshalled above to show its fallaciousness. And it is in a way
worse than a mere interpretational mistake. It deprives Wittgenstein's
ideas of their real depth. Wittgenstein is not rejecting descriptive
meaning in favour of sundry language-games. He is not saying merely
that there are language-games other than fact-stating ones, he is doing
something much more striking. He is claiming that descriptive meaning is itself based on language-games. Instead of eliminating descriptive meaning or relegating it to a subordinate status, language-games
constitute descriptive meaning, according to Wittgenstein. Thus for
Wittgenstein there is no obstacle to saying, for instance, that descriptive meaning is truth-conditional, as long as we realize how it is that
those truth-conditions are determined.

6 LANGUAGE-GAMES AS MEDIATING COMPARISONS BETWEEN PICTURES AND REALITY

One way of looking at Wittgenstein's development beyond the
Tractatus – in some ways parallel to the discussion above – is to start
from the picture view and examine, not the name–object relations,
but the relations of picturing. This leads one to ask: How are the
pictures, which our sentences are supposed to be, compared with
reality? How do we establish whether they are true or false? The
viewpoint defined by these questions is as instructive as any idea that
can be brought to bear on Wittgenstein's development. We saw above
in chapter 7, secs. 3 and 5, that Wittgenstein was led to his crucial step
from a phenomenological to a physicalistic basis language by considerations concerning comparisons between a proposition and reality. In
fact, Wittgenstein's notebook entries from the crucial transition
period in October 1929 are shot through with comments like the
following:[10]

My leading idea is that a proposition is *compared* with the reality. (MS
107, p. 155, 7 October 1929)

> I must after all be able to *compare* reality with a proposition. (MS 107, p. 153)

These quotations also show how little truth there is in the allegation that Wittgenstein's change of his philosophical position went together with a loss of interest in language–world comparisons.

In the *Tractatus*, Wittgenstein's view of language–world comparisons is simplicity itself. By means of his theories of truth-functions and quantifiers, Wittgenstein hopes to reduce these questions to pertain only to elementary sentences and to the way they are compared with reality. Now of these comparisons Wittgenstein says precious little in the *Tractatus*. Virtually the only remark he makes on the subject is the laconic 4.05:

> Reality is compared with a proposition.

Wittgenstein's silence amounts to overlooking an important problem. If one thinks of atomic sentences as small snapshot pictures of possible states of local affairs, one may be led to think that the comparisons with reality can be made at a glance. Wittgenstein is clearly assuming in the *Tractatus* that all comparisons between elementary propositions and reality are trivial, that they are matters of immediate confrontation and comparison. This may be viable in a language in which the atomic sentences deal with our objects of direct acquaintance. However, when Wittgenstein changed his basic language, there was no longer any guarantee that language–reality comparisons are as simple as that. In many ways, they can be effected only by means of rule-governed activities on the part of the language users. And if so, the structure of those activities is an important element in the situation which has to be brought out in the open. The interpretation sketched here amounts to saying, in part, that the rule-governed activities by means of which the sentences of our language can be compared with reality are language-games.[11]

An early stage of Wittgenstein's analysis of the problem of comparison is found in *Philosophical Remarks*, III, secs. 21–3, where Wittgenstein is discussing the problem of intention. His words show that this is essentially the same problem as the problem of picture–world connections.

> What is essential to intention is the picture: the picture of what is intended.

> Hence the connection between intention and intended action is the same as the connection between a picture and what it pictures. But what is that connection?

When a language is first learned, connections are as it were established between language and actions – that is to say, connections between the levers and the machine – the question arises as to whether those connections can break down. If they cannot, then I must accept any action as the right one. If they can, what criterion do I have that they have broken down? For what means do I have for *comparing* the original decision with the subsequent action? It is such *comparison* which is left out in Russell's theory. And comparison doesn't consist in confronting the representation with what it represents and through this confrontation experiencing a phenomenon . . . [Emphases added.]

That an account of the language-reality comparisons is needed becomes even clearer when the picture view is developed further – as Wittgenstein at one point tried to do – and sentences are conceived of, not as ready-made pictures, but as instructions or recipes for constructing the pictures. This way of modifying the picture view is put forward in *Philosophical Remarks*, II, sec. 10:

If you think of propositions as instructions for making models, their pictorial character becomes even clearer.

On such a constructivist view of propositions, we cannot compare a sentence with reality in one fell swoop. For on such a view there is no guarantee that the results of picture constructions are particularly simple or that they can be compared with reality directly, and every reason to expect that they can sometimes be too complicated for this purpose. At the very least, we have to retrace the model-building processes in carrying out language–world comparisons, for obviously it is their outcomes that have the best chance of being comparable with reality.[12]

This way of looking at the development of Wittgenstein's views has the advantage of showing the naturalness of another change in them. If we think of language-games merely as serving to mediate name–object relationships, there is a temptation to assume that in normal cases there is a one-to-one correlation between words and language-games. The change in Wittgenstein's views just referred to is that there is no longer a bottom layer of one-to-one naming relations on which the rest of our semantics is based. Rather, one and the same language-game can serve to link several different expressions to the world and thereby give them their meanings. Conversely, one and the same word can play a role in several different language-games. Wittgenstein seems to have come to view the latter change as a corollary to the language-game idea, as witnessed by the quotes in section 5 earlier in this chapter. More generally, Wittgenstein sometimes used the language-game idea to underline this new, more complicated picture of the language–world relations. Important though this point is, it is for Wittgenstein largely a mere consequence of the much more significant idea of language-games as constituting naming relations.

It is to be pointed out, however, that initially Wittgenstein realized the possibility – and the need – of multiple language–world comparisons before he had developed the full-fledged notion of a language-game, and even at the same time as his new language paradigm and independently of it. This insight of Wittgenstein's was an early result of his struggle with the problem of independence, discussed in chapter 5 above. This is strikingly shown by Waismann's notes of 25 December 1929 (in *Philosophical Remarks,* p. 317), quoted above in chapter 5, sec. 5. In *Zettel,* sec. 644, Wittgenstein writes even more explicitly: 'A language-game comprises the use of *several* words.'

Of course, there is no intrinsic conflict between language-games as mediating the name–object relationships and as mediating the sentence–world comparisons. In fact, the two are bound to merge into one, when the situation is examined more thoroughly. For, since 'only in the context of a proposition does a name have meaning', the only purpose for which the name–object relations are needed is as a part of the sentence–world comparisons. And Wittgenstein never lost his interest in the latter comparisons.

7 LANGUAGE-GAMES OF VERIFICATION

We can also pinpoint more closely an early developmental stage of Wittgenstein's idea that language-games mediate sentence–world comparisons. It is the idea that the meaning (use) of an assertion is shown by the way in which it could be *verified.* Indeed, in chapter 7, secs. 3 and 5, above we saw that it was precisely Wittgenstein's analysis of what is involved in the verification of a sentence (in 'comparing it with reality') that led him to his new language paradigm in October 1929.[13] Hence the idea of verification as giving us the meaning is not only interesting as an anticipation of Wittgenstein's later concept of language-games as constituting meaning relations; it is also vitally important for the purpose of understanding Wittgenstein's development.

What happened later was not that Wittgenstein somehow found the verification idea to be mistaken. Rather, he found that it did not apply to all kinds of sentences. In other words, it is his insight into the variety of different possible language-games (cf. sec. 5 above) that led Wittgenstein to downgrade later the idea that the method of verification of an assertion shows its meaning. His point is merely that this idea does not apply to sentences that are not asserted. You do not try to verify a question, command, or prayer, and even the truthfulness of a confession differs from its literal truth (see *PI*, II, xi, p. 222). But there is little in what Wittgenstein says to belie the idea that, when it makes sense to speak of the verification of a sentence, then it is its verification processes that show its sense. We merely have to remember that games of verification are for the later Wittgenstein only a small subclass of all the language-games which give our sentences their meanings. Historically speaking, it nevertheless appears that the entire language-game idea was originally but a generalization from the language-games of verification and falsification.

In the light of these observations, we can also understand why Wittgenstein could literally to the end of his life use the verification of a proposition as a key to its logic. For instance, in March 1951 Wittgenstein writes:

> The statement, "I see a red circle" and the statement "I see (am not blind)" are not logically of the same sort. How do we test the truth of the former, and how that of the latter? (*Remarks on Colour*, I, sec. 84)

Historically speaking, it is even fairly obvious how Wittgenstein was first led to broaden the scope of his semantical vision. The first step was prompted by his interest in the idea of command (*Befehl*). He was preoccupied with, not to say obsessed by, this notion in MSS 109–10. Significantly, the very first language-game Wittgenstein outlines in the *Philosophical Investigations* is one of commanding and obeying (*PI*, I, sec. 2). It is also significant that as early as in MS 108, p. 190, Wittgenstein says that commanding (*der Befehl*) must constitute a kind of comparison of a sentence with reality. In such statements, one can see the first seed of Wittgenstein's later idea that it is entire language-game like the practice of issuing commands and obeying them that serve as those 'methods of projection' which connect language with reality by facilitating comparisons between the two. (Cf. here MS 108, p. 191.)[14]

8 WHAT HAPPENED TO THE PICTURE IDEA?

At this point, an intriguing conclusion is beginning to emerge.

What has been argued is that the basic name–object relations of the *Tractatus* were thought of in Wittgenstein's later philosophy as being constituted by language-games. Now clearly *this change should not affect Wittgenstein's picture idea at all.* This idea is that *after* (logically, not temporally speaking) name–object relations have been established, one can use these relations to represent facts in virtue of the isomorphism relations between complexes of names and complexes of objects. But if so, the way in which the name–object relations are established does not make any difference in principle. The pictorial (isomorphism) idea should still be applicable.

This conclusion is in the main correct, it will be argued, subject to a number of qualifications.[15] It throws sharp critical light on the widespread view that Wittgenstein later gave up the 'picture theory of language' that he had put forward in the *Tractatus*. It is now seen that this view is deeply misleading, if we understand the picture idea in the same way as Wittgenstein. There were important changes in Wittgenstein's attitude to the picture idea, but they are not relevant to its gist.

What are these changes? First of all, the picture (isomorphism) relations between language and the world lose their primacy. In the *Tractatus,* the picturing (isomorphism) relations which may obtain between sentences and facts are based on naming (name–object) relations. However, Wittgenstein says absolutely nothing about naming relations except that they are there. (Cf. 3.22–3.221.) Hence the pictorial relations between sentences and facts are in effect the ground floor of our logic in the *Tractatus.*

This priority is changed radically in Wittgenstein's mature thought. The naming relations are now constituted by language-games, which therefore are the most fundamental layer of relationships in our semantics (or 'logic', as Wittgenstein might have called it).

Now Wittgenstein was always greatly concerned with the primacy of logic. The very first entry in his *Notebooks 1914–1916* reads: 'Logic must take care of itself.' Hence the change in the order of conceptual priorities meant that the importance of the picture view for Wittgenstein was greatly reduced. It became mere frosting on the real logical cake which consists of language-games and which claimed Wittgenstein's main interest in his later works. As we might put it, taking our clue from Jaakko Hintikka, Wittgenstein's picture theory is like the old soldier of song: it never died; it just faded away. But recognizing this does not imply maintaining that Wittgenstein ever gave up the basic idea of his picture view.

Secondly, another change in Wittgenstein's views has already been registered. It is that, in his later philosophy, the basic semantical links connecting the expressions of our language with the ingredients of our world are no longer one-to-one relations. One and the same language-game can, as it were, mediate the connection of several different words with reality. This makes the application of the picture idea messier, and hence reduces its value and interest. (For further discussion of this point, see sec. 6 above.)

Thirdly, the fact has also been registered that Wittgenstein's language-game idea had other functions than merely to highlight what in the *Tractatus* were the naming relations. It was used by Wittgenstein also to illustrate the fact that our language has other uses than the descriptive one. This change in emphasis does not in itself change the fundamental ideas of the picture view, however. The mere existence of uses of language other than the descriptive one is, for instance, perfectly compatible with Erik Stenius' fascinating idea that these other language-games (we might call them 'modal language-games') are played by means of pictures.[16] Pictures can be used, e.g., to show what someone is told to bring about, not only as a description of how things in fact are.

None of these changes destroys the applicability of the picture idea, however. If so, a prediction ensues to the effect that Wittgenstein never gave up completely the picture idea, even though its importance for his overall philosophy was greatly reduced. This prediction is diametrically contrary to a widespread, influential interpretation of Wittgenstein. It is therefore an important confirmation of the interpretation defended here that this prediction turns out to be correct. The evidence we shall present shows that Wittgenstein's alleged rejection of the picture idea is merely another respect in which Wittgenstein's later philosophy has been misunderstood.

It is, for instance, clear from Wittgenstein's notebook entries that his initial steps away from the philosophy of the *Tractatus* were not due to a loss of interest in 'pictorial' relations between propositions and the reality. If anything, Wittgenstein exhibited an ever keener interest in them than before. This is shown among other things by the quotation above in chapter 7, sec. 3, as well as by such passages as the following:[17]

A proposition is not simply a picture, but a portrait. (MS 107, p. 155, 7 October 1929)

In reality, there is in Wittgenstein's middle-period writings striking evidence that he did not 'give up the picture theory'. For instance, this is shown by his words in MS 219, p. 14:[18]

My *idea* that a proposition is a picture was a good one. It said that thinking is the same as, or something similar to, making a picture for oneself, and thinkable is the same as, or similar to, what is imaginable. And as undetermined as the concept of proposition is, as undetermined is also the concept of picture. I.e., a picture is nevertheless a perfect guidepost to the understanding of how a proposition works.

But how does a proposition (sentence) work in language? We have argued that the gist of Wittgenstein's picture view was the idea that, once the meanings of the simple signs have been established (perhaps ostensively), the meanings of propositions are determined by the requirement of a structural similarity between a proposition and and the possible fact it represents. In this sense, the picture idea is closely related to Wittgenstein's requirement that a proposition is *articulated*. (Cf. *Tractatus* 3.141.) Now this conception of a proposition is affirmed by Wittgenstein in the *Big Typescript* (MS 213), sec. 43, pp. 189–90. There he says in so many words that 'the connection between language and reality' is established by explanations concerning the meanings of words, e.g., ostensive definitions. In contrast, 'there is no ostensive definition [*Erklärung*] for *sentences*'. This is obviously so because of the reasons we have indicated: a sentence has its meaning because its articulated structure matches the structure of the fact it expresses. Wittgenstein indicates this by speaking of a 'similarity' [*Aehnlichkeit*] and of a 'picture' ibid., p. 190). He also emphasizes that the agreement and disagreement between a proposition (or sentence, *Satz*) and the world (reality) is not arbitrary, plainly because it is based on the nonconventional matching (picturing) relation. This helps to confirm both our claim that Wittgenstein never gave up the picture idea and also our original interpretation of this idea (see above, chapter 4, secs. 4–5).

An even more direct assertion of the picture view is found in *The Blue Book*:

> If we keep in mind the possibility of a picture which, though correct, has no similarity with its object, the interpolation of a shadow between the sentence and reality loses all point. For now the sentence itself can serve as such a shadow. *The sentence is just such a picture*, which hasn't the slightest similarity with what it represents . . . This shews you the way in which words and things may be connected. (*The Blue and Brown Books*, p. 37; emphasis added)

In view of such pronouncements, it is simply impossible to maintain that Wittgenstein gave up the picture view in his middle-period philosophy.[19]

There is no evidence in Wittgenstein's later writings either, that he changed his mind about the basic ideas of the 'picture theory', as we have interpreted it. Even the modifications he makes in his views, far from refuting our reading of Wittgenstein, on the contrary confirm it further, and show in fact a remarkable persistence in his central views. Here we shall consider only one characteristic idea Wittgenstein uses in his later writings. It consists in comparing some sentences, not with portraits (historical pictures), as we saw him doing, but with genre pictures. For instance, in *PI*, I, sec. 522, he writes:

> If we compare a proposition to a picture, we must think whether we are comparing it to a portrait (a historical representation) or to a genre-picture. And both comparisons make sense.

A closely related point is made by Wittgenstein as early as in the *Big Typescript*, sec. 22 (pp. 85–6). There a comparison with genre pictures is used to understand the nature of sentences (e.g., sentences occurring in fiction) to which the idea of verification does not apply. His point is that even when the elements of a sentence have not been tied to actual objects in the world, e.g., through ostensive definitions, we can understand it the same way as a historical picture or portrait. But how do we understand the latter kind of picture? Such a picture has its meaning in virtue of its structure, i.e., because it is an isomorphic replica of the possible state of affairs which would make it true. Hence the same must according to Wittgenstein hold of genre pictures – and of the sentences compared by Wittgenstein with genre pictures. Thus Wittgenstein is relying here on the idea that isomorphism is what constitutes sentence meaning, i.e., on the basic idea of his 'picture theory'. Hence Wittgenstein is still swearing by the picture idea here, both asserting it and – what is more important – relying on it in his argumentation.

This observation is worth elaborating. Earlier, we said Wittgenstein's picture idea comes into play only after the basic name–object relationships have been established, and hence is independent of how these relationships are thought of, e.g., whether they are simple two-place relations or constituted by language-games. In his statements about genre pictures, Wittgenstein is saying more: he is saying that the picture idea does not only apply *after* the simple expressions are assigned their particular references, it can apply to a sentence *independently* of the way the references of its basic ingredients are determined, for instance, even if those simple ingredients do not stand for any particular entities.[20]

9 PICTURES INVOLVE LANGUAGE-GAMES

The occasion on which Wittgenstein seems to come closest to renouncing the picture theory is in *Philosophical Grammar*, I,

Appendix 4B (pp. 212–14).[21] Hence it is a good test case for the interpretation presented here. Wittgenstein writes there:

> What gives us the idea that there is a kind of agreement between thought and reality? – Instead of "agreement" one might say here with a clear conscience "pictorial character" [*Bildhaftigkeit*].
>
> But is this pictorial character an agreement? In the *Tractatus Logico-Philosophicus* I said something like: it lies in an agreement of form. But this is an error.

Wittgenstein is here speaking of thinking and not of language. As every reader of the *Tractatus* knows (cf., e.g., 3, 3.01, 4, etc.), thought and language go together for Wittgenstein. Hence his remarks apply also to the picture theory of language; and hence they might seem to indicate that he after all rejected the picture view.

This would nevertheless be a serious misunderstanding of Wittgenstein. Dramatically, just when our interpretation seems to run into trouble, it receives one of its most persuasive confirmations.

For Wittgenstein goes on to explain what he means. First, a picture can be a picture of a possible state of affairs; it does not have to be a picture of an actual state of the world. For instance, an order (command) normally is a picture of the action as it ought to be executed, not necessarily of how it will actually be carried out; and a blueprint is a picture of an object as it ought to be constructed, not of what it actually will be like. (Notice, incidentally, that Wittgenstein is here speaking unashamedly of a verbal order as a picture.) As is implicit in what we found in chapter 4 above, this is precisely the same as can be said of the picture 'theory' of the *Tractatus*.

But what mediates the connection between such a picture and its eventual target in reality? What is the 'method of projection' involved? 'One can compare a method of projection with such lines of projection which reach out from one [geometrical] figure to another one' when the former is projected onto the latter. Such a method of projection is of course what corresponds in language to a system of naming relations.

Such concrete analogies can be misleading, however, Wittgenstein emphasizes. In the case of verbal propositions, it is the *use* of the picture that constitutes this 'method of projection':

> We might now express ourselves thus: the method of projection mediates between the drawing and the object . . . – But if the method of projection is a bridge, it is a bridge which isn't built until the application is made . . . what we may call 'picture' is the blueprint *together with* the method of its application. [Kenny's translation has been modified][22]

Wittgenstein could scarcely have expressed more forcefully the idea that it is the *use* of a picture that mediates between the picture (a sentence, a thought, a blueprint, or an order) and the reality it represents. Even though Wittgenstein does not here use the term 'language-game', it is unmistakable that what he later referred to by this term are here taken to constitute the basic semantical relations. And when this fact is noted, the picture idea is vindicated: the blueprint *together with* an appropriate language-game remains a picture. As Wittgenstein puts it:

> So I am imagining that the difference between proposition and reality is ironed out by the lines of projection belonging to the picture, the thought, and that no further room is left for a method of application, but only for agreement and disagreement.

Thus what prima facie might look like a rejection of picture theory turns out to be not only a qualified assertion of the picture idea, but strong evidence for the interpretation of the semantical role of language-games in later Wittgenstein.

This interpretation is confirmed by Wittgenstein's own statement of what he is arguing for in the passage we have considered:[23]

> As everything metaphysical, so is the "agreement between thought and reality" to be found in the grammar of the language. (MS 116, p. 122)

In other words, Wittgenstein is not denying the agreement (which is essentially just the pictorial relation) between language and reality. What he is doing is to diagnose its nature. The passage we just quoted is in fact Wittgenstein's own way of introducing his discussion of the pictorial character of propositions and of putting it into perspective. It is his own statement of what he is arguing for in the passage we have analysed. It strikingly confirms our interpretation.

These observations show, among other things, that it is not inappropriate to refer to the basic ideas of the picture view in discussing Wittgenstein's development beyond the *Tractatus*. This possibility has been, and will be, made use of throughout this chapter.

What we have found nevertheless shows that an important change had taken place in the picture view which Wittgenstein accepted in his later philosophy. What is a picture is no longer a sentence as a syntactical (formal) entity. The 'projective relations' constituted by use also have to be incorporated in the 'picture' if it is to serve its purpose. This marks an important difference between the *Tractatus* and Wittgenstein's later views.

The precise nature of this difference is nevertheless subtler than one is first likely to think. In the *Tractatus,* too, the projective relations are to be included in the real proposition, as is shown, e.g., by 3.12–3.13. 'A proposition includes all that the projection includes, but not what is projected,' as Wittgenstein sums up his view. What makes a difference is the precise nature of the projective relations. In the *Tractatus,* they are in the last analysis simple two-place relations. Because of this, we have no reason to make a distinction between the syntactic form of a sentence in a logically correct notation and the form of a proposition it expresses. In his later philosophy, the complicated nature of those relations gives the lie to his earlier identification of syntactical and logical form. In the *Tractatus,* Wittgenstein had acknowledged that, in ordinary discourse, 'in order to recognize a symbol by its sign we must observe how it is used with a sense' (3.326) and that 'a sign does not determine a logical form unless it is taken together with its logico-syntactical employment' (3.327). Of course, in a purified logical language can we look at its syntactical form alone. But now that Wittgenstein is during his middle period considering everyday language as his basic language, he suddenly has to heed his own early injunctions. He cannot resort any longer to an ideal language where he could forget use as a determinant of logical form. However, the possibility of his new position had unmistakably been anticipated in the *Tractatus,* which vividly shows that Wittgenstein is not violating the picture idea here.

What Wittgenstein is arguing for in MS 116, pp. 122ff., is therefore not any change in his picture idea, but a modification in the way his idea of logical form is to be applied, due to the change of his language paradigm.

What we have found also shows what Wittgenstein means by those frequent pronouncements in his middle-period and later writings where he seems to discard altogether the idea of sentences as pictures. What is going on in such statements is that Wittgenstein is pointing out the inadequacy of syntactical form for the picturing job which it was supposed to do in the *Tractatus.*

10 THE FATE OF THE MIRRORING IDEA AND THE PROBLEM OF CONVENTIONALITY

All this does not yet close one of the issues which is often discussed under the heading of the 'fate of the picture theory'. In chapter 5 above, we distinguished from each other the *picture idea* (isomorphism as a mark of truth) and the *mirroring idea.* The latter is in a sense a modal idea; it amounts to claiming that in a logically correct language the totality of admissible combinations of symbols ('names') matches the totality of possible structures of entities ('objects') in the world. In most earlier discussions of 'the picture theory', those two ideas are run together.

Someone might argue that, even though Wittgenstein never gave up the picture idea, he relinquished the mirroring idea as a part of his account of the language–world relationship. Did he? This question is not easy to answer. Some things are nevertheless clear. In his transition period 1929–30 Wittgenstein worried about the mirroring idea and was to all practical purposes ready to give it up, as shown inter alia by his 1929 paper 'Some Remarks on Logical Form'. This does not close the issue, for what Wittgenstein wrote in 1929–30 must frequently be taken as a statement of a problem rather than as a ready-made view. The real question is not whether Wittgenstein rejected the mirroring requirement in 1929, but whether his subsequent new ideas, culminating in the notion of language-game, enabled him to regain the paradise of the mirroring idea.

It seems to us that in his mature thinking Wittgenstein in fact again accepted a version of the mirroring idea. The basis of his acceptance was discussed in sections 8–9 above. In a sense, the same strategy by means of which Wittgenstein could still maintain his picture view also serves to vindicate the mirroring idea. This ploy consisted in including as a part of each proposition also the language-game which mediates the 'projective' relations of this proposition to the world. This strategy has an interesting consequence, however, which changes the philosophical situation. The change can be formulated by reference to the problem of the conventionality or nonconventionality of semantical relations. It is quite subtle, but it is nevertheless merely a consequence of the central role of language-games in later Wittgenstein. It was diagnosed in effect above in secs. 8–9. The change is this: As long as the basic language–world links are unanalysed naming relations, the only thing that can limit the possible combinations of symbols is their own intrinsic nature. After the name–object relations are established, names (symbols) are left to their own devices. They must 'take care of themselves', Wittgenstein could have said. All that determines their possible combinations is their own nature. This nature is not conventional, even though the naming relations are. That this is Wittgenstein's view in the *Tractatus* is shown by such propositions as the following:

> 6.124   We have said that some things are arbitrary in the symbols we use and that some things are not. In logic it is only the latter that express: but that means that logic is not a field in which *we* express what we wish with the help of signs, but rather one in which the nature of the natural and inevitable signs speaks for itself.

Similar statements are found in 3.315, which like 6.124 was quoted earlier only partially. The previously unquoted part shows what the nonconventional element in language is according to Wittgenstein:

> But if all the signs in [a proposition] . . . are turned into variables, we shall still get a class of this kind. This one, however, is not dependent on any convention, but solely on the nature of the proposition. It corresponds to a logical form – a logical prototype.

A way of putting Wittgenstein's point is to say that in a truly pictorial language each proposition, being a picture, automatically represents a possible configuration of objects, whereas in our everyday verbal language there are all sorts of meaningless combinations of symbols. They must be ruled out by conventional rules if we are to maintain the mirroring principle. They are not automatically eliminated by the nature of our symbols in their own right. Wittgenstein's view in the *Tractatus* of a logically correct language is that it must be like a picture language in this crucial respect. (This observation deepens further our interpretation of Wittgenstein's mirroring idea.)

What happens in Wittgenstein's later philosophy is that he gives up this idea of (as it were) automatically correct, self-guaranteeing mirroring language. He gives it up, not merely because it is impossible to reach, but because it is intrinsically incoherent.

Language is in the last analysis related to the world, not by naming relations, but by language-games. And these language-games do not leave the symbols of our language to their own devices, unmonitored and governed only by their own laws, because it is only a language-game in use that first determines what the symbol *is* that is used to represent an object or a phenomenon in different situations. As we saw, in the sense relevant to the concept of logical form, language-games must literally be considered parts of linguistic propositions. In other words, the very identity of the symbols of our language is constituted by the language-games. In this sense, the symbols do not exist independently of the language-games which constitute the 'projective relations' of language to the world.

What all this implies is that Wittgenstein is after all free to think of language as mirroring the world in his later philosophy of language. Each possible combination of linguistic symbols can – if we want – be thought of as corresponding to a possibility in reality. But this is no longer due to any metaphysical analogy between language as a self-contained syntactical system and the world. It is true because our language-games serve to define the linguistic symbols involved in them and thereby guarantee them a role in our interactions with reality.

In this sense, Wittgenstein adheres to the mirroring idea in his later writings. This is shown, among other things, by his repeated statements that it is the 'rules of grammar' that determine what is possible and what is not. For instance, in *Philosophical Remarks* Wittgenstein embraces the view that the totality of admissible combinations of linguistic signs must reflect the essence of the world. In V, sec. 54, he writes:

> But the essence of language is a picture of the essence of the world; and philosophy as custodian of grammar can in fact grasp the essence of the world, only not in the proposition of language, but in rules for this language which exclude nonsensical combinations of signs.

Similar pronouncements are found elsewhere aplenty. For instance in *PI*, I, sec. 520, we read:

> "If a proposition, too, is conceived as a picture of a possible state of affairs and is said to show the possibility of the state of affairs, still the most that the proposition can do is what a painting or relief or film does: and so it can at any rate not set forth what is not the case. So also it depends wholly on our grammar what will be called (logically) possible and what not – i.e. what the grammar permits?" But surely that is arbitrary! Is it arbitrary? It is not every sentence-like formation that we know how to do something with, not every technique has a use in our life; and when we are tempted in philosophy to count some quite useless thing as a proposition, that is often because we have not considered its use sufficiently.[24]

This appears to be partly analogous with the *Tractatus*. In that early work, once the basic naming relations have been defined, it is thereby determined nonconventionally which combinations of simple signs are propositions and which ones are mere *Wörtergemisch*. (Cf. 3.141.) In a similar way, once the appropriate language-games of the *Philosophical Investigations* have been set up, it is determined which sentence-like combinations of symbols have a use in the form of life that these games represent. The 'grammar' of these language-games may be partly conventional; what is not conventional is what happens if it is accepted and practised.

A difference as compared with the *Tractatus* is nevertheless the fact that the kind of possibility and necessity defined by a language-game is relative to it. This is not unlike the fact that one language-game defines what is possible in chess and another one what is possible in checkers or draughts. Maybe there are possible moves in chess which nobody ever actually makes. However, this does not vitiate the notion of 'possible in chess' defined by the rules of the game, provided that the overall game has a use in our life. For instance, we read in *PI*, I, sec. 521:

> Compare 'logically possible' with 'chemically possible'. One might perhaps call a combination chemically possible if a formula with the right valencies existed (e.g. H – O – O – O – H). Of course such a combination need not exist; but even the formula HO_2 cannot have less than no combination corresponding to it in reality.

This is also expressed by Wittgenstein as follows:

> The rules of grammar are arbitrary in the sense that the rules of a game are arbitrary. We can make them differently. But then it is a different game.[25]

Here a reader will perhaps begin to appreciate the depth of Wittgenstein's idea of language-game.

NOTES

1 Their role in Wittgenstein's later philosophy was emphasized in Jaakko Hintikka, 'Language-games', in Jaakko Hintikka et al., editors., *Essays on Wittgenstein in Honour of G. H. von Wright* (*Acta Philosophica Fennica*, vol. 28, nos. 1–3), North-Holland, Amsterdam, 1976, pp. 105–25.

2 Cf., e.g., Wolfgang Stegmüller, *Hauptströmungen der Gegenwarts-Philosophie*, fifth edn, vol. 1, Alfred Kröner, Stuttgart, 1975, p. 584.

3 See, e.g., R. Fogelin, *Wittgenstein (The Arguments of Philosophers)*, Routledge & Kegan Paul, London, 1976, pp. 107–8; P. F. Strawson, 'Review of Wittgenstein's *Philosophical Investigations*', reprinted from *Mind*, vol. 63 (1954), pp. 70–99, in G. Pitcher, editor, *Wittgenstein*, The Philosophical Investigations: *A Collection of Critical Essays*, Doubleday, Garden City, N.Y., 1966, pp. 22–64, especially p. 25; Wolfgang Stegmüller, *Main Currents in Contemporary German, British, and American Philosophy*, D. Reidel, Dordrecht, 1969, p. 435; Michael Dummett, 'Frege and Wittgenstein', in Irving Block, editor, *Perspectives on the Philosophy of Wittgenstein*, Basil Blackwell, Oxford, 1981, pp. 31–42, especially p. 40.

4 For Wittgenstein's terminology, see chapter 10, sec. 9, below.

5 See sec. 6 below. It is in order here to comment on an apparent counter-example to our interpretational thesis. When Wittgenstein says in *Remarks on the Foundations of Mathematics*, I, sec. 155, that in logic 'there is no question at all . . . of some correspondence between what is said and reality', he is not there talking about the representation of reality in ordinary factual sentences, as we are. Rather he is talking about *logic* and logical inferences. The entire section reads as follows:

The steps which are not brought in question are logical inferences. But the reason why they are not brought in question is not that they 'certainly correspond to the truth' – or something of the sort, – no, it is just this that is called 'thinking', 'speaking', 'inferring', 'arguing'. There is not any question at all here of some correspondence between what is said and reality; rather is logic *antecedent* to any such correspondence; in the same sense, that is, as that in which the establishment of a method of measurement is *antecedent* to the correctness or incorrectness of a statement of length.

Wittgenstein's last words show that he is not denying in the least that in language in general we are dealing with a 'correspondence between what is said and reality', as little as he would deny that the measurement of length is essentially a comparison between what is measured and the yardstick. Rather his point is that in the special case of logical conclusions we are dealing with something that is antecedent to relevant comparisons because it is part of the framework we need to carry out such comparisons. In general, just because it is language-games that make comparisons between language and reality possible, what is constitutive of a game itself cannot be such a comparison. (Logic, Wittgenstein suggests, is a case in point.) Hence Wittgenstein's statement yields extremely strong evidence for the present interpretation. There is on Wittgenstein's view no question at all of any correspondence between what is said and reality *in the special case of logic*, because logic precedes all such correspondences. (See here also below, sec. 10.)

6 This result is further confirmed by a comparison between *PI*, I, sec. 10, and *The Brown Book*, pp. 171–3, discussed in chapter 8, sec. 6, above. In *Philosophical Remarks* Wittgenstein explains in the same spirit what he means by *use* (*Anwendung*): 'By use [*Anwendung*] I understand that which in the first place makes combinations of *sounds* or marks into a language; the sense in which it is the use that makes a rod with markings into a *measuring-rod*: the superimposition of language on reality.'

7 The German word *Tätigkeiten*, which G. E. M. Anscombe translates as 'actions', could and perhaps should be rendered as 'activities'. This would fit even better with what we are arguing.

8 See Jaakko Hintikka and Jack Kulas, *The Game of Language*, D. Reidel, Dordrecht, 1983; Esa Saarinen, editor, *Game-Theoretical Semantics*, D. Reidel, Dordrecht, 1979.

9 One is tempted to ask here, ironically, 'How do you explain the meaning of lying by reference to the illocutionary force of "I am lying"?'

10 The German of these two passages reads as follows:

Mein Hauptgedanke ist, daß man den Satz mit der Wirklichkeit *vergleicht*. (MS 107, p. 155, 7 October 1929)

Ich muß die Wirklichkeit ja tatsächlich mit dem Satz *vergleichen* können. (MS 107, p. 153)

11 Cf. here Jaakko Hintikka, 'Quantification and the picture theory of language', chapter 2 of Jaakko Hintikka, *Logic, Language-Games, and Information*, Clarendon Press, Oxford, 1973.

238   *Language-games in late Wittgenstein*

12 In the paper referred to in note 11 above, Jaakko Hintikka argued that, if one seriously tries to extend Wittgenstein's picture view to first-order languages (languages whose logic is lower predicate calculus, a.k.a. quantification theory), it is not individual sentences that can be thought of as 'pictures'. Rather, what are known as *model sets* (sometimes also referred to as Hintikka sets) are the best candidates for this role. A sentence serves in a natural sense as a starting-point for constructing (or trying to construct) a number of alternative model sets, especially in our ordinary logical practice. (All logical proofs can be thought of as attempted but frustrated model set constructions.)

This seems to vindicate completely Wittgenstein's ideas of propositions as instructions for 'making models'. However, this happy state of affairs is marred by the necessity of comparing such 'pictures' or 'models' with reality. They are now sets of sentences, and as such they can be quite complicated and even infinite. They cannot be compared with the world without further ado. The only realistic view on these comparisons is that they are mediated by certain rule-governed activities. In brief, we cannot dispense with language-games in comparing language and the world.

13 Similar ideas about verification as a clue to the meaning of a sentence are found in *Ludwig Wittgenstein and the Vienna Circle*, pp. 47, 79, 227, 243–4; *Philosophical Remarks*, II, sec. 27; XIV, sec. 166; XXII, secs. 225, 232; *Wittgenstein's Lectures, Cambridge 1930–1932*, pp. 5–7; MS 107, p. 151; etc. During this period, Wittgenstein is putting his argumentative practice where his mouth is. He asks frequently how some particular sentence or kind of sentence could be verified (cf., e.g., *Ludwig Wittgenstein and the Vienna Circle*, pp. 71, 97–8, 126, 221, 226) and infers a difference in meaning from a difference in the verifications procedures (ibid., pp. 46, 48, 53–5, 70–1, 98, 158–61, 186, 204–6, 245–6, 258–9, etc.). Cf. also MS 113, p. 417 (6 May 1932).

14 This idea may perhaps be traced further back in Wittgenstein's development. One kind of symbolism which is used to guide action is a musical score when it is used as the basis of a performance of the composition in question. Musical notation (*Notenschrift*) and its relation to a performance is in fact mentioned by Wittgenstein as early as in the *Tractatus*; see, e.g., 4.0141: 'There is a general rule by means of which the musician can obtain the symphony from the score . . . And that rule is the law of projection which projects the symphony into the language of musical notation . . .'

Later (in MS 107, p. 243) Wittgenstein notes that musical notation can be thought of as a set of instructions for acting in a certain way: 'Die Sprache der Notenschrift [ist] eine Anweisung für das Spielen eines Instruments.'

Thus musical notation provided Wittgenstein with an interesting example of how a symbolism can be a part of a complex which includes human activities guided by this notation.

15 A similar thesis has been argued for by Erik Stenius; see his paper, 'The picture theory and Wittgenstein's later attitude to it' in Irving Block, editor, *Perspectives on the Philosophy of Wittgenstein*, Basil Blackwell, Oxford, 1981, pp. 110–39.

16 Erik Stenius, 'Mood and language-game', *Synthese*, vol. 17 (1967), pp. 254–74.

17 The German reads: 'Der Satz ist nicht einfach ein Bild, sondern ein Portrait.'

18 The German text reads: 'Mein *Gedanke,* der Satz sei ein Bild, war gut. Er sagte, denken sei dasselbe oder etwas ähnliches wie, sich ein Bild machen, und denkbar dasselbe oder etwas ähnliches wie vorstellbar. Und so unbestimmt der Begriff Satz, so unbestimmt ist ja auch [übrigens auch] der Begriff Bild. D.h. das Bild ist allerdings ein perfekter Wegweiser zum Verständnis der Funktion des Satzes.'

19 The picture 'theory' could not be asserted more emphatically in Wittgenstein's lectures in Cambridge in 1930–2:

A proposition is a picture of reality, and we compare propositions with reality. (p. 1)

The proposition is a picture of reality. – Two senses of picture – (1) A portrait, which is like, resembles, is similar to that of which it is a portrait. (2) Something which is intended to be a picture of another without resembling it in sense (1). That it is a picture consists in intention. (p. 4)

True propositions describe reality. Grammar is a mirror of reality. (p. 9)

"A proposition is a picture of reality" – but only if we do not take "picture of" to mean "similar to" in the ordinary sense. (p. 63)

See *Wittgenstein's Lectures, Cambridge 1930–1932.* In *Philosophical Grammar,* IX, sec. 123, Wittgenstein likewise writes: 'Let us imagine a picture story in schematic pictures, and thus more like the narrative in a language than a series of realistic pictures. Using such a picture-language we might in particular e.g. keep our hold on the course of battles . . . *And a sentence of our word-language approximates to such a picture of this picture-language much more than we think.'* [Emphasis added.] Other relevant passages here are *Philosophical Grammar,* III, sec. 37 and *Philosophical Remarks,* II, sec. 10.

20 There is, admittedly, one way of understanding the claim that 'Wittgenstein gave up the picture theory of language' which is correct and indeed related closely to the role of language-games which we have emphasized. What it is can be seen from our discussion above in chapter 4, sec. 5, of the different things that have been included under the ill-defined heading 'Wittgenstein's picture theory of language'. One of these different assumptions was that the pictorial relationship between propositions and states of affairs is a *complete* account of language understanding. This implies that the name–object relationships on which the 'picture' (isomorphism) relations are based do not presuppose any activities on the part of the language users and hence can be understood once and for all without further ado. This simplicity assumption was rejected by Wittgenstein when he introduced language-games as mediators between language and reality. On the construal of 'picture theory of language' which takes it to put a premium on the simplicity of name–object relations, his later philosophy of language does indeed involve essentially a rejection of the 'picture theory'. However, this way of

trying to save the claim that Wittgenstein 'rejected the picture theory' is subject to a simple but crucial objection. There is no evidence whatsoever that this construal of the picture idea has anything to do with Wittgenstein's use of such terms as 'picture' and 'depict'. For this reason, it is misleading to use the role of language-games to suggest that Wittgenstein ever abandoned the 'picture theory'.

21 This passage is from MS 116, which has been edited by Heikki Nyman. (His valuable edition has unfortunately not been published, however.) In Nyman's text, the sections included in *Philosophical Grammar* and discussed here are 176–7 and 251–4. Other sections of MS 116 are also relevant here. We are most grateful to Heikki Nyman and G. H. von Wright for an opportunity to use the edited text.

22 Instead of our '*together with*' Kenny has merely the unitalicized word 'plus'. This seems to be too bland a rendering of Wittgenstein's underlined word *mit*.

23 Cf. note 21 above. This passage is inexplicably omitted by Rush Rhees from the fragment included in *Philosophical Grammar*. This passage also occurs in a different context in *Philosophical Grammar*, VIII, sec. 112 (p. 162). We are using our own translation rather than Kenny's.

24 G. E. M. Anscombe translates *Verwendung* as 'application' rather than as 'use' in the last sentence of the quote. Both translations are possible, but it seems to us that 'use' captures Wittgenstein's point more fully.

25 See *Wittgenstein's Lectures, Cambridge 1930–1932*, p. 57.

10
Wittgenstein on Private Experience

1 WHY IS A PHENOMENOLOGICAL LANGUAGE NOT POSSIBLE?

One important aspect of the odyssey which took Wittgenstein from the philosophy of the *Tractatus* to that presented in the *Philosophical Investigations* remains to be investigated. If we are right, the crucial step in Wittgenstein's development was his rejection of a phenomenological basis language in favour of a physicalistic one in 1929. But what was the basis of this rejection? More specifically, what arguments could Wittgenstein offer to show the impossibility of a purely phenomenological language? It might seem surprising that in his early middle period Wittgenstein does not offer any major general arguments to show that a language of immediate experience is impossible in its own right. We have even found some indications which suggest that Wittgenstein hesitated between calling a phenomenological language impossible and calling it unnecessary.[1] However, in the light of what we have found in chapters 6–9, this absence of proof should not be hard to understand. In chapter 7, sec. 3, we saw that Wittgenstein was originally led to reject phenomenological languages by the requirement that an atomic sentence be directly comparable to the corresponding fact. But such comparisons soon turned out to be far from direct in physicalistic languages, too. As Wittgenstein expressed his point, the actual application of language is part of the 'projective' connections between language and the world.

Wittgenstein may have believed very strongly in the impossibility of a phenomenological language, but he did not yet have available to him conceptual tools for proving his point. For there is nothing in the main ideas of Wittgenstein's early middle-period philosophy of language that prima facie rules out a language of the immediately given. For instance, one of the key concepts of this period in Wittgenstein was ostension. Now surely one can point to an object of immediate acquaintance. Indeed, such 'phenomenological' objects were in Russell's philosophy of 1913 and in Wittgenstein's philosophy in the

Tractatus the archetypical objects that *can* be pointed to. An emphasis on ostension therefore favours a phenomenological language, and does not discourage it.

Likewise, there is prima facie nothing in the concept of rule that implies that a language of acquaintance (a 'phenomenological language') cannot be subject to rules. Certainly every self-respecting phenomenologist has believed in a rule-governed phenomenological language.

In his early middle-period writings, Wittgenstein often argues that this or that concept has been illicitly extended from its normal uses in physicalistic contexts to a purely phenomenological application.[2] Even though such arguments concerning particular concepts undoubtedly tend to speak against the primacy of a phenomenological language, they do not amount to a genuine refutation of the possibility of a phenomenological language.

It is undoubtedly this lack of strong general arguments against phenomenological languages that explains Wittgenstein's comparative silence on the subject in his middle-period writings.

The situation was changed by the ascendancy of language-games and especially by their role as constituting the crucial language–world links. For even though ostensions and rules can perhaps be private, language-games cannot be. If what one has to witness (in principle and in the last analysis) in order to understand a word is not merely its ostensive definition or a rule for its use, but the entire language-game which is its 'logical home', then the language in which that word plays a role cannot be private. And if language-games are the heart of all semantics, it is in the most literal sense of the word nonsensical to think of any language as being purely phenomenological, that is, as dealing in the first place with what is immediately given to each of us.

In his 'Notes for Lectures on "Private Experience" and "Sense Data"' Wittgenstein makes the point vividly that it is the primacy of language-games that forces us from the private phenomenological realm to the public one:

> Die Auffassung der Solipsismus erstreckt sich nicht auf Spiele. Der Andere kann Schachspielen so gut wie ich. [The conception of solipsism does not extend to games. Another person can play chess as well as I.]
>
> I.e., when we play a language game we are on the same level.[3]

However, the mere introduction of the idea of language-game does not yet provide a basis for rejecting phenomenological languages. For the purpose, language-games must reign supreme. It is important to realize that Wittgenstein could use the language-game idea as a means of refuting the possibility of a phenomenological language only because he believed that language-games are conceptually prior to their rules. This primacy claim, we suggested, is what Wittgenstein argues for in his famous 'following the rule' discussion in *PI*, I, secs. 143–242. Thus this discussion is vital for Wittgenstein's defence of the most important single idea of his later philosophy. For if language-games were not prior conceptually to their rules, one could perfectly well define private languages by specifying their private rules. It is only when the entire language-game, with the variety of different modes of behaviour it involves, becomes the highest court of semantical appeal that the true basis of all semantics must be public. If Wittgenstein had a rock-bottom 'private language argument', that is, an argument against the possibility of private languages, it is his discussion of rule-following in *PI*, I, secs. 143–242.[4]

This can be seen in a number of different ways. In MS 116, pp. 205–7, Wittgenstein asserts virtually in so many words that it is the reliance of language on language-games, not the role of rules in language, that makes language public:[5]

> "There is surely [such a thing as] subjective rule [*Regelmäßigkeit*], a rule which exists only for *me*." That is: we frequently use the word "rule" thus: someone imagines to himself a rule; he sees something rule-governed; something strikes him as rule-governed; etc. But that does not mean that he has in mind an object which is unknown to all of us and which is called "rule". If, over and above the game which I see, he is also playing a game with himself which I know *nothing* about, I don't know either whether it is to be called a "game". If, over and above the public language, he also speaks a private language which I know nothing about, why do I call it a language?

There are of course games one can play alone, and games in which some of the moves are private. But they are parasitic on public games, and they cannot perform the semantical function which public language-games serve in Wittgenstein. He discusses such games in MS 116, pp. 256–60, and points out the dangers inherent in attempts to speak of *innere Spielhandlungen*. His inimitable way to make his point is to invite the reader to envisage 'a ball game in which the other player throws the ball to me and I throw it back to him in imagination'.

In fact, in *PI*, I, sec. 202 Wittgenstein infers in so many words the public character of rule-following from the subordination of rules to language-games ('practices'):

> and hence . . . 'obeying a rule' is a practice. And to *think* one is obeying a rule is not to obey a rule. Hence it is not possible to obey a rule 'privately' . . .

2 THE FUNCTION OF WITTGENSTEIN'S 'PRIVATE LANGUAGE ARGUMENT'

This leads to a somewhat surprising conclusion. Usually, it is Wittgenstein's discussion of private experiences in *PI*, I, secs. 243–315,[6] that is taken to be his attempted refutation of the possibility of a private language. What has been found shows that this common view is misleading. Wittgenstein's so-called 'private language argument' is not a self-contained refutation of a purely phenomenological language. This argument is based on Wittgenstein's earlier discussion of rule-following in *PI*, I, secs. 143–242.

Hence we have to be very careful in interpreting the argumentative structure of Wittgenstein's *Philosophical Investigations*. His explanations may appear to suggest that the so-called 'private language argument' is about the impossibility of a phenomenological language. In *PI*, I, sec. 243 he writes:

> A human being can encourage himself, give himself orders, obey, blame and punish himself; he can ask himself a question and answer it. We could even imagine human beings who spoke only in monologue; who accompanied their activities by talking to themselves. – An explorer who watched them and listened to their talk might succeed in translating their language into ours. (This would enable him to predict these people's actions correctly, for he also hears them making resolutions and decisions.)
>
> But could we also imagine a language in which a person could write down or give vocal expression to his inner experiences – his feelings, moods, and the rest – for his private use? – Well, can't we do so in our ordinary language? – But that is not what I mean. The individual words of this language are to refer to what can only be known to the person speaking; to his immediate private sensations. So another person cannot understand the language.

However, this formulation is somewhat misleading, as far as the presuppositions of Wittgenstein's argument are concerned. In fact, Wittgenstein continues (in *PI,* I, sec. 244) as follows:

> How do words *refer* to sensations? – There doesn't seem to be any problem here; don't we talk about sensations every day, and give them names? But how is the connexion between the name and the thing named set up? This question is the same as: how does a human being learn the meaning of the names of sensations? – of the word "pain" for example.

Here Wittgenstein makes it clear that he is raising questions which presuppose the framework he has set up earlier. Wittgenstein is not, and cannot be, asking questions like 'how is the connexion between the name and the thing named set up?' in a vacuum. He is asking them against the background of the views which he had carefully expounded earlier in the *Philosophical Investigations* and which we have discussed in chapters 8–9 above. He is assuming that what mediates that connection has to be a language-game. Indeed, he immediately goes on in *PI*, I, sec. 244 to sketch such a language-game. (We shall return to this particular language-game later in this chapter; see sec. 10 below.)

But if this role of language-games is already assumed by Wittgenstein in *PI*, I, secs. 243–315, he cannot be conducting there an argument against private language *ab ovo*. Notwithstanding the prima facie suggestions of sec. 243, he is not mounting his main attack on private phenomenological languages there. He is assuming that that campaign has already been won, and he is launching a mopping-up operation to show how the job of phenomenological languages can be done in the important special case of private experiences by languages based on public language-games. He is not in reality arguing against the possibility of private languages in general, but against their necessity in the particular area of the language people use of their inner sensations and feelings.

The presuppositions of Wittgenstein's 'private language argument' are revealed by the fact that, in the course of his examination of private experience, Wittgenstein repeatedly appeals in effect to specific conceptions he thinks he has established earlier. For instance, in *PI*, I, sec. 261, he says, " 'Has' and 'something' also belong to our common language." Why? Wittgenstein does not give any reasons in this passage. The real reason can only be his general rejection of phenomenological languages.

Further analysis is nevertheless needed here. For prima facie it might seem that Wittgenstein is in fact putting forward at least two different arguments (or kinds of arguments) in his private language discussion to disprove the feasibility of private phenomenological languages. On the one hand he is discussing the idea of private ostension and arguing that there cannot be any such thing, and more generally discussing the problem of naming one's sensations and describing them. On the other hand, Wittgenstein appears to be putting forward epistemological arguments based on the difficulty of remembering a particular sensation or even attending to the right sensation. Hence the burden is on us to prove that these two Wittgensteinian lines of thought in fact rely on his semantical views, including the primacy of language-games as semantical mediators between a language and whatever aspect of reality the language is used to speak of. Accordingly, the target of Wittgenstein's remarks on ostension and naming will be discussed in secs. 8–9 and his apparently epistemological arguments in sec. 11 below.

Furthermore, if a language-game is always necessary to establish and to maintain language–world links, the paramount question for Wittgenstein in his discussion of private experiences is: what are the language-games that connect our talk of private experiences to their subject matter and hence lend this talk talk its meaning? This question will be discussed in sec. 10.

3 PRIVATE EXPERIENCE AND THE RECEIVED INTERPRETATION OF WITTGENSTEIN

The mistake we have criticized – that is, the mistake of thinking that Wittgenstein attempts in his discussion of private experience a self-contained refutation of phenomenological languages – is not the only way his discussion of private experiences has been misunderstood. Indeed, the interpretation of this part of Wittgenstein's late philosophical *oeuvre* is particularly interesting in the present context, because the conflict between the received view of Wittgenstein's later thought and the one outlined in the preceding chapters comes to a head there. In the light of what was said earlier, it is not hard to see how the usual interpretation of Wittgenstein's views on allegedly private experiences is on the received view a consequence of this overall philosophy of language. On this interpretation, in order to grasp the meaning of our sentences we must attend to the roles which different utterances play in our lives. Hence, in the special case of a vocabulary which apparently refers to private experiences, we ought to forget (on this construal of Wittgenstein's purpose) those private experiences and focus exclusively on public utterances and public behaviour in different public contexts. In brief, on the received view private experiences disappear from the picture. To use Wittgenstein's own analogy (*PI*, I, sec. 293), private experiences are on this interpretation like a beetle in a box which each person can see only for herself or himself. "The thing in the box has no place in the language-game at all; not even as a *something* . . . No, one can 'divide through' by the thing in the box; it cancels out, whatever it is."

If we are right, the received view is not just wrong, but diametrically wrong, in so far as Wittgenstein's views of private experiences are concerned. One of the tasks of this chapter is to show how and why.[7]

In doing so, one of the most important clues to the correct understanding of Wittgenstein's discussion of private (internal) experiences is what we have found about his change of position in October 1929. As we have seen, in replacing a phenomenological basis language by a physicalistic one Wittgenstein did not want to alter the ontological status of phenomenological objects, including private experiences. The world we live in remained for him a world of phenomenological objects; but we must talk about them in the language we use to talk about physical objects.[8] The real purpose of Wittgenstein's 'private language argument' is to show how people manage this neat trick.

Another way of formulating the same point is this: What faces Wittgenstein here is a problem which inevitably confronts anyone who has rejected phenomenological languages in favour of physicalistic ones. How is the job which the former ones seem to do accomplished by the latter? In order to defend his language of acquaintance, Russell had to attempt a 'reduction to acquaintance', that is to say, he had to try to show that the job of language of physics can be done by a language of immediate experience. Conversely, in order to defend the primacy of an everyday physicalistic language, Wittgenstein had to show how we can speak of 'what is given' to us, that is to say, of our immediate experiences, in a physicalistic or at least behaviouristic language. He had to carry out, not a 'reduction to acquaintance', but a reduction away from acquaintance and to an everyday language of everyday public objects and public events.

4 THE PRIVACY PROBLEM AS A PROBLEM OF INTERPERSONAL COMPARISON

In earlier chapters of this work, especially in chapter 9, an interpretation of Wittgenstein's later philosophy of language has been outlined which differs radically from the received one. On our view, far from trying to get rid of vertical links between language and reality, the later Wittgenstein emphasized them. On our interpretation, the first and foremost function of Wittgenstein's languge-games is to serve as such links.

Thus there really are private experiences, and there really are expressions naming them and referring to them. These observations suggest a way of reading Wittgenstein's remarks on sensations and other private experiences more instructively than on the received interpretation, so as to bring out the logical (conceptual or 'grammatical') foundation of Wittgenstein's 'private language argument'. If

Wittgenstein had been willing to use discardable conceptual ladders as he did in the *Tractatus,* he could have tried to speak realistically of private experiences and of their properties as actually existing entities to which each of us has privileged access. In the terminology of Wittgenstein's own analogy, there *is* an actual beetle in each person's box visible only to that person. From this perspective, the entire problem is to *compare* different speakers' beetles with each other so as to establish interpersonal ways of speaking of them. Since by assumption one's own beetle can be witnessed only by its owner, comparisons are feasible only by reference to some publicly available framework. What this framework is in different cases requires a separate examination. The crucial point is that the necessity of resorting to some such public framework does not in the least obviate the reality of private experiences or our ability to speak of them, to refer to them, to describe them, and to name them. For instance, an ostensive definition of a word that is supposed to apply to one's beetle is a futile gesture, not because there is nothing there to be pointed to, because one cannot refer to it, or because what is pointed to is somehow elusive, but because such ostension is by definition private, and so cannot help to compare your beetle with mine in any way.

Wittgenstein acknowledges repeatedly that the problem of private experience can be thought of as a problem of comparison and re-identification. In *Remarks on Colour* he writes (III, secs. 314–15):

What actually is the '*world*' of consciousness? . . .
The question is clearly: How do we compare physical objects – how do we compare experiences?

Wittgenstein makes the same point by reference to a special case in ibid., sec. 78:

The indefiniteness of the concept of colour lies, above all, in the indefiniteness of the concept of the sameness of colours, i.e. of the method of comparing colours.

The comparisons which Wittgenstein has in mind are in the first place interpersonal. However, he points out time and again that comparisons between my own experiences at different times are also problematic. The reason is not that my memory can deceive me, but that it has not been defined what it is that we are supposed to remember. The following is an example of Wittgenstein's formulations of this aspect of his problem:

"Imagine a person whose memory could not retain *what* the word 'pain' meant – so that he constantly called different things by that name – but nevertheless used the word in a way fitting in with the usual symptoms and presuppositions of pain" – in short he uses it as we all do. Here I should like to say: a wheel that can be turned though nothing else moves with it, is not part of the mechanism. (*PI*, I, sec. 271)

If this crucial role of comparisons is Wittgenstein's meaning (or a part thereof), why does he not say so? One reason is that, according to his lights, an account of the kind we sketched above is unsayable. In order to put Wittgenstein's point in the way just done, one must first speak of individual private experiences (individual beetles in their respective boxes) in their unsullied state, untouched by any reference to a public framework. One must then think of the problem merely as one of co-ordinating different persons' references to their respective beetles. But of course these two steps are exactly what the end product of Wittgenstein's line of thought (on the right interpretation of it) declares to be absolutely impossible. One cannot, according to his doctrine, refer to sensations except within an already established public framework. Such a framework, Wittgenstein reminds us, we certainly do have for our ordinary sensation language.[9] However, such a framework, he asks us to suppose, is initially absent in the beetle case.

5 PRIVATE EXPERIENCES DO NOT CANCEL OUT

What can one say in the light of these observations of Wittgenstein's discussion of private experience in *PI*, I, secs. 243–315? It follows from what has been said that much of the literature on this allegedly Wittgensteinian 'private language argument' is beside Wittgenstein's point. Wittgenstein does not deny the reality of sensations or their role in the semantics of our talk about sensations. There are several passages in the *Philosophical Investigations* which show that sensation words can, and do, refer to sensations.[10] Wittgenstein holds that we can form images (*Vorstellungen*) of sensations (*PI*, I, sec. 300), give names to sensations (*PI*, I, secs. 257, 270), and give vocal expression to our inner experiences (*PI*, I, sec. 243).[11] The beetle in the box does not disappear, except when we try to speak of it independently of a public framework. The 'beetle' passage mentioned above in section 3 in explaining the received view was, as the reader may have noticed, quoted there out of context. Wittgenstein is there speaking conditionally. In fact the passage continues:

That is to say: if we construe the grammar of the expression of sensation
on the model of 'object and name' [*Bezeichnung*] the object drops out
of consideration as irrelevant. [Emphasis added]

Indeed, sec. 293 is worth quoting more extensively:[12]

> Now someone tells me that *he* knows what pain is only from his case! –
> Suppose everyone had a box with something in it: we call it a "beetle".
> No one can look into anyone else's box, and everyone says he knows
> what a beetle is only by looking at *his* beetle. – Here it would be quite
> possible for everyone to have something different in his box. One might
> even imagine such a thing constantly changing. – But suppose the word
> "beetle" had a use in these people's language? – If so it would not be
> used as the name [*Bezeichnung*] of a thing. The thing in the box has no
> place in the language-game at all; not even as a *something*: for the box
> might even be empty. – No, one can 'divide through' by the thing in the
> box; it cancels out, whatever it is.
> That is to say: if we construe the grammar of the expression of sensation
> on the model of 'object and name' [*Bezeichnung*] the object drops out
> of consideration as irrelevant.

There will be occasions for us to return to this passage later. One can
see from it at once that the private objet (the beetle, the sensation)
drops out of semantical consideration according to Wittgenstein *only
when the semantics of sensation-talk is construed on an incorrect
model.* We shall later spell out what this incorrect model is. At the
present time, it suffices to emphasize that when the wrong semantical
paradigm is applied to our sensation-terminology, it results in relegating the putative representative relationships between sensation-
language and sensations entirely to the realm of the private and thus
in rendering these relationships otiose. It is the privacy of these
semantical relations, not the privacy of what is represented by their
means, that Wittgenstein is critizing. (*Sensations* are private; *sensation-
language* cannot be.) This incorrect model is the basic source of the
problems which manifest themselves as an apparently private language.

In the famous 'private language argument' (*PI,* I, secs. 243–315),
Wittgenstein was thus not essentially modifying the Cartesian account
of our inner life (at least not in the case of pains, other sensations, or
other particular private experiences), insofar as this account does not
involve any assumptions as to how our language works.[13] He was in
this part of his work criticizing Cartesian semantics, not Cartesian
metaphysics. For instance, he was not denying that mental terms can
express occurrences rather than dispositions. All he was doing was to
examine the language in which we can speak of internal (private)
entities and events and to show how such a language must operate. As

Jaakko Hintikka emphasized as early as in 1976,[14] Wittgenstein's ideas about private experiences are little more than a corollary to his more general views concerning language-games, rules, and rule following.

Wittgenstein himself in so many words countenances internal (private) facts in MS 173, pp. 72–3:[15]

> There are internal and external concepts, internal and external ways of looking at people. There are even internal and external facts – as there are e.g. physical and mathematical facts. But they do not stand next to each other like different kinds of plants. For what I said sounds as if one had said: all these different facts occur in nature. And what's wrong about that?

Wittgenstein answers his own question as follows:

> The internal is not only connected with the external by experience, but also logically.

Wittgenstein's point in *PI*, I, sec. 293 and in similar passages is made clear by an earlier formulation of his. It occurs in MS 116, pp. 206–7. It is an immediate continuation of the quote in section 1 of this chapter:

> That is: We use the *picture* of a 'Private Object' which only he and nobody else can see. It is a picture – make sure you are clear about that! And now it is essential to this picture that we make further assumptions about this object and about what he does with it; it is not enough for us to say: he has something private and does something with it.[16]

Wittgenstein's point is plainly, not that a private object cancels out from our language, but that its 'picture' must have other roles in our language-games than just to stand for a private object.[17]

All this serves to confirm resoundingly the veracity of our initial clue. For the Wittgenstein of the *Philosophical Investigations* no less than for the Wittgenstein lecturing in Cambridge in 1930–2, the world we live in is the world of sense-data. His problem is to show how I can speak of them in the only language I understand, which is the language of physical objects.

6 THE RELEVANCE OF PRIVATE EXPERIENCES FOR PUBLIC LANGUAGES

A telling corollary to these observations is the importance of the actual private experiences for those public languages by means of which we can speak of them, according to Wittgenstein or at least according to his unspoken assumptions. The problem he is considering in the notorious 'private language argument' is not, so to speak, how one's private experiences are to be handled in an already existing language of the physicalistic sort, but how a new public language could be invented to express them. Less metaphorically put, differences between different public language-games are frequently due, not to differences in the way in which the different communities of speakers organize their speech-acts in relation to each other and to the social context in which they are performed. These differences may be due to differences in the ways the members of disparate language groups perceive their environment. There is therefore a sense in which philosophers' recent emphasis on language users' 'way of life' as the ultimate arbitrator of semantical issues in Wittgenstein is misleading. If a lion could speak, we could not understand him, Wittgenstein avers. Why? Not only, and perhaps not even mainly, because the social life of a lion pride is organized differently from a human society. The reason may very well be that the sense-data which constitute the world of a lion are different from the sense-data of human beings. Playfully expressed, Wittgenstein perhaps ought to have used as an example, not lions, but organisms like flies whose perceptual apparatus is more blatantly different from the human one.

Our attribution of this view to Wittgenstein is not an instance of speculative overinterpretation. Wittgenstein makes a closely similar point himself in emphasizing the conceptual connection between colour-blindness and the languge-games a colour-blind person can or cannot play.[18] Ironically, the real import of such Wittgensteinian remarks is precisely opposite to what it is often taken to be. Wittgenstein is not denying the semantical relevance of colour-blindness, i.e., denying that our language serves to reflect actual differences in the sense-data of a colour-blind and of a normal person. He is emphasizing the way this difference must be manifested in order to be expressible in an interpersonal language. Wittgenstein is sometimes taken to suggest in his remarks on colour-blindness and other similar matters that differences in people's colour experiences must 'cancel out' from the public language. On the contrary, what Wittgenstein is pointing out is that the public language must adjust itself to the nature of those very experiences and of interpersonal differences in them.

7 THE POSSIBILITY OF PRIVATE LANGUAGES
FOR WITTGENSTEIN

Another way of seeing the logico-semantical character of Wittgenstein's argument is by noting the precise force of Wittgenstein's words. 'Public' means for him 'publicly accessible', not necessarily 'publicly used'. 'Private languages' in the sense of languages *used* by only one person were not denied by Wittgenstein, but were countenanced by him in so many words in the *Philosophical Investigations*, I, sec. 243, quoted above in sec. 2. Language may be an essentially social phenomenon, but Wittgenstein's comments on privacy neither are predicated on this thesis nor do they yield it as a conclusion. As sec. 243 shows, the whole (apparent) problem with our discourse about private experiences is, not that it is a privately used language, but that it does not seem to be a publicly accessible language. This is why the unproblematic 'private' language of sec. 243 can serve in Wittgenstein, by way of contrast, as an introduction to the real problems he is discussing. The point Wittgenstein emphasizes about the unproblematical 'private' languages of sec. 243 is that the criteria of their use are public, e.g., accessible to a resident explorer. The real problem does not lie in the direction of the language of a Robinson Crusoe, but in that of the language of an autistic child. Indeed, Wittgenstein is on the record as saying:

> We can indeed imagine a Robinson [Crusoe] using a language for himself, but then he must *behave* in a certain way or we shouldn't say that he plays language games with himself. (MS 148, p. 24)

This need of an appropriate sort of behaviour on the part of the speakers of a language we are trying to understand is of course but another formulation for the need of a language-game which could lend Crusoe's words their meaning. Whether or not such a language-game is played for the gallery is immaterial for the conceptual situation.

8 WITTGENSTEIN'S TARGET:
THE *BEZEICHNUNG* MODEL

Perhaps the most telling way of seeing how Wittgenstein's argument in *PI*, I, secs. 243–315, is based on his idea of the primacy of language-games is to examine his view on how the basic semantical relations are

254   *On private experience*

not established and are *not* maintained. That is, it is instructive to spell out what the wrong model of relationships between sensation-language and sensations is that is Wittgenstein's primary target in what has been called his 'private language argument'.

The wrong model is fairly obviously the model of 'object and *Bezeichnung*', that is, the model of reference unmediated by any languge-game or, as one might say, the model of object and designation. It is a model on which a name refers to its object directly, without the mediation of a public framework. It is of this model that Wittgenstein says in sec. 293 that *if* the grammar of the expression of sensation is construed as it prescribes, sensations would drop out of consideration as irrelevant. Of course, this 'dropping out' of sensations is intended by Wittgenstein as a *reductio ad absurdum* of the doctrine he is criticizing, not as a part of his own view.

To understand more precisely what model Wittgenstein is rejecting in *PI*, I, sec. 293, one may consider *PI*, I, sec. 15, where he explains that the cognate verb *bezeichnen*

> is perhaps used in the most straightforward way when the object signified is marked with the sign . . . It is in this and more or less similar ways that a name signifies [*bezeichnet*] . . . a thing.

In *PI*, I, sec. 256, Wittgenstein implies that the relation of a name to a sensation is private only if this relation is construed on the *Bezeichnung*-model, i.e., so as not to rely on the natural expressions of a sensation:

> *How* can I refer to [*bezeichnen*] sensations by means of words? – As we ordinary do? But aren't my words for sensations therefore connected with the natural expressions of sensations? – In that case my language is not 'private'. Someone else might understand it as well as I.[19]

It is becoming obvious here that Wittgenstein's rejection of the *Bezeichnung*-model was a consequence of the development of his views 'from ostension to language-games' that was discussed in chapter 8 above. If the basic semantical relations between a name and an object were of such a nature that they could in principle be established ostensively, the *Bezeichnung*-model could in fact serve as a paradigm for semantics in general and for the semantics for our sensation-talk in particular. Hence to say that the *Bezeichnung*-model was what Wittgenstein was opposing in the so-called 'private language' discussion is to say that this discussion is Wittgenstein's rejection of ostensions and rules as the primary mediation of meaning.

Thus we have further evidence for what was said above in sections 2 and 4 about the aims and presuppositions of Wittgenstein's discussion of private experience. For Wittgenstein is not really presenting any major new arguments against the *Bezeichnung*-model in the 'private experience' section of the *Philosophical Investigations* (I, secs. 243–315).[20] Rather, he is assuming the inadequacy of the *Bezeichnung*-model and the consequent need of a language-game to do the job ostensively introduced name-labels cannot do. Moreover, since the *Bezeichnung*-model is the gist in the idea of 'private language' which Wittgenstein is opposing, we can see once again that his ultimate reasons for rejecting private phenomenological languages are not expounded in *PI*, I, secs. 243–315, but in his discussions of ostension, language-games, and rule-following.[21]

9 WITTGENSTEIN'S TERMINOLOGY AND DOCTRINE

If there is any terminological generalization to be gathered from Wittgenstein's pliant usage, it seems to be the following: When Wittgenstein is speaking of *bezeichnen* or *Bezeichnung*, he does not stray very far from the etymological connection with the idea of a *Zeichen* (a mark or a sign) standing for some one entity. (Cf. *Tractatus* 3.322.) The paradigm case is putting a label or a chalk-mark on an object as its designation.[22] Even though such words as *bezeichnen* are not technical terms for Wittgenstein, the use of this verb typically suggests that the sign–object relationship he is considering is supposed to be an unmediated, direct two-term relation.[23] This observation helps us to appreciate certain interesting uses of the *bezeichnen* terminology in the *Investigations*, including Wittgenstein's use of it to pinpoint one way in which sensation-language *cannot* be connected with sensations. For a simple relationship of the *Bezeichnung* variety is vacuous unless the object exists and is publicly accessible. As Wittgenstein puts it, a *Bezeichnung* merely serves 'to avoid continual pointing'.

In contrast, when Wittgenstein wants to speak of the relation of a word to what it represents in neutral terms, which among other possibilities allow the representation to be mediated by a language-game, he typically speaks of names (*Namen*) and naming (*benennen*).[24]

For evidence concerning Wittgenstein's usage, one may turn to his *Remarks on the Philosophy of Psychology*, vol. 1, sec. 589:[25]

> Example of the names that have meaning only when accompanied by their bearers, i.e. that is the only way they are used. So they serve merely to avoid continual pointing. The example that always comes to

my mind is the designation [*Bezeichnung*] of lines, points, angles by
A,B,C . . . a,b . . . etc. in geometrical figures.

With these observations in mind, let us look again at the beetle
passage of *PI,* I, sec. 293. As Wittgenstein constructs the example, it
would be quite possible for everyone to have something different in
his or her box. We are asked then to suppose that the word 'beetle'
has a use in these people's language. If so, Wittgenstein says, the word
'beetle' would not be used as the *Bezeichnung* of a thing. Now we can
see what his point is. In order for the word 'beetle' to have a use in our
imaginary informants' language, it needs a public language-game to
back it up semantically. But it is precisely the absence of such a
language-game that Wittgenstein highlights by the term *Bezeichnung.*
It is thus highly significant that in sec. 293 Wittgenstein is speaking not
of names (*Namen*) of sensations, but of their *Bezeichnungen* – a fact
that is completely lost in the Anscombe translation.

Thus Wittgenstein's thesis in the beetle-passage is that a public
language-game is needed to constitute the meaning of our sensation-
talk. Wittgenstein is not in *PI,* I, sec. 293, arguing for such a need in
general terms. He is pointing out that an interpersonal framework is
especially urgently needed in the case of people's talk about their
private experiences. Wittgenstein is turning around his earlier priorities. In the *Tractatus,* it was the relations of a word to the object of an
immediate experience that were the self-explanatory rock bottom all
semantics. Now Wittgenstein is turning the tables and pointing out
that it is precisely in connection with such phenomenological terminology that the need of semantical mediation is keenest. But even
though the reasons why an interpersonal language-game is necessary
are illustrated here, no overarching argument of their indispensability
is given. The real shortcomings of the *Bezeichnung*-model are argued
for in *PI,* I, secs. 143–242, not in secs. 243–315.

10 PHYSIOGNOMIC LANGUAGE-GAMES

After Wittgenstein's problem has thus been clarified, using *PI,* I, sec.
293, as the paradigm example, it is time to analyse his solution,
especially his positive doctrine about private experiences, by reference to other Wittgensteinian passages. What we have found shows
what the thrust of Wittgenstein's discussion is. He admittedly offers a
number of explanations and reminders calculated to show that the
Bezeichnung-model cannot do justice to the language we use of our
private experiences (see, e.g., secs. 258, 264–5, 293, etc.) or that we

need a public framework for speaking about them, independently of which our sensation-vocabulary has no function (see, e.g., secs. 253–4, 270–1, 281, 283, etc.). However, these arguments are supplements to what he thinks he has already established. The most important novel element in what Wittgenstein is doing in *PI*, I, secs. 243–315 does not lie in these criticisms, but in his constructive account of what the language-games are like which can lend our talk of pains and other sensations its meaning. This account is given mainly in sec. 244, that is to say, in the very beginning of the so-called 'private language argument' and well before any criticisms of phenomenological languages Wittgenstein offers in the course of this argument.

In other words, what is important in Wittgenstein's 'argument' is his account of the nature of the particular public framework we in fact rely on in speaking of our private experiences. Wittgenstein proffers strong indications to the effect that there are several different possibilities here. (Cf. his words 'here is one possibility' in *PI*, I, sec. 244.) Perhaps because of this emphasis on the variety of ways (the variety of language-games) which link our language to reality, Wittgenstein does not discuss systematically what kinds of public frameworks there are that connect our psychological jargon with its subject matter. However, his several remarks add up to a remarkably coherent overall doctrine.

As was indicated, Wittgenstein's first and foremost example of 'how words *refer* to [more accurately: "are related to", in German *beziehen sich auf*] sensations' is found in sec. 244 of the *Philosophical Investigations*:

> How do words *refer* to sensations? – There doesn't seem to be any problem here; don't we talk about sensations every day, and give them names [*benennen*]? But how is the connexion between . . . [such a] name [*Name*] and the thing named [*Benannten*] set up? This question is the same as: how does a human being learn the meaning of the names [*Namen*] of sensations? Here is one possibility: words are connected with the primitive, the natural expressions of the sensation and used in their place. A child has hurt himself and he cries; and then the adults talk to him and teach him exclamations and, later, sentences. They teach the child new pain-behaviour.

This is an apt example of *one* kind of public framework which (to use the realistic talk Wittgenstein shuns) enables different persons to compare their respective sensations. On this model, a sensation is an instance of pain, if it is of the kind that typically goes together with what is normally taken to be, and is responded to, as pain-behaviour. Wittgenstein's main point is that this 'going together' is conceptual ('grammatical') rather than factual. Such a framework of spontaneous expressive behaviour (including facial expressions, gestures, and other bodily movements), will be called a *physiognomic* framework and a psychological language (or language fragment) based on it will be called a physiognomic language.

It is to be noted that for Wittgenstein such physiognomic language-games do not depend only on the spontaneous expressions of sensations (e.g., pain). They can, and do, involve also other persons' reactions to someone's expressions, as is shown by *PI*, I, secs. 286–7 and 310. (This illustrates also the sense in which an entire language-game is involved in what Wittgenstein calls pain-behaviour.)

Several further observations can be made on the basis of sec. 244 and related Wittgensteinian passages. First of all, Wittgenstein is not denying the reality of private experiences or even their role in the relevant language-game. What he is saying is that they enter into this language-game via their natural physiognomic correlates. As a consequence, the relation of these correlates to private experiences themselves is not a contingent or epistemic one; it is a logical (semantical) connection, constitutive of the language-game in question. As Wittgenstein puts it in *Zettel*, sec. 543: 'My relation to appearances is here part of my concept.' Another way in which Wittgenstein expresses his point is in the form of a reply to an imaginary objection in sec. 281 which could have been levelled precisely at what Wittgenstein says in sec. 244:

> But doesn't what you say come to this: there is no pain, for example without *pain-behaviour*? – It comes to this: only of a living human being and what resembles (behaves like) a living human being can one say: it has sensations; it sees; is blind; hears; is deaf; is conscious or unconscious.

We shall return to this passage later, especially in section 12 below.

Here we have finally found a respect in which Wittgenstein is in fact revising philosophers' customary ideas. We found that he is not denying that there are private experiences or that they play a role in our language-games. However, Wittgenstein is looking at their relation to their behavioural and other observable counterparts in a new way. What is crucial, according to him, is that the relation of private experiences to their public manifestations is not a contingent one. These 'external manifestations' are needed in the language-games which give our talk of our private experiences its meaning. They are therefore logically (semantically) connected with the experiences themselves; they enter essentially into the relevant language-games.[26] It is in this sense that Wittgenstein is denying the possibility of private languages.

11 THE PRIVATE LANGUAGE PROBLEM IS SEMANTICAL, NOT EPISTEMOLOGICAL

We can now put into perspective Wittgenstein's repeated thought-experiments about naming or re-identifying private experiences privately. These are often taken to lead to, and to illustrate, insuperable epistemological problems about private languages and private objects, and perhaps even to constitute an integral part of Wittgenstein's criticism of private languages. Admittedly, Wittgenstein does speak repeatedly of the apparently epistemological problems into which we would run if we tried to base our language of inner experiences on private definitions and private criteria. For instance, in the paradigmatic beetle example (sec. 293) he writes: 'Then it could very well be each person has a different thing in his box. One could even imagine that such a thing is constantly changing.' This corresponds to different persons' private experiences being different from each other and to their constantly changing, without outsiders' being able to find it out. In sec. 271 Wittgenstein invites us to '"imagine a person whose memory could not retain what the word 'pain' meant – so that he constantly called different things by that name – but nevertheless used the word in a way fitting in which the usual symptoms and presuppositions of pain" – in short uses it as we all do.' Furthermore, the epistemological problem of justifying one's memory-knowledge is apparently discussed by Wittgenstein in sec. 265.

Appearances notwithstanding, Wittgenstein's concerns are nevertheless semantical, not epistemological. For instance, the possibility that the 'private object' might be changing is intended by Wittgenstein as a semantical thought-experiment, not an actual epistemological difficulty. He confesses this in *PI*, II, xi, p. 207:

> Always get rid of the idea of the private object in this way: assume that it constantly changes, but that you do not notice the change because your memory constantly deceives you.

In other words, Wittgenstein's point is not that I cannot remember what my private experience was like, but that such an act of remembering cannot be a move in a language-game that would link my private experience to its name. The apparent epistemological problems he raises are thus merely an expositional device to dramatize semantical facts of life.

This will in effect be shown in the next section about Wittgenstein's line of thought in *PI*, I, sec. 270. Similar arguments may be levelled at other Wittgensteinian scenarios. For instance consider *PI*, I, sec. 265, where Wittgenstein criticizes the idea that the correctness of memory could be tested by looking up 'a table (something like a dictionary) which exists only in our imagination'. Wittgenstein's criticism is not that such a procedure is too fallible to serve its purpose. For on a number of occassions he makes it quite clear that identifications of colours on the basis of memory (remembered colour images) is as a matter of fact no less reliable (albeit no more reliable, either) method than identification by means of actual colour samples. Indeed, the point sec. 265 unmistakably makes is not that looking up a table in imagination is a more fallible test than a physical test of correctness, but that it is not an independent public test. If Wittgenstein's problem is formulated in terms of skeptical doubts concerning mental identification, then what the introduction of the public criterion envisaged by Wittgenstein there brings about is not that a skeptic's doubts are removed, but that they turn out to have been senseless.

Thus Wittgenstein's thought-experiments as to what would happen if our sensations were subject to systematic mistakes, for instance in analogy to the possibility that the beetles in different people's boxes might be changing all the time, are not calculatd to highlight any elusiveness of our sensations or any difficulty in perceiving or describing them. These Wittgensteinian scenarios instantiate the shortcomings of any alleged semantics that does not rely on a public frame of reference even when one is speaking of one's own private world. The reason why Wittgenstein's semantical experiments have so frequently been misunderstood is that in them he is illustrating the need of an important assumption rather than trying to prove its unavoidability. This is the assumption that a language-game is needed in each and every case to mediate the language–world links. This assumption is not justified by Wittgenstein's apparently epistemological thought-experiments. It is justified by Wittgenstein, if anywhere, in his analyses of language understanding, language learning, and rule-following.

Thus the variability of one's sensations is a semantical thought-experiment concocted by Wittgenstein to confound his opponents, not a doctrine or even a problem of his own. Wittgenstein's main concern in his discussion of private experiences is the need of a public language-game in speaking of them, not their inaccessibility or inexpressibility. To assimilate Wittgenstein's arguments to skeptical ones is radically to misunderstand their nature.

There is excellent evidence right in Wittgenstein's own writings to show that his apparent epistemological criticisms of private experiences were little more than an expository device. In the next chapter it will be shown that such epistemic concepts as knowledge, error, truth, belief, certainty, verification, etc., do not apply in what we shall call his primary language-games. Physiognomic games connected with sensations are typical examples of primary language-games. It follows that Wittgenstein is not intending his own words to be taken literally when he apparently voices doubts about the certainty of our knowledge of our own private experiences in introducing such primary games (cf., e.g., *PI*, I, sec. 265). Such doubts would be senseless according to his own lights. In reality, these apparent doubts are merely illustrations of the need of a public framework and of the impossibility of construing sensation-talk on the wrong model of a private object and its *Bezeichnung*. Once again, the true premises of Wittgenstein's private experience arguments can be traced back to his semantical views.

12 WITTGENSTEIN'S DEEPER REASONS

We have not yet exhausted the import of Wittgenstein's 'private language argument'. It remains to examine what is in some ways his most ambitious and most original point concerning the privacy problem. Wittgenstein's arguments can be construed so as to deal with the interpersonal comparison of languages, as we initially did. This way of looking at them is not the whole story, however, and in certain respects it focuses one's attention in a wrong direction.

In order to see what the right direction is, we can raise once again the question: Why was a discussion of private experiences needed in the first place? In rejecting a phenomenological basis language in 1929 Wittgenstein had in effect rejected the possibility of speaking of our private experiences except by means of a public language-game relying on a public framework for interpersonal comparisons. What need could possibly remain after that rejection for a separate 'private language argument'?

The answer is that Wittgenstein's original grounds for rejecting phenomenological languages in 1929 did not prove to be binding. His premises were, as we saw in chapter 7 above, essentially two: the need of language–world comparisons and the public character of language. We have discussed at length the vagaries of language–world comparisons and the ways in which Wittgenstein overcame them by means of his idea of language-game. It remains to have a closer look at his other premise, i.e., at his assumption that language itself is inevitably public.

It was noted above in chapter 1, sec. 9, and again in chapter 7, sec. 6, that this assumption was encouraged by Wittgenstein's idea of language as the universal medium. As was also noted, his premise was nevertheless not implied by the 'universality of language' idea. In order to see this, we can recall one of the most memorable remarks Wittgenstein ever made, quoted twice above:

> But if one says "How am I supposed to know what he means, all I can see are merely his symbols" then I say: "How is *he* supposed to know what he means, all that he has are merely his symbols."[27]

In spite of the persuasiveness of Wittgenstein's words, they beg the real question here. For imagine that Wittgenstein's notional interlocutor had retorted: 'No, he does have something more than his symbols. He has his private experiences. They can serve as references of his symbols.' In order to parry this riposte, Wittgenstein would have had to rule out private languages. But their possibility is precisely the moot point.

This observation shows that Wittgenstein's assumption of the public (physicalistic) character of language in 1929 rested on inadequate grounds, even granting to him the idea of language as the universal medium. This reinforces what was said above in sec. 1 about the weakness of the original reasons for which Wittgenstein rejected phenomenological languages and about his subsequent thought as being to a considerable extent a quest for firmer grounds for his new position.

In fact, this objection to Wittgenstein's early reasons for rejecting phenomenological languages can also be levelled at our construal earlier in this chapter of Wittgenstein's private language discussion as turning on the problem of interpersonal comparisons. On such a construal, Wittgenstein's argument would still leave untouched a philosopher who maintained that he could develop and use a full-fledged language for the purpose of speaking of his beetle, and of his beetle alone. We might be able to convict him of solipsism, if he refused to relate his language to ours, but not yet of bad philosophy of language. Did Wittgenstein himself not confess in the *Tractatus* to an unspeakable version of solipsism? Is not the possibility of such solipsistic language the real issue here? Thus Wittgenstein's reasons for not formulating his problem as one of interpersonal comparison include more than the initial inaccessibility of the languages to be compared. He believes that such private languages are impossible in a strict sense of the word. Thus we have to go beyond what was said earlier in this chapter, now that we have discovered a deeper layer of Wittgenstein's concern with the possibility of private languages.

It is in fact unmistakable that this problem of solipsistic languages was one of the issues, perhaps even the most crucial issue, in *PI*, I, secs. 243–315. If an example is needed, *PI*, I, sec. 257 will do. There Wittgenstein pushes his quest beyond questions of interpersonal cummunicability of sensation-words to the nature of 'grammar' in general.

> "What would it be like if human beings shewed no outward signs of pain (did not groan, grimace, etc.)? Then it would be impossible to teach a child the use of the word 'tooth-ache'." – Well, let's assume the child is a genius and itself invents a name for the sensation! – But then, of course, he couldn't make himself understood when he uses the word. – So does he understand the name, without being able to explain its meaning to anyone? – But what does it mean to say that he has 'named his pain'. – How has he done this naming of pain?! And whatever he did, what was its purpose? – When one says "He gave a name to his sensation" one forgets that a great deal of stage setting in the language is presupposed if the mere act of naming is to make sense. And when we speak of someone's having given a name to pain, what is presupposed is the existence of the grammar of the word "pain"; it shews the post where the new word is stationed.

But what is this 'grammar'? One way of seeing what it is is to consider the next section (*PI*, I, sec. 258), where Wittgenstein describes one's attempts to name a certain recurrent sensation and argues that private definitions cannot serve the purpose. Wittgenstein continues this thought-experiment in sec. 270:

> Let us now imagine a use for the entry of the sign "E" in my diary. I discover that whenever I have a particular sensation a manometer shews that my blood-pressure rises. So I shall be able to say that my blood-pressure is rising without using any apparatus. This is a useful result. And now it seems quite indifferent whether I have recognized the sensation *right* or not. Let us suppose I regularly identify it wrong, it does not matter in the least. And that alone shews that the hypothesis that I make a mistake is mere show. (We as it were turned a knob which looked as if it could be used to turn on some part of the machine; but it was a mere ornament, not connected with the mechanism at all.)

What Wittgenstein is saying here is not that the sensation drops out of consideration as irrelevant, but that it can be spoken of only by means of some public correlate. Since the correlation is logical, not contingent, the sensation-term does not make any sense independently of this correlation. This is what Wittgenstein means by saying that it does not matter whether the sensation is identified correctly after the correlation has been established. The clincher is Wittgenstein's statement that it is mere illusion (*Schein*) that one can speak of mistakes here. This shows that his point is completely independent of all epistemic difficulties in identifying a sensation. Before the correlation has been established, there is nothing to know or to make a mistake about. After it has been established, the connection between the public correlate and the sensation is not subject to epistemic mistakes, because it is a conceptual connection.

Here we can see what the 'grammar of the word "pain"' is for Wittgenstein. It is constituted by a language-game which essentially includes, over and above having certain sensations, also their normal spontaneous expressions.

What happens in the *Philosophical Investigations* is that Wittgenstein's criticism of the *Bezeichnung* model cuts deeper than any analysis of interpersonal comparability could. For the problems of reference, of name–object relations, and more generally of language–world links apply to a solipsistic language just as much as to an overtly public one. If even a putatively solipsistic language must be connected with the world through language-games, and if these games, qua games, must be public (see section 1 above), then a private language is impossible in a strong sense.

This, we suggest, is the most important step in Wittgenstein's line of thought concerning private experience. It is also the step for which he needs the conceptual priority of language-games over their rules. It is the premise of his refutation of phenomenological languages which he could not justify in 1929.[28] By relying on the primacy of language-games and their inevitably public character, Wittgenstein was finally able in 1944 to justify the step he took in October 1929 and to reject private (phenomenological) languages lock, stock, and barrel.

Now we can see why Wittgenstein had to push his argument beyond the problem of interpersonal comparison of initially idiosyncratic languages. This problem is unmistakably part of Wittgenstein's agenda in his discussion of private languages. But it does not exhaust the relevant problems. In particular, Wittgenstein's analysis of the comparison problem could not provide an answer to his most urgent question, which was to show the impossibility of phenomenological languages.

This two-layered structure of Wittgenstein's privacy discussion has helped to hide the dependence of his argument on his antecedent analysis of rule-following. For the conditions of interpersonal com-municability do not all depend on the primacy of language-games over their rules, argued for by Wittgenstein in *PI*, I, secs. 143–242. In contrast the impossibility of solipsistic languages does depend on the results of that earlier rule-following discussion. It is this conceptual formulation of Wittgenstein's privacy that lends it its true depth and interest. If Wittgenstein's privacy problem were construed as a question of interpersonal comparison, it would seem that he is arguing merely from the possibility of interpersonal communicability to the public nature of all language. If so, his argument would still be interesting, but it would not be nearly as radical and as sweeping as it is in reality. If we are right, in the last analysis Wittgenstein does not want to use the interpersonal communicability of language as his premise in his refutation of phenomenological (solipsistic) languages even though he sometimes clearly does rely on it for other purposes.

13 THE PRIVACY OF INNER EXPERIENCE

The most surprising, and the most controversial, thesis of this chapter is likely to be Wittgenstein's metaphysical Cartesianism, that is to say, the claim that for Wittgenstein there really were private event-like experiences, including pains and other such sensations. This thesis is so important that it deserves a few additional comments.

What is likely to be agreed on is that according to Wittgenstein the language we use of sensations has to rely on a public language-game. What is controversial is what follows from this fact for the privacy of one's sensations. Does the need of a public framework imply that these experiences themselves, be they objects, events, or whatever, are *not private*? This has been taken to follow by a large number of philosophers, perhaps most notably by G. E. M. Anscombe. On one occasion she writes: 'If a word stands for a private object, it must have a private ostensive definition.'[29] Since private ostensive definitions are impossible, there presumably cannot be any private objects, according to this view. It is not hard to see that the implication fails, however.

Let us first get a subsidiary point out of the way. Of course we cannot *say* in language that sensations and their ilk are private, according to Wittgenstein. But this is not the problem. It is only one of the consequences of the ineffability of semantics. The real question is: Are those philosophers right who say that *there are no private experiences* according to Wittgenstein? Fairly clearly that does not follow. An instant counter-example is offered by *PI*, I, sec. 272:

> The essential thing about private experience is really not that each person possesses his own exemplar, but that nobody knows whether other people also have *this* or something else. The assumption would thus be possible – though unverifiable – that one section of mankind had one sensation of red, another section another.

But even if you discount such direct evidence, or try to explain it away, there are reasons for holding that for Wittgenstein private experiences are indeed real events, and private.

Our opponents could try to defend their position by saying that by a rejected private object they mean something that is *logically* imposs- ible for others to witness. But suppose it were logically impossible for others to see my beetle in my box, but that I could compare it with public beetles outside the box. Why could I not then speak of my beetle and also of yours? It is in fact quite clear that there will in such circumstances be no impediments to my speaking of my private beetle in a manner intelligible to others. For Wittgenstein, the crucial question is not whether it is logically impossible for me to witness another person's beetle, but whether it is logically impossible for me to relate my beetle to publicly accessible objects of comparison. If so, the indispensability of a public framework (needed to enable us to speak of beetles) does not entail that these beetles themselves have to be public.[30] In other words, it is compatible with Wittgenstein's ideas to imagine (along the lines of *PI*, I, sec. 293) a situation in which each person has access only to his or her own beetle, but that beetle-owners can nevertheless happily converse with each other about their pets by relating their own beetle to suitable public objects of comparison.

But can we be so sure what Wittgenstein's reaction to such a scenario would have been? It might appear that he would have wanted to challenge the comparisons each person is supposed to be able to make between her or his beetle and the outside world. Cannot each of us be systematically deceived in making those comparisons?

Perhaps, but it is important to notice that the inaccessibility of my beetle to others does not imply that it is impossible for me to compare my private beetle with public ones or for you to test my comparisons. There are public ways of checking my skill and veracity in making such comparisons, such as testing my eyesight, calling character witnesses, administering lie detector tests, etc.

By the same token (our imaginary opponent's token), one ought to be able to ask, by way of criticizing Wittgenstein, why one cannot be systematically wrong about one's pains. Wittgenstein's answer is that one cannot drive a wedge in language between pain and pain- expression. But if so, the same situation could in principle obtain in other cases, e.g., in colour ascriptions. Given suitable background assumptions, my ascriptions of colour to my private beetle could be as spontaneous (and as incorrigible) as my pain-expressions.[31]

To put the same point in another way, once a suitable language- game has been established in a public domain, it can in special (and admittedly parasitic) cases be extended to private objects. Notice that there is in principle no problem of teaching and learning a language-game of the kind we have envisaged, even though that can happen only after one has first learned the corresponding game as played solely with public objects.

It is indeed quite obvious that Wittgenstein himself countenances such secondary language-games as we have described, played with private objects and events, e.g., with sensations. For instance, in *Zettel*, secs. 75–7, 81–3, he is clearly assuming that I can attend to my sensations (pains, auditory impressions, etc.) and even use a stop-watch to determine their duration (sec. 82), unlike the duration of knowledge, ability, or understanding. Such a determination need not be any more difficult than the determination of the duration of an observable physical process. It is the precise analogue of my looking at my private beetle in my box and, e.g., timing its activities. Whether others can or cannot attend to my sensations does not make any difference to this possibility. It is amply clear, furthermore, that by timing a sensation Wittgenstein does not mean timing its natural expressions (moaning, scratching, etc.).

The important general point illustrated by this section is this: What follows from Wittgenstein's general philosophy of language is not that there are no private objects or that we cannot speak of such objects. All that follows is that we can use language to name them, to describe them, etc., only by means of a public framework. But from the public character of this framework it does not follow that the experiences themselves are not completely private. (Of course, that cannot be *said* in language according to Wittgenstein; but that is merely another corollary of the ineffability of all semantics.)

Hence no reason emerges for thinking that we cannot, according to Wittgenstein, have private experiences in a perfectly straightforward Cartesian sense. The whole problem is how we are to talk about them. Sensations (pains, itches, hot flushes, twinges of pleasure, etc.) do not admit of private ostensive definitions. I cannot refer to them without enabling you to do likewise. But from the public nature of the framework needed to do so it does not follow that the experiences themselves are public; or that they do not play any role in public language-games.

NOTES

1 See p. 140 above.
2 Examples of this were registered above in chapter 6, sec. 4. Others are found, e.g., in *Philosophical Remarks*, VI, sec. 57, and XX, sec. 213.

3 This passage occurs in MS 149, p. 69. It was inexplicably omitted by Rush Rhees from the version he edited. The first two sentences are in German, unlike the bulk of MS 149. The translation is ours.

4 Admittedly, Wittgenstein first tried to base the public character of language on its rule-governed character. In MS 109, pp. 284–5 (dated 30 January 1931) he writes:

> D.h. die Sprache funktioniert als Sprache nur durch die Regeln nach denen wir uns in ihrem Gebrauch richten. (Wie das Spiel nur durch Regeln als Spiel funktioniert.)
>
> Und zwar, ob ich zu mir oder Andern rede. Denn auch mir teile ich nichts mit, wenn ich Lautgruppen ad hoc mit irgend welchen Facten assoziiere.
>
> Ich muß, wenn ich zu mir rede, schon auf einen gegebenen [bestehenden] Sprachklavier spielen.

It is interesting that an emphasis on the public character of languge and the idea of language-game here seem to enter into Wittgenstein's speculations together. This way of arguing against private languages did not satisfy Wittgenstein in the end, however.

5 See MS 116, pp. 205–7 (sec. 407 Nyman):

> "Es gibt doch eine subjektive Regelmäßigkeit, eine Regelmäßigkeit, die nur für *mich* existiert." – D.h.: wir verwenden das Wort "Regelmäßigkeit" manchmal so: jemand stelle sich eine Regelmäßigkeit vor; er sehe etwas regelmäßig; etwas scheine ihm regelmäßig, usf. Aber das heißt nun nicht er hat ein Objekt vor sich, – das keiner von uns kennt und er "Regelmäßigkeit" nennt. Spielt er außer dem Spiel, was ich sehe noch eins mit sich selbst, wovon ich *nichts* weiß, so weiß ich auch nicht, ob es ein 'Spiel' zu nennen ist. Spricht er außer der öffentlichen Sprache mit sich selbst noch eine private, von der ich *nichts* weiß, warum sage ich, es sei eine Sprache?
>
> D.h.: Wir gebrauchen das *Bild* vom 'Privaten Objekt', welches nur er und kein Anderer sehen kann. Es ist ein Bild – werde Dir klar darüber! Und nun liegt es im Wesen dieses Bildes, daß wir noch weitere Annahmen über dies Object, und was er damit tut, machen; es genügt uns nicht zu sagen: Er hat ein privates Etwas und tut etwas damit.

6 Important material is also contained in MSS 148, 149, and 151, partly published as 'Notes for lectures on "private experience" and "sense data"'.

7 By speaking of 'the received interpretation' we do not intend to imply that all philosophers have accepted it. On the contrary, there are remarkable anticipations in the literature of many of the points we are arguing for in this chapter. Among several such anticipations, perhaps the most striking ones to have come to our attention are Bernard Gert, 'Wittgenstein's private language arguments' (1967–8, unpublished) and Alan Donagan, 'Wittgenstein on sensation', in George Pitcher, editor, *Wittgenstein: The Philosophical Investigations*, Doubleday, Garden City, N.J., 1968, pp. 324–51.

8 *Wittgenstein's Lectures, Cambridge 1930–1932*, p. 82.
9 See *PI*, I, secs. 257, 256, and 244.
10 See, e.g., *PI*, I, sec. 244.
11 See also *PI*, I, secs. 257, 261, and 384, inter alia.
12 In section 9 below we shall comment on Wittgenstein's use of the word *Bezeichnung*, wich G. E. M. Anscombe here misleadingly translates as 'name'.
13 Cf. here Colin Radford, 'Wittgenstein and Descartes: the best of both worlds', in E. Leinfellner et al., editors, *Wittgenstein and His Impact on Contemporary Thought, Proceedings of the Second International Wittgenstein Symposium*, Hölder-Pichler-Tempsky, Vienna, 1978.
14 See Jaakko Hintikka, 'Language-games', in Jaakko Hintikka et al., editors, *Essays on Wittgenstein in Honour of G. H. von Wright* (*Acta Philosophica Fennica*, vol. 28, nos. 1–3), North-Holland, Amsterdam, 1976, pp. 105–25.
15 The German text reads:

Es gibt innere und äußere Begriffe, innere und äußere Betrachtungsweisen des Menschen. Ja es gibt auch innere und äußere Tatsachen – sowie es z.b. physikalische und mathematische Tatsachen gibt. Sie stehen aber nicht nebeneinander wie Pflanzen verschiedener Art. Denn was ich gesagt habe, Klingt als hätte man gesagt: In der Natur kommen alle diese Tatsachen vor. Und was ist nun daran falsch?

NB Inneres ist mit Äußerem nicht nur erfahrungsmäßig verbunden, sondern auch logisch.

16 The German text of the passage quoted from MS 116, pp. 205–7, is given in note 5 to this chapter.
17 The only respect in which Wittgenstein changed his mind about the quoted passage was to become disenchanted with the term 'picture'. Wittgenstein's change of terminology is expressed in *PI*, I, sec. 301: 'An image is not a picture, but a picture can correspond to it.' This is anticipated by a marginal comment in MS 116, p. 207: 'Das Vorstellungsbild ist das Bild, das beschrieben wird, wenn man die Vorstellung beschreibt.' His reformulation is found in *PI*, I, sec. 300: 'It is – we should like to say – not merely the picture of the behaviour that plays a part in the language-game with the words "he is in pain", but also the picture of the pain. Or, not merely the paradigm of the behaviour, but also that of the pain. – It is a misunderstanding to say "The picture of pain enters into the language-game with the word 'pain'." The image of pain is not a picture and *this* image is not replaceable in the language-game by anything that we should call a picture. – The image of pain certainly enters into the language-game in a sense; only not as a picture.' In MS 116, our quotes from pp. 205–7 are followed immediately by what in the *Philosophical Investigations* became I, sec. 297. Ironically, this section has become one of the favourite passages of those who think that Wittgenstein is trying to exorcise private objects (acts, experiences, etc.) altogether:

Of course, if water boils in a pot, steam comes out of the pot and also pictured steam comes out of the pictured pot. But what if one insisted on saying that there must also be something boiling in the picture of the pot?

We are now in a position to see that the accepted interpretation of this passage is precisely the wrong way round. All one needs to do to reach the right interpretation is to take Wittgenstein's analogy literally. Wittgenstein is not suggesting that the actual private experience (the analogue to the real water boiling in the actual kettle) must fall out of the semantical picture, but that a part of its alleged one-to-one representation or 'picture' (pictured water boiling in the pictured kettle) is redundant. We must not expect, Wittgenstein is saying (or suggesting), that each element in the actual situation corresponds to one and only one distinguishable element in the representation. (Cf. chapter 9, sec. 6, above.) The point of the analogy is thus to criticize the simple object-label model of our language of private experiences. (More will be said of this inadequate model in secs. 8–9 below.) It does not tell at all against the reality of private experiences – or against their privacy. The original role of *PI*, I, sec. 297 as an illustration of the unmistakable passage on pp. 205–7 of MS 116 conclusively confirms our interpretation of this section of the *Philosophical Investigations*.

18 See chapter 11, sec. 11, below.

19 Sec. 256 is quoted here only partially. G. E. M. Anscombe's translation has been made less literal to bring out what obviously is Wittgenstein's intention.

20 What look like epistemological arguments propounded by Wittgenstein for his view on privacy turn out to be in reality conceptual (semantical) thought-experiments. See sec. 11 below.

21 In view of what was said of Wittgenstein's development in chapter 7, it is of interest to see that in *Philosophical Grammar*, IV, sec. 56, Wittgenstein is still in the hold of the *Bezeichnung*-model: 'To give a name to an object [*Gegenstand*] is essentially like hanging a name-tag [*Namenstafelchen*] on it.'

22 Wittgenstein mentions such a case in so many words in his important discussion of naming in *The Brown Book*, pp. 172–3, which was analysed in detail in chapter 8, sec. 6, above.

23 In a number of passages in the *Philosophical Investigations* Wittgenstein apparently uses the terms *Bezeichnung* and *bezeichnen* in a way which does not prima facie square with our reading of these terms. They include *PI*, I, secs. 13 and 273–4. However, in none of these passages is Wittgenstein speaking on his own behalf; rather, he is in all of them merely putting forward what we are tempted to say. Notice, for instance, that sec. 13 could equally well be translated 'If we say, "Every word in language signifies [*bezeichnet*] something", we have so far said nothing whatever . . .', instead of 'when we say . . .', as G. E. M. Anscombe's translation reads. Hence these passages do not tell against our interpretation.

Conversely, when Wittgenstein says in *PI*, I, sec. 26 that 'naming [*Benennen*] is something like attaching a label to a thing', he is again putting forth a view he is criticizing, not one he espouses.

24 This extraordinarily wide sense of 'name' (*Name*) is reminiscent of the sweeping sense of the same term in the *Tractatus*.

25 We can now also understand precisely what Wittgenstein means by *PI*, I, sec. 239: "'Red' means the colour that occurs to me when I hear the word 'red'" – would be a *definition*. Not an explanation of *what it is* to use a word as a name [*Bezeichnung*].' This passage loses its intended force if *Bezeichnung* is taken to mean a name here, for a definition of a designating word presumably is supposed to tell precisely what it is for the word to operate as a name. Wittgenstein's point is that even a perfectly successful definition does not tell what it is for the *definiendum* to refer to its object directly, i.e., without the benefit of a language-game.

26 Wittgenstein sometimes even speaks of the transition from gestures to words as a replacement of 'one set of symbols by another', thereby highlighting the conceptual rather than evidential connection between the two in physiognomic language-games. See *Wittgenstein's Lectures, Cambridge 1930–1932*, pp. 43, 62, and 102.

27 This quote is from MS 108, p. 277. The German text is reproduced in the Appendix to chapter 1 above.

28 It is hard to see, pending closer examination of the unpublished materials, when precisely the link between the privacy problem and the supremacy of language-games first began to dawn on him. It is highly significant, in any case, that Wittgenstein worked out at one and the same time his definitive analysis of the privacy problem and his examination of rule-following, which serves to establish the logical primacy of language-games. Most of *PI*, I, secs. 198–330 (85 out of 132 sections), go back to MS 129, which was written from August 1944 on. (We are relying here on published and unpublished information from G. H. von Wright.)

29 G. E. M. Anscombe, 'On private ostensive definitions', in Elisabeth Leinfellner et al., editors, *Language and Ontology, Proceedings of the Sixth International Wittgenstein Symposium,* Hölder-Pichler-Tempsky, Vienna, 1982, pp. 212–17.

30 To take a different kind of example, we may ask: Is it *logically* possible for me to witness your mental arithmetic? Scarcely, for if I did, it could not be your private calculation any longer. Yet I do as a matter of fact speak legitimately of, e.g., doing sums in my head.

31 In chapter 11, sec. 13, below, we shall in fact argue that for Wittgenstein colour ascriptions can exhibit such immediacy.

11
Differences and Interrelations among Language-games in Wittgenstein

1 BACKGROUND SUMMARY

It was argued in the preceding two chapters that Wittgenstein's later philosophy has been sorely misunderstood. There an attempt was made also to outline a more faithful overall picture of some of the most important aspects of Wittgenstein's mature thought. To sum up briefly the results of this attempt, the later Wittgenstein did not forget or lose interest in 'vertical' connections between language and reality as distinguished from 'horizontal' relations between different occasions of language use. One of the main purposes of Wittgenstein's language-games was to constitute these very vertical relationships. The main reason why Wittgenstein does not say this in so many words is merely his consistent adherence to the view of language as the universal medium.

Concerning sensations and other allegedly private experiences, Wittgenstein is not arguing for their nonexistence, nonprivacy, variability, elusiveness, unknowability, or anything else derogatory. He is merely arguing that we need a public framework, a public language-game, to give the vocabulary and the syntax of our talk about sensations and other private experiences their meanings. What is denied by Wittgenstein is hence that we can speak of our private experiences without the mediation of a public language-game.

It was also pointed out above what the most important language-games are that provide a framework for speaking of mental events. As shown by such passages as *PI*, I, sec. 244 (quoted above in chapter 10, sec. 10), they are what we have called physiognomic language-games. They rely on the natural expressions of one's sensations and emotions, such as facial expressions, gestures, expressive bodily movements, grunts, exclamations, and other modes of comportment frowned on at Wimbledon. Such language-games can be called *physiognomic,* even though this term has to be understood in a rather wide sense, for in its normal usage it pertains primarily to facial expressions only. The appropriateness of this term is nevertheless vindicated by *Zettel,* sec.

225, where Wittgenstein assigns to facial expressions a crucial role in connection with emotions:

> "We *see* emotion." – As opposed to what? – We do not see facial contortions and make inferences from them (like a doctor framing a diagnosis) to joy, grief, boredom. We describe a face immediately as sad, radiant, bored, even when we are unable to give any other description of the features. – Grief, one would like to say, is embodied in the face.
> This belongs to the concept of emotion.

The passage quoted from *PI,* I, sec. 244 in chapter 10, sec. 10, vividly illustrates the nature of Wittgenstein's physiognomic languge-games.[1] These physiognomic language-games constitute the most important kind of a public framework that makes it possible for us to speak of our private experiences. In the preceding chapter, some characteristics of such physiognomic language-games were discussed briefly. This discussion now has to be generalized. At the same time, we shall try to put physiognomic language-games into a wider perspective by comparing them to several other types of language-games Wittgenstein considers in the *Philosophical Investigations,* and by examining the interrelations of all these different language-games. We are venturing into uncharted territory here, for there are few discussions in the literature of the interrelations among different language-games in Wittgenstein, and almost as few discussions even of distinctions and differences between different language-games.

2 THE THESES OF THIS CHAPTER

To facilitate the reader's task, some of the most important theses that will be defended in this chapter will be listed now.

(1) Physiognomic language-games are not the only possible public frameworks which primarily give our talk of private experiences its meaning. However, they seem to be considered by Wittgenstein as by far the most important ones in our actual discourse.

(2) A possible alternative framework is offered by the physiological correlates of private experiences. This framework operates by and large in a way analogous to physiognomic language-games. Other parallel frameworks (neither physiognomic nor physiological) are used in our discourse about colours and other visual phenomena.

(3) In general, we have to distinguish from each other such primary language-games as were mentioned in (1) and (2), and certain other kinds of language-games which can be built on them and which will be called secondary language-games. (The primary–secondary terminology is not employed consistently by Wittgenstein.)

(4) The basic reason why Wittgenstein makes the primary–secondary distinction is that the 'moves' in primary games have to be taken to be incorrigible. Otherwise they could not serve as the basic language–world links.

(5) Private experiences and their behavioural manifestations can be separated from each other only by moving into a secondary language-game. Since a secondary language-game is different from primary ones, such a step leaves the primary games intact. Thus the relationship of a private experience to its accompanying behaviour depends essentially on the language-game which is being presupposed.

(6) The relation of a 'move' in a secondary language-game to a similar 'move' in a primary game is not epistemic (e.g., evidential), but semantical (logical or 'grammatical'). It involves the two language-games as wholes.

(7) In primary language-games, criteria and rules play no role in the sense that they need not be used by the players of these languge-games in making their moves. In such primary language-games as deal with private experiences, the relation of mental events and their 'external manifestations' is a logical (necessary) one: one cannot use language to separate the two. In this way, a primary language-game taken as a whole can provide *criteria* for mental events in one of the senses of the word.

(8) Many important concepts can be used only in a suitable secondary languge-game. They include knowledge, belief, doubt, correctness, and mistake.

(9) Physiognomic language-games have to be distinguished from the language-games which lend a meaning to our discourse about such propositional attitudes as belief, expectation, hope, etc.[2] These language-games operate in a way different from both physiognomic and physiological language-games.

(10) According to Wittgenstein, people's colour-vocabulary is parallel with their vocabulary for sensations. An important part of this parallelism is that in primary language-games with colour-terms one cannot drive a wedge between physical and phenomenological colour attributions.

(11) For other kinds of mental experiences further language-games may be needed.

These points will be discussed one by one.

3 WITTGENSTEIN PREFERS PHYSIOGNOMIC LANGUAGE-GAMES

Thesis (1): Wittgenstein acknowledges, as was already noted, that the physiognomic framework of spontaneous expressions of sensations (as well as other psychological states, processes, and events) is only one possible public reference frame. However, his commendable caution is sometimes forgotten, both by his commentators and by Wittgenstein himself. There is in Wittgenstein's basic insight nothing that precludes, for instance, the possibility of using the physiological correlates of various sensations as the public semantical coordinate system one needs when talking about sensations. It may be that such a physiological framework is not at all, or not primarily, what we rely on in our ordinary discourse. It is far from clear, however, that some such physiological framework is not the most relevant one when we are discussing, e.g., scientific research into neurophysiology or discussing the philosophical mind–body problem.

In any case, it seems that Wittgenstein preferred physiognomic language-games to physiological ones, and thought of them as the 'logical home' of the terminology we use about our private experiences. It is not clear why this should be the case. Wittgenstein's preference may be connected with the idea that it is through physiognomic language-games that children learn the meaning (use) of the jargon we use of our particular private experiences, e.g., sensations.

However, physiological language-games are in principle quite as learnable as physiognomic ones. One probable reason why Wittgenstein opted for physiognomic language-games is their everyday, humanly central character. Wittgenstein is a closet Tolstoyan in his philosophy of language, it may thus be suspected. This strain in Wittgenstein's central theoretical philosophy is elusive, but it seems to be very real indeed. Witness, for instance, passages like the following one from *PI*, II, xi, p. 200:

What we have rather to do is to *accept* the everyday language-game, and to note *false* accounts of the matter *as* false. The primitive language-game which children are trained in [*beigebracht*] needs no justification; attempts at justification need to be rejected.

Thus Wittgenstein's philosophy of language seems to be based in part on his moral and cultural stance. The effects of this moral and social preference on Wittgenstein's theoretical philosophy remain to be disentangled from the rest of his philosophy.

This suspicion is strengthened further by such statements of Wittgenstein's as the following:

> For words have meaning only in the stream of life. (*Remarks on the Philosophy of Psychology*, vol. 2, sec. 687)

> Instinct comes first, reasoning second. Not until there is a language-game are there reasons. (Ibid., sec. 689)

In the second quote, we must take 'a language-game' to mean 'a *secondary* language-game'. (Cf. sec. 8 below.)

4 ALTERNATIVE LANGUAGE-GAMES

Thesis (2): In any case, Wittgenstein occasionally countenances in so many words physiological language-games as an alternative basic link between our private experiences and their linguistic expressions. This is by any token a viable link. Even in our ordinary discourse, physiognomic frameworks sometimes yield to somewhat more physiological ones. A small reminder of this is perhaps obtained by reading John Aubrey, who reports that William Harvey used to walk around in his nightshirt whenever he could not sleep, 'till he had a horror'. Here we can see how our word for extreme fear came to have its present meaning through the physiological manifestations of intense terror, principally the characteristic shivering which in Aubrey's time was still what 'horror' meant. This illustrates on what kinds of manifestations physiological language-games for private experiences could rely.

In sec. 270 of the *Philosophical Investigations*, I, Wittgenstein in fact adumbrates an example in which a sensation-word receives its meaning (use) via the physiological correlates of the sensation in question. This important section was partly quoted and discussed above in chapter 10, sec. 12. One of the most remarkable things about the physiological language-game described there is that what can be said about it parallels closely what Wittgenstein says (or implies) about his basic physiognomic language-games. These parallelisms are quite striking. The dropping out of the allegedly wrongly identified sensation in section 270 parallels the dropping out of the beetle in sec. 293. In both cases, this apparent vanishing of the private object is a consequence of a wrong model, which in sec. 293 is traced to the *Bezeichnung–Gegenstand* model (which overlooks the role of language-games), while in sec. 270 it is diagnosed as being due to the introduction of the concept of mistake without the requisite language-game. (Cf. 'that is enough to shew that the hypothesis that I make a mistake is mere show.') In neither language-game does one use criteria, as is shown by the following parallelism:

Sec. 270:	Sec. 290:
And why a "particular sensation", that is, the same one every time? Well, we are supposing that we write every time [the same sign] "E".	What I do is not, of course, to identify my sensations by criteria, but to use the same expression.

In neither languge-game is the relation of the external manifestations of a sensation and the sensation itelf evidential or justificatory, nor is there room for doubt or mistake in either of the two cases. And, last but not least, in neither type of language-game is there a hint that the private experience itself is not real and important.

The possibility of physiological basis languages is also acknowledged by Wittgenstein in MS 169, pp. 129–30:[3]

> If people really could, as I assumed, see the working of the nervous system of another person and adjusted their behaviour toward the other, they simply would not, I believe, have our concept of pain, though perhaps a related concept. Their life *would look quite different from ours.*

> That is: I consider this language-game as autonomous. I only want to describe it, not justify it.

There are also primary language-games which are neither physiognomic nor physiological. One of the most clear-cut games of this kind is connected with colours and other visual phenomena. In his *Remarks on Colour* Wittgenstein indicates that he wants to deal with colour concepts in the same way as sensation concepts. In secs. 12–13 below, we shall show that this does not mean that the basic language-games played with them are physiognomic. There we shall also discuss a number of other problems concerning our discourse about visual phenomena.

5 PRIMARY VS. SECONDARY LANGUAGE-GAMES

Thesis (3): Most of these common features of basic physiological and physiognomic games also serve to distinguish them from the secondary language-games which can be built on them.

But where in the first place can one find the distinction between primary and secondary language-games for private experiences in Wittgenstein's texts? Wittgenstein explains the difference (without using the term 'game') in *PI*, II, xi, p. 216:

> Given the two ideas 'fat' and 'lean', would you be rather inclined to say that Wednesday was fat and Tuesday lean, or *vice versa*? (I incline decisively towards the former.) Now have "fat" and "lean" some different meaning here from their usual one? – They have a different use. – So ought I really to have used different words? Certainly not that. – I want to use *these* words (with their familiar meanings) *here*. – Now, I say nothing about the causes of this phenomenon. They *might* be associations from my childhood. But that is a hypothesis. Whatever the explanation, – the inclination is there.
>
> Asked "What do you really mean here by 'fat' and 'lean'?" – I could only explain the meanings in the usual way. I could *not* point to the examples of Tuesday and Wednesday.
>
> Here one might speak of a 'primary' and 'secondary' sense of a word. It is only if the word has the primary sense for you that you use it in the secondary one.
>
> Only if you have learnt to calculate – on paper or out loud – can you be made to grasp, by means of this concept, what calculating in the head is.
>
> The secondary sense is not a 'metaphorical' sense. If I say "For me the vowel *e* is yellow" I do not mean: 'yellow' in a metaphorical sense, – for I could not express what I want to say in any other way than by means of the idea 'yellow'.

In order to obtain another example, we may think of *PI*, I, sec. 244, as being immediately followed by sec. 290: 'What I do is not the end of the language-games: it is the beginning.' There is a terminological difference present here, however. We are here calling a primary language-game what Wittgenstein calls the beginning of a language-game.

By and large, Wittgenstein emphasizes the dissimilarities between primary and secondary games. This distinction is nevertheless easily misunderstood in different ways. Wittgenstein may be thought of as denying the possibility of what we are calling secondary language-games. Alternatively, the features he insists are characteristic of secondary games may be attributed to the primary ones. One particularly important point is not to overlook the legitimacy of secondary language-games according to Wittgenstein. Their being secondary in the present technical sense does not mean that they are in any way suspect or inferior.

6 THE INCORRIGIBILITY OF PRIMARY LANGUAGE-GAMES AND THE PRIMARY–SECONDARY DISTINCTION

Thesis (4): A general explanation may be in order here. What conceptual situation led Wittgenstein to postulate secondary language-games? This problem is one which confronts every serious student of Wittgenstein's later philosophy. His fundamental reason is nevertheless not hard to grasp. Since primary language-games are what mediates the relation of language to reality, there is not, and cannot be, any way of challenging what happens in such language-games. For such a challenge would presuppose an independent link between one's language and the world, a link that would by-pass these language-games. But when they would no longer be the primary vehicles of our semantics.

What this means in practice is that, according to Wittgenstein, primarily language-games are incorrigible. This is in fact one of their most characteristic features.

In view of this observation it is interesting to see how the problem whether 'an expression can always lie' occupied Wittgenstein intensively, and how it was one of the considerations which led him to his tacit distinction between different kinds of language-games. This is dramatically shown by his 'Notes for Lectures on "Private Experiences" and "Sense Data"', e.g., p. 250. He realizes there that

> The language games with expressions of feelings are based on games with expressions of which we don't say that they may lie.

As Wittgenstein puts it a little later (p. 252), we cannot say, 'expressions can always be lying' when it comes to 'the expressions to which we fasten our words'.

Thus the plain fact that there are also language-games with corrigible 'moves' serves to demonstrate the need of a distinction between primary and secondary language-games. It is, for instance, no accident that, in the very next paragraph after the quoted one, Wittgenstein describes how a child might come to learn a secondary language-game (even though Wittgenstein does not there use the term) of misleading adults about his or her sensations, in contrast to the introduction (teaching) of a primary language-game with pain-expressions, essentially in the same way as in *PI*, I, sec. 244, which Wittgenstein sketches in the paragraph after that.

Another, related way in which Wittgenstein indicates the need of further (secondary) language-games is found *PI*, I, sec. 288. Speaking of a physiognomic language-game for sensations Wittgenstein writes:

> The expression of doubt has no place in the language-game; but if we cut out the expression of sensation, that is human behaviour, it looks as if I might *legitimately* begin to doubt afresh. My temptation to say that one might take a sensation for something other than what it is arises from this: if I assume the abrogation of the normal language-game with the expression of sensation, I need a criterion of identity for the sensation; and then the possibility of error also exists.

The context shows that the elimination of the normal physiognomic language-game is not supposed to result in a semantical state of nature, but to be an abdication (or 'abrogation', as G. E. M. Anscombe translates *abgeschaffen*) in favour of another language-game. Indeed, this passage must be taken to be a part of the preparations for Wittgenstein's comment only a few lines later that a physiognomic game 'is not the *end* of the language-game: it is the beginning'.

It is in any case clear that Wittgenstein acknowledges all sorts of language-games which presuppose the basic physiognomic language-game for sensations and hence are conceptually secondary with respect to it. They include lying (*PI*, I, sec. 249), pretending (*Zettel*, secs. 568–72), simulating (*PI*, I, sec. 250), etc.

Wittgenstein formulates his claim that such secondary language-games have to be learned over and above the primary ones in a particularly vivid way in *PI*, I, sec. 250:

> Why can't a dog simulate pain? Is he too honest? Could one teach a dog to simulate pain? Perhaps it is possible to teach him to howl on particular occasions as if he were in pain, even when he is not. But the surroundings which are necessary for this behaviour to be real simulation are missing.

7 THE RELATION BETWEEN PRIMARY AND SECONDARY LANGUAGE-GAMES

Thesis (5): The next question we face here is what happens to primary language-games when secondary frameworks are superimposed on them. This question, too, is among the most central issues concerning the interpretation of Wittgenstein's mature philosophy.

Why must we postulate secondary language-games? This question was answered in the preceding section. Now we have to put the line of thought offered there in a wider perspective. Suppose that Wittgenstein is right about the role of physiognomic language-games, that is, suppose that our terminology of pains is given its primary meaning by people's spontaneous reactions to pain, such as exclamations, bodily movements, facial expressions, and so on. They constitute the primary language-game to which our pain-vocabulary belongs. The pain-reactions they involve are logically (semantically) and not only contingently connected with our language of pain. But apparently this connection, though conceptual, is not invariable. Someone may, for instance, pretend to be in pain and exhibit all the outward signs of pain. How are we to handle such a situation conceptually? What sense can we make of a logical connection which is not incorrigible and which hence cannot give us a criterion of pain? What *is* the relation of the 'moves' in the primary languge-game to pain?

Later philosophers have tried to answer these questions in various traditional terms, such as evidence, justification, criteria, symptoms, etc. The outcome has been slim. The true nature of Wittgenstein's answer has scarcely been appreciated. What happens when the primary logical connection between pain and pain-behaviour is seemingly broken is, according to Wittgenstein, that this break is only an apparent one. It does not mean that the primary language-game in question has been modified. Wittgenstein never admits that we can, for instance, drive a wedge between pain and pain-expressions in primary language-games. What happens is that *another (secondary) language-game is superimposed on the primary one.* It is therefore misleading to formulate the problem as one concerning the relation of pain-terminology to pain-behaviour or the relation of pain to pain-behaviour. The relation which is to be studied in the first place is a relation obtaining between different language-games. This is a problem of an entirely different logical type than any problem pertaining to the nature of some one language-game. It involves, e.g., problems which differ from all the traditional epistemological problems of evidence and justification.

For instance, if one wants to claim that someone is in pain without exhibiting pain-behaviour, one's reasons cannot lie solely in our evidence for connections between pain, pain-language, and pain-behaviour. One's reasons must be partially couched in terms of the language-games (e.g., the language-game of simulating) which the person in question has to have learned, and in terms of her or his reasons for practising those further language-games on that particular occasion.

In his *Last Writings,* vol. 1, sec. 203, Wittgenstein presents a vivid thought-experiment concerning one possible way of moving from a primary language-game to a secondary one:

> A tribe unfamiliar with the concept of simulated pain. They pity anyone who indicates that he is feeling pain. They are unfamiliar with the suspicious attitude towards expressions of pain. A traveller coming from our culture to theirs frequently thinks that a complaint is exaggerated, indeed, that its only purpose is to generate pity; the natives don't seem to think that way. (In their language they have an expression corresponding more or less to our: "to feel the pain".) A missionary teaches the people our language; in the process he also educates them. Under his tutelage they learn to distinguish between a genuine and a pretended expression of pain. For he mistrusts many an expression of pain and suppresses it, and teaches the people to be suspicious. – They learn our expression "to feel pain", and also "to simulate pain", and the question is: were they taught a new concept of pain? Certainly I won't say that they only now know what pain is. For that would mean that they had never felt pain previously. – But they had to receive a new kind of training for the use of our words. This was similar but not the same as the previous training.

This thought-experiment shows what kind of change is involved in the transition from a primary game to a secondary one.

Thesis (6): That this transition cannot be described in traditional epistemological terms, but only by reference to the nature of the entire language-games involved, is in effect stated by Wittgenstein in *Remarks on the Philosophy of Psychology,* vol. 2, sec. 684:

> If it is said, "Evidence can only make it probable that expressions of emotions are genuine", this does not mean that instead of complete certainty we have just a more or less confident conjecture. "Only probable" cannot refer to the degree of our confidence, but only to the nature of its justification, to *the character of the language-game.* [Emphasis added]

To illustrate: if it suspected that someone, for instance a child, is exhibiting pain-behaviour without pain, our reaction should not be a second look at our knowledge about the relation of pains to pain-behaviour or even less a revision of our standards of inductive inference. The right questions to ask (barring physiological anomalies) are, for example: Is the child lying, simulating, or play-acting? Could the child have learned these more complicated language-games? If so, how? Why should the child be 'playing' those language-games now?

There is characteristic behaviour which goes together with having a toothache, and there is both characteristic behaviour and characteristic antecedent learning experience which go together with hiding a toothache. Suppose we discover that someone is exhibiting the hiding behaviour. Does this observation change the evidential situation? Does it make it harder to discover whether he or she really is in pain? Not necessarily. Such signs can in principle be quite reliable indications as to what the person in question feels. As Wittgenstein says in *Last Writings,* vol. 1, sec. 901, 'from a person's behaviour you can draw conclusions not only about his pain but also about his pretence'. The crucial difficulty (if any) lies in ascertaining which game the person is playing. But this is a partly semantical problem, and epistemic questions are to be addressed to that difficulty.

For instance, suppose that a child does not want to be taken to a dentist and therefore hides his toothache, but that his parent has learned to tell when this is happening. Need the evidence for the child's actually having a toothache be any less strong than in a case where the child tells that he has a pain? Obviously not. As soon as we know which language-game is being played, we might have equally good evidence in the two types of cases (primary language-games and secondary ones).

Such considerations show that what one is dealing with in the distinction between primary and secondary language-games is *not* a matter of evidence or justification within either primary or secondary language-games.

One way of seeing that the relation between the 'moves' in primary and secondary language-games cannot be epistemic is the following: Wittgenstein indicates in *PI,* I, sec. 282, that we can legitimately use sensation-words when the behaviour that normally goes together with the sensation in question is absent. All we have to realize is that 'this use [e.g.] of the concept of pain is a secondary one'. Besides partly vindicating the terminology used here, this shows strikingly that the relation of pain-behaviour to pain in Wittgenstein's theory is not an evidential one, for an evidential relation could not be so affected by the imposition of a new conceptual perspective on pain and its expressions.[4]

What has been said in this section shows that the distinction between primary and secondary language-games was for Wittgenstein not merely a way of finding a niche for semantical phenomena that have no place in primary language-games. It is an absolute necessity for him if he is to maintain his conception of primary languge-games, prominently including the physiognomic ones. For the only way for him to maintain the inseparable conceptual tie between sensations and their expressions in the teeth of various prima facie counter-examples to refer to these apparent counter-examples to secondary language-games.

Further evidence for what we have argued for here is found when we examine thesis (7) below.

8 DIFFERENCES BETWEEN DIFFERENT LANGUAGE-GAMES AND WITTGENSTEIN'S NOTION OF CRITERION

Thesis (7): Now we are also in a position to see what Wittgenstein is often, perhaps typically, highlighting by the term 'criterion'. Primary language-games do not operate by means of criteria in the sense that criteria are conceptually subordinate to language-games. Whether a criterion is satisfied does not depend on the local phenomena alone; it also depends on the overall language-game that is being played. Hence one characteristic use of the term 'criterion' in Wittgenstein serves to call attention to this language-game, to its global features.

However, as ingredients of primary language-games one also finds criteria of sorts, in the sense that certain phenomena, e.g., pain-expressions, are inextricably tied to what they are criteria of in the particular language-game in question. For instance, in a primary language-game, we cannot even try to use language to get between pain and its expression. Thus one thing Wittgenstein sometimes marks by using the term 'criterion' are these intrinsic and inextricable ties between a criterion and what it is a criterion of. In short, this term serves to call attention to the incorrigibility of primary language-games.[5]

In the light of this observation, we can understand many of those other uses of the term of 'criterion' in the *Philosophical Investigations* which are not covered by the explanations which we gave in chapter 8, sec. 10, above, for instance, *PI*, I, sec. 354, where Wittgenstein contrasts to each other 'criteria' and 'symptoms'. The point made by means of the former term turns out to be that sense-impressions do not always deceive us, but sometimes are what helps to define a phenomenon.

The force of the term 'criterion' is nevertheless weaker in such late passages than in Wittgenstein's middle-period writings. For one thing, there is no implication that the so-called criterion need not play any role in a speaker's mind in applying a word. For another, an originally inseparable tie between a 'criterion' and what it portends can be severed by moving to another, secondary language-game. But then we do not in reality have the same criterion any longer, for it is a criterion only in a primary language-game. A characteristic pain-expression is not a criterion of pain in a language-game of play-acting or simulation. What happens then is that a new kind of criterion – a criterion characteristic of the secondary languge-game in question – will be needed. And sometimes Wittgenstein is indeed signalling by the use of this term the use of a word is governed by such a second-order 'criterion'. By and large, it is only by reference to secondary language-games that Wittgenstein uses the term 'criterion' in its narrower and stricter sense. This is the sense in which the criterion for an expression is actually involved in its use. (In the parallel case of rules, this would mean that a rule is not followed blindly.) We have seen that primary physiognomic language-games do not operate by means of criteria in this strict sense. One of the characteristic differences between primary and secondary language-games is that, by and large, secondary language-games are much likelier to rely on criteria in the strict sense of the word than primary ones.

Several occurrences of 'criterion' in the *Philosophical Investigations* in fact belong to Wittgenstein's discussion of secondary language-games. Typically they involve notions like correctness. Often there is an unmistakable suggestion that primary language-games get along perfectly well without criteria. The following are cases in point: I, sec. 258 (where not being able to talk about 'right' means that we have not got the appropriate secondary language-game going); I, sec. 322 (comparing experiences for identity belongs to secondary language-games, not to primary ones, for clearly we do not compare, e.g., two fits of crying for their identity); I, sec. 376 (similar); II, p. 222 (where the different criteria considered are all criteria for correctness); I, sec. 580 (it will be shown below by reference to the context that Wittgenstein is there discussing secondary language-games); I, sec. 573 (criteria of someone's having a belief); I, sec. 253 (identity criteria for different persons' experiences); and I, sec. 572 (criteria for being in the state of expectation).[6]

Now we can also see an important reason why it is misleading to attribute a criteriological relation to Wittgenstein. The reason is that according to him the nature of this relation depends on the particular language-game that is being played. Consider again the relation of characteristic pain-expressions to pain. In primary physiognomic games, the relation is in a sense a necessary one: the two are conceptually inseparable. However, the relation of the two in a certain secondary game may be partly evidential in nature. Is it likely that the person in question is not pretending? In other secondary games, e.g., in play-acting, normal pain-expressions may even be counter-evidence to the actor's really being in pain.

Hence the alleged 'criteriological relation' is at best not one but many: as many as there are language-games in which the word connected with the criterion can play a role.

9 DIFFERENCES AND SIMILARITIES BETWEEN PRIMARY AND SECONDARY LANGUAGE-GAMES

Thesis (8): Several ways in which primary and secondary language-games differ from each other in Wittgenstein have been reviewed so far. Here is a list of a few differences, some of them noted above and some of them new:

(i)   Primary language-games – at least physiognomic ones – do not rely on criteria in the stricter sense of the term.
(ii)   The notions of error, correctness, and verification do not apply in primary games.
(iii) This absence of the notions of correctness and mistake from primary language-games is closely connected with another remarkable feature of Wittgenstein's views. In the primary language-games for sensations, there are no criteria for the *identity* of sensations which different persons have or the sensations one and the same person has on different occasions, independent of the characteristic physiognomic correlates of these sensations.
(iv)   Likewise the notions of evidence, belief, justification, and knowledge are not applicable in the primary physiognomic games.
(v)   In secondary games in which, e.g., words for such sensations are pains are used, the utterances containing such words need not be construable as instances of pain-behaviour.

These differences will be discussed briefly in this order.

(i) *Criteria.* This point was argued for in section 8 and in chapter 8 above. Only a couple of supplementary remarks need to be made here. In contradistinction to the received interpretation, there is in any case good evidence that according to Wittgenstein the primary physiognomic language-games do not utilize criteria. Most of the relevant passages of *PI* have already been discussed. Some of them are nevertheless worth quoting again and considering together:

> To use a word without a justification does not mean to use it without right. (*PI*, I, sec. 289)

Instead of 'justification' Wittgenstein could have said 'criteria' here. For witness the following:

> And what is our reason for calling "E" a sensation here? Perhaps the kind of way this sign is employed in this language-game. – And why a "particular sensation", that is, the same one every time? Well, aren't we supposing that we write "E" every time? (*PI*, I, sec. 270)

> What I do is not, of course, to identify my sensation by criteria, but to repeat an expression. (*PI*, I, sec. 290)

> . . . if I assume the abrogation of the normal language-game with the expression of the sensation, I need a criterion of identity for the sensation; and then the possibility of error also exists. (*PI*, I, sec. 288)

Defenders of the received interpretation will have to say that in such passages as have been quoted Wittgenstein is merely rejecting alleged private criteria. There is no evidence for this claim, however, and in some cases it is obviously wrong. For instance, this interpretation can be seen to be impossible in the last passage quoted (*PI*, I, sec. 288). In order to save the orthodox view, a defender would have to say that in sec. 288 Wittgenstein is envisaging a reversal back to a state before (as it were) the normal physiognomic language-game had been launched. Similarities between sec. 288 and other quoted passages show that the attempted abrogation mentioned in sec. 288 is not abdication in favour of a gameless situation, but in favour of second-order language-games. This is shown especially clearly by the words 'possibility of error'. There is no such possibility in the 'semantical state of nature' before primary language-games or even in primary language-games, only in secondary ones.[7]

(ii) This point was registered in the discussion of primary language-games in section 7 above. Further evidence is forthcoming, for instance, from Wittgenstein's *Remarks on the Philosophy of Psychology*, II, sec. 315, where Wittgenstein lets us understand that what he calls 'the rather fine distinction between seeming and being' does not belong to the first language-games of a child who is learning the language.

(iii) Evidence for this point is found, e.g., in *PI*, I, secs. 253–4, 272, 377–8, and 398–411. Of these, sec. 253 was mentioned in chapter 8, sec. 11 above.

(iv) That the concept of knowledge does not apply in primary language-games is seen from such passages as *PI*, I, sec. 246:[8]

288 Interrelations among language-games

It can't be said of me at all (except perhaps as a joke) that I *know* I am
in pain. What is it supposed to mean – except perhaps that I *am* in pain?

What goes for knowledge goes also for doubt, belief, and justifi-
cation almost *a fortiori*.
Highly relevant evidence is also found in the *Remarks on the
Philosophy of Psychology*, II, sec. 342:

> So how does the doubt get expressed? That is, expressed in a language-
> game, and not merely in certain *locutions*? Maybe in looking more
> closely; and so in a rather complicated activity. But this expression of
> doubt by no means always makes sense, nor does it always have a point.
> One simply tends to forget that even doubting belongs to a language-
> game.

(v) One kind of secondary language-game in which sensation-words
play a part is one in which one speaks of one's sensations hypotheti-
cally or in the past tense. Then the use of words like 'pain' cannot be
construed as pain-behaviour, however acquired or extended we may
allow it to be. This is ipso facto a sign that we are not dealing with a
primary language-game.
Wittgenstein comments on this difference between primary and
secondary games in *Remarks on the Philosophy of Psychology*, vol. 1,
sec. 479:

> "Suppose I have a pain . . ." – that is not an expression of pain and so is
> not a piece of pain-behaviour.
>
> The child who learns the word "pain" as a cry, and who then learns to
> tell of a past pain – one day this child may declare "If I have a pain, the
> doctor comes." Now has the meaning of the word "pain" changed in
> this process? It has changed its employment [*Verwendung*]; but one
> must guard carefully against interpreting this change as a change of the
> object corresponding to the word. [G. E. M. Anscombe's translation
> has been modified slightly.][9]

This difference between primary and secondary language-games connected with sensation-words has its analogues elsewhere. For instance, a similar difference is found between the language-game of
promising and the language-games of speaking of past promises or of
hypothetical ones. The former is of course primary in relation to the
latter.
Our latest quote also shows what the most basic similarity is
between primary and secondary language-games. Whatever differences there are between the two, the differences are semantical, not

ontological. Primary and secondary language-games *deal with the same objects*. Hence, in so far as references to past pains speak of events rather than dispositions, then so must do references to my present pains.

This point is further confirmed by other statements of Wittgenstein's. For instance, the thought-experiment we quoted from *Last Writings*, vol. 1, sec. 203 (above, sec. 7), continues as follows (secs. 204–5):

> Had these people overlooked something, and did the teacher bring something to their attention?
>
> And how could they remain unaware of the difference if sometimes they would complain when they were in pain, and sometimes when they were not? Am I to say that they always thought it was the same thing? Certainly not. Or am I to say that they didn't notice any difference? – But why not say: the difference was not important to them?

The differences between primary and secondary language-games which we have noted have important consequences. One group of problems for which these differences are crucial was discussed in the preceding chapter. The distinction between primary and secondary language-games is, for instance, vital for understanding Wittgenstein's views on private experiences.[10]

10 WITTGENSTEIN ON PROPOSITIONAL ATTITUDES

Thesis (9): A discussion of Wittgenstein's views on propositional attitudes can conveniently start from a passage in Wittgenstein which is all too often taken to support the criteriological view of private experiences, viz. *PI*, I, sec. 580:

> An 'inner process' stands in need of outward criteria.

The briefest way of explaining the real force of this sentence is to say: commentators have overlooked the inverted commas. What Wittgenstein is dealing with here are not really inner *processes*. Hence the need of criteria here, according to Wittgenstein, does not tell in the least against the interpretation outlined in the present work, where we have so far discussed only Wittgenstein's views on genuine inner processes.

In other words, the context of the quoted passage has invariably been overlooked in the recent literature. What Wittgenstein is discussing there are not private experiences and the language we use about them, but what philosophers often call propositional attitudes, such as belief, hope, expectation, etc., and the way we speak about them.[11] The view which he criticizes is that each of such propositional attitudes is characterized by a special feeling or some other distinctive private experience, and that it is these experiences that we mean by speaking of believing, hoping, expecting, etc. Wittgenstein denies that this is how propositional-attitude words are used, that this is their meaning. He denies, for instance, that someone who says, 'I hope he'll come,' is typically reporting his or her state of mind, either to others or to herself or himself. (Cf. *PI*, I, sec. 585.) Wittgenstein's point is that this meaning has to be seen from the whole language-game in which words like 'expect' are used.

> An expectation is imbedded in a situation, from which it arises. The expectation of an explosion may, for example, arise from a situation in which an explosion *is to be expected*. (*PI*, I, sec. 581)

There could scarcely be a sharper contrast between what Wittgenstein is doing here and what he is doing in his earlier discussion of private experiences and our ways of speaking about them. In his earlier analysis, Wittgenstein addresses himself to such language as we in fact use to talk about sensations and other private experiences, to give them names, etc. (Cf. *PI*, I, sec. 244.) Here Wittgenstein is analysing concepts of an entirely different kind. His main thesis is that these concepts do *not* refer to any particular private experiences. They may be said to pertain to states (cf. sec. 572), but only in roughly the sense in which we speak of states of inanimate bodies. These states may even involve sundry feelings and other private experiences, but having these feelings are not what it means to be in the state in question. This has to be spelled out by means of the associated behaviour. A belief in, say, Goldbach's theorem (cf. sec. 578) does not consist 'in a feeling of certainty as we state, hear, or think the theorem'. One is closer to truth if one says, 'it makes me search for a proof of the proposition.' Wittgenstein's comment is: '. . . let us look what your searching really consists in. Then we shall know what the belief in the proposition amounts to.' The same point is made in such passages as the following:

> If someone whispers, "It'll go off now", instead of saying "I expect the explosion any moment", still his words do not describe a feeling; although they and their tone may be a manifestation of his feelings. (*PI*, I, sec. 582)

> When someone says "I hope he'll come" – is this a *report* about his state of mind, or a *manifestation* of his hope? – I can, for example, say it to myself. And surely I am not giving myself a report. It may be a sigh; but

it need not. [But] [i]f I tell someone "I can't keep my mind on my work today; I keep on thinking of his coming" – *this* will be called a description of my state of mind. (*PI*, I, sec. 585)

One remarkable thing about such passages is that in them Wittgenstein speaks completely realistically of feelings (cf. also *PI*, I, sec. 578), states of mind, of descriptions of such states of mind, etc. His critical point is merely that such feelings or states of mind are not what our talk of propositional attitudes pertains to.

Wittgenstein's remarks about criteria in sec. 580 and in sec. 572 are calculated to serve the same purpose. They are intended to be applied to concepts like hope and expectation, not to genuine private experiences. If such propositional attitudes are called inner states, then these states are in need of criteria, not because they involve private experiences, but because they don't – at least not in a way that would allow them to serve as criteria. Passages like sec. 580 are irrelevant to Wittgenstein's discussion of private experiences, not because in them he is denying that propositional attitudes are private, but because he is denying that they are experiences. A comparison between sec. 572 and sec. 580 is especially instructive here. It shows that the 'inner processes' or 'inner states' Wittgenstein is talking about in the latter are 'processes' like expectation, belief, hope, etc., not processes or states like pains or other sensations. Hence sec. 580, rightly understood, has no force against the interpretation defended here, but supports it.

As far as *PI*, I, sec. 572 – a passage which also has been taken to favour the criteriological interpretation of Wittgenstein – is concerned, Wittgenstein's initial point admittedly is that expectation is grammatically a state. But this is merely his starting-point. He hastens to point out that any state – including physical states like hardness and weight – has to be specified by reference to its manifestations. Wittgenstein's word 'criterion' in sec. 572 is meant to be taken generally to stand for any such manifestations. It is not restricted to criteria in the narrow sense of 'crucial experiments' (once-and-for-all tests) for the states in question. After all, there is no decision method for the physical states Wittgenstein mentions, either. Hence sec. 572 does not tell against the present interpretation, for Wittgenstein is clearly using there the term 'criterion' in the weaker sense which was commented on in chapter 8 and in sec. 8 of this chapter and in which it basically serves merely to call attention to the public language-game which is being presupposed.[12]

In the same spirit, Wittgenstein writes in *Remarks on the Philosophy of Psychology*, vol. 1, sec. 311:

"Understand" just is not used like a word for a sensation.

More generally, it is vital in interpreting Wittgenstein to distinguish from each other two quite different things, viz. his discussion of inner *experiences* (sensations, feelings, etc.) and his remarks on *propositional attitudes*. What was just found out illustrates the difference between these two discussions in Wittgenstein. Many of those pronouncements in which Wittgenstein seems to deny the reality of sensations and other similar private experiences, or to deny their role in the relevant language-games, are in reality aimed at propositional attitudes, not at sensations.

In the case of sensations, the private object is really there, and the whole problem is to find a public framework by means of which we can speak of it. In the case of notions like hoping or expecting, Wittgenstein's thesis is quite different. He is denying that they *are* private experiences, that having these propositional attitudes means or involves having a sensation or feeling of a certain kind. Here the private object legitimately disappears. In a sense, it is true, according to Wittgenstein, that there is no expectation without expectation-behaviour, but in this sense it is not true to say that there is no pain without pain-behaviour. Even though Wittgenstein warns us that the concept of thinking is not especially closely related to propositional-attitude notions (see *PI*, I, sec. 574), nevertheless in the specific respect here considered Wittgenstein's warning about it applies more widely:

> Misleading parallel: the expression of pain is a cry – the expression of thought, a proposition. As if the purpose of the proposition were to convey to one person how it is with another: only, so to speak, in his thinking part and not in his stomach.

In *PI*, II, xi, p. 217, Wittgenstein says that even 'if God had looked into our minds, he would not have been able to see there what we are speaking about'. The context shows what kinds of things Wittgenstein has in mind here: speaking, thinking, remembering, meaning, intending, etc., in other words, propositional attitudes and concepts closely related to them. Wittgenstein's statement does not belie his analysis of sensations in which he did not depart radically from Descartes as far as metaphysics is concerned, only as far as semantics is concerned. According to Wittgenstein's rightly understood view, if God had looked into your mind he would have been able to see there what you sense or feel. Now it can be seen, however, that Wittgenstein's closet Cartesianism does not extend from sensations and other episodic private experiences to thinking or to propositional attitudes. As far as propositional attitudes are concerned, Wittgenstein is after all an anti-Cartesian. Thoughts, meanings, beliefs, expectations, and the like are not 'ideas' that could be reified into items in the inventory of our inner world. The usual interpretation of Wittgenstein's treatment of sensations and other private experiences thus applies much better to his views about thinking and about propositional attitudes than it does to its alleged primary target.[13]

11 COLOURS AND PRIVACY

Thesis (10): An interesting and historically important example of a class of concepts which prima facie differ from all the ones we have so far discussed are colours. What kinds of language-games do we play with them according to Wittgenstein?

Wittgenstein discussed colours more than any other comparable complex of concepts. We have repeatedly come upon conceptual problems connected with colours in this work. Toward the end of his life, Wittgenstein even devoted three separate manuscripts to the subject of colour. They have been published as a volume entitled *Remarks on Colour.* In surveying all this material, one can soon see that an exhaustive treatment of Wittgenstein's views of colour and colours would require a more extensive discussion than we can undertake here. What we shall do is merely to try to show how Wittgenstein's remarks on colour find a niche in the overall interpretation we have presented.

One reason why such a discussion is called for is that it is not immediately obvious that what Wittgenstein says is compatible with our interpretation. For one thing, Wittgenstein makes a large number of comments on colours which prima facie seems to support the received view of his privacy discussion. He seems to say, or imply, that all that matters in our discourse about colours are certain modes of behaviour, certain language-games, and that colour experiences 'cancel out' from our discourse in the last Wittgensteinian analysis.

For instance, Wittgenstein writes in *Remarks on Colour,* III, sec. 112, apropos the difference between a colour-blind and a normal person:[14]

> The one can learn a language-game that the other one cannot. And indeed *this must* be what constitutes colour-blindness of all kinds. For if the "colour-blind" person could learn all the language-games of normal people, why should he be excluded from certain professions?

It might thus seem that all that is involved in our colour-language are certain public language-games and that in philosophy we must look away completely from colour-impressions. For instance, it might seem that colour-blindness is not a matter of the colour experiences which a colour-blind person has and which differ from those of a normal person but merely a matter of a difference in the language-games which he or she can learn.

Wittgenstein nevertheless makes it clear that he is not dealing (in his remarks on language-games with colour-words) with the reality or unreality of colour-impressions but with the ways speak of them:

> Couldn't seeing be the *exception*? [I.e., rather than blindness being the exception.] But neither the blind nor the sighted could describe it, except as an ability to do this or that. Including e.g. playing certain language-games; but we must be careful how we describe these games. (*Remarks on Colour*, III, sec. 332)

The right way of looking at Wittgenstein's comments on language-games played with colour-words is as an illustration of what he says in *Philosophical Remarks*, I, sec. 1:

> A recognition of what is essential and what is inessential in our language if it is to represent does the same job as the construction of a phenomenological language.

> Each time I say that, instead of such and such a representation, you could also use this other one, we take a further step towards the goal of grasping the absence of what is represented.

12 ANALOGY BETWEEN COLOUR-CONCEPTS AND SENSATION-CONCEPTS: WHAT IT IS NOT

Indeed, colour experiences cancel out as little according to Wittgenstein as pains and other such sensations do. Wittgenstein explicitly asserts that the two sets of concepts, colour concepts and sensation concepts, operate in analogous ways:

> I treat colour concepts like the concepts of sensations. (*Remarks on Colour*, III, sec. 71)

> The colour concepts are to be treated like the concepts of sensations. (Ibid., III, sec. 72)

This parallelism helps us to appreciate both parties. On the one hand, it helps us to understand how colour concepts operate according to

Wittgenstein, i.e., what the language-games are that give these concepts their content. On the other hand, the comparison will turn out to confirm further our earlier analysis of sensation concepts.

At first blush, the analogy nevertheless looks wrong-headed and even paradoxical. We have seen that the primary languge-games which (according to Wittgenstein) establish the semantical links between private sensations and the language we use of them rely on the characteristic spontaneous expressions of different sensations. This idea has no counterpart in Wittgenstein's philosophy of colour. On the contrary, he clearly signals his disapproval of purely psychological colour theories which concentrate on the 'sensuous and moral' effects of colour (Goethe).[15]

Furthermore, even without knowing the precise nature of the language-games which connect our colour-language with the world, it is easy to see that they are in one apparently crucial respect radically different from the physiognomic games considered in chapter 10. In a physiognomic game, it may be the case that 'the verbal expression of pain replaces crying and does not describe it' (*PI,* I, sec. 244). What this means is that in physiognomic games the requisite public framework can consist of modes of behaviour which can be replaced by speech-acts, or else of behaviour which is closely related (from the viewpoint of the language-game in question) to speech-acts. In the case of colour-words, the idea that the basic language-games that give them their meanings rely on expressive behaviour in general or linguistic behaviour seems absurd. Wittgenstein's favourite, albeit admittedly oversimplified, example of such a language-game is a game of colour comparisons played by means of colour samples or colour charts. The public framework (samples or charts relied on in such games) is of course nonlinguistic and nonbehavioral.[16] Hence it may seem again that the analogy Wittgenstein sees between sensation-language and colour-language is spurious.

13 ANALOGY BETWEEN COLOUR-CONCEPTS AND SENSATION-CONCEPTS: WHAT IT REALLY IS

What Wittgenstein aims at in emphasizing the parallelism of colour-words and sensation-words is something more general than the physiognomic character of basic language-games with sensation-words. Part of what he means is the need of a public framework in both cases – in both, because a public framework is needed in all cases. One way in which Wittgenstein introduces this requirement is to ask what the language-games are in which colour-words play a role. For language-games are for him always public in principle, as we have seen.

The simplest public framework for colour-words is one which uses physical colour samples.[17] Wittgenstein often discusses colour concepts as if this were how colour concepts operate. If we want to emphasize the parallelism between physiognomic langue-games for emotions and such language-games for colours as rely on colour samples, we might imagine that physiognomic games, too, rely on samples, say pictures of facial expressions exemplifying different emotions, perhaps in the manner which was popular in the days of Lavater and his 'science' of physiognomy. The applicability of an emotion-word to a person would on this model be judged by comparing his or her expression with the chart of facial expressions.

The ridiculous character of this thought-experiment illustates the fact that colour-words do not in our actual colour-discourse rely on colour samples or colour charts. What, then, is a better account of the 'grammar' of our colour-words? There is a tempting next step, which is nevertheless sharply rejected by Wittgenstein. It consists in saying that our colour-discourse operates, not by means of actual physical colour samples, but by means of remembered colour-images. What is wrong with this idea is that colour-images, because they are private, cannot be the tools of any language-games, which must be public. As a part of this discussion of the alleged indestructibility of simples, Wittgenstein writes in *PI*, I, sec. 56:

> But what if no such sample is part of the languge, and we *bear in mind* the colour (for instance) that a word stands for? – "And if we bear it in mind then it comes before our mind's eye when we utter the word. So, if it is always supposed to be possible for us to remember, it must be in itself indestructible." – But what do we regard as the criterion for remembering it right? – When we work with a sample instead of our memory there are circumstances in which we say that the sample has changed colour and we judge of this by memory. But can we not sometimes speak of a darkening (for example) of our memory-image? Aren't we as much at the mercy of memory as of a sample? (For someone might feel like saying: "If we had no memory we should be at the mercy of a sample".) – Or perhaps of some chemical reaction. Imagine that you were supposed to paint a particular colour "C", which was the colour that appeared when the chemical substances X and Y combined. – Suppose that the colour struck you as brighter on one day than on another; would you not sometimes say: "I must be wrong, the colour is certainly the same as yesterday"? This shews that we do not always resort to what memory tells us as the verdict of the highest court of appeal.

Wittgenstein's criticism of the remembered-images account of our colour-discourse parallels his criticism of the ostensive model of the teaching and learning of sensation-words. For instance, the quoted passage is analogous to *PI*, I, sec. 258. It is also significant that Wittgenstein comments on colour-words in the middle of his discussion of the language of sensations in *PI*, I, secs. 273–8.

How, then, can we describe the primary language-games with colour-words? What was wrong with the colour-sample idea is that it was an attempt to describe the rules of a language-game, not the game itself. What can the right characterization of the basic language-games of our colour-discourse be if it does not refer to colour-images? Basically, the only thing one can say (according to Wittgenstein) about such a language-game is that it is one in which colour-identifications are made correctly. An early expression of this view is found in *The Brown Book*, pp. 85–8.

Thus we can see, in terms of the illuminating example of colour-words, what Wittgenstein means by saying that certain rules are followed by people 'as a matter of course' (*PI*, I, sec. 238) or 'automatically' (*The Brown Book*, pp. 87–8). He is not describing the psychological character of such rule-following, but is making a conceptual point. He is saying that such rule-following is constitutive of the language-game in question, and that nothing more can be said of it than 'a language-game is being played'. As he puts it elsewhere, the primary rules are followed 'blindly'.

Thus, according to Wittgenstein, the only adequate description of a basic language-game with colour-words is to say that in it these words are attributed correctly. This is also the real reason why he says the things which one is initially tempted to understand as a rejection of inner experiences, e.g.,

> . . . the language-game with colours is characterized by what we are able to do, and what we are not able to do. (*Zettel*, sec. 345; *Remarks on the Philosophy of Psychology*, vol. 1, sec. 619)

(Cf. here also the quote and references in sec. 11 of this chapter, above.)

Wittgenstein is not even denying that mental images of colours can play a *de facto* role in our language-games with colours. All he is arguing for is that they do not play a *de jure* role in our semantics of colour-words. As he writes in *PI*, I, sec. 239:

> How is he to know what colour he is to pick out when he hears "red"? – Quite simple: he is to take the colour whose image occurs to him when he hears the word. – But how is he to know which colour it is 'whose image occurs to him'? Is a further criterion needed for that? (There is

indeed such a procedure as choosing the colour which occurs to one
when one hears the word ". . . .")
" 'Red' means the colour that occurs to me when I hear the word 'red' "–
would be a *definition*. Not an explanation of *what it is* to use a word as a
Bezeichnung.

Here it is especially clear that Wittgenstein is not denying the reality
or relevance of private colour-impressions, only their semantical
primacy. (For the meaning of *Bezeichnung,* which we have left
untranslated here, see chapter 10, secs. 8–9, above.)

One of the main points Wittgenstein makes by emphasizing the
analogy between the primary uses of sensation concepts and those of
colour concepts is that in both cases the basic attributions are made
without any further justification. (Of course, 'to use a word without
justification does not mean to use it without right', as Wittgenstein
says in *PI,* I, sec. 289.) This is not a feature of these two language-
games only. It is a characteristic feature of the basic moves in many
primary language-games, and distinguishes them from moves in more
complicated secondary games. Wittgenstein discusses this distinction
in *PI,* II, xi, p. 197, in the case of different language-games connected
with the expression of visual experiences.

> I look at an animal and am asked: "What do you see?" I answer: "A
> rabbit". – I see a landscape; suddenly a rabbit runs past. I exclaim "A
> rabbit!"

> Both things, both the report and the exclamations, are expressions of
> perception and of visual experience. But the exclamation is so in a
> different sense from the report: it is forced from us. – It is related to the
> experience as a cry is to pain.

Thus the analogy which Wittgenstein sets up between our colour-
discourse and our sensation-talk extends to those features which make
a language-game a primary one. What he is saying that people's verbal
reactions to their colour experiences can be fully as spontaneous and
primitive as their reactions to sensations. This observation helps us to
see what Wittgenstein's overall analogy amounts to.

14 INSEPARABILITY OF PHYSICAL COLOURS
AND COLOUR-IMPRESSIONS

In the light of these observations, several pieces of our puzzle fall into
place. Among other things, we can find counterparts for colour-words
to several characteristic features of the basic language-games for

sensation-words. Here is one of these analogies between colours and sensations: Whatever the precise mechanism is that gives colour-terms their meaning, it is like a physiognomic language-game in one important respect. Just in the same way as it is impossible in primary physiognomic language-games to make a distinction between having an expression and giving it its natural expression, in the same way it is impossible in the primary colour-games to drive a wedge between physical colours and colour-impressions. This is shown by the remarks on colours and colour-impressions which Wittgenstein sandwiches in the middle of his discussion of sensation-language in *PI*, I, secs. 273–80. (He is discussing sensations like pain in so many words in sec. 271 and again in sec. 281.) Wittgenstein mentions the idea that a word like ' "red" designates [*bezeichnet*] something "we all face", and that everyone should really have another word, besides this one, to designate his own sensation of red?'[18] as well as the alternative idea that 'the word "red" designates something known to everyone; and that for each person, it also designates something known only to him.'[19] He rejects both views, and even offers an explanation why one might be tempted to adopt the one or the other. This temptation he describes in terms of an attempt as it were to detach the colour-impression from a coloured object, like a membrane. (Cf. sec. 176.) This explanation turns on the degree of attention a colour-perceiver is paying to what he or she is doing.

I don't turn the same kind of attention on the colour in the two cases. When I mean the colour impression that (as I should like to say) belongs to me alone I immerse myself in colour. (*PI*, I, sec. 277)

In contrast to such misconceptions. Wittgenstein emphasizes firmly the inseparability of physical colours and colour-impressions. He illustrates his point by a striking analogy:[20]

Someone paints a picture in order to shew how he imagines a theatre scene. And now I say: "This picture has a double function: it informs others, as pictures or words inform – but for the one who gives the information it is a representation (or piece of information?) of another kind: for him it is the picture of his image, as it can't be for anyone else. To him his private impression of the picture means what he has imagined, in a sense in which the picture cannot mean this to others." – And what right have I to speak in this second case of a representation or piece of information – if these words were rightly used in the *first* case? (*PI*, I, sec. 280)

This inseparability is an integral part of the analogy between sensation-language and colour-language in Wittgenstein. Wittgenstein's point is obviously parallel to *PI*, I, secs. 273–80. Wittgenstein could have expressed his general point in the same way we earlier saw him express his overall view: 'The visual world we live in is a world of colour-impressions, but we can speak of them only by reference to physical colours.' (Cf. above, chapter 6, sec. 3.)

No essential difference (in Wittgenstein's view) is apparently generated between sensation concepts and colour concepts by the fact that colours have a clearer structure than sensations.

15 THE COMPLEXITY OF THE SYSTEM OF COLOURS

All this does not yet show what the real nature of colours is according to Wittgenstein. For him, this question amounts to asking: What are the most important language-games played with colour-words? We have seen that for Wittgenstein they are roughly analogous to the language-games people play with sensation-words, and we have even seen what that analogy consists in. However, Wittgenstein never tells us directly what the language-games with colours are really like.

It is nevertheless easy to see why he does not attempt anything like a full description of these language-games. The reason is their enormous complexity and subtlety. Wittgenstein's *Remarks on Colour* are to a considerable extent an attempt to remind his readers of this complexity and subtlety. Not only are we dealing with a space of colours in which such things as the relative proximity of one shade of colour from another one play a role. We have to understand the dimension of pure vs. impure colour. Furthermore, colours interact conceptually with other visual phenomena, for instance transparency and opacity. Hence the language-games we play with colours must overlap with the languge-games that are connected with other concepts from the world of vision. Because of this many-dimensional character of colour concepts, Wittgenstein follows his wonted strategy of merely assembling reminders of the relevant conceptual points concerning colours. We, too, have to be satisfied with the same.

16 OTHER CONCEPTS

Thesis (11): Instead of discussing the general problem of the different conceptual frameworks one can use in speaking of private experiences, Wittgenstein comments on several specific psychological concepts: remembering, dreaming, thinking, understanding, etc. It seems that these Wittgensteinian case studies are best approached by first discussing such wider theoretical issues as are illustrated by our comments on the objects of perceptions and the language appropriate to them. That is too large a problem for this occasion, however, Suffice it to voice the suspicion that Wittgenstein relies here, too, far too heavily on physiognomic frameworks at the expense of others which may be farther removed from ordinary discourse but no less in keeping with his basic insights.

Perhaps one should nevertheless register here the fact that Wittgenstein himself thought of his enterprise in his last works very much in the spirit of a comparative investigation of different language-games. Admittedly, he typically expresses himself by speaking of different psychological concepts rather than different language-games; but no Wittgensteinian can deny that the two ultimately amount to the same.

Another complex problem area which Wittgenstein leaves to the care of case studies and *obiter dicta* rather than systematic theorizing is the distinction between the descriptive and modal elements of a sentence. Wittgenstein's main point is that even the descriptive component receives its meaning from certain language-games. Thus a public framework is needed, not only for the semantics of a propositional-attitude word like 'knows' or 'believes', but also for the specification of what it is that someone knows or believes.

NOTES

1 Cf. here also, e.g., *Zettel*, sec. 537; *Lectures and Conversations on Aesthetics, Psychology, and Religious Belief*, p. 31.

2 The term 'propositional attitude' is not Wittgenstein's. We do not want to imply that all the concepts falling under this term exhibit the same logical behaviour, either.

3 The German text of this passage reads:

Wenn Menschen wirklich, wie ich annahm, das Nervensystem des Andern funktionieren sehen könnten und danach ihr Verhalten zum Andern einrichteten, so hätten sie, glaube ich, gar nicht unsern Schmerzbegriff (z.B.), obgleich vielleicht einen verwandten. Ihr Leben *sähe eben ganz anders aus* als das *unsre.*

D.h. ich betrachte dieses Sprachspiel als autonom. Ich will es nur beschreiben, oder betrachten, nicht rechtfertigen.

4 Wittgenstein also indicates, again in *PI*, I, sec. 282, that even where the secondary language-game could stand on its own feet, without the primary language-game it is based on, the presence or absence of the primary game

makes a difference: 'When children play at trains their game is connected with their knowledge of trains. It would nevertheless be possible for the children of a tribe unacquainted with trains to learn this game from others, and to play it without knowing that it was copied from anything. One could say that the game did not make the same *sense* to them as to us.'

5 This is what Wittgenstein is telling us in passages like his 'Notes for lectures on "private experience" and "sense data"' (p. 250). There he argues that in our language-games dealing with sensations and feelings there are 'expressions of which we don't say that they may lie'. As he also puts it,

> When I say that moaning is the expression of toothache, then in certain circumstances the possibility of its being the expression without the feeling behind it mustn't enter my game.

> Es ist Unsinn zu sagen: der Ausdruck kann immer lügen. [It is senseless to say: the expression may always lie.]

By 'certain circumstances' Wittgenstein clearly means primary physiognomic language-games.

6 The index to the *Philosophical Investigations* lists 'criteria of pains' as being discussed in part I, secs. 350–1. However, this is not a registration of the facts of occurrence, but an exegetical judgement, and a hasty one at that. In reality the term does not occur in either section, and in sec. 350 Wittgenstein is in any case discussing the criteria of *identity* of pains, which involves an entirely different language-game from the primary one which gives pain-terminology its meaning.

7 A comparison with sec. 290 is instructive here. On the received view, Wittgenstein would have to speak of alleged private criteria also in sec. 290. There is no indication of the alleged privacy in the text, however, and a comparison with neighbouring passages shows that there cannot be. For one thing, in the preceding sec. 289 Wittgenstein is defending the use of a word 'without justification', obviously meaning 'without *criterial* justification'. He cannot be here referring to private criteria. It would be very odd for Wittgenstein to use the same terminology in entirely different senses in adjacent paragraphs. Furthermore, a comparison between sec. 290 and sec. 270 shows a close parallelism, which vindicates the reading of 'criterion' in both cases as an external criterion. For in sec. 270 Wittgenstein's whole point is to study the use of an external criterion for a sensation.

8 Similar evidence is found in much of *PI*, I, secs. 316–87; cf., e.g., sec. 363.

9 G. E. M. Anscombe translates the words "Hat nun in diesem Prozess des Lernens das Wort 'Schmerz' seine Bedeutung geändert . . ." by 'Now has the meaning of the word "pain" changed in this process of learning the word? . . .' The context nevertheless shows clearly that what is supposed to be learned is not the word 'pain' but a new use of the word.

10 Perhaps the briefest way of illustrating this fact is to point out that even some of the best existing discussions of Wittgenstein's views on privacy usually suffer from a failure to distinguish primary and secondary language-games from each other and to appreciate the differences between them. To take one example, John W. Cook ('Wittgenstein on privacy', *Philosophical*

Review, vol. 74, 1965, pp. 281–314) shows very nicely that the alleged use of the verb 'to know' in the typical formulations of the alleged 'private language argument' is, in Wittgenstein's eyes, 'not a use at all but a confusion'. (This goes for such statements as 'No one can know that another person is in pain.') On the other hand, Cook wants to argue, partly on Wittgenstein's behalf, for 'the "incorrigibility" of first-person sensation-statements'. Both arguments are well taken, but only in so far as primacy (physiognomic) language-games dealing with sensations are concerned. It simply is not true that according to Wittgenstein we cannot speak of knowing what other persons feel. His point is merely that this cannot happen in the primary language-games. (Cf., e.g., *PI,* I, secs. 288–9.) Likewise, the vaunted incorrigibility of first-person sensation-expressions is restricted to primary language-games. Wittgenstein is not denying the reality of play-acting, simulating, or lying.

11 Cf. especially *PI,* I, sec. 574, where belief, hope, and expectation are mentioned. Moreover, belief is discussed in secs. 575, 577–8, 587; opinion in sec. 573; expectation in secs. 572, 576–7, 581–3, 586; hoping in secs. 572, 574, 583–5; etc.

12 Excellent additional evidence to the same effect is obtained from *Zettel,* secs. 75–86, where Wittgenstein discusses the difference between, on the one hand, such sense-impressions as pains (secs. 75, 84), hearing something (secs. 81, 83), after-images (sec. 77), etc., and, on the other hand, such prop-ositional attitudes as belief (secs. 75, 77, 85), knowledge (secs. 75, 77, 82, 83), hope (sec. 78), intending (sec. 85), and understanding (secs. 82, 84). The former, or at least some of them, can be attended to (sec. 75, 81), have a continuous duration (secs. 81–3, 85) that may even be measured by a stopwatch (sec. 82), can be called (albeit not very informatively) states of consciousness (sec. 84); all these unlike the latter. These Wittgensteinian remarks all illustrate the very contrast between inner experiences and propositional attitudes which we have been pointing out.

13 There is a subtle mistake which it is very easy to fall victim to here. Wittgenstein's primary physiognomic languages make essential use of the *natural expressions* of sensations and emotions. It is also eminently natural to speak of certain kinds of behaviour as the *natural expressions* of expecting, hoping, fearing, and of several other propositional attitudes, and hence to suggest that the language-games which lend a meaning to the two kinds of concepts – i.e., sensations and emotions on the one hand and propositional attitudes on the other – work similarly in both cases. There are in fact similarities here, but they should not overshadow the clear differences. These differences are crucial for the overall interpretation of Wittgenstein, for they relate to the question whether there really is 'a beetle in everyone's box', in other words, whether the terms in question are really names of particular private experiences or not. The relation of the 'natural expressions' to what is being expressed is different in the two cases.

14 Similar remarks are found in *Remarks on Colour,* III, secs. 281, 284, 286, 292, etc.; *Zettel,* sec. 345, etc.

15 Cf. here *Remarks on Colour,* I, sec. 73.

16 Thus it is not the case that our basic language-games with colours rely on the characteristic modes of behaviour of the differently coloured objects. Admittedly, there exists, for instance, a theory according to which the

ancient Greek colour-words (i.e., words which we are normally inclined to think of as colour-words) operated somewhat in this way. See Eleanor Irwin, *Colour Terms in Early Greek Poetry,* A. M. Hakkert, Toronto, 1974; and cf. R. M. Dancy, 'Alien concepts', *Synthese,* vol. 56, 1983, pp. 283–300. But the very difficulty of interpreting ancient Greek 'colour-words' which modern scholars face is a vivid illustration of the fact that *our* colour-words do not operate functionally.

17 See, e.g., *PI,* I, secs. 48–9; *Remarks on Colour,* I, sec. 59.

18 As we saw above in chapter 9, secs. 7–8, *bezeichnen* does not mean for Wittgenstein 'mean', even though G. E. M. Anscombe so renders it. Her translation has accordingly been revised here.

19 See *PI,* I, sec. 273. – We can here see that G. E. M. Anscombe's translation is impossible. For the word 'red' cannot on any view *mean* two different things to each person, whereas it might be thought of to serve to label or designate two different objects. (One can tie the same name-tag on two different objects.)

20 Wittgenstein makes the same point in his *Remarks on Colour,* III, secs. 322–4, 326:

Is it a phenomenon that I see the tree? It is one that I correctly recognize this as a tree, that I am not blind.

"I see a tree", as the expression of the visual impression, – is this the description of a phenomenon? *What* phenomenon? How can I explain this to someone?

And yet isn't the fact that I have this visual impression a phenomenon for someone else? Because it is something that he observes, but not something that I observe.

The words "I am seeing a tree" are not the description of a phenomenon. (I couldn't say, for example, "I am seeing a tree! How strange!", but I could say: "I am seeing a tree, but there's no tree there. How strange!")

Or should I say: "The impression is not a phenomenon; but that L.W. has this impression is one"?

To observe is not the same thing as to look at or to view. "Look at this colour and say what it reminds you of".
If the colour changes you are no longer looking at the one I meant.

One observes in order to see what one would not see if one did not observe.

Name Index

Subject Index

primary, 261, 273–4, 277, 280–3, 298, 302
primary language-games
incorrigible, 274, 279
primary vs. secondary, 274, 278–80, 282–3, 286, 288–9
primary and secondary deal with the same objects, 289
secondary, 274, 276, 278–83, 298
secondary language-games legitimate, 279
technical languages as language-games, 192
with feelings, 279
with private objects, 267
language learning, 167, 179, 200
as key to meaning, 192
as training, 200–1
language–world comparisons, 164–5, 168–9, 171, 177, 208, 221–4, 261
holistic, 131
take place in the present, 169
language–world relations, 1, 3, 6, 8, 10, 12, 50, 164, 171, 176–7, 179, 184, 186, 192, 195–8, 208, 212, 233, 242, 272, 279
as a problem for Wittgenstein, 177
as mediated by language-games, *see* language-games
set up in the teaching of a language, 192
life (stream of life), 276
limits
of language, 4–6, 16–18, 57, 166, 171
of thought, 16
of world, 57, 65, 67
linguistic relativity, 5, 21–2
logic, 10, 52, 65, 153
and experience, 56–7
and grammar, 168
and phenomenology, 61
as a study of logical form, 100
as calculus, 1, 27
as empirical, 153
as language, 1–24, 27
as mirroring the world, 120
determined by the forms of objects, 100
infinitary, 110
of criteria, not Wittgenstein's leading idea, 206

pervades the world, 65
prior to every experience, 56
propositional, 100
universality of, 1, 3
logical
axioms, 10
categories, 94
constants, 100, 102, 104, 110
grammar, 90
impossibilities, 126, 128
inference, 236–7
language, 87–8, 90
necessity, 70, 111, 116, 123
notation, 94, 126, 169
operations, 100, 114
pictures, 8, 94
proper names, 63–4
semantics, 2–3, 94–7, 102
space, 117
structure of phenomena, 76, 126
syntax of language, 10, 90
truth, 52, 62, 103, 114, 117, 120, 127
type, 34, 94, 281
logical form(s), 8–9, 31, 40–1, 49, 52–3, 55, 64, 72, 75, 79, 100, 102–5, 116–17, 121–3, 127–8, 137, 149–50, 182, 232, 234
as independent entities, 54–5
as modal notion, 118
of colour ascriptions, 123, 127, 130, 133
of colours, 123, 128
of complex propositions, 52–4
of elementary propositions, 53
of proposition, 9, 56, 81, 103
of simple objects, 53–6, 80–1, 134, 148–9
lying, a secondary language-game, 220

mankind, 209
material mode of speech, 11
mathematics, Wittgenstein's philosophy of, 22, 25–6
meaning, 62, 155, 162, 228
and use in language-games, 217, 275
and verification, 171, 224
as use, 21, 190–1, 193
descriptive, 221
explaining meaning, 19, 178, 180, 190
of a sign, 11

Index of Passages from Wittgenstein